COFI
CONSCIOUSNESS

The Application of
Perspective to Reality

VITO MUCCI

Vito Mucci

Acknowledgments

Very simply, without Claudia Coniglio breathing life back into my mind and rescuing my soul from the brink of oblivion, neither I nor this book would be here. To her I owe all my present and future selves. Whatever bounty I bring to the world or harvest I reap will be solely a footnote to the world created by my love and devotion to her.

I would like to bow before those who guided me through the times in my life that I can scarcely remember, those who listened to me: my mother, who brought me in and let me wrestle my demons without asking anything in return, and my therapist Cynthia Higgins, who was the first person to actually understand where I was and what I was going through. Without you two, I would not have made it to Claudia.

I would like to thank my nuclear families, those now, and those of the past. Bert Wheeler and the boys of the family five that we have now, who welcomed me, and who continue to welcome me even though I have issues reaching the top shelves. I want to thank my brother and sister-in-law, Adam and Diedre Bryant, who showed me first-hand what healthy marriage and intimacy looked like. I would like to thank my father for his intelligence, as well as the money and energy he put up over and over for my health, safety, and finally, the making of this book. I would like to thank my stepfather Duncan MacNichol for showing me how to be silent, strong, and what the definition of "calm" was. Thank you to Sierra Heuermann for growing strong, and for being healthy and awesome. I also want to thank Jim

Dietrich (and co.) and Shannon Hazlehurst (and co.) for never giving up on me. It mattered.

I also want to thank my inspiring voices. These men have, throughout my life, enabled me to feel at home and hopeful in a world that was very foreign and hostile to me. Maynard James Keenan, Joseph Campbell, Alan Watts, Chino Moreno, Carlos Castaneda, Abraham Maslow, C.S. Pierce, Fyodor Dostoevsky, and Thom Yorke.

Finally I want to speak out to those who have befriended me and listened to me in one form or another over the past decade, whether on social media or otherwise. All of you have helped me refine my voice, my message, my temper, and my ability to manage myself while trying to create Synergy of Commune in the world around me. Specific thanks to my brothers Stephen Hubbell and James West, along with sister Ganin Lovell, as well as anyone who has trusted me enough to engage in a Rebinding treatment. Also thank you to anyone who has adopted one of our art pieces. For all of you that were not named here—seriously, there's like a million of you--thank you. Love you sillies.

Table of Contents

Section 2

Section 3

Section 4

We do not create our world, our Perspectives do.

I am going to bounce back and forth between essays and a conversational narrative over the next 500 or so pages to show that mind expansion is normal, meaning is readily available through experience and Resonance, and that forming relationships with engaged presence makes us capable of Influence in our lives where we feel powerless now.

I am going to address our addiction to certainty and fairness, as well as how we lose our individuality when we allow ourselves to be overwhelmed by fear.

I am going to show what tools we can use on a daily basis within our bountiful consciousness. Then I will show what primary purposes they can be applied to.

This life is art...and we make more of what we are.

Section 1

Chapter 1:

Opening ... Experience, Resonance, Rapture, repeat ...

Welcome to the playground! This is how I greet new people, new ideas, and realities into my world. This is a Perspective I have been afforded over a long period of study, and a great deal of experience. I am very comfortable in my world, and very comfortable with the tools I must use to make sense of reality, and to make adjustments where necessary.

This entire book is based on getting us in touch with our most intimate selves, without abstracting our minds out of our everyday lives. Everyone in developed countries has the necessary support and experience to become more engaged and invested in the world around them, and in their rich mental reality. Individual spiritual health and emotional presence is the first step to global health.

There are big questions and big answers in this book. They are not final answers, or Universal answers. They are Perspectives. They are meant to be used. Using Perspectives gives us a powerful tool. This tool enables us to ask questions that we may not have answers for (or those that have answers we cannot use), and find answers that can help us in specific situations, so we can proceed with our lives in a healthier manner.

These are vitally important because it is not necessarily answers that we lack. Answers like "The Golden Rule" have been around for millennia. Kindness and love are pretty commonly held as innately good things. We do not need answers. What we need is the motivation to act in accordance with the answers we believe to be right, even when it is difficult to do so. Generating Motivation is tricky. And finding a way to translate our answers into the everyday moments we are faced with…that takes an entire book to describe.

So let's start out with something easy. Let's just begin with the meaning of life. Remember, you do not have to agree or disagree, so there is no need to react or judge. You just have to try it on to see if it fits, and see what happens in your world when you're wearing this Perspective. It is a tool.

Experience, Resonance, Rapture, repeat.

Experience: Contact with incarnate phenomena

Resonance: Integration of the phenomena

Rapture: Creation of new consciousness as a result…one that feeds itself into the grid of all consciousness and expands the self and the universe.

I was asked by my ten-year-old son recently about the meaning of life in reference to the simple propagation of the species ("We're just here to breed…or what?"). He was curious about the survivalist attitude, which seems to have the most stable foothold for an idea of "purpose" within the realm of explainable reality. I used this opportunity to let myself explore how the idea of *thriving into existence* can be communicated.

I started by supporting the idea that "having fun" was an

inherent good that deserved regard. But I had the speaking space to go deeper, and I did.

Why experience Resonance and Rapture? The idea is simple ... **Commune Imprinting.** From the most basic relationship that exists in our species (mother/child) we see imprinting and unconditional positive regard relating directly to heath, specifically that of the child. The shared experience of an intimate and loving reality is a Creative experience, wherein, at the very least, brain growth and organ health are direct results for the child.

Looking at Commune and Imprinting, hugs are a great example to showcase. Loving touch stimulates the release of healing chemicals in the bodies of those who participate in the experience. The moment of the Commune is a physical imprint that leads to increased comfort. Is that not experience, then Resonance, then Rapture?

While the universe does not lose mass or energy, it does gain it. The conservation of mass and energy law seems to miss that, as any contact creates a third physical reality (waveform) that can communicate the transaction of the contact to the farthest reaches of the universe. Newton did not have the instruments to measure this. We have only just discovered that Consciousness has mass through waveform, and that recognition of reality is a creative action.

But what does this mean for our lives?

We are each genetically unique, experientially unique, and have a singular Perspective that has never existed in the history of the universe. At the same time, we contain matter that has been drawn (continuously throughout our lives) from other particles that have served many purposes over their existence in the Universe.

So we have **permanently unique and temporarily imprint-able** realities passing through us at all times, which brings us to Resonance and intimate experience. We are more distanced from this than we think.

It is common to see Virtual Reality devices as technological advances in our near future. These devices in science fiction films are meant to grant the user an experience. The funny thing is, we already are having a virtual experience within our own bodies. There are temporarily imprint-able particles that make up our body. So not only are we carrying borrowed encoded cells that we may be able to tap into and use for instinctual information, we are carrying a record-keeping system that holds our experiential information and transmits it via waveform throughout the universe after its passage through our bodies.

Why not experience our touches with vulnerability, and with the intent to disseminate our Perspectives and intimate realities into wellsprings of cosmic consciousness? Why not also enjoy this Commune Imprinting with the people who are sharing our realities, as they carry the actual particles that end up being the stuff our cells are remade of every 48 hours or so?

We can use these moments to become more united. These Commune moments are intimate expressions, shared moments. Whether mental, physical, or spiritual, they cross the threshold of a lonely singular existence, dipping us into a well of shared reality. This is how we make contact and become present, even if only for a brief moment.

The "one love" stuff? This is what it's supposed to mean. Not that we are *blandly* all one, but that we are united in our understanding of how we correlate to the universal energy we share, and we can experience it in a capacity that transmits permanently through ourselves and the world around us.

The universe is made of energy, and we are made of star stuff. We can imprint our joy, bliss-realities, and deep experiences onto the very particles that make up the new and ever-changing worlds. We can do it every second. We don't just feed the grid with our emotional/metaphysical states, but with the actual cells that are passing through our bodies. We can share these with everyone.

I personally want the well of matter that we draw on to make our ever-changing bodies that of shiny pixie stuff. I dig that. It's healthy and fun.

This idea is **Healthy Runoff** from living a good life. You don't have to focus on anything but your innate experience and reality. Your Perspectives and the shared realities you are fortunate enough to have are enough. So Touch the world; imprint your positive regard and intent. EXPERIENCE. RESONANCE. RAPTURE. repeat.

I wrote this essay a while back. I have a real love of giving direct links to my ideas as they introduced themselves to me, as my thoughts at specific intense and focused moments are my most loved. This essay is one of my favorites.

I know where these ideas come from, they come from myth. They come from the "field of myth," wherein the subjects of many stories can be used in concert to create a narrative of "how people have learned to talk to themselves" over the course of human history (at least those which contains storytelling aspects). So I learned, over many years of putting my ideas together, that the many studies of human beings can be strung together in the same manner. I learned that the subject of Human Consciousness is not the amalgamation of humanities, psychology, mysticism, and hard sciences. It is their synergy.

Synergy is part of **The Process**. This does not just mean "a way to do something." The act of taking incorporated lessons and ideas in one area, and using that energy in other areas to develop our reality, is part of the creative foundation that we can tap into with every breath we take.

And there is one of my favorite words: incorporation. There are extensive internal and external realities that I want to talk about, but it's the inclusion of these ideas/phenomena/stimuli/sensation in the guts of our machinations that concern me. I want life to matter. I want it to matter to everyone. I want it to matter in any schemata we use to translate the world from an external source of stimulus, into a motivational mechanism. These mechanisms are at the root of our behavior and every decision we make. *That* is what demands our ability to incorporate ideas.

This gets us to the next section, an idea that started by taking transcendental meditation and looking at a whole being. This includes the part of our being experiencing the *all-encompassing oneness* **and** the part of our being that drove home from work in stifled rage after having a bad day at work. ***This is about rejoicing in the AMOUNT of experience that whole being was able to incorporate***.

This is about combining realities within ourselves. It is about becoming the tactile matter that makes us up, as well as becoming what that tactile matter is capable of spiritually, and doing it simultaneously. We must do this without being exclusive, focused on incorporation.

The word "ascension" has been used to describe a trip to "heaven" and AWAY from this physical plane. And that is exactly what I don't want: exclusion. Especially the exclusion of the physical, as it is the one thing that separates this from every other reality (whether real or imagined).

Ascension vs. Ascend In

Hmmm . . . I think I've finally found a nice way to describe the versions of spiritual growth by slightly altering a word while keeping its basic spirit association.

Ascension becomes **Ascend-In**.

We know that we use only a fraction of our brain, that our experience for the 99% worth goes into the subconscious mind because we are not able to process it consciously. Or, at least, we "weren't" able. I doubt that is true anymore to that extent, and I want to start cutting into it.

I have always felt the desire to get *into the flesh* more than the desire to exit. Many promote the exit as not only desirable but the greatest possibility for consciousness (Ascension, Transcendence). I like to promote the abilities of consciousness, like connecting with source, but I don't need to leave my body to do it. Source is in my body too, so why want out?

Then I figured, while walking to get my mail, that **THE ONLY PLACE IN THE UNIVERSE WE DONT FULLY EXIST IS IN OUR OWN BODIES**. We can always connect with the infinite, but we can't seem to use more than 10% of our brains?

It's like this human body is a glove and we're wearing it draping off the tips of our hands instead of fully immersed, fitting it tight and snug. How much are we missing?

It seems that as children (being newly incarnate) we get a leg into these bodies, get scared, begin to lose trust, and start pulling out. It seems that we begin pulling out in every aspect, from soul engagement to physical sensation.

This is not simply a "fear is unhealthy" thing. The fulfillment of our bodies with source is what we were given to do upon being born. We're basically not following orders, and *they are orders we gave ourselves*.

So this is the idea of embodying a Now is expanded into *how much Now are we having*? We were given a body--how much of that body are we experiencing? We were given a world to Commune with--how much of it are we resonating with?

We are like plants. Our roots are source energy and the tips of our branches are these bodies. Are we filling up with the deliciousness of both ends? Are we just going in one direction? Are we pushing growth both ways?

I get the feeling that the less healthy we are, the closer we are to the seed core (distant from the nourishment of the body at the branches and soul at the roots). I also get the feeling that the more fully resonant our reality is, the more likely it is that we can reach all the way to source/creation energy at our roots, and encompass that, while simultaneously feeling the whole of our bodies in its most distant branches.

If we can fully get into our bodies we can have deeply rapturous experiences. They will be tactile and yummy, from so many conscious Perspectives, but only as rich as we are deeply related to our bodies. Not a penny more. Our Resonance and Rapture depends on our engaged presence.

This is Incorporation. This is an investment. It is a willingness to experience and inhabit a mess and try to make sense of it. It is the Process of Entropy-Refinement.

What do we love to taste? What do we love to feel? What emotion floods us with joy? Which feelings are less than desirable? This is observation now, not judgment. This is refinement after the "allowance" of entropy. Our spirit is in the mix for all of this, all that comes to us, and the ability to refine and choose that which we desire most depends on our conscious involvement in the process of experiencing and integrating the experiences. This is Commune with the self.

Being present for this Commune gives us the ability to improve the quality of our existence. It gives us opportunities for embodying Grace.

Grace. Make Us More Alive!

Grace. For me it's always been the best parts of magic, the ones that I associated with the most power because they were a state of being instead of an action.

There was a Bose commercial in the '90s where they went through an entire self-description. They exclaimed: "We don't make the stereo, we make it louder," and "We don't make the pillow, we make it softer." Finally they closed with "We don't make a lot of the things you buy, we make a lot of the things you buy...better." That really hit me in a solid way.

How do we take something given to us, like our daily experience here, interwoven with millions of co-creative consciousnesses, and make it better? This is not a search for a philosophy or something vague and ambiguous. It is asking *"How much energy do we put into making things a bit better?"*

That has always been Grace to me. Attention within motion, like the focus within the dance. The pained expression within a heartfelt song lyric, the excited anticipation of the chef while mixing the ingredients, and the deep breath in the hug. It's the spoonful of sugar I was looking for as a child (and then later as an adult for a long time). It is Grace. It makes our world easier, more rich, and thus, more alive.

We are looking for Rapture through Experience and Resonance. Commune gives us that. Grace makes it richer, more available. And all of it takes place when we give ourselves fully to our bodies, and the chaos that lies within. That is why we Ascend-In to this opportunity.

The presence of purpose, for me, lies simply within that opportunity. It lies in making the most of what we are presented with. There is a Perspective I hold that is fully correlated to that. It is the idea of our lives, and their relevance when placed next to the Universal Consciousness, and its expansion.

Chapter 2:

The Course Curriculum and the Host of the Party

I've always felt safe. Not the small safety that comes with food and shelter and caring individuals (though I did have that), but the BIG safe. Death was something I was forced to confront at a young age, something we dealt with as a family through multiple advanced-stage cancer scares with my brother. These started when I was seven. By the time he had beaten the disease a couple more times I was sixteen. That is when I started, for the first time, putting the "Where do we come from?" answer into my own creative words (I had felt the question's presence since I was a toddler...I know it sounds weird, but I remember the feeling). It is the same picture now that it was then, but I am much better at feeling out the language of the details, and much better at translating the elegance of the picture into something that I can share.

Translation is a key...literally. It unlocks ideas from the abstract space of the mind and drops them into your lap while you're driving to the grocery store. There are so many quotes that fit the description of what I am trying to describe that I could fill an aisle at a metaphysical Hallmark with them.

... "You are not a body having spiritual experience, you are a soul having a material experience."

... "You are the universal consciousness experiencing itself subjectively."

... "Enjoy the ride."

... "We are all students of the Universe."

... "There is a vitality, a life force translated through you into action, and this expression is unique...."

All of these quotes are hinting at ideas--ideas of something larger that we are a part of, and our relation to it. They mean to tap into our innate sense that we come from something big, and express that Source uniquely through a vessel body. They mean to tap into this because there can be so much more ease and joy in our lives when we shift our focus from our **Urgently Mortal Seriousness** into something larger. Something that is more fitting to a cosmic being.

This is what I can put into words now.

It all makes sense to me now....

So, in general, I do not like to write essays this fluffy. My picture of the origination of all energy in the universe, and the way in which the soul comes into being, is simply not concrete enough (as it is based mainly on the faith I have in my Intuition). But the Perspective this affords us is worth the effort of translation. I got a really clear picture of it the other day while coming back from the grocery store. So here it is.

When I was eighteen, I postulated happily that I believed the soul was made up of "universe parts," in the same way molecules of water make up a glass of water. I also theorized that the soul water that fills us up was made of "soul molecules" or "spirit" that the creative intent of the Universe scooped up and dumped into our bodies like liquid filling a vessel.

I was fuzzy on how genetics worked into that picture, so I was curious about a possible concentration of "family spirit" that might all rest near each other.

Well, after fifteen years of not really thinking about it, I found a deeper understanding.

I had been thinking of the nature of soul contracts, and I came across some of Dr. Brian Weiss' and Abraham Hicks' work (I was familiar with them, of course, but had not used their work in this manner). Weiss very much thinks of existence as a teaching element, and the learning of lessons as the karmic debt to be paid. Abraham mentioned that certain souls come in with specific qualities for the effect they are going to have on life as a whole. That is simply what they sign up to do.

I have also always felt that certain people are carrying more spirit around with them (this would explain the "fact" that everyone can remember being someone famous in another life. We all were. They had a bounty of spirit in them that many of us are carrying around now).

Well, the combination of all that hit me. And instead of thinking of the spirit contained in a person as an un-arranged grab bag that has something to do with genetics and purpose, I immediately saw it as...wait for it...

...AN ACTUAL COLLEGE.

The allotment of spirit that makes up a soul is a mix of mostly student soul-molecules and a few instructor soul-molecules. The body-and-mind vessel is the classroom where the instruction and testing takes place.

Classes range from "Remedial Suffering 1a," an African child born into slave labor that dies young, to the "PhD delegation" housed in a public spiritual master like Jesus or the Buddha.

Every little bit of spirit in me signed up for the "Vito Mucci" class. The soul contract is actually a class description and syllabus. The karmic debt lesson is the course objective, and the pass/fail/grade of the class *is how fully I live my life*.

The completion of the course objectives manages multiple aspects. Not only do the problems tied to karmic debt get released, but the Universe gets to experience that growth from an individuated state (where the experiences are more powerful). The students get first-hand kinesthetic knowledge of working through deeply personal issues. They also achieve cathartic relief and sense of empowerment. They are given exactly what students in college hope for in every class.

The Universe also gains knowledge of itself through this medium, that of our individuated experience. We collect the experience of our lives for the expanding Universe like video cameras all shot into the same open field from different angles. The gathering of empathic Perspective within us is used to capture a previously unmapped representation of reality in the Universe. This *entropy* is then *refined* through awareness.

We are thousands of souls, not one. We are a small number of teachers and masters, and an enormous number of students. Over our lifetimes we are capable of having the expansive experiences that the Universe has a passion for. Our Rapture has creative energy.

Our experience builds the universe, soul by soul, turning students into teachers, and slowly the masters can spread, *upgrading the overall quality of the learning experience across the complexity of creation*.

Now stop. Yes, this is kinda pretty...look at it. Look at how it works in conjunction with what we love about living, the joys of incarnation and experience...the richness. Feel how the different aspects of yourself are brought out by the nature of those you love and the recognition of other spirit in the world. Feel how you are teaching yourself. Feel how the experience, then Resonance, then Rapture gets set deeply into the hearts of thousands of souls.

We are not just bowing to the God in others. We are not simply believing in the deified nature of the creative self. **We are the subject, teaching expression to the universe, as it creates itself.**

Look inside yourself. Look at your classroom, the guides and the eager eyes on them as they learn you, see reality through you. This "I" that has made up what you identify as yourself is the class description. Your creative expression is the vocation, your experience the only teaching tool, and your body the only vessel.

All of everything that is "you" signed up for this. The universe is reflecting back upon itself through you. Experience it. The prerequisites you met in order to be here are the fundamental values you express in this limited and impermanent mortality. The fullness of your life is the very thing that moves all the universe forward through the vitality of the spirit housed in you.

We are the curriculum.

This description gets me somewhere. It gets me relaxed, and focused. I am HUGE on ideas that change Perspective. That is the moment when an idea by itself becomes a tool, a platform from which to operate. I like that it's approachable and friendly, not exclusive or divisive. I also do not see it being mutually exclusive from some of the more rigid belief systems that are in place, whether religious or scientific.

For me this idea is like mental yoga. And like yoga, it can be as powerful and meaningful as is needed for what you want to use it for. You wanna get limber? You got it. You wanna learn to meditate and relieve stress? You got it. You wanna become one with your body to learn to self-heal? This is a great place to start. You wanna be Batman? This certainly can't hurt.

This changes our focus. It can change our vision in the same way goggles do underwater, and putting these goggles on for Perspective is vital. I call them **Distance Goggles**, as they can give us a larger picture, from a greater distance. This is a priceless tool. We can easily get lost inside a powerful moment or get caught up in Urgently Mortal Seriousness without it.

So, to give an example, we can think back to one of our first relationships. Let's think of the first one that knocked us on our ass. Standing where we are right now, we know that relationship was a lesson. *We didn't feel like that at the time, though.* We were "inside" the moment, which is where we belonged. From the inside it felt wrong. Now that we are "outside" of that moment and we have a larger picture, we see something different. It fit. It did exactly what it was supposed to. It was one of many experiences on the way to where we are now. That is the gift of Perspective, and how we use it is a divine aspect of our reality. Perspective will show us that we could have done a lot of things better had we donned our Distance Goggles.

When we're inside the moment, we become its victim. We try to control, and can't, so we give up rather than trying to work with it. We could try to work with it, but we don't. We don't say to ourselves

"Hey, I'm seventeen, this situation could use way more patience and understanding than I am capable of having naturally, BUT NOT MORE PATIENCE AND UNDERSTANDING THAN I COULD IMAGINE." Existing fully within the body of a hurt seventeen-year-old boy was the lesson. That's the "class" my soul was attending, and I would not change that. What I could change was the amount of Influence those feelings of anger, sadness, and hopelessness had on my thoughts and behavior.

If I could have said to myself "This feeling is what you signed up for, this is you teaching yourself about the world," I could have begun to work WITH my reality. The second that pain, anger, and frustration are not our enemy, that's the second we become ten times as power-ful. That's the second that our mind opens up to creative ideas and appreciation and gratitude for the wealth of experiences we are being blessed with at any given moment. That's the second when we can be kinder, more attentive, and more loving to everyone. That is what Perspective can do. That is why it matters. It can alter what aspect of ourselves we are identifying with.

We can identify with the crude tactile body, or the mind, or our circumstances. It's all limiting. When we take all of those things--the body, the mind, and our circumstances--and add them to the plethora of hungry viewers drinking in every second of experience that we are affording them, we have the choice to identify as more than a victim--more than a participant. We can identify with being the **Host of Universal Creation Energy Incarnate**.

We can be whatever kind of Host we want. This is OUR party. Our venue. These energies gathered FOR US. We are the unique owners of a singular experience, and only we can bring vitality to that experience.

Chapter 3:

Parenting Through the Relationship of Influence

Relationship. It's a description of how we connect with…well… everything. Relating is something we do to such an extent that it can't be quantified. It is something more easily referenced by time and place (less about "the thing" and more almost completely about "the thing in a certain situation"). The way I relate to my cat is much more about whether it is relating to my cat "on my lap during a cozy after-noon" or "on the dining table during dinner." If you think that just has to do with your cat, try it with a person or a television.

Nonetheless we have ideas about relating that seem consistent. We consider the way we relate to things to be part of who were are, something we identify with, and it is precisely that identification that is reallllly begging to be expanded. Our conscious relation to reality needs to be less about place and time, and more about who we want to be, and what kind of world we want to create.

And there is that word "create." It is very different from the word "react." That distinction is the point of this section. When you are relating by the means used above with the cat, you are making "re-action" your primary means of relation. How much of your world is reaction? How much should it be?

Parental Walk-in. A Story.

I was thinking about my manner of relating to the world, the way I feel it is necessary to treat everyone with the same respect for growth as I would my own children, and I remembered exactly the moment when I started doing it.

My mate mentioned that I often use rhetoric and flashy analogies to describe things, and that I may want to relate this story in a different way. This is about the birth of Vito as a father.

I had really awesome parents. They took good care of themselves and I got the joyous and supportive runoff. It was plenty. That was my model for parenting: that there is a lot of soul nourishing energy in the world, and those who take good care of themselves can easily manage gifting their excess to those closest to them. My parents used the passion of existence to fuel their internal fires, and the winds of change to fan the flames. As a result, I was always warm. As a result, I knew I had the means to house a strong fire for myself that would warm others. I was about fourteen when it came into play . . . .

So, this is Vito twenty years ago.

Summer of...some year in the early nineties (I'm thinking '93. Kurt Cobain was still alive. That's how I mark time around that period). My brother had been cancer-free for six years. That horror of my childhood and the horror of my mother's life had been gone for the entirety of my middle school years, and I was totally ready for high school.

I went to California every summer and stayed with my brother--he's fourteen years older than me. While at the gym one day (it was my first real stint working out), in between sets on the rowing machine, he looked at me and his best friend that was with us, and said "Hey...ya know...I think I have cancer again." This time I wasn't seven, so I knew what it meant. No one survives the second round (he did, and the five rounds after that).

My reaction was not only worry and anxiety, but a new feeling, which was "Hey, he's scared, and I'm going to make sure he isn't any more scared than he needs to be, and I'm gonna make sure I don't make his life harder." I don't know where that voice came from, but I remembered it. I knew it. I incorporated it.

That summer there was a family wedding. My uncle was marrying my aunt, and it was being held in Sedona where they lived. We had all planned on going out, but my brother stayed back with my sister-in-law to get a biopsy and wait for the results. My mother and I, and the rest of the family (there's a bunch on the West Coast, so it was a two-car affair from Southern California across the desert), went to the red rocks and set up camp.

The wedding was gorgeous. I met new people and had new experiences. I knew something was growing in me. It was palpable. Maybe it was an influx of serotonin from puberty, or adrenaline from the excitement of being older. I can't be sure. But it mixed with the energies of Sedona, and culminated in a moment that I remember very clearly.

We were waiting for a phone call. My brother was going to get the results. He was going to call my mom. She was holding it together really well, but she didn't have much left in her, and I knew it.

So, he called. The room was full of loving people and she answered the phone. She immediately picked up a pen, and her grip got tight on it, nodding and adjusting her glasses on her head. Then she started writing ....

That's the second it happened. Awareness and focus and care and confidence all melded into this magnificent feeling, and a set of simple thoughts rushed warmly over me. My brother had cancer. This was too much for my mom to handle, and it was too much for my brother that she had to handle it. Only I had the energy and love to take care of everyone in this moment. It was clear. It wasn't difficult. It wasn't a sacrifice. It was the most natural thing I've ever felt, and having that specific combination of thoughts and feelings felt so right, I was almost overjoyed.

I grabbed the phone from my mother as she started to break down. I kissed her head (which we really never did as a family, so I was already working outside the box) and blasted her with father energy. It was the first tangible father energy that came out of me, and I knew at that second that it was going to be something I engaged in forever. I clutched her for a second and she settled. I felt everything in the room so much more clearly, and that everyone had bowed to that moment. I knew that I could expand this feeling for whatever distance I wanted, so I let it fly and it covered the globe at light speed. I could see it. It was powerful and vital.

I was almost giggling when I got on the phone with my brother. I said, "So . . . see any good movies lately?" That cracked him up. The tension he had over having to tell his mother that he had cancer left. We talked about fifteen more minutes until I was sure he had settled down, and we got off the phone.

I had protected my mother, and I had protected my brother. The immensity of that expression was intoxicating and life-affirming in a way I had only dreamt of.

Why was this? Why did this feel so powerful? It was because I had tapped into divine masculine energy. I became a father to everyone in that moment. This is something that everyone can do.

The Grid of Divine Vitality is available to all of us, all the time. I may be special in many ways, but not this way. I didn't do anything that day but dip my human consciousness into a river of permanently flowing energy that is always here. I loved it, and the Grace that comes from it is different from anything else I have experienced.

This energy is HUGE. It will change your world completely when you engage in respecting the growth and change around you through the expression of your own divine presence. Whether it is masculine or feminine energy, behaviors that are parental, protective, and nurturing are the main components.

So when I talk about the importance of Parenting, I'm actually talking about a main facet of tapping into your divine energy.

So, this is what we want to grow into, and a Perspective we want to mark. In general, the situations that inspire this happen with family first. We become wholly different as protectors. I want to say we become "big," but what we truly become is creative. It is a catalyst that changes the magnitude of the situation we see ourselves in from ordinary to mythic. Instead of being a fourteen-year-old in my uncle's living room as my mother was finding out my brother had cancer, I was ageless and conscious (Distance Goggles). This gave me the whole story of my family over the span of the experiencing my brother's cancer. My reaction to the situation was no longer relating to just chapter and verse.

I created an idea of who I wanted to be during that harrowing experience, and it became a permanent Influence on my every behavior. I had begun my myth. That is creation.

So where there was once a "behavior in reaction," the *behavior of a moment in a situation*, there becomes the **behavior within a story**. This is expansion in identity (I did say I wanted to expand it), and through creative focus it allows us to write new ideas and roles into every area of our lives. It also allows us to map out our story in such a way that our behaviors and experiences source out of that intention. That is creative living. It is a focus. It is a habit. And it can be Influenced.

The most direct example of this creative focus is with a child. Your child. There is a chance that you stepped into a healthy parenting role in another way, as I did, but there is no way after bringing a child into this world that this is a foreign concept. The ideas you generate, and imaginations of their future that you hold dear, are the brightest and most beautiful example of creative relation in the world. It is through this imagination that we permanently connect deeply with something that is not us.

How does this relate to relation? How does this define a role within the matrix of reactions and creations? It gives you something that you can never forget. Ever. It is a permanent Perspective. The example I like to use for this is specific; it puts the period at the end of the sentence.

Imagine making sandwiches, and going out to dinner, and buying groceries. Really, *stop and imagine it*.

Now, imagine the same things, but know your child is deathly allergic to peanuts. Your sandwich is no longer a peanut butter and jelly, your trip out to eat includes a short discussion with the waitress about what types of oils are used for cooking, and your trip to the grocery store includes checking the back of packages for ingredients.

You cannot forget. The way you go about everything is altered... *and that is just a peanut allergy*. This is what a change in the way your consciousness relates looks like. This is an example of a "situation" that contains specific attributes common to the parent, not just the environment. The attribute of focus, in this case, supersedes the situation presented by the environment, by becoming a part of the consciousness that is addressing it. All of us are capable of weaving more focus into our matrix of behavior if we take a moment here and there. That is an upgrade of the relationship between consciousness, and the reality it is presented with.

Imagine if we realized that love was allergic to fear, or that creative thought was allergic to anger.

Imagine if we could activate the parent in us for more than just our children. Imagine if we could activate the themes we cared about most, and put them in *every story*. Imagine if we could activate the parent in us when we dealt with our own raw emotion and life circumstances. Imagine how much patience would source from that creative focus. Imagine how deeply we could Influence ourselves.

Soul Presence and Patience for the Rotating Lock.

One of my favorite parts of instinctual living, source-related action, etc., is that being patient, and understanding the role you play in the many worlds surrounding you, gets really easy, and the process of changing the world in the way that is unifying to our soul becomes easier to trust. Acting out of the relationship we want to form with the world becomes second nature, even though it is frustrating.

The world, when it comes to the people we live with and around, always seems to be difficult to Influence. That is because we want to be able to "work" them like we would a machine. We expect that if we give someone an answer, and they conceptually understand it, that it will affect their behavior. Why we think this is BEYOND me. It is grossly inaccurate.

This is why I stand for parenting of all people, including ourselves. We make the mistake of assuming that as we grow, we gain control. But while we gain greater control of parts of the body and mind, we don't gain control over the forces that motivate our actions. Because of this, we can only hope to use **Influence** in these areas.

Our lack of control over our world, and the limitations of Influence are why I started leaning into ideas that eventually led to Psychological Determinism. Our lack of control over how we integrate information is more than frustrating, as understanding concepts does not translate directly into behavioral motivation. That fact is like an **_injury_**. It is infuriating, and a prime component in the often- present Cognitive Dissonance that gums up the gears of our creativity.

Motivations are like a revolving lock in a door. Even if we are key masters, we have to wait for just the right multiplicity of combinations in order to get helpful information to ANY consciousness, _including our own._

This fact leads to a ton of frustration, because we can either try a bunch of times (most ending in failure), or stare and wait. Neither is appealing.

Many of us have tried a bunch of times with significant others. The "I just can't get through to them!"… the "I've tried to get them to understand!" … and the "They don't listen!" echoing through the house. That is frustrating. The inability to unlock understanding through communication is destructive for both sides of any relationship, but the frustration that comes from it is even worse.

If we go for the "stare and wait" option, we are less likely to be visibly frustrated, but we are consistently let down when our minds aren't read, and changes aren't made. This makes everyone feel helpless, and for the most part, we are helpless. We cannot control other people. The more we try, the more frustrating everything in our world will be.

But we aren't completely helpless, and we certainly do not want to feel helpless in our lives. So, what on Earth do we DO?

Patience, preparedness, willingness to love, willingness to act when the time comes, and learning to recognize THOSE EXACT MOMENTS when a person is pliable: these are payoff moments.

I have no idea how they happen, but I know that they do happen. If these moments are used for changing programming in anyone's personal matrix, they happen more and more often. This means that the more we can access ourselves or others in a meaningful way, at the right moment, the more often meaningful moments will present themselves. *When Resonant moments lead to Rapture, more Resonant moments present themselves.*

That is Influence. It is the expression of our **Observer Consciousness** when given a voice for Commune in our external reality. It is our parent-self, the nurturing identity listening to and observing the fullness of our reality. This expression is capable of coming to life through every relationship we form, if we are consciously engaged. Its loving attention is **soul presence**, and its ability to Influence our lives, and bleed through all environmental circumstances, is **soul expression**.

This is important, because the Observer Consciousness, which can act from within us, for the betterment of our reality through Influence, is the best representation of parenting we can bring forth. It is nurturing and patient, observant and accepting. And whether or not we actively engage in focusing on this, we are still influencing the world with our presence. It just may not be parental or nurturing if we are not using soul expression to relate to it.

As parents of this world, it is our job to be patient, and ready. The moments of action have their specific windows of opportunity. All changes we wish to make in our lives, and in the world as a whole, are based on momentary Resonance, and capacity for Rapture. So through training to be able to adjust to our immediate environment, we are training to be able to change the world.

All we can do is listen, and be open. It's worth it. The mind's eye trains to observe through soul presence, and as the lock tumblers spin into place...the key fits.

Involvement of this nature is Commune. The benefit of long-term relationships of Influence that are centered on nourishment is that they are a wealth of focus in peace of mind. The benefit appears as "ease, calm, joy, and contentment," but it results in the fruition of what those states are the foundation for: "growth, creativity, problem-solving, and adjusting to an ever-changing world." It is a solution based mentality. It creates a solution-based reality.

Chapter 4:

I'm Happy

Why am I writing a book? I made sure to ask myself before I started writing. I have always been an outspoken person. I have always had luck expressing myself in psychological and spiritual matters. But that is not enough for me. I also know I can write a book. I am not writing to challenge myself to see if I can do it. That is not the reason. I did find the reason, and it matters to me that it was this reason, and not any of the myriad of other possibilities.

I'm happy. Nothing else matters as much as that. The Perspectives, tools, and knowledge I am referencing here wouldn't have a leg to stand on if I weren't happy. Very simply, I would not be writing. But what does Being Happy mean, and why is that important for this book?

Expressive Happy

This is a list of the reasons why being happy is necessary for me to write this book.

1) **I am fully focused on satisfied and joyous living.** How focused? So focused that if I were not totally happy, I would not have the time to write. Because I'd be building up the areas of my life that were asking for my attention, as that

is WAY more important than writing. This expression has to be an overflow of love and care. For that I need to have filled up everything I need, and all for those I hold dear, before it can spill out on to the page.

2) **I am advertising something**. It is what I am, not what I think or write. You can only make more of what you are. Art is a perfect example of this idea in one genre of expression, an example of someone expressing and making more of what they are, often in a beautiful and abstract way.

I have been thinking the way I am writing for a long time, and it was not enough. I slowly come to believe it through experience, and then I became it over time.

3) **The Vibration of my expression needs to match the focus of my expression**. I want you to be happy, so I have to be happy while I'm giving you tools to that end.

4) **I don't believe that you can explain something that you don't know intimately**. Joyous living is what I want to explain, because that is where I find value. There are messes of things we think we should want as well as lists upon lists of goals that supposedly get the job of satisfying ourselves done, so we stop when the job is done without taking any notice of whether or not any of it actually improved our level of happiness.

There are lots of ways to hint at it and basically everything we do is a means of getting to it, but it is rare that we are conscious of what we're doing. We think we're buying a can of soda, or an apple, but what we're paying money for is satisfaction. It IS the only thing of value. If you buy a can of soda and drink the whole thing, you define that as getting your money's worth. If you drink a sip and throw the rest out, that is "waste." That is because society has some valuation issues.

I use soda as the basic idea here because it's the first item I used this with in my life. When I was fourteen, I would get a soda and finish it, because as it was finished fully that is when I had "proof" that I was happy. The soda mission had been completed. When I was seventeen I realized: "Hey... soda hurts my stomach, and makes my teeth feel weird." Did that stop me from finishing a soda? Nope. I was wasting them if I wasn't finishing them.

A few years later I paid $3 for a huge soda. I was a meager three swallows in when I realized it had worn out its welcome. It tasted so good, but if I had another sip it was gonna be no fun anymore, and I thought to myself: "Great. I just paid $3 to get unhealthy and then feel like crap as a direct result. What a stupid thing to do." Then I had a moment of clarity. I put the soda down, and walked away. I realized that I was spending money to procure happiness, which the soda created for the first three sips. I set the soda down, and walked away. While the fluid inside was wasted, my happiness was valued above it. *As it should be.* I chose to waste the fluid in the soda rather than waste my joyous state of mind, which I no longer needed proof of from external sources.

Is having our perceived needs met always positive? No. If it makes us happy, then yes. If it doesn't, then we have to investigate. We have to investigate whether our perceived needs can make us happy, and if not, then we have to try to use our imagination to find what can, because until we find it, we are incapable of being happy through our own intended actions. That is a powerless feeling. We have to ask those questions, but we also have to realize that everything we do that does not lead us to joy is a DISTRACTION FROM ATTAINING IT. **I am no longer distracted**.

5) **I am sure that I have no motives involved in this expression that could undermine the message**. I am not writing this to "fix" anything, or "fill" anything. Nothing is broken and nothing is lacking. There was a movie wherein staring in a mirror would show you what you wanted most to have or be...and it was noted that a happy man would stare into the mirror and see nothing but his own reflection. I have that, and I want that for everyone.

6) **This is a book to tell everyone how I got somewhere, so that place better be awesome**. There has to be a focus on solutions, not a focus on problems. I cannot be focused on what's wrong and feel confident that it could help anyone.

7) **How we feel about ourselves, especially our weak areas, is always a part of our expression**. Respect for our Audience in this life includes making sure that our love for ourselves is complete through and through, to ensure the genuine nature of our message, if our aim is teaching.

8) **I can fully see how everything fits, because I'm happy**. That's not for anyone but me--I cannot describe it, but I couldn't do this without it.

9) **I know it's possible to be happy**. I know it deeply. It is not an *EQUAL* possibility. It is a unique experience and journey for everyone, but I know it is available.

10) **We can truly inspire through joy**. It's the difference between gifts and lessons. It's the difference between a teacher or mentor that teaches you an "object" and one that teaches "You." It is the difference between a rock band that plays their music, and the rock band that plays to affect the listener. It is the difference between me expressing artistically as if no one were listening, and me having a conversation with you.

This is a conversation. I'm not writing "at" you. *I'm writing to you*. Your part of this is vital to my expression.

11) **This is between you and me.** You're in my living room with me as you're reading this, in the same way I am wherever you are as I'm typing. I know you can feel that. That is a Vibration, a reality, a connection that is unhindered by secrecy and judgment, one that is as intimate as a conversation with oneself.

I decided to write the closing to this section when I was done with the book, and in edits. So, here I am, still happy. I was happy all the way through writing, even if I did get exhausted by some of the more challenging chapters.

My life is still joyous, and expansive. I'm confident about you reading this. It was therapeutic for me to write it and the amount of discovery was beyond my greatest expectation. I owe that blessing to your presence in my world, so thank you for that honor. It is a great joy to have shared this process with you. It is the joy of Commune, even if it stretches across time and distance. Bless your journey. May it bring you joy.

Chapter 5:

The Business of Accountability

PART 1: SYNERGY OF COMMUNE AND AUDIENCE

What are we capable of being accountable for? Growing up, my mother told me I was accountable for everything in my world. I didn't understand why she would say such a thing. Certainly, not everything was my fault. But that's not what accountability meant. It meant that I had the honor of being present for everything in my life, and my choice to engage it or not had consequences. That is accurate.

When we discussed Parenting the World a couple chapters ago, we got a peek at the kind of focus we can employ across our entire reality, and I wish to tap that focus again. The entirety of this chapter will deal with our **Relationship of Accountability**, as it pertains to our environment. Our Relationship of Accountability is a description of the degree to which we "take into account" our ability to impact the world around us as we move throughout our daily lives. This is a level of accountability that runs in very low percentages right now. We are a global society that shrinks from accountability, and we do not need to continue that trend. Our Presence and Potency in the world allow us the confidence and safety needed to undertake larger tasks. The Business of Becoming Accountable is the expansion of accountability through our personal world, and outward through the rest of the social reality.

We are going to talk about communication. In this area we are going to shift the focus from honest expression to results. That is a shift from "where our focus is" to "where it can be" when we undertake a larger role in our Relationship of Accountability. Effective Commune lies in the results of our expressions, not in their mere existence. We are going to talk about our recognizing our **Audience**, adjusting to them, and creating timing within a conversation. This can create **Synergy of Commune**.

We are going to get started by looking at simple one-on-one communication. I hinted at this at the end of last chapter in the description of my writing this book "to you," rather than just expressing myself. That is a heightened level of accountability. It is an exciting proposition. The reason I focus so much on **Parenting the World** is that being nurturing and divinely present is a powerful motivator. It is a Perspective that can Influence us whenever we are inspired to tap into it.

When we look at communication from a parental standpoint, we may see that we fall short. We mean to *express ourselves fully **and be received fully***. If we feel that we are not being received fully we may want to incorporate a higher level of sophistication. **Sophistication in Communication** is when the source (feeling), voice (expression), and reception of an idea (understanding) are all tied together with care.

Feelings within us demand that we accept them in their raw form. But expressing those exact sentiments may or may not work, depending on our audience. Raw expression has great value, and let me say specifically that I am not undermining its role in communication. It has a role to play--that of a tool. Insofar as it serves that purpose, it is valuable.

Fear of expression has led to a focused movement in society, one where expression is valued and encouraged. I love this. It is a movement toward the art and soul of expression and away from the repression and limited scripts that have left us lacking as a global society.

However, as most movements are fond of doing, it has over-stepped its boundaries from encouraging expression to exalting care-lessness. There is no reason for this--we don't need to be an either/or consciousness. The movement of the universe is creation to entropy to refinement, in cycles of spirals outward moving and unending, and this seemingly mundane topic can be nurtured in the same manner.

We don't want to just express, *we want to express and be under-stood*. This is a refinement of the entropy of expression.

Hitches in Models for Expression, and Ivan the Cat's Sophisticated Meowing

"You must, at all costs, express yourself while not taking responsibility for the reaction...."

"I can explain it to you, but I can't understand it for you...."

"You can lead a horse to water, but you can't make him drink...."

Regardless of how accurate these may be, they are not the way we want to connect to our expressions. We can see this more easily if we replace the words say, explain, and ex-press, with "try to communicate." It is important because we can totally fail at trying to communicate without failing at the other descriptions, and trying to communicate is actually what we're going for.

The story of Ivan the cat:

Ivan can tell me all day he wants milk, but, since he's a cat, I just hear him meow.

Ivan can either be fine with that, or think, "*Can I do more to communicate that idea?*" and being a cat, he does the latter.

He goes and sits by his milk bowl, then meows.

I think he's just standing there meowing, as I'm not paying attention to where his milk bowl is.

Ivan is frustrated. After calming down and taking a few shots of cat vodka Ivan comes to me, stops, and meows. Then he goes to his milk bowl, stops, and meows. And finally, it clicks.

"I bet if I put milk in that round thing that little fella will stop meowing."

Ivan gets his milk.

I love the story of Ivan the cat. It's simple. His raw expression, obvious as it was to him, was insufficient for Commune synergy. He was motivated by hunger, and while that's something that is not going to be a serious thing in our world, the creation of a more delicious reality is one of the things we strive for. This being the case, we should find a way of focusing on getting into a better relationship with our expressions and their reception. Ivan's not gonna get fed if he isn't understood. We're not going to have a steadily improving reality if we are not understood, and synergistic Commune is not achieved. We have to follow Ivan's lead. We have to learn our Audience. We have to communicate to them specifically. We have to do more than simply express ourselves. We can do a lot more than just leading a horse to water. It is not beyond our reach.

Synergy in Commune is what we are going for. Synergy of Commune is "a mutual goal of understanding between people that are communicating." This means that someone is giving me directions to their house and I am listening with the intent of learning the directions (rather than thinking about anything else). In the story of Ivan the cat, Ivan was forced to work without Synergy of Commune. If Ivan's owner had been focused on Ivan, and looking for signs of hunger, that would have been Synergy in Commune.

So without further ado, let's play some baseball.

Home Runs and Synergy of Commune

Home runs are beautiful things. They are glorious displays of power, grace, flight, and sound. If you have ever been to a baseball game and seen a home run, you know that it can bring a sleeping crowd to its feet in a matter of seconds. It is something that is naturally engaging. So, how is this related to Synergy of Commune? A home run can't happen without two people. You need a pitcher and a batter.

Communication should be seen for what it is: one person sharing something specific and integral to their reality with someone who has only a meager tool (their mind) to attempt to connect to it on a deep level. That is a daunting task. Communicating is much more like hitting a baseball traveling 90 miles per hour than we give it credit for. Some specific difficulty areas need our continued attention.

"Dog." Yep, I said it. I really haven't communicated anything, though, have I? I can guess that upon reading that word you thought of a dog, but very likely not the dog I was thinking of when I wrote it. Now if you were thinking of a white and brown spotted border collie facing to the right that weighed about thirty-five pounds, that would be amazing, wouldn't it? If you were, we would be rejoicing in the synchronicity. It could be something that could land someone a second date (or at least a phone call). It could be the first step to a relationship between friends. That is the importance we already place on sharing our inner realities, and the difficulty we know to be inherent in doing so. That's why I use a home run to exemplify Synergy in Commune. It is complex, takes focused combined effort, and has a payoff we all understand and value.

So, what role do we play in actualizing this idea? We are notably the pitcher or batter in the analogy, depending on whether we are the one expressing, or the one attempting an attitude of reception. I want to deal with the pitcher. I want to focus on the one expressing.

For a pitcher, if you are going for a home run, your first job is to make sure there is a batter available. Expressing to be understood requires an Audience. This may seem obvious...but it's not. There has to be a batter there waiting to hit what you're pitching. He has to be focused on what he's doing, and ready to hit. This means that everything about his state of mind comes into play. Is he distracted? Is he angry, scared, hungry, manic? Does he have an ideology that makes his presence in the Commune impossible? This is not about what the batter says, this is about how the batter actually is. It is rare that a person is truly in a receptive state, given the chaos of everyday life.

The next thing we need to do as pitchers is have some working knowledge of the batter. We need to know what pitches he likes. Does he like high fastballs? Hanging curve balls? Is he the kind of person that responds best to fast

pitches, or does he want a lob? This relates to everyone, because everyone has a preferred method of taking information
in. Everyone has a learning style, an area where their focus is
maximized. We can be accountable for this also.

Then we have to deliver the pitch. We have to take all
of what we know about who we are communicating with,
and translate our raw expression into something they can
integrate.

Communication is difficult. We want to keep this in mind when
we begin to devote energy to creating a fertile environment for its
existence. It is easy to get frustrated and give up. It is also not always possible to succeed, even if we focus. The degree to which we
make ourselves accountable for **Creating a Fertile Environment for
Communication** does lead to a proportional amount of opportunity
for Synergy of Commune. The more energy we put into it, the more
likely we are to get something good out of it. It matters every time we
try.

The presence of the batter in the Home Run analogy is a huge
issue. How many conversations do we have where the other person
is not focused or mentally present? How many conversations do we
have where the other person has an agenda they are acting out, or an
ulterior motive? How many are so affected by emotion or stress that
they cannot engage our efforts?

Over years spent observing both sides of the communicating
landscape I have found that the largest issue is not just *being able to
adjust to who we are talking to,* but **being able to adjust to that person's state of being**. That is Creating a Fertile Environment.

Creating Timing. Batter Availability.

A responsible communicator WAITS for timing, and the gifted one CREATES the timing. This may seem a like a bit much to be accountable for, so I'll give a direct example. I'm not saying it's easy, **but I am saying it's necessary**.

It might be a tad abstract … the whole *"wait for timing or create the timing"* aspect. Even the unavailability of a person in an emotional state may be a bit abstract. So, let's break it down.

I have PTSD. I am bipolar. So, when I get stressed by whatever it is that stresses me out, I have a panic attack. There are lots of types of panic attacks. But, in all of them, the person experiencing it is out of commission from a logistical standpoint. They are incapable of taking in and processing information beyond the immediacy of the moment. If you have been around someone who has panic attacks, this should be obvious. Panic attacks are emotional states that occur when your body is reacting faster than the frontal lobes are capable of processing information.

My mate has taken the necessary steps to work with me during these moments. She is limited with what she can do logically, because although I am rather intelligent, I am crippled in that area during a panic attack.

So, as someone handling me, she creates the timing and environment wherein I can be helped. She observes that I am not available, and instead of simply banging both of our heads against a brick wall by going into the "logic" behind why I don't need to be panicking, she deals with the physical response first. She sits me down, and just chills with me until my heart rate gets back under control, and I stop shaking.

Then she can talk to me. Not until then. I can't hear a thing. The world is crashing in on my brain like a collapsing star, and there is nothing that anyone can say or do that is not an attack.

She doesn't just wait for good timing, she doesn't just wait for me to be better (which is really all right also; most of my family has done that). What she does is infinitely more engaging and loving. She does not ignore my mental state. I can't describe how important this is. I am not a nameless entity receiving her expressions. I am Vito, *at a certain time with certain characteristics*, and I am her Audience. If she wants to have a discussion with me and my characteristics are not in line with that interest, we either don't have the conversation, or she gets me where she wants me first.

We are more than just people. We are people, **at a certain time, in a certain mental state**. If we want to improve communication, this is the Perspective we have to start with.

This was an introduction to the idea of being accountable to our Audience. We want them receptive. We want them present and focused, and capable of integrating our expressions. This means that we want them to end up with the same picture in their heads that we started with in ours. That is quite specific.

Being able to manage this Perspective is not easy. It takes energy. We have to be motivated and focused. We have to be able to recognize our Audience, understand their state of being, and be willing to adjust our behavior to translate our expressions.

This opportunity exists all day, every day. The empathic people I know walk around sizing up everyone's mood and focus and trying to ease into those worlds when a shared moment comes into play. Now, not everyone is going to analyze the mood of their waitress upon sitting down for dinner, and adjust to her state of being, *but that does not change the fact that everyone is capable of doing so*. And if we want the best restaurant experience possible, we are accountable for it. If our waitress is upset, it might be a good idea to let her vent or go out of our way to say something kind to her. Not only is this just a nice thing to do, it will make it less likely that her state of mind distracts her from doing her job well. We have an opportunity to do something to try to ensure her presence.

Our opportunities to recognize, adjust, and create are countless every day. ***Every person we come in contact with is a new Audience***.

Vibration of Reception

Whether we like it or not, we are teachers. Period. Just by living on the planet. The more we voice our opinions, the more we engage fully, and the more ideas that we give life to, the more active we are making ourselves reality's final design. Everything we do has a Vibration of intent, and a Vibration of reception.

When we choose to share things with individuals we become teachers. We should also become parents. A parent understands that there is a responsibility to the Vibration of the sharing and how it is received. But a great parent also knows that the resulting Vibration will change the Vibration of the world as a whole, making the resulting Vibration in our children's lives priceless. Vibration is a pretty common term, but I am going to give it a hard definition so there is no confusion. **Vibration** is the waveform identity of a reality. It is a material reality that has its own specific characteristics and qualities. Successful communication occurs when our expression creates the identical Vibration for our Audience that we have within us.

As we practice our ability to recognize, adjust, and create our environment, we get better at successful communication. We owe the knowledge and Perspective we have its Vibration. As parents and teachers we owe our Perspective the honor of delivering it in a way that will create a Vibrational match. This also demands that we understand that we are accountable for the Perspective's existence outside of our own reality.

We must express our internal realities in a way that will cause a Vibrational match. We owe it to ourselves. We are not pitching ideas to wear ourselves out, or to be repetitive because we are bored. We want the contact. We want to change the external reality.

I can psychobabble about the intricacies of expression and what any specific person's actual intentions are when analyzing any conversation. We are completely capable of undermining and sabotaging, being passive-aggressive and manipulative. But that is not what we're talking about right now. We're not talking about everything that can go wrong. We are just trying to find ways it can go right.

We want the contact and connection. We want the home run. So we make sure we have our batter, and we throw them a pitch they can let loose on. We throw it at *their* sweet spot. *It doesn't matter whether we think it's a strike or not.* This is not a game…this is home run derby.

This is a huge distinction. Your goal includes another person, or an entire Audience. If they don't connect, it doesn't matter if we said it "right" or not. We might as well have been speaking to them in another language. If we throw a strike, and the batter whiffs, no connection was made, and everyone loses. We are aiming to be accountable for something we CANNOT CONTROL. *This is not easy to make peace with.* It's easier to just say "I threw a strike," and walk away with no connection. But it doesn't work. It just doesn't. When we do that, things we want, and that we care about, don't happen. Connections are not made, and growth is not achieved. IT IS OUR JOB TO DO EVERYTHING WE CAN TO ADJUST TO THE PERSON WE CANNOT CONTROL. And after all of that, it doesn't guarantee any success at all. ***But it does do great honor to our Vibrational intent by giving it the best possible foundation for success.*** That in itself is evolution of consciousness. That is how our Vibrational consciousness becomes an embodiment of Synergy of Commune.

Audience and the Responsible Teacher Principle

The **Vibration of Intent** is like a signature for expression. It is distinct in each moment, and for the creation of Commune synergy it has to include others. This is our Audience. The amount of care taken with Audience is a direct reflection of our dedication to expression and Commune. When we think about Audience, and we think of speaking to our friends and those we share space with, we rarely think of ourselves in the way that a kindergarten teacher thinks of herself when speaking to her class containing two dozen five-year-olds. This highlights the differences in the way we view our roles as expressive beings.

So, it's clear that we don't talk to a group of five-year-olds the same way that we talk to adults, but how much effort do we put into adult Audiences, if any?

It has been said that when one reaches enlightenment, that everyone becomes your guru. Everyone is a great teacher to the enlightened through the sharing of Perspective. We can visualize this enlightened person. A person who uses every bit of contact with the world to vivify reality is not far from imagination (Dalai Lama, anyone?).

What I want to show is that in the enlightened society we all want to create, we are all gurus, as all are experiencing different Perspectives of shared enlightenment, and the effort we put into addressing our Audience has a direct correlation to the quality of the ever-changing reality we are creating.

We can include Audience in every expression. The **Responsible Teacher**, at any level (not just kindergarten), can do it all day. Every student presents a different challenge. We are no different. In the world we want to create, we are all gurus sharing Perspective and changing the realities of those around us. This means that whether we like it or not, the world is our classroom, and everything we do is nourishment. We can connect with our Audience, and adjust to our Audience. This is good faith behavior.

Man, that is a lot of terminology. I have used **Synergy in Commune**, focus on **Audience**, being a **Responsible Teacher**, the presence of a community of gurus, and even home runs to get at what I'm going after here. That's because I know how important it is to me, and how important it was to my own personal development. Things that were furiously frustrating became easy. I know how building a foundation for a creative mental environment works. I know it. And I know that the way we are habituated into doing it now, from adults in a working environment, to psychologists dealing with clients, parents with children, etc. ...all of that falls short of the basic requirements of successful communication.

We have simply not been told how difficult it is to communicate. If what we are expressing is important, we don't need to just say it. We need to say it, feel it, be it, vibrate it, and glow it in neon through our eyeballs. Then, after we have nailed the ability to do ALL of that, we need to be able to motivate understanding by making attractive what we are communicating.

All of this is leading us to the integrity of a group, as a focused creation. It starts with the self, how we maintain our expressions and creativity, and moves through how we seek to communicate with each other. It can expand to a larger picture of families, and groups of people, who have become involved with the creation and maintenance of growing ideas for common goals. It also gives us the ability to test the integrity of the groups as people move in and out of close contact with each other. Synergy of Commune demands that we are active in refining our world, and it gives us tools to do so by accessing the motivations of those we are close with.

PART 2: GROUP EXPRESSION

We have accountability within our environment. In the first part of this chapter, we were looking at the creation of a fertile environment for communicating. In this part we are looking at the types of relationships and people we have in our world, hoping to discern their nature, and refine our experience. Rather than wanting clarity of Vibration within a momentary idea, it is clarity over a long-term vision of who we want to be. The reason these ideas belong together is that **we are communicating our relationships' validity to the rest of the world** through our experience.

There are people who simply may not fit with what we want to do. This is not a judgment on them, but a judgment on how they fit with us. They may not be building material for the structure we are trying to create. They may be damaging to us...*or not*. But it will be impossible to communicate the Vibration of what we want into an external reality with their presence. We are Accountable for our world. We can recognize, adjust, and create. But we cannot control...*we cannot make someone fit.*

Every relationship we engage in carries a Vibration that is validated through our continued engagement. This means that the nature of how we relate to our family, our friends, and our coworkers carries a Vibration that is transmitted to the world as a whole. This is why we must become more accountable for the people in our environment, and refine our engagements in accordance with what we most want to validate. We need to make *our world* the way we want **the world** to be.

It's important to have mission statements about what we want in our lives. The following essay is basically the one I wrote for myself on this subject.

Group Refinement for Heightened Synergy.

So, I was talking about mood and focus, especially in reference to what we bring to those around us and what we want others to bring to us.

There has been confusion in this area and I'm looking to clean it up. This has to be taken into account alongside the need for people to be able to share their truths and be vulnerable. That is necessary, as is our focus on the type of vibe quality we want in our relationships. We want people to share their lives with us, but we don't want to be brought down. This is not a conundrum. It is not impossible. It is Perspective. We are often too busy and distracted to make discernments in this area, but we can get better at it. Let's look at the subtleties.

There is a huge difference between someone who is sad, or unhappy, or angry, and someone who is *getting off* on being sad or unhappy. The former is someone who generates happiness from deep down even when their external circumstances create discomfort for them. The latter is someone who is latching on to external realities to base their pervasive mood on, because they don't have the well of internal fortitude or volition to really BE happy. It is time in our evolution that we discern between these descriptions, and begin making alterations in our lives so that the former is validated and the latter is not.

I don't mind being around a person who is sad. I don't like being around **sad people**.

I don't mind being around a person who is angry. I don't like being around **angry people**.

I don't mind being around a person who is sick. I don't like being around **sick people**.

I don't mind being around someone who is in a fight. I don't like being around **fighters**.

So how do we look at this stuff? Some situations are obvious. Really angry or really sick people are obvious. Eeyore is pretty obvious. We needn't start with the obvious. We need to acclimate ourselves to finding subtlety, and in order to find subtlety, we need to start with ourselves.

Just yesterday I came across a great example. I found myself aggravated (by the cost of tires to be exact), and not only did I let myself get angry...*I was getting off on being angry*. I was happy that I was angry and was looking for any reason to be rude to someone and mess with their day. I did that. Yesterday. Now, I know myself pretty well, and this behavior is inconsistent with the type of person I like creating daily. So, I made sure to do nothing, give the urges no energy, and wait until they were gone.

We all do this. We all get angry. We may even get titillated by our emotion and want to stoke the fires (*some people enjoy this more than others*). What we are talking about is not how we initially respond. What we are looking at is who, through habitual thoughts and behavior, we are willing to become.

We don't ever get past reactivity. We get better at managing what it leads to. This is about Influence and movement, not control. It is a creative effort to build a life that vibrates in tune with love and joy being permanent, and everything else being temporary. Loss, pain, anger, fear, sickness, struggle... we want these, as they are a part of the life matrix we have come for. But they are NOT the stasis. They are temporary. Love is what we are born of and die into, and we can have that be the fertile space from which our life spirals.

So who brings what into your life? Everyone in your world is an author of incoming energy for you. If what they are bringing in is negative, are they trying to do anything about it? Or are they addicted to the dramatic experience? We know what the media embodies, especially after last week's _____ (insert tragedy here). Did you notice which people in your world wouldn't let it go? Do you notice who doesn't want to move on? We need to notice those we are close to. We should be asking ourselves some questions.

Do you notice someone who has experienced loss and never gets over it?

Do you notice angry people always trying to make you angry?

Do you notice sad people always bringing you bad news?

Do you notice sick people always bringing in new ailments?

DO YOU NOTICE PEOPLE WHO NEED YOU TO FEEL A CERTAIN WAY ALWAYS BRINGING YOU EVIDENCE THAT YOU SHOULD FEEL A CERTAIN WAY? DO YOU NOTICE THAT THEY ALWAYS HAVE EVIDENCE?

That's because there is always evidence that the world can totally suck, that things are unjust or imperfect. But that is not nourishing or enriching. Besides that…it is incomplete. There is plenty of evidence that the world is beautiful also.

We are going to be affected. That is the reality of living. The people around us help shape and Influence our view of the world. We want to be able to create a joyous world, though, and doing that means we are going to have to discern the nature of the people we have close to us, so we can limit negativity and foster health. This is the Parenting of our own environment.

So how do we tell the difference between someone who is getting off on negativity and someone who is getting over negativity? The difference is good faith. My family spoke of it when I was young and it has been burned into my psychological views since then. It is the person who is taking the given reality as it is, and seeking the best and most loving Perspective from which to deal with it. This is a theoretical person. This is an unattainable goal, but a very worthwhile focus. This is not something that can be pinned down. It is not a Perspective that can be controlled. It is a desire to move in ways that are consistent with joyous creation rather than ones that are distracted and crippled by parasitic negativity.

The process of refinement is a key element to all expansions. It is a key to healthy growth. It is a system that seeks to manage how our interactions with the world serve us when the social edges of our reality are malleable.

We are accountable for the quality of this "mix." I do not mean we should be accountable. I mean that this accountability is wholly ours. We are the only ones that get to deal with our reality directly, thus we are the only ones that can Influence changes within its matrix. We are expressing the whole of this matrix to everyone in our environment, and that environment is now global because of technology. We cannot control how much of our reality is transmitted (all), we can only Influence it toward a refined ideal of what we want to embody the most.

Here is an example of how it's done.

Parental Environment Self-Refinement.

I have gotten some harsh criticism in my life about the manner in which I remove people from my world. It is a deeply personal thing to edit someone out of our experience, but it is one of the most important tools we have for creating our reality. So ...let's get to a quote from the Invitation by Oriah Mountain Dreamer:

"Can you bear the accusation of betrayal without betraying your own soul?"

When I first read this at fifteen, it didn't seem like it was going to be a huge deal. The first time I acted on it I was eighteen years old, home for the last time before moving to California from Florida. A kid I didn't enjoy so much was hanging with all my friends, and I didn't really know him. After giving it the ol' college try, I decided I didn't want him in my house. So one night he came knocking, and I said, "No you can't come in, we're chillin', thanks dude, see ya later."

He was stunned. You can't just say no to someone for no reason!

Yes, I can.

It was my house. It was my time with my friends and family. I'm not going to miss an opportunity to make a magical moment. It is simply not my duty to do things I don't want to when there are other options available. And though I totally care how others feel, I also know that time is short. Quality of life and vibe is precious…and I act accordingly.

Now I want to address adult social settings, especially social media. I remove a lot of people. A lot. This is my party, and I am constantly re-upping on invitations for it. I used to figure this was natural, and that everyone sees it this way. I'm guessing now that many do not.

I am sitting in my house right this second. My family is all around me. This is literal. If someone upsets me, presents a vibe I don't like, or brings me down, my family has to pay. My kids and my mate are the first to foot the bill when my mood is messed with. I am accountable for my mood, and responsible for managing my environment so that moments like this are rare to nil. So how do I respond to people in those moments? I don't invite them to my next party. That's all. I can still love people and not invite them into my world. No one is assured access to me, and honestly, no one should be assured access to anyone.

Is it unconditionally loving to behave like this? Hmm... good question. Let me first point out that I am not a believer in unconditional love, though I strive for its unattainable beauty. However, I don't know that this situation applies. I don't consider it loving to allow "unconditional access" to my reality. I don't think anyone should do that. I don't consider it loving of the self. Healthy boundaries are present to protect and honor everyone.

Behaving the way I just described gave me the best summer of my young adult life. It was six weeks and I've never forgotten a minute. It was epic. The vibe was flawless, and I never got another opportunity like it.

I really hope we all take our world as seriously and preciously as I took mine that summer. Please don't be afraid to bear the accusation of betrayal for defining the boundaries of your reality, not with anyone in your world.

We would jump at the chance to choose the friends for our children and loved ones, to protect their peace and foster their creativity. We would streamline a glorious environment for them. This is something we must do for ourselves. Those closest to us deserve the best of us, and the company we keep goes a long way toward influencing that.

Healthy discernment is a continuous process. It is necessary for health. This is what the Business of Accountability entails. When realized fully, it is a process by which strengths within the self, or members of a group, are shared and enhanced. It is also the process by which illness, in all its different expressions of negativity, can be separated and removed. In this way our lives are refined.

Refinement is a natural process if we allow it to be. When there is something foreign in the body, inflammation is the result. This draws attention to that which is causing friction and allows the body to resolve the issue. As we create more healthy realities in our lives, the unhealthy realities begin to cause this friction.

As we become happier, unhappy people begin to stick out. This can be resolved by removing the people, or limiting our involvement with them.

As we create more joyous thoughts, our own unhappy thoughts become obvious to our consciousness. This can be resolved by limiting the amount of Validation we give those thoughts. That is the nature of creating a healthy internal and external environment.

Working to create this type of environment on the micro scale, in conversations, gatherings, internal meditative dialogue, and the whole of our expressions from moment to moment, is conducting harmony into the orchestra of our lives. We are accountable because we live in the music. This is the business of creating a society with a more harmonic shared reality.

Chapter 6:

Why Bad Decisions Are Attractive: The Hangover Proposal

We know that health is a positive thing, and we know that harmony in our lives comes from a combination of qualities that require a certain amount of focus. We also know there are a lot of maps and guidelines to healthy and happy living. We are then presented with a pretty unhealthy and unhappy world that seems to have completely ignored the many maps at hand. This juxtaposition has got to seem strange to someone besides me.

I have a hard time believing it's a lack of intelligence, or a lack of information. I know that it is a lack of knowing oneself, but the idea of "knowing yourself" is about as specific and helpful as telling someone that what they are looking for is "in the last place they will look for it." In this case, the issue is personal motivation. We don't have it, not even when it comes to happiness and health, because like most things that are glorious in this life, nothing guarantees it.

The following is an essay I wrote after responding to a question from a frustrated therapist.

The Therapist's Query ...

So...a therapist put out an open question last night in frustration: "*Why does someone come to therapy, pay me money, listen to my advice, and then completely ignore it in the face of all evidence over a long period of time?!*"

This is a good question, and the answer is not super obvious until you hear it. Afterwards, it is forever super obvious. We have been distracted by individual psychoanalysis and missed a commonality that has far-reaching affects. Everyone ignores advice, and everyone finds a way to not do what's best for them. The reason, however, is not specific to the person.

DOING WHAT'S BEST IS NOT A SURE THING. THERE IS NO GUARANTEE IT WILL WORK.

SABOTAGING OUR LIVES WORKS EVERY TIME.

The second behavior is simply more satisfying.

Happiness is not guaranteed, no matter what. You can do your absolute best, study and practice and meditate and focus all your positive energy on loving the world and healthy relating...and get the short end of the stick.

THAT IS HORRIBLE!!!!!! It's simply too much to take. I still can't handle it as well as I'd like.

So what do we do with that knowledge? What do we do knowing that we don't have the power to ensure the happiness and safety we crave?

We decide that we'd rather prove we're powerful by deciding to sabotage our lives by making bad decisions, as bad decisions almost always lead to negative consequences. We choose to be powerful instead of taking a chance at being happy. We can always cause ourselves pain. So when we feel *(past)* helpless and scared, we load the gun and shoot our own feet.

Homer Simpson to Lisa on *The Simpsons*: **"Aww, Lisa, look here now, you tried your best, and you failed miserably. The lesson is...never try."** *Self-sabotage*

That's literally what we do. We choose a risk-free option.

We do make ourselves feel better by asking for help, venting, and going to therapy. It's the same as having a gym membership and never going. It makes us feel good to use it as defense if people question our commitment to health and well-being (and you'd better have a defense...because you can't righteously complain without one...oops). *? (the 'central' issue.)*

So when we look at someone who won't take advice, and we are resentful toward them for sabotaging their lives, it's important to know why. Is it just because we are empathically tied to them and their shoddy decision-making? No. We are also upset because we are doing the same thing in at least a couple areas, and being reminded of that leads us into Cognitive Dissonance, the brain's most uncomfortable state. *We do what we judge...*

We have a strong drive to *ignore* our role in the perpetuation of this reality, because it is our consciousness' weakest link. The need for power and control looms large in our frightened adult consciousness. It will keep us from ever taking the chances our soul came here to take. *UCS (for primary + secondary gain)*

So, this is why we can ignore good advice and sabotage our lives. This is a very seductive power we wield, and I fully understand that no one wants to give it up. But now we know why we bail on good advice, and knowing why will Influence every conversation we have from now on (internal and external conversations).

When someone says "it's too hard," they don't mean it's actually too difficult. They mean there's no assurance it will make them happy, so it's not worth how hard it is.

⟡⟡⟡⟡

So when we look at the people in our lives through this Perspective, the mistakes everyone makes and the advice they ignore becomes less of a mystery, and more of a simple behavior pattern. This Perspective has helped me refine my environment a lot. When someone is not ready to help themselves and we don't know why, it is difficult to make a judgment call on whether to keep helping them or not. But when we know why they are not helping themselves, we can take action more easily...and we should.

It is frustrating when someone screams for food, and then tosses the three-course meal we've set in front of them in the garbage. We don't have to be frustrated, though. We can just know that they are afraid of the risk and afraid of giving up certainty. I want to use another analogy to highlight the issue, and in this analogy I will use myself as the example of the person ignoring advice. I call this the Hangover Proposal.

⟡⟡⟡⟡

The Hangover Proposal

For many years in my twenties I was a drunk. Not just a year or two, but many. During this time I discovered many a things about myself. I became well-acquainted with my personal psychology, not just as an addict (which is really informative on its own), but as a person with a mixture of needs and compulsions that expressed themselves in many ways. Drinking was always an answer to a problem, but I was very focused on what all of these "problems" were. And, because I had no intention of "not drinking" anytime soon, the pressure was off for me to bullshit myself, and I was afforded the ability to watch the natural expression of my psychology. *I'm in the "split mind"*

Every day I had a choice: "Stop drinking if you want to feel better." This is a true dictate I considered every day. True as the world turning. But I didn't stop. I didn't stop drinking for so many reasons that the number of reasons I didn't stop became a reason to drink. It was obvious that I should stop drinking if I wanted to feel better, but there was a catch. While you feel bad when you drink, it doesn't mean that if you stop drinking you will feel good. D'oh! *(reasons to avoid change)*

So, let's take a look at detox. It's SOOOO fun. You feel awful for two or three days, and then you feel better. It's really great to feel better. Every day you wake up early, can participate in life, can complete basic tasks, etc. As you are going about being sober, you are faced with a question every day. "I am starting to feel bad, and I don't like it. If I drink, I'll feel better." This is another true dictate. I'll feel better for a short time, in trade for how I will feel the next morning. I'll be useless and unhappy most of the next day, in fact, and I know it. *avoid; temp, pain*

Let me say right now, this is me after drinking for 5-6 years straight. That is a ton of liquor, all day. Many people can drink and be fine the next day. So when I say "I'll be useless tomorrow if I drink," that's just me.

So, knowing I would literally be "taking myself out" for the entire next day if I drank, I resisted temptation and worked through it. I stayed sober so that I could feel better the next day. But then, after resisting the urge to remove myself from an issue, the unthinkable happened. I woke up in a bad mood and had no energy. **WAIT, THAT WASN'T THE DEAL I MADE!**

I made the deal that I wasn't going to drink so that I would feel good the next day. This was just crazy and infuriating. I didn't feel good and I didn't even do anything wrong! Rude.

I felt betrayed. So, the next time I was faced with that decision, the nature of my options was different. I had what most see as a choice between feeling good and feeling bad, but it was actually the choice between *"maybe feeling good,"* and *"definitely feeling bad."* This choice was *very different.* I know what a hangover is, and I can choose it. I CANNOT choose to feel good with certainty. It is not an option that is guaranteed.

This is the **Angst of No Promises**. The stress of facing the world without certainty is so damaging that we do not address it. Angst is truly the best word to describe it. We would have to accept that reality is not fair to be able to live with this, not just conceptualize it, but believe it. And accepting unfairness is untenable to most. This inability to accept unfairness is not only a human trait. It has also been documented in the animal kingdom, as well. Any form of consciousness capable of conceptualizing action and reward has an issue with unfairness. It is not surprise, given this fact, that our logic-driven minds cannot manage the stress that comes from accepting a world without certainty in actions and results. This leads us to the Hangover Option.

The Hangover Option makes sense. It is choosing the certainty of feeling bad over the possibility of feeling good. It has certainty, and the alleviation of risk equals alleviation of stress. It gives us a sense of power, which will be more attractive than the possibility of happiness much of the time. It is more attractive in the moment, but ineffective for creating sustained satisfaction in our lives.

There is never, and will never be a guarantee that we will feel good. Ever. So when anyone we advise "does the completely wrong thing," we can look at the hangover principle and understand that *it is never an obvious option to opt for a healthier and more difficult decision, as it may not lead to the desired result.* But also, understand that because the decision to sabotage has merit, that there is less motivation to ever make the healthier choice. *very little to depend on God-centered*

From this angle, every bad decision makes sense. Every bad decision grants the person making it the illusion of control--a fantasy of certainty in an uncertain world. When a bad decision makes sense, we are left without the recourse of externalization. We cannot say "That just makes no sense," and be done with it. This means we have to deal with the fact that it could be us and engage its possibility in our reality. We share this reality, the one where bad decisions are more attractive because they offer consistency, control, and the illusion of power. We must be careful of our potential to act in this manner. *relat: & others to blame? (addicts)*

Chapter 7:

Psychological Determinism

We have gotten through adding a lot of Perspective to our reality in the first six chapters. This is going to continue throughout the book. In this chapter we are also going to lose some Perspectives because of the additions we make. This is the nature of refinement, and it is time we take a close look at some commonly held beliefs. What we are adding is **Psychological Determinism**, a theory postulating that every individual action is the result of our environment combined with our specific momentary Perspective.

Now, how I go about this refinement is significant, because subtracting belief is a violent act. We have a lot of emotional attachment to our constructs due to fear of change (a valuable survival trait). Altering or removing our ways of thinking can come with a sense of loss and distress. I am NOT a fan of either of those feelings, so before I go about ripping up certain thought matrices, I will promise you that *the removal of these devices will be through the growth of other ideas* such that no distress or sense of loss should accompany them. I am going to deconstruct in such a way that we are able to see the beauty and power that the present point of view has hidden from our sight. It will be like tearing down small buildings right in front of our face so we can see the entirety of the cityscape, in all its breathtaking glory.

I am tearing down **Free Will, Control, and Responsibility**. They do not exist, and come with a high price for our consciousness that far outweighs the value of their façade.

I am going to show that the city behind these ideas is strong, alive, and powerful. This city is based on **Observation, Influence, and Accountability**. The city is our consciousness, and after Free Will, Responsibility and Control are no longer confusing our focus, *we will be able to explore it.*

I am doing this because we, as people, need to feel "in control." If we need to feel "in control," then we are incapable of unbiased observation of our reality, and everything affecting it. If we are incapable of seeing and getting to know our consciousness, we are simply *unqualified to Influence our world.* Losing the idea of Free Will is a prerequisite for full self-analysis because the world we live in does not contain control. In order to maintain that illusion we have to shrink our focus mightily.

"Unqualified to Influence our world" sounds pretty harsh, doesn't it? But how often do people ignore sound advice? How often does telling someone that a stove is hot keep them from touching it? How often do people, in all areas of their lives, try to put square pegs into round holes? How likely are we to ignore when things are not working? How often does conceptual knowledge and experience fall short of motivating healthy behavior?

My frustration over these questions formed the basis for my future investment in Psychological Determinism. It began when I was a freshman in high school, and led to my first attempt at a philosophical essay. It was titled "The Jar Theorem." It likened understanding abstract concepts to filling up jars of unknown depth, and the inspirations/information that led to the filling as ping-pong balls. That is "ping-pong balls flying into jars." It developed over years of focus in psychology and several really tasty philosophical essays on Epistemology. Finally, about five years ago, I landed on **the Shoulder Surfer** description.

Psychological Determinism and the Shoulder Surfer

Common logic says that we have x options...however many we can consciously recognize. I say that we have only one. That is the one we end up choosing--the one that we value most. The others are never real options, no matter how real the "choosing" feels. This is why good psychoanalysts know what their patients are going to do in advance, and why the entire field of psychology is predicated on being able to predict and Influence behavior.

The Shoulder Surfer

Let's say that a small being lived on your shoulder and was invisible. This watcher has two defining characteristics:

1) It understands your genetic code, along with how that code will process experience from a genetic standpoint, and all of your natural tendencies.

2) It has been with you since the moment of your conception, and experienced every moment of your life with you, and thus seen how your experiences have shaped you.

Is there a doubt that at ANY GIVEN MOMENT the Shoulder Surfer could tell an independent party exactly what you were going to do next? I would say there is no doubt. I would say that, given any set of recognizable choices, this watcher will have guessed the choice you would end up making, *every time, forever.*

If this watcher can do that, in what way were you free in making those decisions? *In fact, in what way were **you** making those decisions?*

Decisions are seen to belong to us. In the sense that they belong to no one else, this is true. *In the sense that our identity*

authors *our behavior,'it is not true*. We may take part in some way, but we are not the **Authors of Our Behavior**. ✗ A∪T

This does not mean that PRE-destination exists. That is a completely different idea having to do with cosmic intent. What I am speaking of are the laws of behavior when put to scientific ends within the realm of personal psychology.

If we are not Authors of Our Behavior, this calls many ideas into question. It leads us into inquiry and examination. One of the ideas that must be adjusted (or in this case eliminated) is Free Will. Responsibility, guilt, shame, and judgment all undergo mutations. Mostly, they become simple descriptions of unjustified emotional states (guilt, shame), or tick-like habitual reactions to common situations (responsibility, judgment). *to eliminate*

Are we accountable? Physically, in this world, yes. We, and only we, are accountable for our realities. This includes everything from our behavior to the entirety of our internal and external environment. Are we Responsible for all of that? No. And those two ideas are not mutually exclusive.

The language that I hear in my head is English. Heck, I even dream in English. I was given a childhood, filled with a bounty of experiences across an enormous environment made up of people and things not under my control. I have the genetic disposition of my ancestors, and the social disposition of an American growing up in the '80s. My personality was shaped by my parents and family. My values were created by my experiences and my internal reactions. My entire subconscious mind is filled with a blueprint of experiences that is unique to my life. Think of your life, your history, and the bounty of experience you moved through to get to where you are. Think of the people in your life that helped shape you.

At some point I realized that nothing is beyond those Influences. I looked at myself, and saw the insanity of the belief that I could be free of (completely unInfluenced by) everything that had been given me. I realized that the mind I identified with was not under my control. I began to think that the mind I had considered my identity might not even be "mine."

This creates Cognitive Dissonance, but what beyond the love of our own thought processes can tell you that you are making these choices you make?

The Shoulder Surfer, and his well of knowledge....

Let's start with an obvious one, an example of a Russian citizen walking up to me and asking me a question in Russian. The Shoulder Surfer would be accurate in saying that I wouldn't be of much help (I do not speak Russian). That's not too much of a stretch. So when I looked at choosing one partner over another, one meal over another, it became less of a stretch to think that the knowledge of "Russian language" may be a lot like "most desired partner," or "most wanted meal." Maybe such things would be obvious to us if we spent more time observing our behaviors. But there is no reason to think that patterns hadn't emerged over years that the Shoulder Surfer was privy to.

My lack of understanding of the Russian language leads to the Surfer being able to predict that I won't be able to reply. My tastes and interests based on my experience will dictate what food or people I will yearn for at any given moment, and the Surfer knows those too. I am not the author of the experiences that led me to my wants, values, and abilities. If I had full access to my genetics and subconscious mind, the sources of these motivating factors in my life would be present to me at all times, and I would have more to work with mentally. This would give me the insight that the Shoulder Surfer has... but it would still not give me control or authorship over my motivations. X

The absence of the possibility of free will is a tough pill to swallow, though. Why is it hard to accept that the sum of our experiences plus our genetic disposition combine to make our decisions for us? Why must there be so much dissonance over our lack of control? The Angst of No Promises, where unavailable certainty is concerned, turns into the Fury of No Control where illusory freedom is concerned.

The Fury of No Control occurs because we need to feel Potent in our reality. This is an emotional need, something survival-driven that is coded into our DNA. We have to address this with Influence. That is the tool we do have. Control is an illusion. Influence is real. We can safely remove our attachment to the idea of control only by replacing it with the power of Influence. Then the Fury of No Control can abate.

There is a genealogy to experience. Adding to the already-unique nature of our body's genetic structure, our experiences provide a reality-footprint that has no match in its intricacy. The raw data that we have taken in JUST TODAY is not quantifiable in its largeness, and it is unlike that of any other consciousness in the Universe. It's time to stop thinking of our experiences as just *"things that happen,"* and more like *"**the motivational DNA of conscious reality.**"* (Level II)

This puts control squarely out of our reach. It puts choices, behavior, and attitude into a great mire of subconscious motivations. If anything today had happened differently than it had, we would not be where we are right now. If we had almost gotten into a car accident this morning, our inner mental reality (thoughts and chemistry both) would be altered, thus every outgoing expression would have had a different quality. Every interaction we would have had throughout the day would have been different. The crux of Psychological Determinism lies in the realm of this logic.

Free Will's Myth rests in the idea that we are free to act beyond our environment's Influence on us. It is built on the idea that something separate from the EVERYTHING-that-makes-us-who-we-are is capable of being **unInfluenced** by our environment. Because our society believes in Free Will's Myth, instead of finding Commune with everything we are Influenced by and relating to it, *we think that we can free ourselves* from it when making decisions in our reality. This is crippling.

We are in an endless discussion with ourselves about the world around us, and the world inside of us. The character of that relationship is what Psychological Determinism is describing. As I said once when asked about the likeness between Psychological Determinism and Definition, "Definition is how you and I talk about a third thing. Psychological Determinism is how I and I talk about Everything Else."

Psychological Determinism looks at a moment and sees the multitude of information that led to a single consciousness acting in a specific manner at a specific time. The multitude of information does not include anything external to the environment of the person (although that environment is gigantic). Our Perspectives and subconscious mind hold all the motivating factors for our behavior.

So, where does that leave us? It leaves us in a state of inquiry with a lot to focus on. It leaves us with a lot of relationships and motivations to figure out. It leaves us with the impetus to relate and reflect. It leaves us with observation and Influence as hopeful tools for managing expression. That is our job. We are accountable for the management of the internal voices and external phenomena coming into our reality (our thoughts and surroundings). We are also accountable for the Influence that our outgoing expressions have on the matrix of society. The results of our behavior and the example that we set become our offering to the whole of the world.

Chapter 8:

Relationship to Determined Action and Responses

The relationship we have with our actions changes in the language of Psychological Determinism. For me it was the end of looking at my decisions as "things I did," and the beginning of looking at them as "things that happened." A whole new focus was demanded about my behaviors, as their motivations were thrust completely into doubt. The name of the state of mind that is created by doubt is Inquiry. Its goal is to track "Influence."

Tracking Influence leads us to discussions of sobriety, as "Influence" by unconscious motivators or subtle mental states can easily be matched with the effects of more obvious substances and the accompanying problems that come with them.

Drunk driving is a very obvious case...one defined by societal law through science. Operating an automobile at .08 BAL is illegal, as your focus is dimmed and your reaction times are slowed to an unacceptable extent. You are "Influenced" by alcohol in a way that makes you a "worse" driver than you are. And that is what is illegal--not being a "bad" driver, but through direct action becoming a "worse" driver than you would be normally. Here's where it gets fun.

It is not illegal to be a *distracted* driver, an *angry* driver, a *sad* driver, a driver *with the flu*, a driver *with a headache*, a driver who is *too hot to be comfortable*, or even a *tired* driver. Those are all Influences too, but are considered unintentional in the eyes of the law.

Now, looking at all of these, from alcohol in the bloodstream, to a dog in the backseat, or a headache, there is one thing that we can do as conscious human beings to ease the power of the Influence. That is to **adjust for its presence**. If we know we are being affected by something it becomes much easier to maneuver more carefully to keep from having an accident. We can take different roads, we can play appropriate music, roll the windows down (assuming you, like me, still have crank windows), and put extra energy into our focus. I don't know if anyone reading this has ever driven under the Influence of the aforementioned things, but odds are you have, and odds are you know what you need to do in order to stay safe and have a "focused, sober attention" when driving.

eg, of depr)

Being able to adjust for a known Influence is HUGE. For that, we do have to know we are being Influenced, and that is not always the case. So, let's look at the best example of this: roofies. The date rape drug, known to completely rob someone of awareness of what's going on, is the most viable example.

So, let's go to a party. We have our keys, and we plan on having two drinks over two hours and driving home. We know from our body weight and previous experience that this will have us well under the legal limit and totally capable of operating a car safely. So, we drink our two drinks over two hours and get in our car. But, someone has drugged us by slipping us a roofie. Because of this we are totally incapable of driving, BUT WE DON'T KNOW IT. Can we drive safely? Nope. Can we make an informed decision on whether or not to drive? Nope. Can we have the accurate amount of trust in our abilities? Nope.

2nd logt

Imagine it. We've been drugged, and have the consciousness equivalent of someone who has downed a bottle of whiskey, while believing that we are sober enough to drive. We are in trouble. I get scared just thinking about this kinda stuff, especially with my kids. If we haven't been drugged before, odds are there is no way we'll notice. Imagine it. Imagine watching going through all this.

Now imagine that we could reach into the world we are imagining and scream "HEY, YOU'VE BEEN DRUGGED!"

That would change everything, wouldn't it? We'd walk away from our car and find help. We would adjust accordingly. ***Knowing that you are being Influenced IS THE BIGGEST INFLUENCE*** on decision-making. Knowing that all of our decisions are based on our momentary matrix of consciousness, genetics, and experiential DNA is the key to making changes in our reality. We can set down the keys whenever we want, and the person who can scream at us, same as we screamed at ourselves that we'd been drugged, is the Observer Consciousness.

The following essay examines how meditative exercises can bring the Observer Consciousness forward.

Meditation and the Observer Consciousness

Let's examine meditation and other similar models of consciousness- expansion/heightened awareness.

The thing I noticed when I started meditation (at age ten) was that it seemed weird that it was something you would "do." It was spoken of like a task or event, like watching a movie, planting some flowers, or throwing grapes at an antelope. Go Meditate. It seemed to be abstracted and separate from second-to-second mental realities. Well, I didn't like that after about six years of practicing, so I started doing it differently. This is not to say that I don't get "still" sometimes…just that I try to lend my focus toward my meditative reality, that of observing the self, body, mind, and world, *all the time.*

The growth of the Observer Consciousness is learned in Meditation, but does not fully actualize until we can take it with us through daily activities. That, in my opinion, is the natural expansive use of the tool of Meditation. Having access *mindful-ness* to the Observer Consciousness throughout the day, to any degree, is going to enrich our life.

I've found that this style of observation is the most effective way to get at self-knowledge. This is because when you watch your actions with unconditional positive regard, and curious wonder, you can more easily shut down reactive systems of judgment that can keep you from experiencing yourself fully. That is a pivotal statement about what the Observer Consciousness is capable of.

This was my first conscious concept for the Observer Consciousness. This is the backbone of self-awareness. It is the tree from which all roots and branches spring. It is not "talking to yourself about your world," it is *identifying the one who watches* you talk to yourself about your world. This Observer has to be coaxed into action. It has the power to validate thoughts and actions. He has to be coaxed from voicelessness into the present through the mind's commitment to inquiry. The **State of Inquiry** that must be accepted is the one that is birthed from the fact that we are simply never sober. Never. We are always drugged.

We are, every second of our lives, being Influenced by the chemicals in our brain and the presence of our recent and long-term histories. This is an overwhelming state of affairs. It's scary. It tells us that there is a powerful complexity beyond the scope of our cognition that has a masterful hand in every single thing we have ever done, and will ever do. It is a fact that bothers us so much that we trivialize it, marginalize it, or ignore it.

In this way, "I am thinking" is accurate in the same way that "music is coming from that speaker" is accurate. *Sound* is what is coming from the speaker. Music is something being played by fifty people in a room, being recorded by men in another room, and mixed by another set of people at a whole different time, before being placed on something portable, and transferred to whatever is playing music through your speakers. The only minor things wrong with the declaration "I am thinking" are the definitions of the words "I," "am," and "thinking."

Meditation, as it allows a de-identification process with the childhood attachments to "I" as the self, allows us to understand our Influences. We begin by not marginalizing the aspects that are frightening, or different, or seemingly trivial...and we begin opening to learn the complexity and beauty of the full orchestra going on in our minds.

The Orchestra of the Influenced Mind

Listen to an orchestra. It's nearly impossible to pick out a single instrument; there are dozens.

Now imagine that meditation consisted of hearing "ONLY" the third violin, and you got to *fully observe* that third violin.

Now imagine every time you meditated you got to hear another instrument.

Imagine that after years of practice, you could listen to the orchestra as a whole and be able to pick the individual instruments out, specifically hearing their offering to the group (I know this is possible; it's why conductors make the big bucks).

Our motivating Influences can be tuned
Meditative states, and during any moment of
Consciousness. This practice allows us to learn our
orchestra without being overwhelmed. It is not a
possibility to be able to receive any of our subconsci
tivations without practicing consciousness. Meditation
that: consciousness practice. We are afforded the tim
opportunity to practice extensively, and we should make
most of it.

Thinking, *though we believe it to be "us," is not us.* It
not our identity. It is a conglomerate of noisy-and-irrevere
internal voices, whose source is elsewhere in our environ
ment. Learning how to discern the nature of the voices is what
meditation does. Making good decisions and improving our
ability to manage reality is what it allows us to do.

Thinking of a single instrument within an orchestra shows how the
relationship with the **External Mind** (that is the part of our own mind
we have to work with) must be cultivated. The External Mind consists
of a multitude of thoughts generated by the mechanisms and habits of
our brain. It is what we are listening to when in meditation. It must be
managed in the same way the external environment must be, through
observation and Influence. It is the **Conductor Consciousness**, the
"participating observer," that must manage the External Mind. He
works for harmony in the overall sound of the orchestra by giving
specific attention when necessary. He does not get lost and distracted
trying to micro-manage everything. That would be akin to trying to
play all of the instruments of the orchestra himself rather than guiding
specific conscious Perspectives within the group of musicians and

eir part of the whole.

78 e to trust them? First he has to understand

trum him. It is vital that they are, for only to-

n confluence the totality of whatever art is

he gets to know them.] He forms a relation-

t a working basis.

w the parts of our mind (all of the differ-

an take part in what reality they are creat-

t do this because reality is fragile and easily

g making noise within us, whether we want it

ou.

is jus,

e and

e the

is

t

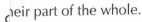

.n of Expecting Mastery

we are not in control of ourselves, what exactly is
 we've gotten ourselves into? The best way I've been
o see/experience/share this life is through the idea of a
.tionship, a Commune/co-op with a semi-malleable host.

Now, I just said our life is taking place within a semi-malleable host. That's kind of a big deal. **You are not a body with a soul, but a** **soul that happens to be riding in a body**.

I think that if we understand our relationship with things outside of our control, and do what is necessary to Influence those realities, we can take more of an active role in what we ultimately cannot control. The achievement of cooperation and acceptance can lead to heightened Influence. Heightened Influence can be habituated and expanded. That is as close to controlling this *wild-incarnated-bunch-of-chemistry-and-genetic-memory* as we're ever going to get.

The aspect I want to highlight here is that mastery is not an option. We're dealing with cooperation here, at best. The idea of mastery is a description of a disrespectful cooperation with the body. This is another area where **Synergy of Commune** really matters, as we are *turning the focus of conversation inward* to deal with motivational aspects of personality and behavior, *rather than outward at a society* that, like the self, is not controllable and is hard to communicate with.

The problem with expecting mastery is the creation of Cognitive Dissonance. **When we believe we are in control, and that belief is VITAL to our reality matrix, we are forced to ignore evidence of our role within our world.**

Our Perspective of the role we play in our world leads to our belief in how much power we have, and how accountable we make ourselves correlates to how powerful we believe ourselves to be. The more powerful we believe ourselves to be, the more we can creatively engage with our lives and the world around us. The downside to this is that we must take on the damage our lives cause others in order to have the fullest and most powerful Perspective. This is daunting.

To highlight the fragility of this situation I'm going to move away from the orchestra and the Conductor Consciousness, because it does not address the nature of our surroundings, and the damage that carelessness causes daily.

We are social beings with fragile egos. This is okay. It's not a failing of society that we are fragile. It is a gift of incarnation that we are sensitive. It allows us to experience deeply and resonate with our lives. But it has the downside of leaving us vulnerable to the whims of our minds, fear through misunderstanding, and the carelessness that comes with having a limited amount of conscious focus to draw on at any given point.

The hand we are dealt includes this. So when we think of how to manage our mind, we will want to think of a beautiful piece of music being conducted, but when we think of our ability to impact the world around us, it's best to think of ourselves in a wholly different and destructive manner. Dog in a china shop sounds about right, doesn't it?

Dog in a China Shop

So, let's imagine ourselves the owner of a well-trained police or service dog. Then let's imagine we're the owner of an untrained Dalmatian. And let's imagine that we have to take our dog into a china shop. The dog in this analogy represents the parts of ourselves that we cannot control, and the china shop is the feeling-world around us.

The goal of much of the work we do with ourselves as Conductor Consciousness is to reduce the amount of damage we are capable of inflicting on our surroundings as we move through them.

So we engage our world, and go into the store. We may get frustrated if we go into a store and our well-trained service dog breaks something. But ultimately it is not our action that destroyed the item, and we have done all we can in our power to train our dog. We don't have to feel bad, but we do have to pay for the damage, as that is a part of our accountability.

That doesn't seem like such a bad situation. That is how our interactions can be if we have put time, effort, and care into the training of our dog. If we do not, how other story altogether.

If we take an untrained, anxious dog into we are obviously taking a larger risk. Most of to some extent when letting ourselves loose in social situations. If we do not acknowledge that we are not in control of ourselves, as well as not close to being able to manage our own emotions, we have put ourselves in the position of being able to damage a large amount of our surroundings without having the fortitude to be accountable for all. So, when our "dog" breaks something we "externalize" the event. This means we blame the dog (can you hear yourself cursing your dog in your head?). We weren't responsible for the breakage, but do not realize that we are nonetheless accountable for the clumsiness of our dog. So we refuse to pay. In doing so, we refuse our own power and disrespect the world around us.

In the situation of china shop damage, blame and guilt are externalized onto the poorly trained dog (who had no business being in the store). This is analogous to our damaging behavior that can be externalized onto our anger, or whatever we believe caused it (as if that mattered). In doing this, we deny our own power. This is self-nullifying in the largest sense, as well as disingenuous. We bring all of ourselves into a situation, and then deny our relation to the part of ourselves that caused the damage.

It is such a powerful activator of Cognitive Dissonance to cause harm, that we would rather deny our power in a situation than face it. This is fear expressing itself through our denial of reality, and our power in it. In the end, this denial is also useless, as we still feel guilt and shame (just a repressed, subconscious, and perverted version).

When we do not engage in accountability for the damage we cause (pay for broken items), we are not engaging in the relationship we have to form with the parts of ourselves that we cannot control. This is dismissive of the self. This is dismissive of our power. It also makes it difficult to form a relationship with our uncontrollable selves, because once a type of power is dismissed, it is difficult to get back.

The reason I use a dog in the analogy is vital. Our body does not speak our language. It speaks in energy and chemicals. It knows what we do and how we feel, not what we say to ourselves. This is why making decisions about our lives is silly when we are not in complete Commune with ourselves.

"I don't know why I keep making the same mistake!" ... I do. **We keep letting an untrained dog run our lives because we deny the fact that he is ours to train.**

We are accountable for everything in our reality. We are not the cause, but it is all ours to deal with. This is because we are the **Primary Caregiver** for our mind. Whether we are thinking of conducting an orchestra, training a dog, or trying to get through to a drugged party-goer, we are the Primary Caregiver in every situation, and we have the most powerful Influence. Knowing this should put us back into the Parental role we have been getting more comfortable with since Chapter 3. We want to become vitally present and engaged Primary Caregivers. In doing so, we step into our power.

When we come to terms with the existence of the world of Influences beyond our control, and we refuse the natural tendency to dismiss and externalize that which we are accountable for, we can become a manager and harvester of our motivations. We can attend to and validate that which serves what we believe to be our best nature, and ignore or alter that which we do not wish to promote. That is Conductor Consciousness. It is birthed into existence through our commitment to **Influence**. Influence is the effect of taking an active role in our many matrices of thought and behavior. *It is the part of our full environment of Influences that is authored by us*.

We are either conductors working divinely with a group of skilled musicians, assuming we are in correct relation to our External Mind, or we're irresponsible owners of a pack of untrained dogs. We have a relationship with our mind as Primary Caregivers, and those are the opposing poles of its description. Conscious-and-engaged or unconscious. We want it to be that of a Conductor rather than that of a careless pet owner. The difference in those relationships is simply how much we wish to work with and Influence ourselves on a deep level.

Chapter 9:

Influence

I'm overwhelmed. It's the truth, you know. I'm frightened by the magnitude of existence every time I think of it. Every new piece of information makes the world a bigger place...makes the idea of remaining stable and independent more difficult. I want there to be answers and rules. I have always wanted them.

When I was young, my brother and I would have conversations about the existence of God (back when we were still enticed by the philosophy of the idea, all politics aside). My brother always told me he was very careful when it came to thinking about such things, because of how bad he wanted them to be true.

I have always wanted to believe that control was achieved with practice, skill, mastery, and focus, and that there was a "right way." Not a "find your own," but a "right way." I want someplace to put my feet so I can always be ready emotionally, mentally, and spiritually. But it's not there. It's just not.

So what is there? We want something. We want to feel good about who we are and where we are going. And while we cannot have certainty, we should be able to come up with something that stays the awfulness of the void that we carry around with us long enough to be able to manage to enjoy the world. I think we have some power there. We also want to be able to know what to do whenever anything happens around us or inside of us, to keep negative or destructive results from getting in the way of what we want. I think we have some power there too. We also want to be able to stop bad things from happening in our world. In all of these areas we will never have as much power as we want, and *we will certainly never have anything close to control*. But we do have something.

Have you heard the Serenity Prayer? Grant me: *The serenity to accept the things I cannot change, the courage to change the things I can, and the wisdom to know the difference*. Yeah, those are kinda all over the twelve step meetings I've attended. You know, those meetings you attend when your entire life is REALLY on the line, and you don't have the luxury of making a mistake? Psychological Determinism and its acceptance is part 1. Choosing to take part in influencing your world takes courage (part 2, the courage to change the things I can) because there is no guarantee, and we risk ourselves by becoming vulnerable when putting our heart into making changes and decisions. Part 3 (the wisdom to know the difference) is to save our strength. The "wisdom to know the difference" means we are committed to not being wasteful with our energy by trying to change things that cannot be changed.

We need our strength because we do not have control. *We need our strength because learning to Influence our world does not reward us immediately, obviously, or often*. This strength is the dividing line between being momentarily frustrated or disheartened, and becoming bitter and shutting down. So, as we look at the meaning and manner of influencing our reality, we have to respect our psychological needs as human beings, and make sure to tend to them as we work ourselves into these behaviors.

I am going to go over a few main types of Influence in this chapter, and throughout the rest of this book it will be a common theme. I focus on this heavily. I do so because once we have acclimated to using Influence in our lives, it becomes present in every conscious act.

The News Feed, the Crawl, and the Act of Conscious Validation

The ideas of the crawl and the news feed came up long ago for me. I was meditating, and learning to harness internal monologue and thought reaction in an attempt to slow them down, so that I could attain some control over the link between my conscious mind and the thoughts it had. I liked to picture the thoughts as moving in a direction across my brain, left to right. I also learned that if thoughts appeared in chunks of information, I could separate them like stories, and scroll through them mentally. I could see the errands I had to do that day in the section just above how I slept, which was in turn above what I wanted to eat that day. In another section I'd be worrying about money, happy about the weather, happy about my weight and strength, etc. Then there would be a section of loneliness and alienation hanging around. The sizes of certain sections would grow and shrink in correlation to my moods.

I was doing this before CNN started the news crawl at the bottom of the screen. This was also before social media had me reeling down an entire never-ending news feed. Now, this description that I had used to make sense of how I managed my relationship with my awareness has turned into an easily applicable description for anyone wishing to discuss or analyze their relationship with their mental activities. Priceless.

Conscious Validation is a means of Influence. Conscious Validation is the act of engaging with a subject or reality, and investing in it on a specific level. **Passive Validation** is a common thing. It takes no investment, and does not engage us consciously. There is a huge difference between the two, but they are both powerful creators. We are still a culture that passively validates at too high a ratio to Validation that occurs consciously. We are simply not as involved and engaged as we can be. This is the difference between being present and potent, and not being so.

So let's take a moment to examine the Validation of our inner realities, both Conscious and Passive. The easiest way to see the power and violence of our naturally active minds is to take a look at how we judge other human beings. We all judge everyone. We make assessments about everyone we come in contact with, first impressions, and these impressions are powerful (which is why it is important to make a good first impression).

If we are looking at a passive version of creating an impression, we can easily put ourselves at a mall. We size up every person we walk past. We can all remember doing this when we think about it for a moment, but the snap judgments we make seem to flow through us…that is because they are passive, for the most part. This does not mean they are not powerful. This just means we are not engaged in how powerful they are, or in the final expression of their content. We walk past someone, make a judgment, and then that judgment exists through us for a powerful moment, casting a Vibration in still space.

We give everyone a grade. We do this unconsciously, but it does not have to be this way. We can grade like it matters. We can pretend we are grading a bikini or muscle man contest. We can take in the entire person, write down notes, and have a reaction before we move forward with our thought's final expression. Think of the same person you passed in a mall, imagine a short interview with them, and imagine every note you would take about them. Then move forward with your final assessment of their entirety. Have that final thought be a thought you would be happy about expressing to the world. Be proud of it. That is Conscious Validation.

Whether Passive or Conscious, what we validate imprints on the world around us, and has effects. It matters that we engage ourselves for the sake of others as we move through the world. Not only do our judgments affect the external world through us, they also affect us. The first reason is that our judgments are permanent fixtures within our subconscious. If we assess negatively often, we are building evidence that the world around us is not a very good or safe place. That leaks into our beliefs and feelings as we move through our world. Also, if we partake often of negative judgments and comparisons, it makes us more likely to assume that we are being judged in the same manner. This leads to anxiety and stress.

At the moment we have them, our thoughts are pure energy and Vibration that not only exist physically, but that carve out a space in our subconscious, **becoming a permanent part of our influential matrix**.

Now let's look at one specific moment.

We are in a mall, and pass a grossly overweight man. "What a sickly and disgusting person; I cannot believe anyone would let themselves look like that." *That is a reaction, and we've all had that initial reaction once.* Our judgmental attitude from that moment is now permanently in our mind. It is physically present. That's awful, and it leads to insecurities in other areas of our lives. Not only do we feel guilty for the harm our judgment has caused another, but we become more afraid of it happening to us because of how quickly and easily we engaged in it. Ew. That leaks into our world...gets us sticky. Being honest about that reaction is the only way to address its presence, in the same way that noticing differences in races and types of people is the only way to adjust for our confusion about their differentness (or lack thereof). If we do not address that moment, we are Passively Validating that reaction, and *it becomes our opinion*. If we are practicing Conscious Validation, it never gets that far.

So we have the "He's disgusting" reaction, then Conscious Validation stops the reaction from expressing itself fully. We are not fans of how that reaction made us feel about another person, or about ourselves. So we take a moment, and engage the reaction. This frees us from our unconscious judgments. We can then empathize and give out some love, making the world a better place inside and outside of us. We can find a different reaction to counter the first one. "This man is probably doing the best he can and it's not uncommon for trauma and stress to show up in physical form." Conscious Validation changes *"He's disgusting"* to *"He's got his own battles, and I'm going to respect that,"* and the *disgust is replaced by unconditional positive regard of his humanity*.

Behaving in this manner leaves a wholly different mark on the world, your subconscious mind, and in your habit-creating Matrix. Also, if you've done it? It feels REALLYREALLY good. Taking back a judgmental reaction and replacing it with a conscious and loving one feels unbelievably healthy. That is a great example of Influence.

It is obvious, when reacting judgmentally to another person, that it is a perpetration of violence. But this exercise in Conscious Validation is not meant solely for external unconscious judgments. This process can be turned inward on every thought, and *our External Mind's reaction to those thoughts*.

Our brain always has a crawl going, and the groupings of consistent thoughts are always sectioned into their own little clusters. When someone asks us what we're doing, and we say "nothing," or, "thinking," odds are it is going back and forth between those two things at different speeds and levels of intensity. Our level of engagement and investment, however, can be anywhere on the scale. And that is the real issue, because **the tendency of the passively validating mind is to attend to fear and worry first and foremost,** as it is the most emotionally relevant as a survival instinct. It is the dominant emotional activator in our behavioral matrix. However, that is simply not where we need to be spending our mental energy. The Validation of fear reactions is crippling.

There are many inspirational quotes about why worrying is not a good idea, or a healthy use of energy. Worrying is a Validation of a fear reaction in the External Mind. It is very literally "praying for what we do not want." But my focus is on the *manner in which we attain the Influence necessary to lessen our worry.* That is Conscious Validation. Without a mechanism in place to engage and adjust our reactions, knowing how destructive worry is leads only to a shame spiral. If we do not know how to stop or adjust our thought matrix, we just feel bad for not being able to stop worrying, creating a shame spiral on top of everything else...greaaaaat.

The reactions we have are all parts of the orchestra, and they need our affection and attention whether or not they have our best interest in mind. Observing them is how we become acquainted with them, and learn the way they work. This is how we learn the specifics of the instruments and musicians in our music-making reality. Conscious

Validation is how we adjust their playing styles, and manage their Influence on the sound of the whole.

There are more than a couple Perspectives available to us for this exercise of Consciousness. The more we are capable of using, the more sophisticated our relationship with ourselves becomes, and the more Influence we can have over the shape our reality takes. The next description expands on Conscious Validation by examining the act of validating, and the abilities we have when validating.

The "Like" Button as Conscious Validation.

So let's use the "like" button on social media to use as the primary metaphor for this section. Every part of the crawl in our mind, and every section of thought clusters, comes with a little button (I actually visualize mine) that says *"like"* or *"ignore."* Conscious Validation consists of using that button as often as possible. More in-depth answers are available, also, such as *"I do not agree with this reaction," "I am excited about this thought pattern," "That external reality resonates," "This internal judgment serves no positive purpose and though it is a part of me, I am not going to base my future on its presence."*

We do not have to worry about whether these reactions are right or wrong; they are simply Perspectives with power. As we consciously click the imaginary buttons in our brains that validate, we are changing the matrix that motivates and Influences our behavior. This is because every thought we have is a part of the whole, an active ingredient in the creation of our moment-to-moment mental structure.

Treating our thoughts like active ingredients in our Reality Matrix is Authoring our Consciousness, and partaking in

Accountability. Conscious Validation is quintessentially Parenting our thoughts. Our thoughts are not our identity, and they are not solely sourced from our identity, but they are ours to Influence, in the same way our children are ours to raise. Conscious Validation is one of the tools.

Let's take a quick look here at a way we all do this, and how powerful the results are in such obvious situations. Conscious Validation is an "in the moment" practice, something that we can exercise in the same way one would learn to improvise during a dance. This may be something we are unfamiliar with, depending on how we have been brought up to deal with our consciousness. It was something I developed for some time before becoming adept at it. I realized later that I used a primitive, pre-emptive form of it much earlier.

I am speaking of the ability to adjust to our reality. If we are going to be "not at our best," we can prescribe adjusted behavior patterns for our immediate future. This is an excerpt from an old essay on consciousness. It served as a guide for managing consciousness in times of "obvious unwanted Influences." We have all done this, and Conscious Validation is very closely related to this.

Pre-emptive Adjustment Awareness

What did I do when...

I was scared? *I told myself I was scared, judged my reactions accordingly, and told myself I was free to use my brain when it passed.*

I was chemically altered? *I told myself I was not seeing things clearly, judged my reactions accordingly, and told myself that I was free to use my brain when it passed.*

I was drunk? *I told myself I was impaired, judged my reactions accordingly, and told myself that I was free to use my brain when it passed.*

I was stunned? *I told myself that I was in no shape to respond to anything, judged my reactions accordingly, and told myself I was free to use my brain when it passed.*

I was furious? *I told myself that I was reacting from fear, was a danger to myself and others, and told myself I was free to use my brain when it passed.*

This mechanism is the same one we use when we are driving, and come to a place where speed traps are often set. Marking the spot on the freeway is the same as marking a feeling. We make mental notes of danger areas, and use these notes to trigger behavior in order to protect ourselves. That is **Pre-emptive Adjustment Awareness**. It is an Influence.

When these obvious examples from all over our worlds (from childhood to adulthood) are included, hopefully it makes the daunting task of managing such a complex and chaotic system more accessible and inviting.

A great example happened to show up recently for me. I believe it showcases close to everything I have said in this chapter, as well as how using Influence has changed my thinking over the past few years. Holidays, in general, are emotionally loaded experiences. The recent Father's Day gave me enough raw intel to create a sophisticated example to share.

This is a good example because of my relationship to fatherhood. I am the stepfather of two awesome boys. I am very close to my step-sons' father. I have had issues with my own father. I consider my brother to be my father also. I have not spoken to my own stepfather in nearly a decade. I consider my relation to the world as one of parenthood …always have. I also believe that fatherhood has been the most damaged role in human society since the birth of the industrial revolution, and the least-forgiven throughout time. So…my brain came up with lots of good stuff to toss at me.

The sentences listed below are the reaction thoughts of my External Mind, things that came to me throughout the day as feelings or ideas. That is the "crawl." The percentage they got out of 100 (the number listed next to them) was how often they showed up in my reality. So, the ones with higher numbers got the most airtime. That is my "news feed," the groupings of thoughts scrolling across my brain throughout the day. Then I did one of three things with the thoughts. I will describe that operation in depth.

I either 1) *Validated the thought*, as it resonated with who I want to be and how I want my world to be; 2) *Allowed the thought* to have its moment, acknowledged it, and then **adjusted** it to a healthier Perspective. Then, after it was adjusted, I Validated the healthier Perspective (this operation was performed every time the thought came up); or 3) *Ignored* the thought, as I could simply do nothing healthy with it, and **gave it zero energy or validation**.

So here's the list:

First, the Validated Affirmations …

(25) *I'm truly grateful to be gifted two amazing boys to father.*

(15) *My boys' father is a wonderful man, and it is a great joy to honor him.*

(10) *I'm so thankful for my love, who not only gave me the opportunity to become a father, but put me close to a great father to learn from and made me realize how much I loved my own father.*

(9) *This society is starting to father more consciously, and that is awesome.*

(7) *My brother not only lived long enough to father four children, but he is an amazing symbol of strength and courage for them and me.*

(4) *My best friend is now a father, and I think he will be a great father.*

(2) *My father's feelings toward me have totally changed, and I am thankful.*

Those above get straight Conscious Validations. They get checkmarks and go through clean, and each time they come up they get automatic Validation from me. I really like that they make up 72% of my natural reactions. That is just a good life to have. I like those odds. The fact that this is the case now, *where before it was not anywhere near this high,* is a direct result of the work I've done influencing my reality with Conscious Validation and other tools.

Next batch: **The Reaction-Adjustment use of Cognition.**

(8) *I wish there was a Stepfather's Day.* (Feeling unappreciated, projecting, spiteful, petty)

(6) *Fathers are the biggest jackasses in society, and are not worthy of their offspring.* (Judgmental, critical, angry, lacking hope)

(3) *I wish my dad had been supportive in the exact way I wanted when I was a young man.* (Judgmental, bitter, unsympathetic)

(2) *I have not done my part as a stepson by keeping some form of contact with my stepfather...and now I am a stepfather.* (Guilt, fear that what I did will happen to me)

These can be adjusted. All thoughts are natural reactions to our history, but we can really have an effect on what kind of power they wield. So...I'll adjust them:

-*Stepfather's Day issue*: "Hey, relax. They honor you every day, and have a great time with you. You may not have your own day, but you are dearly loved. That is all you really want, and you know it." (Recognition and appreciation of love, realization of wants being achieved)

-*Fathers are jerks*: "Hey, it's not their fault, they were removed from parenting in the Industrial Revolution and their role in the family has been decreased to having been ostracized. They are getting better now, and the hurt from previous generations is being washed away." (Hope, faith in humanity)

-*My dad's perceived lack of support*: "Dude, hush. Your dad did the best he could, and he wasn't wrong. Besides, everything turned out fine and he's a great father to have. Oh yeah, and he saved your ass countless times." (Understanding, mercy, forgiveness, respect, gratitude)

-*My lack of contact with my stepdad*: "Hey, you tried for a while. It just got too difficult logistically. You still love and honor him (and draw from his teachings now that you are a stepfather). You are doing the best you can with that and maybe one day you'll track him down. Besides that, there's no reason to worry about that with your boys now, the circumstances will never match the ones that split you two up." (Allowance, self-acceptance, safety, hope)

After these sections are consciously adjusted, or "re-written," the accompanying "rewrite" replaces the initial reaction so that the final product of the reaction is healthy. This is imperative. It is a movement from judgmental and resentful to grateful and accepting. This may not always work, mind you. We cannot always forgive, or be accepting of ourselves or others. But we really need to try. We need to do this as often as possible because this operation is what changes our mental environment from overwhelmingly fearful and resentful to healthy and manageable.

Case in point: Three years ago my thought process was 85% "Angry at my dad." It took me a full year of not allowing those thoughts to pass unadjusted to even get to where the "Angry at my dad" number was manageable. Now it's under 10% and my appreciation for my dad is so much higher. That took years, support, and focus. My life is better as a DIRECT RESULT of my attitude toward my thoughts, and my unwillingness to allow negativity to be validated with the whole of my being. My entire mental environment in a very tender area was altered for the better. That is what Influence can accomplish.

Final Group: **The Poison Thoughts**

(5) *God, no one even notices me. What's the point.* (Ewwwww … whiny awful brat?)

(3) *I am a crappy father, I can barely even get the things done I need to, and I have no idea what I'm doing.* (Ewwwww … inaccurate, self-loathing crap)

(1) *I'll never be as important as their real father.* (Ewwww .. I don't even know what that is. Self-pity? It's really unsexy, and I can't believe I'm sharing it)

These happen. It's just our nature. I remember a lecture by a prominent and well-spoken Buddhist monk, where she mentioned "wanting to smack the shit out of her grandchildren" as one of her impulse responses to reality. I don't know if the Dalai Lama has moments like these also, but my bet is he would if he were engaged with small children over a long enough period of time.

What to do here is just hit the "ignore" button in our brain. We can't do anything with self-nullifying thoughts like these except let them be spoken and move on without giving them a split second of our emotional energy. And that, like everything else in the realm of Influence, takes practice. It takes practice to do this because these thoughts are the result of feelings (not facts) and we believe them deeply, the same way we believe hunger. And while these thoughts are the results of feelings, we can always find evidence to justify them as fact-based. Since feelings that are unjustified create Cognitive Dissonance, we are driven to use whatever evidence we have to support these feelings instead of blessing and dismissing them. So here's the example...ready?

"I'll never be as important as their real father."

He was there at their births. He raised them as babies. He taught them to walk and talk. He changed their diapers, has years of protecting them, and shares DNA with them. If I wanna get personal about it I can go further. He's taller than me, can fix things, is better with computers (which they love) than I am, makes more money than me, and is a more capable a human being in many areas.

Those are all facts. Nothing I said above is false. Not a one. I even have to ask him to get stuff off the top shelf for me and the boys laugh and joke about my height in a good-humored manner. It doesn't matter that those things are true. They don't make my role as a stepfather less. They are of no concern to my future reality. They do no one any good and they specifically make me feel bad. That makes me a less awesome person to be around.

So…I hit the "ignore" button. I still have to read the thoughts as they creep across the crawl in my mind, but I can hide them from my news feed. That way the damage they cause can end with me at an ineffectual level, one where I have begun to laugh at them. Their Influence over my present and future realities gets lessened every time they are hushed. It takes time and practice, and it never goes away. Ever. It does get lessened, and the lessening of self-nullifying voices makes me feel powerful within my small world of Influence. That is priceless.

Life will keep going. The orchestra is not going to stop. We are part of this process. The role we play varies greatly, depending on our ability to use tools for the purpose of managing our focus and awareness. Slowly, over time, we create healthy habits by using Influence. This is the building of a relationship.

Our lives are a broadcast to the world around us. The tools we have allow us to edit the final product before it goes on the air. There are a myriad of pitfalls, and it takes a ton of effort. It can be utterly frustrating, and discouraging. But if we handle all the steps properly, and the things outside of our control do not all work against us, we will have something solid we can count on for some time. It is a foundation.

PART 2: BREAK-IN MOMENTS AND ZOOMING OUT

We are trying to create an environment within us that is fertile for creation, and capable of adjusting to a chaotic reality. Using Conscious Validation allows us to help shape our thought matrix and manage our External Mind. Pre-emptive Adjustment Awareness gives us a head start on managing the overwhelming number of thoughts and reactions in stressed or altered states of consciousness.

But what are we using? It is not constant, and we are not always in control of it. The mechanism by which we awaken within our External Mind to our Observer Consciousness is called a **Break-In Moment**. These are moments where we jump from a busied brain wave pattern and deliver ourselves to another Perspective within that. In meditation, we move from Beta waveform to Alpha waveform, and if we are going to get deep, Delta waveform. The goal is to be able to access a light meditative state at any point during the hustle and bustle of our day. We are literally breaking into our Beta pattern thoughts and inserting Alpha waves. Doing this allows us to enact Observer Consciousness within the madness of the Busied External Mind.

Break-In Moments are vital for the awakening of our soul during the drudgery of daily life. They are one of the main mind-expanding techniques available to us. I will be discussing a few types of these Break-In Moments in the coming essays in this chapter. Pivot Points are first.

Pivot Points

The issue of control being gone, and management and Influence in mind, we are left with very few options other than the all-encompassing (and tedious) Conscious Validation model for habit alteration/creation. That model involves constantly focused work on adjusting our thoughts throughout all of every day, with the goal of a new reaction matrix as its endgame.

But we do have something else, something difficult to quantify. This tool, which acts like a reflex within our consciousness, can be used if and only if it presents itself. I call these moments **Pivot Points**. I cannot explain why they happen, or why they are offered to us when they are. However, I have no reason to believe that either of those issues should stop us from understanding and using this magnificent tool to reshape the way we are capable of thinking about our reactions.

Pivot Points are moments within a Perspective when we get the opportunity to interrupt ourselves. We can stop, while inside the flow of consciousness, and make a change in the Perspective we are using for the situation. As an alcoholic, I knew this as a "moment of clarity." Now, having laid those experiences alongside others, I can see that it was part of a larger, more powerful set of abilities. These abilities, when recognized, can be trained. When they are trained, they become a huge ally in the constant relations we have with the multiple facets of our consciousness.

"Count to ten. Bite your tongue. Check yourself. Suck it up. Hold your horses." These are things others—usually parents--have said to us, to keep us from acting impulsively to our detriment. We may even develop a way to speak to ourselves in this manner that keeps us in check. However, *it is not common enough for us to count on it in every situation.* We do not have enough healthy respect for our motivations, and as a result we do not have this toolbox open all the time.

We may notice when we're about to punch someone, or call someone we care about an awful name. We may notice when we begin getting lost in self-pity and depression, or react explosively in a public situation. We have been trained not to follow through on those impulses (hopefully).

This training falls short because it is often paired with a recognizable emotional/chemical state. This state is one where *excitation and impulse* are powerful enough to remind us of our youngest, most impressionable experiences with behavior. To do that, they have to be 1) extreme, and 2) immediate. Even then, the voices that come to us in these moments are not our own. They belong to those who trained us: those we respect, fear, and listen to. They don't come from us because we do not have a *healthy enough relationship with **our** self-parenting voices* to interject, and that is where we must focus.

The Pivot Point is when we get struck by the awareness of a different Perspective within a situation. We are mad at someone, but realize we don't have to act on it. We are drunk and realize that we should not drink more, or that we should not drive. We are freaked out in a panic attack and remember to breathe and calm down. These are Break-In Moments.

When we are happy or manic or energized, Break-In Moments can remind us that we have healthy limits to keep in mind. When we are upset, mad, sad, guilty, or ashamed, they can come in to tell us we are not thinking straight, and that the evidence we are receiving is skewed toward our mood. The more excited we are (happy/joyous or angry/scared/sad), the more we are being motivated by those feelings, rather than by our Consciously Validated Reality. This does not mean that the feelings are wrong to have...*in fact, they are a non-negotiable part of life.* It also does not mean that the current course of thought is not accurate...it very well may be. **But it is NOT a Perspective that is being checked against and validated by the whole of our Perspectives**. It is just the one we are in right this second. It is limited, and it doesn't have to be.

So... *"It's now."* I have heard it spoken by my mate thousands of times. It's a cry for help from herself to herself. It is her way of asking for more Perspectives, because the one she has now is not creating a healthy mental environment for her to work with. She is unwilling to validate her thoughts in the frame of mind she is in, and *simply asks for another one*. She may be frustrated or angry, feel trapped or depressed. It may be a mood fluctuation due to energy levels, chemicals (how are you before your coffee?), or external circumstances, like a flat tire or traffic.

It doesn't matter what it is. It has moved her off her "calm and happy" spot, which is where she is able to manage her motivations, and put her someplace where she is less capable. So, now that it has been confirmed that she is not in her spot, she asks for more Perspectives in order to get back to where she feels comfortable.

This is not easy, and is more akin to lucid daydreaming than "being aware." She is attempting to inspire a Break-In Moment for herself by saying *"It's now."* In lucid dreaming training, one of the tools we utilize is to look at our hands.

Looking at our hands is a reminder to change Perspectives, and if we can habituate the act of looking at our hands, we will be capable of triggering a Break-In Moment and altering our Perspective should we need to do so.

Lucid Daydreaming

In lucid dreaming we are attempting to gain heightened Perspective (that of consciousness) within a reality that is being fueled by our subconscious mind. The technique we are going to employ is looking at our hands. The idea is that before going to sleep, we raise our hands, and mentally note that we are conscious. The purpose of this is to place the image of raising our hands to our face close to our sleeping state of consciousness, so that it is more likely to occur in a dream state. There are other techniques, of course.

The idea is that if we are dreaming, and see our hands, we may have a chance to expand our Perspective, or even become fully conscious. I have done this. It does work. The aim is to exercise Influence within an altered state. We see our hands, and it clicks. Being able to get a message to ourselves from an expanded and more actively participatory state of consciousness, with more information and Perspectives to work with, is a vital exercise. This is what I call **Lucid Daydreaming**. And it is just that…an exercise. We cannot control whether or not we will raise our hands in our dream, or if we will click into a more active and focused plane of experience when we do raise our hands, but we can Influence the probabilities.

The idea is that we also need to Break-In to our unconscious motivations when we are in our normal waking state. We can also guarantee that if we never work on waking ourselves from an "immersed" state of mind, that we will often fall victim to whatever whims that Perspective is sourcing from our pool of motivational attitudes. Our daily Perspective, while engaged in trivial realities, is also an immersed/altered state, even though we are not used to thinking of it like that. That is why Lucid Daydreaming is the best description for this practice.

We've been happy before, right? We can remember how being happy felt, like ...really deeply happy. Yes? Now imagine that when we looked at our hands we could have that exact Perspective for a few minutes. No matter how angry or sad or hopeless or depressed we were, we could have that internal reality for a short amount of time. In the same way that we can attain consciousness in a dream, we can expand our Perspective while awake, even if only for a few moments.

This is not power, this is just Influence. We cannot control this. We can practice, and engage, and hope. That's it. That is the nature of Influence.

Your presently conscious mind? The one reading this book right now? It is ONE Perspective. If we learn to create Pivot Points in our world ... we can have access to every Perspective we've ever been a part of. **That is evolution of consciousness**.

Cultivating this relationship is important for many reasons, not the least of which is that the voices of others we can draw on are static. They are created through conditioning, and thus are limited and non-adjustable. That is not good enough. The issues we face throughout our lives change, and with them, our responses. We also have many more subtle ways of creating damage as we age. There is more to managing our mind and relating to our thoughts than just trying to avert catastrophe. We are moody. We are not emotionally sober beings.

Most of the decisions we make and the plans we set into action *source from mental states that do not contain any observational oversight.* Adults are also skilled at lying to themselves and others to keep their realities less turbulent. This creates a matrix of thought that leans away from confrontation, ensuring there are no signals that anything needs to be questioned. We have to be proactive in creating comfortable avenues for these questions, and Lucid Daydreaming offers us a shot at that. It creates the avenue; then we must train our way into being successful operators of those moments.

ZOOM OUT!

There was a story about someone who could see the future, and one of the ideas that drive the use of Pivot Points is one that I gleaned from that story. Except, instead of the future, I use it with the reality of Perspective in the present. At any given moment we are making decisions from one Perspective... the one we are in. Pivot Points allow us Break-In Moments to alter our source Perspective. But the nature of what happens when we are allowed to make that change is intricate. I now have the analogy that describes its nature in depth.

Imagine a map. You are focused on the section of road you are on, looking for the next turn. You are also looking at landmarks near you so you know how to navigate. This is normal and healthy. This is our **Perspective Map**. It is how we navigate our daily lives with the least amount of mental energy. However, it does not afford us the totality of our knowledge--just the one from the Perspective we are using at the moment. We may have other Perspectives on hand, just like there may be other roads and types of landmarks on a map. So what are we talking about altering?

Every map is different. It includes different features, and thus presents different challenges. As adults, we are often multitasking, which makes navigating even more difficult. Where we get into trouble is that on top of multitasking, we also have to try to adjust for our mood, and other irritants.

Our focus on the tasks in our Perspective Map brings us closer and closer to the exact spot we are in. If I am making dinner, my eyes are likely on pans, and my mind is likely timing the cooking. My map is small and efficient. But what if my boys come in and start creating a fuss about something? That's not on this map…this is the dinner-making map.

My patience, my care for my boys, and my restraint in my behavior is not on the dinner map. It's probably close by, but it is not here right now, and I'm deep in this map. My life got more complex, and now I am trying to perform an operation that is not at the forefront of my consciousness. If I am lazy, or tired, or not at my best, I will likely respond by barking at my boys and telling them to leave me alone for a minute. Is that a huge deal? No, but it's not the way I'd like to handle it. I'd rather have a soft voice and quickly and efficiently explain that I'm busy and I'll work to meet their needs in just a moment. This is difficult. Trying to manage such a thing from within the sole Perspective we are operating from is not effective. But we have options, and we can all get more adept at bringing them to the forefront. We do not have to habituate "barking" in situations like that. It makes us pretty close to untrained dogs, acting out of reaction without any depth of presence. We can get better here.

So, let's imagine we're looking at a map on our computer. Rather than the dinner-making map, let's just make it a feeling. We are up close on something we don't really want to see, just like being all up in some mood that is not the best to deal with the situation we are in. Anger while driving would be an emotional state at an inopportune moment. The Break-In Moment in this situation affords us the opportunity to use the **Zoom Out** button. It lets us drop all the way back out from where we are focused, and allows us to take in a much larger section of the map. This does not necessarily give us *every-thing* we need at the moment, but it provides options. First, it reminds us that this is only one moment in one day of a long and glorious life. This is often enough to deflate the power of our present mood. I remember this as I'm about to raise my voice at my boys, and that alone can stop me dead in my tracks. Zoom Out. This does not always afford us exactly what we need, *but it definitely gives us a chance to take healthier action than what our unconscious reactions would be*. It can get us out of a spot that is basically wrong every time, by giving us a larger landscape to visualize.

Getting back to the story I was thinking of, and the idea it gave me in reference to singular momentary Perspectives. **"*Every time we look at reality, it changes, because we looked at it.*"** The determining factors of our mood and mental matrix cannot stay exactly the same when we widen the gaze to include more.

Whether it is more time or the addition of different reactions … it is MORE. Once we include tomorrow, and yesterday, and five years ago, and five years from now into our view, *we completely change the character of our momentary reality*.

We can't get there from here. We have to go somewhere else first.

Every time we look at a reality, it changes, because we looked at it. Changing Perspectives is the goal, honestly. It is. But we cannot get into a new Perspective without getting out of the one we are in first. That is the first move.

We've heard the seemingly insane statement *"You can't get there from here. You have to go someplace else first?"* I used to laugh about it. It came up a few times in commercials as I was a child growing up in the South and I underestimated its viability. It has a very exact meaning when it comes to mood, reactions, and behavior. If you don't think that's the case, next time you are road raging…try to belly laugh. Can't do it, huh?

We have to get out of being mad before we can even hope to get into a space that will allow such an honest and vulnerable reaction. This is true in the same way that we can't go from "running" directly to "sleeping."

This looks really simple when it's broken down like this, and pretty obvious. But that doesn't make it easy to manage. There is a lot inherent in our mental framework that makes this difficult, most of which I am going to cover in other places. But I will mention a bit here so that we know what we are up against, and why it is such a worthy adversary.

Our body is built to self-support its "feelings." If we are in a negative mood, something that is created and held in stasis by a chemical reality (lack of dopamine plus some adrenaline-based anxiety, for example), then our brain's job is to justify that feeling with every bit of information it can gather. It will Zoom In on things that bother us, keeping our field limited to justify our feelings. Our mind is built to make it difficult to "break in" and "Zoom Out" if doing so creates dissonance with our mood. This is why it is difficult to say *"Hmm, that guy must be in a real hurry"* about the guy who cut us off on the freeway. It doesn't justify our rage.

This is why people who have Influence over themselves adjust to reality so well. They can escape the **prison of momentary focus**. We can all get better at this.

Like everything in the arena of Influence, this behavior is like a muscle, not a button. We make it stronger every time we exercise it. The more we focus on it, the more our body feeds its existence with nourishing energy. There are times, always, for anyone, where we simply cannot get out of a mood. We cannot Zoom Out (or when we do Zoom Out, it still all looks pretty bad). That comes with the incarnation. There will always be something too heavy for us to lift. But we get better at it...every time.

PART 3: THE POWER OF INFLUENCE AND THE UPWARD/OUTWARD SPIRAL

I have been speaking about tools within our reality that allow us to engage the mire of cognition that we call mind, and the matrix of Perspectives that make up our motivational realities. What I will describe now is how it is supposed to look when it is working brilliantly.

It's a hot mess. It never really looks all that good. It is not unlike several ethical problems in philosophy (particularly the trolley car problem) that are so viciously uncomfortable that they are self-polarizing.

This is the reason that we have so many protest thoughts to ideas that course through this vein of our psychological machinery. This is why we have the illusions of paradoxes. We have to work through these protests within ourselves while we are dealing with everything else on our plate. It is no easy task. So let's deal with the paradox of psychological determinism first, and get it out of the way, as it exists only within a hypothetical reality, not a real one.

The Illusion of Paradox Within Psychological Determinism

I find Psychological Determinism to be self-evident, in the same way I find Utilitarianism to be flawless, and every protest against it must be based on an assumption not included within the idea. They are descriptions, not prescriptions. We don't have to wonder if they are correct or not; they are observations of reality.

The tough part of Psychological Determinism is the **imagined** correlation between *"not having free will or choice"* at any given moment, and *"not having an effect."* Not having free will often leads people to *"If that is true, then I am helpless and I cannot do anything."* That is false. That is making a straw man out of Psychological Determinism, and I detest straw man arguments.

First off, we know that everything we do matters. So postulating that we are helpless is hypothetical evasion to begin with. Being limited, even so severely that we are not the authors of our decisions any given moment, **does not mean that we are ineffective at making changes in the matrix**. The decision you are going to make now, the reality that you are experiencing right this second, you are incapable of altering it right this second. But that does not mean that you have no hand in future realities. That is what Influence is. It is preparation for realities that you are simply not in yet.

We do this through **Decision Validation**. It is a form of Conscious Validation that we perform when we become accountable for the entirety of an action and its effects. I am not going to devote more time to the Validation process here, because Validations are all about the same, and they all shape our future values and options. Let's get back to how to envision our power.

The best analogies for this are used in maps and the gym. I have expressed that our conscious mind is like a muscle, and like machinery in a co-op, so let's use both ideas.

We are at the gym. We can lift a certain amount. There is in fact, an *exact amount that we can lift*. Psychological Determinism is telling us one thing about ourselves, and one thing only. That is that WE CANNOT LIFT SOMETHING HEAVIER THAN WE CAN LIFT. No matter what. That's why I always put this out as a description of reality instead of a theory. Our ability to lift determines...wait for it...EXACTLY HOW MUCH WE CAN LIFT. That is true in the same way that our experiences and genetics determine...wait for it... EXACTLY WHAT WE ARE GOING TO DO.

So what can change? Our continued engagement changes our depth of experience, and the immersion that creates Resonance expands our mind and world. Basically, we can keep working out and keep our muscles growing. We can keep focusing and augmenting experience to enhance our genetics and experiential DNA (which is what "living" is, honestly). But that's it. We get to pay attention only to what we're doing now, and continue it if we want to (that is where Decision Validation comes into play).

So let's look at a vehicle now. We are driving. We are going to our friend's house, and we are halfway there. Can we go toward our friend's house? Yes. Can we be there right this second? No. That option is simply not available if we are only halfway there. Our ability to even maneuver the car, or go forward, depends on things completely outside of our control. Stopped at a red light? Guess we're not going anywhere, are we? We cannot make a turn that is not presented to us, and we cannot make a decision that is not within our realm of motivations to make. This does NOT mean that we are not going to our friend's house, or that we will never get there. It means that if we have a goal in mind, we have to work with our present circumstances until the focus of our travels presents itself. We will always, when driving a vehicle (or a human body), be restricted by the location and environment of our vehicle, and our ability to maneuver it. Does this mean that we are not driving our car and that it doesn't matter what we do? GOD, NO.

Now imagine whatever our goals are happen to be "our friend's house," or "225 pounds on the bench press." If we want to get there, everything we do matters, even if it does not get us directly where we want to be right this second. That is not a paradox. There are a couple nice new-agey quotes that can be used here …

"Do something today that your future self will thank you for." That is mainly an implication that now has an effect on our later well-being. Nice one.

"Who you are now is a result of who you have been, and who you are tomorrow will be a result of what you do now." Pretty basic thought that we accept. It is exactly in line with Psychological Determinism.

We are a reacting consciousness, and everything we are focusing on is building our muscles and keeping our car on the road. Influence takes our reacting consciousness and makes it into a creative entity that builds our muscles and manages the many maps of all the places in our mind and heart that we want to be. That is the moat of self-awareness.

The paradox does not exist. The illusion of it is used to dismiss the discomfort of not being in control. I understand that. Not being in control is an awful feeling that takes a long time to get *close* to being used to. I don't know that we are ever *fully* used to it. The real problem is something all of us know to be true but cannot do a thing about from moment to moment. **It is the frustration of being alive in a limited vessel, and knowing that we cannot make immediate changes to our reality, even while in full awareness of where we are and what needs to be done.**

We cannot undo what has been done, inside or outside of us. We also cannot skip the steps required to create a situation where better decisions are available for us. We cannot control the environment of our present reality.

The best example of this is dating, or mate selection. We think of our choices as very personal to us, very representative of who we are. There is one thing that makes a person "good" at this. That is practice and experience. Just like throwing a strike as a pitcher on a baseball field.

Does this mean an inexperienced person cannot make the right decision about someone? Nope. A person who has never thrown a baseball before can throw a strike. True story.

Does this mean that someone with a ton of experience can throw a strike every time without error? Nope. Good pitchers miss the plate.

We don't get guarantees here. We don't get assurances. And if we have succeeded at something in the past, it is not evidence that we won't suck at it in the future. Everything deserves its due diligence and there are *always* things that we are simply not ready for. This presents us with a pretty harrowing proposition. ***"If we are not ready for something, and make a mistake, we have to make the most of it and experience it fully, no matter how uncomfortable and painful, to limit the odds of it happening again."*** Even that does not come with a guarantee. Great.

The Problems in Our Perspective

So here the problems one must accept as par for the course when utilizing a Perspective with Psychological Determinism, and creating a Relationship of Influence with our consciousness.

The problems line up as follows:

1) **No guarantees.** We may work hard and succeed. We may work hard and fail. We may not do any work and succeed. We may do any of the previous listed things and be happy or unhappy. There is no way to predict how a body and mind will grow and react. We are not guaranteed anything.

2) **No way of knowing where we are.** In relation to learning the lesson needed to achieve what we are focused on, we simply cannot know where we are. We don't know if we're ready for a relationship or not, ready for children, capable of doing a job, etc. We can hope, and we can be positive and confident, but we will have to live our lives

without that certainty.

3) **No ability to conclude** from the results of actions, thoughts, or behaviors, that our preparation and readiness for something was what directly created the result. Thus, there is no certainty of continued success in the same areas of consciousness. We may have had excellent results in a previous situation, and find that the next time we are in the exact same spot, life takes our lunch money.

4) **This reality is a Lesson-Based Reality**. Learning and growing, for the most part, results from integrating mistakes, and cannot be separated from the negative feelings that come with those mistakes. We may be able to learn to interpret the feelings in new ways through using Perspective Adjustment and Pivot Points, but *failure is the key ingredient to growth*. And the feelings that come with failure cannot be completely shut out without losing parts of the growth experience. So, pain is a necessary part of the journey. How we manage it matters, and is another aspect to consciousness that we will cover later.

5) **Sometimes there is absolutely nothing to do**. Sometimes we are not given any ideas or direction, and just have to sit and wait. Ew. We can work only with what we have, and like surfers waiting for waves in the ocean, we cannot ride what is not there. We can exhaust ourselves paddling and trying to stand on our board, but we cannot surf without waves. Growth and action are both dependent on forces we cannot control, *whether they are within us **or** outside of us*.

Living in a Lesson-Based Reality through Conscious Validation, and using what courage we have to try to stay engaged, places us firmly in a relationship with ourselves. This means that we have Synergy in Commune available to us internally, as the communication with the self is the vessel through which growth occurs.

Synergy in Commune is necessary because this idea is as overwhelming and daunting as tightrope walking across the Grand Canyon. Success is embodied in that idea. That is what all the tools of Influence gather together to form. It is an endeavor, highly specialized and integrated within the self, *meant to create a symphony of adjustments in an ever-changing landscape* that gives us little or no certainty for support.

The Tightrope

A Lesson-Based Reality is very simply the *reality of the existing universe*. It is creation and subsequent refinement. The expansion of the universe continues and the overwhelming amount of information we are presented with obfuscates the obvious and recurring theme.

We are born, and through a life of constant contact with external realities, we are sculpted. Our Perspective on this procedure is often one of frustration. This is because in order to perform the task of learning, we are given the small picture, one where our movement is dependent on a goal or "finished object." Every such task is similar in that it requires us to move through our time with awareness and creativity. Through every task and focus we are continuously creating ourselves (and in doing so, the Universe), albeit with seemingly little of the big picture within our grasp.

We are of consciousness, a balancing act over the Grand Canyon, wherein we are gene-and-experience specific, within an enormous sky of possibility that is not our focus, not our path, not our job.

Every Influence on us can be balanced. Every external reality is part of a matrix of learning and creating. But our movement is the goal, not our perceived finish line, because for every step we are weathered by our minds and the world around us, refined in the fire of the world's attention and violent affection.

So we fall. But we never start over. Our balance improves with every moment and step, and each new challenge catches our attention at the exact moment the weight of it becomes vital to us. We cannot ever become less strong, less experienced. Less of what life is. We cannot. Our perception of failure is useful in youth because it pushes us, but it is not the truth. The truth is that engagement on one task is preparation for another, and training for anything is training the whole of consciousness.

So how do we fail? We fail by refusal. We fail by rejecting. We fail by turning away from the external within us, and the external outside of us, and it is not because "giving up is bad." Giving up is also an experience, and is logged and used as refinement by us and the Universe.

So why is it failure? **Because all abstention is the same.** There is nothing added to the scope of reality. The moments when we are tied up, running from the world inside us and around us, we are denying the world our presence. That is exactly the same when anyone does it. It is not unique regardless of what justifications we believe exist. Justifications exist only to shield us from the Cognitive Dissonance associated with relinquishing our divine presence to fear. It's the "**It's not you, it's me**" **of breaking up with life**.

Rejection of the experience is always the same. It adds nothing. Going back over our lives we will sympathize with all of these moments, all of the times we gave up. When you look at the device that is present, it is the same. Repetitive. Disengaged.

It has its place. We need to feel it, be reminded of it until it no longer suits us. It is part of the experience here. But in transmuting the old world to the new, we can eliminate this boring side effect of consciousness and become more in touch with the glory and bounty of the balancing act, of the grandeur of tightrope walking, adjusting to all that surrounds us until we become one with it, the external realities of our mind and its matrices.

This is the gift we are here to give, our Influence to our matrix of consciousness. Our creation. Our willingness to participate within a vast and uncontrollable environment is what our life is. Influence is the participation, and instead of being merely the Conscious Validation of thoughts, it is the BIG Conscious Validation of our own existence. It is the big yes…the one that ripples the fabric of the cosmos, and molds together *the joy of expansion* and the *refinement of cosmic chaos* into art.

The refinement of chaos into art, the accepting of Influence in all its forms, including an investment in the love of failure as Grace within a Lesson-Based Reality, becomes the **Upward/Outward Spiral**. This spiral is not just a different direction from a downward spiral, it is fundamentally different. It is creative, and unlimited; unique, and indefinable. Downward spirals are plotted along a specific course where everything funnels into fear, regret, and self-nullification, in the same way that spiraling toward the center of the Earth from gravity simply gets you to a single point on the map of the Universe.

Upward/Outward Spirals go out in all directions. And the coolest thing about them in my opinion is that I cannot tell you a definite single thing about them. It's not because there is an answer I don't know or can't share or put into words. It is because the practice is as creative as the Universe is infinite. Its main attribute is that it gathers new realities and Perspectives (matter and energy) that are unique to the self-translating consciousness. Thus it is our experience, Resonance, and Rapture spiral.

That is one example of how we get from action within the consciousness to Universal Action.

Chapter 10:

Body Sovereignty

We've talked about the mechanics of consciousness, as well as how it relates to the world around us. We've talked about how our momentary realities are formed and processed. We have also talked about how viewing those through specific lenses and honoring the nature of the mechanics are important. Now it's time to turn our focus to the body and vessel we are filling up with that consciousness. This, most importantly, includes the mind: a mind that we consider to be our own, a source of "us," but that is actually as foreign as the tissues surrounding our bones.

We are a subjective bunch, and we simply cannot get out of the mindset that all this stuff belongs to us...that all the voices we hear in our head are coming from us. So, given that we can't get out, it's important to understand how this relationship works.

Our bodies are a bridge to experiencing the outside world. Our minds are the manner in which that bridge translates reality into soul experience. Neither the mind nor the body is actually us. But our inability to separate from them is a key element to experiential information. So even if we can elude being present and three-dimensional for a time (through meditation, mind-altering drugs, etc.), that is not where our destiny or enrichment lies. Our destiny and purpose lie within the fulfillment of embodying our realities fully. Knowing that our subjectivity needs its own Perspective is a key element to that fulfillment.

Body Ownership...or Lack Thereof

"Your body is a temple."

"Your body is your home."

"You are a soul within a body."

These clichés seem thousands of years old. Now, given remote control, virtual reality, and robotics, the new generations will be more capable of grasping the Perspective (not the idea, everyone knows the idea) of *our body as a machine or avatar*. The older we are, the less likely we are to be able to handle such a Perspective. It causes too much Cognitive Dissonance. That is the nature of massive evolutions.

Everyone gets the *"our body is like a car"* analogy to an extent. We get to "drive" our bodies, and need to take care of them with fuel-food and checkups blah blah blah.

But we have far less control over our bodies than we do a car, and that is not the Perspective that we now hold as a species, for the most part.

Most people make the analogy of food to gas as fuel for the operating system. Many see that, in some sense, we "steer" our bodies, but assume we have greater control over the direction we take than we do. Our bodies are subject to a limitless host of internal demands, and they do not respond to the application of our will unless they are agreeable to the demands. They also do fifty times more to organize and sustain themselves than a car does. We have systems working constantly in our bodies to sustain life, systems that we have no access to (we can forget popping the trunk to have a look at our endocrine system).

If we want our hearts to stop beating? We're gonna have to fight our bodies hard, and odds are we're going to lose.

Hold our breath until we die? Can't.

Wanna grow up quickly? Wanna stay young? Nope.

We can turn a car off. If we feed a car bad gas or mess with the engine, we can permanently damage it. It takes a lot more time and effort than that to take our bodies out. We can do it with the aid of tools (guns, pills, razors), but we weren't born with those.

See, our cars serve us. Our bodies DO NOT. *They serve our **lives**, not our **minds**,* in the same way a rollercoaster serves the track it is on. It cannot be steered. We can work with it or against it, but it has its own plans.

That's just our bodies. Our minds are an external force occurring within our bodies that we often mistakenly identify with. It shows us such a tiny percentage of what's being taken in that we should seriously sue our brains for obstruction of reality, and demand that the subconscious mind give up the goods! Now! It must obey! It has all that great information, every memory stored. It has all the pieces of the puzzle!

Oh, and while we're at it, let's change the ocular reducing valve so we can see all the visual energy/information our minds filter out! Let's demand it all!

This is a **Semi-Malleable Host** body. That's it.

We can have Influence here, though. We can increase the amount of our brain that we can experience, and with that, the amount of the world around us that we can take in. But we cannot do so if we are fighting for dominance, only if we are in relationship. Only if the goals we have are closely aligned with those of our bodies.

Our minds are tools. They are tools for the spirit consciousness utilized to experience and make sense of reality. It is my goal here to *depersonalize* it. I want this because it's much easier to heal a machine, and understand a machine, than it is to understand an awkward combination of "self" and "tool."

The reason it is so confusing and difficult to know and understand our realities is that we do not know where to draw the line between what *is* us, and what **is happening to** us. And there is much more happening to us than actually IS us. Identification plays a huge role in organizing and compartmentalizing our inner experiences so that we are more capable of understanding what's going on.

Myth of the Five Senses: The Mind as a Bridge of Translation

I want to speak about the power of the mind, by discussing its ability to create our world for us. To start this endeavor I will take something commonly understood, and destroy the way we think about it in order to see if that opens up any new opportunities for expansive and creative ways to relate to the world.

How about the five senses? The idea of having five senses…
is ridiculous. The only thing more ridiculous is calling Intuition
a sixth sense. I'm not going to get to cursing and throwing
things this early in the morning, but such a thing is totally possible given my frustration at how this basic and common sense
Perspective is completely skipped over. End rant.

We do not have five senses, and Intuition is not a sixth.
We have one sense. It is contact. Everything that we experience is **Contact Translation**. Sight: light waves and photons
hit our eyes and are transmitted to our ocular nerves, and then
into the vision centers of the brain. Hearing is sound waves
contacting our ear drums. Taste is particles registering on our
taste buds, and smell is the same mechanism in our olfactory
nerves. That is the touch of an external reality, and our nerves
translating that to our brain. That is Contact Translation.

Given the fact that our bodies are organized with mag-
netic fields external to our skin, and given the presence of
Vibrational realities all around us, getting to an expanded
Perspective of Contact Translation should not be difficult.
Engaging in trying to pick up more information requires a
certain type of relationship with the physical experience of
living, and I will get to that, but for now let's look at a couple
of examples.

Dogs can smell fear. We always knew it, but now it's been
proven that they have receptors in their noses for picking
up adrenaline in floating sweat particles. This is how police
dogs track fleeing suspects. That is just a heightened ability to
translate.

Another example is from the plant kingdom, and the
awareness that plants have of human intention, as recorded
and measured in studies by Cleve Baxter in the '60s. The plants

can't see. But like any situation where one manner of experiencing reality is not available, others are heightened. Plants can pick up the Vibrational intent. The thoughts of the scientists performing the tests are present in reality, and translate into a primitive plant reaction that can be measured by the weak instrumentation we had in the '60s. Contact Translation. The contact can be energetic, and it is not limited by distance.

The idea of Contact Translation gets easier to picture when dealing with hallucination effects. The world does not change. Our ability to translate it changes. Our brain lets more light in to be translated. Got big pupils? Yep. More light. You are not hallucinating; you are seeing more. The hallucination happens in translation, and based on the chemical you are dealing with, the translation occurs and is distorted (or not) in correlation.

Before going into this, I will give a short lesson on serotonin. All habituated feeling, thought and movement skills, sleep, confidence, and comfort are associated with serotonin.

The first type of hallucinogen is a serotonin blocker. This is acid, psilocybin, mescaline, peyote, etc. These take the serotonin centers in our brain and cover them up, so the serotonin released in our brain cannot be absorbed. As our brain gets confused from lack of serotonin, it begins to panic. In its scramble to figure out what's going on, it lets in more external information from every avenue. It does this successfully. This mechanism, letting in more information, is the case in all three examples I am going to share. But in this case, without serotonin, our mind is hooked into *mental unease*. Because of this, as it tries to translate reality for you, it scrambles to make pictures out of everything. This is why we see entire figures in minor shadows, or make faces into angels or monsters. That is the *translation only*. Not our eyes. That's why the monsters and angels are specific to our inner realities.

The extra information in the air that we are picking up is physically there (electromagnetic, Vibration energy), but there isn't actually a dragon in the room. We just need to make sense of the light information coming in because without serotonin, our brain is struggling to ease doubt. So we get a dragon, or an angel, or a '67 Chevelle depending specifically on how we feel at the moment. Our brain will make pictures that reinforce how we feel (that's why it's common knowledge in the drug-taking world that you must be confident and in a safe environment before any experimentation). The external realities will mirror our inner realities. Our mind creates reality for us...sounds eerily familiar.

The second are serotonin reuptake inhibitors (Ecstasy is the main example here). This removes the ability for the brain to clean out the serotonin present (which it does at regular intervals, in normal circumstances), resulting in a huge surplus. As the brain is off-balance chemically, it again attempts to take in more information, but opening sensation to higher levels of influx. But since serotonin is flowing all over the place and flooding the receptors, we feel really really confident. We feel hopeful and undistracted by stress. We do not need to make pictures out of things, because we are not mentally uncomfortable. We just take in all the light. That allows us to see through layers of skin, and translate far beyond the norm, without even having the realization of an extrasensory experience. The translation is far more open and not relegated to "something being wrong" because we feel so awesome. We can focus on all of our senses, allow ourselves to inspect anything we feel, and have the time and energy to analyze mentally. But to show how excessive serotonin can affect the brain in a less-desirable way, I will remind that the serotonin neurotransmitter is fully engaged while sleeping. The hallucinations that show up deep into an Ecstasy experiment are dreams that we have while awake. Our brains release the rules of conscious thought, and instead of making pictures out of light, it takes symbolic objects, and makes them perform like the phenomena in a dream. We are awake, but instead of being in our living room we are in a volcano, and the volcano is like a nice Jacuzzi. The mind, being in a state of ease, simply accepts the new reality, and when we finally come out of it (as evidence to the contrary is presented and finally accepted) we feel startled, as if waking from a dream. But we weren't asleep; our translation devices were simply stimulating the visual centers of our brain in the EXACT same way they would have if we had been asleep.

That is how powerful the translation is.

Sleep deprivation causes the third manner of hallucination. Sleep deprivation forces the same confusion that causes heightened sensation without too much or too little serotonin, and lets in higher amounts of contact information in to be translated. This usually happens about 36--48 hours into the deprivation. In this case, we just see more. The easiest things to notice are the energy and magnetism surrounding our bodies, specifically in areas of high focus and coordination (hands and eyes). Tiny particles, like flashes of light, become present and are obviously in motion in an organized manner and in rhythm. With Intent, these can be Influenced. These energies can also form schemata for receiving information.

We can receive information through our energy field, with no skin contact, that can be translated into our brain. That is not the sense of touch as we know it. *But we all know when someone in a crowd is looking at us, when we are being watched, and when there is danger.* While we chalk all this up to instinct, we should realize that our culture has not defined what instinct is. ***This is instinct. This is Intuition***. The ability to use non-physical contact to interpret information through the Contact Translation of our energetic field IS instinct. That is NOT a sixth sense. It is the same single sense. It is Contact Translation, but it is hampered *in most* by a mediocre translation system that is not fully developed. *Hampered in most*. We ALL have the capability to Influence the growth of this tool. We can do this through validating the information we are given by recognizing it, and by slowly uncluttering our minds so that we are available for subtlety.

To finish this up, and to get back to the myth of the five senses, we are experiencing particles or waveform, and translating that through sensory mechanisms. But that does not mean our ability to translate is limited in any way. We have energetic fields. Energy, intent, thought, and attention each have a specific Vibration that can be translated. Receptivity to these Vibrations can be trained, just like someone can be trained to hear intricate music. But some people have a natural genetic likelihood of ease (as even within groups of musicians, some have perfect pitch, and some don't). While it's more likely for someone to become a quality musician with naturally great pitch, it is not a prerequisite. This is a demystification of the psychic world. We are not magic. We are just people who can translate energetic Vibration. No one bats an eye when a sommelier can do a blind tasting of red wine and tell you the country and region it is from, and what year the grapes were harvested. But try to expand on interpreting realities through energy, which we are surrounded by at all times, and it gets rejected. That's vestigial psychological thinking, and we're past it.

The reason that these distinctions matter so much is not that we need to do one thing or another about our ability to sense the world. It's true that we may be able to Influence ourselves there, but in the end it's not the most important feature--not in comparison to what this Perspective means for our consciousness.

We have contact with the world through a liaison, and ALL of our thoughts are a result of that liaison's ability to translate reality into usable pieces of information. The brain part of this affiliation is where we get into a real mess.

One of the issues of this relationship has to do with understanding that the body and External Mind have prime directives that have nothing to do with our soul Identity, are consistent from human being to human being, and are simply stronger than we are. This is **Body Sovereignty**.

This is the role of the *vessel* our souls inhabit. This role is in place, with volition separate from our momentary whims, and has survival of self and species as its priority. Our confusion over this role is the source of endless confusion, distraction, fear, feelings of powerlessness, and depression. *Our role is to honor this vessel, and its volition.*

Emotion and the Locomotive

We cannot stop emotion. We cannot. Even so, we do not want to stop it, it is life. It is emotional connection, and it is a rich and powerful feeling-experience. Even pain, grief, and fury grant us a huge depth of experience. Trying to stop emotion as it is coming through us is akin to attempting to stop a locomotive by standing in its way.

Not only will it not work, it will leave us battered and torn up in frustration, feeling completely POWERLESS. Run over.

However, if we allow emotion to be what it is (part of our nature), instead of trying to stop it, we may learn how to work it. We can learn to manage its power...by, say...climbing aboard the train and utilizing the control switches. When we learn how to stop the train when it does arrive, not only will we not be torn up by the fear, we will have gotten what we wanted. *We will have attained the power to Influence our reality by working within the natural order of the body, **rather than against it**.*

We cannot control the mind's attachment to human emotion. We can learn it, and work with it, and *in the fruition of that relationship* we can alleviate the crushing feeling of helplessness.

Or we can keep trying to reject our body's responses and keep getting our butts kicked. Knowing this gives us the option to form a relationship, and hopefully makes that option more attractive.

The main issue to grasp when looking at our emotional reactions is that when we can tell ourselves consciously that *we are not capable of stopping them, only using them for information and possibly influencing them slowly over time*, we can naturally let go of a large amount of the frustration. Mind that I said *"a large amount"* and *"over time."*

The reason that we can dump the frustration is that we can unhook guilt, at least logically (we can still feel guilty over anything; I felt guilty this week because it didn't rain when I predicted. That actually happened.). When we logically unhook guilt we can stop validating it as something our mind is *required* to deal with in the crawl of our mental sphere. It does not eliminate guilt completely, but it limits its presence, and undermines any power it may have. It allows us to dismiss it through Conscious Validation. So the thought *Dangit, I can't believe I still love him/her after all they've put me through!* doesn't draw the same Audience in our mind anymore. It can be ignored, or easily altered into *I know my heart is still attached for whatever reason, and it is a beautiful thing that it is beyond my control, and whether or not I agree with its choices, love is a beautiful thing to feel, regardless of the object.*

The body's emotions, like the weather, are a part of our environment. The only thing that we can do is slowly, over time, make ourselves a large part of your environment too. It may not feel like it right away, but this truth about our relationship to our emotional environment grants us our release. We don't have to try to stop the rain anymore.

"Wisdom is not about waiting for the storm to pass, it's about learning to dance in the rain." –B.J. Gallagher. That works pretty well here.

The relationship between the Soul Identity and its bodily emotion is vital.

Emotion...Our Wild Horse

To put it very bluntly, everything that matters in our lives will come from our emotions. Everything. The chronology of our life, if written out upon our death, would consist of a list of emotional realities and their effects over time. Our most important relationships (life partner and children specifically), our ability to function and thrive in a working environment, and our ability to enjoy everything begins with emotion, and ends with how we relate to it.

There is an African proverb I love: "If you want to travel fast, travel alone. If you want to travel far, travel together." This is even more suited to the relationship one has with their own emotions than it is to working together in a group of people. So now that we are struggling less with our exterior world (fewer tigers chasing us) as a society and global culture, it is time to show this internal relationship the respect it deserves. It deserves a voice.

The relationship of human consciousness to its emotional realities is best compared to the relationship between man and a horse. But we are forming a healthy relationship. So we are focused on winning the respect and cooperation of a majestic and powerful animal, rather than attempting to control a beast. That is what "travelling together" means.

Before I get into the specifics of this relationship, I wish to mention **how far we are from grasping its nature**. We have about the same comprehension of this situation that a five-year-old has, while watching a John Wayne movie, of how difficult it is to handle a horse. It's probably tough when we think of it, but it's *totally do-able with a little effort*. Yeah…not so much.

The first thing to realize is that the horse is way bigger than us. It can not only beat us silly and toss us anytime it pleases, but it can destroy everything near us. We cannot make it do anything, ever. Beyond that, even after we have managed to master our horsemanship, any horse can get spooked and throw us. No rider is above being thrown. We have to come into this relationship with awe and humility. Our body has feelings. They are derived from chemicals in our brain, and they follow a pattern in reaction to our environment that is millions of years of evolution in the making. Whether we believe that we came here for the purpose of experiencing emotions and learning to relate and refine our role in the development of universal consciousness, or not...our emotions are bigger than we are.

Second thing to realize is that the horse is gonna be with us all the time. It's not going anywhere, ever. We can drug it to sleep, we can ignore it, we can abuse it, neglect it, and compartmentalize it...but we can never be rid of it. If we build habits of avoidance, and work our lives around having to deal with our horse's presence, that limits our ability to create our world. If you have a horse in your house and don't want to be bothered with it, you're going to have to go way out of your way in every area of your life to ensure that stays the case. ***That is a lot of effort spent making our world smaller and safer.***

Another thing to realize is that we want to get places. Love and marriage, our Primary Relationships, these matter to us more than anything else in our lives. Work and career demand our motivation and emotional investment, and even if they are a means to an end, they need to be an end we are motivated to attain. We need to engage our emotions to get there.

We want to ignore our emotions *and have access to love*? **Not a CHANCE.** Without love we will not form close bonds, experience empathic and vicarious joy, or share any of our precious inner realities with anyone. The odds of living a happy or creative life without love have got to be only slightly lower than a snowball's chance in hell. If we want to ride across our world and see unrestrained new and beautiful places? Do we think we're going to do that on foot? Really?

If we want to have a life that is shared, meaningful, creative, and joyous, we need love. And that leads us to the next section....

If we are going to invite love into our reality, all of the emotions come with it. This is why every serious relationship is a large opportunity for change in our lives. We will naturally hide every unpleasant emotion initially, but once we unpack our love everything opens up, and we have *every little bit of mess* to deal with. This means that once we start dealing with our horse, we have to focus on nourishing it and cleaning up after it. That means that we have to deal with transmuting the waste matter, and have to be motivated to protect, house, and feed it. Our emotions need our Parenthood.

With it we can go really far, though. That's what emotion is: motivation for everything we will ever do. We can use our emotion to drive our thoughts and behaviors. Our horse can get us farther in *every direction over any terrain* than we could by ourselves, and this is not limited to love. A trained consciousness turns **fear into courage** rather than hopelessness, **crisis into opportunity** rather than paralysis, **anger into focus** rather than chaos, and everything into the emotional content that lights up our every movement with soul immersion.

On the reverse side, there are a couple things to mention also. If we don't nourish our relationship with emotion, we are likely to be victim to its whims, and remain frustrated and stupefied by our powerlessness within our own mind. Ouch. Also, since our emotions are powerful, if we have no relation to them, we will be manipulated by everything in our world that evokes any response from us. Not "we *can* be"…but "we *will* be."

This is a serious issue. Because not being in relationship with our emotions is not just unhealthy or "something we may need to work on." It is life-destroying.

If you think that might not be the case, I'll just tell you the short story of how I punched a hole in every wall at every house I lived in until I was thirty-two. Short story, huh? At thirty-two I fell in love and thus was dealing with my emotional realities more often. So I didn't punch stuff anymore.

Seems basic, but I didn't fully get it for thirty-two years in a way that actually protected my walls from my fist, or my roommates from watching me explode in anger. Everyone needs help with their emotions, but ask people in anger management classes how their lives have been affected by their emotions. Ask people in addiction recovery. It's not pretty.

If we do not get into good relation with our emotions, we really might as well have a horse inside our house. It's gonna do the same amount of damage. Any relationship can be destroyed by anger, or fear (which leads to escapism). No matter how well we take care of our connection to love (our horse and joyous travels), if we cannot manage our anger and fear (horse waste management and cleanup), we're going to be living in a mess very soon, and it's going to stain all the good stuff in our world and the people around us.

This is why I translate the statement *"The most creative and loving people have the worst demons"* into *"The people with the biggest horses...**have the biggest horses.**"* Yeah, I know, I'm silly. Gets the point across, though.

But we can ride this thing. We really can. Of this I have no doubt, and we are continuously given examples. We can find ways to reinterpret fear and anger, and we can give ourselves fully to love. The more we become confident in our relationship with pain and fear and anger, the more aggressively we can dive into being loving people. We must do the following:

Approach with humility. Understand the power we are dealing with. Be gracious (this means stop complaining).

Accept all parts of the experience. Realize we cannot do anything by ourselves. Realize that every positive feeling we will ever have is being felt through this relationship, and can be enhanced and augmented. Also realize that every negative feeling we will ever have comes through the same way, and only in good relation can we hope to dim the destructive power of pain, fear, and anger.

We have to earn the respect of this powerful creature we share space with. This means we have to listen. This means we have to value the expressions. This means we have to foster its growth. This means we must bask in the richness of externalizing and integrating simultaneously. The *externalizing demands our respect*, and patience, and the forming of a relationship. The *integrating creates trust*, intimacy, connection, and Influence. This is why simply calling these aspects the "ego," then brutalizing and compartmentalizing them, does not work. It creates hostility. It does not integrate the need for, or value the strength of, such a wonderful natural source of expression and energy. "Travel together if you wish to go far."

PART 2: THE CONVERSATION.

What can help us, and why understanding the nature of our internal realities is important, is that we need to be humble before our internal counterparts. Just like on a playground, sharing has to do with mutual respect. And to be honest, our brains and bodies don't share with us because we are bossy. You…and I…are bossy. We are also rude and unappreciative. True story.

This chapter I am going to keep coming back to a Conversation between parts of our matrix of consciousness. It will take place between the Observer, Logic, and the Feelings Guy.

Conversations Part 1:

"Hey, I hate all that emotion craziness you got going on. And brain, why don't you have all the answers I'm looking for?"

The brain and body, were they active in the conversation, would likely say "Hey, ummm...who do you think you're talking to? This is our playground. This is all our stuff, and not only are you using it without being appreciative, but now you're trying to boss us around? Thanks, but we'll keep all the cool stuff over here until you learn some manners."

"But...but...you guys belong to me!"

"Yeah dude, you just keep telling yourself that. We'll just be over here, doing exactly what we want to no matter what you tell us. And instead of coming over here kindly and learning to play with us, you'll sit over there and bitch and moan."

"But I can make decisions!"

"Not without us. The thing that you can do without us...is *talk*. But if you say words without our participation, they are just meaningless words."

"But I can play any game I want!"

"All the games you want to play take three and you only have you. That's just one."

"I don't need you to play 'go to work,' or 'be in love'!"

"All right, you can try--go ahead and tell us how far you get playing 'go to work' without any emotional energy, and please tell me how playing 'be in love' is without emotion. We're looking forward to hearing all about that."

We must be humble before our Body Instinct, and Mental Instinct reactions. Our Body Instinct is emotion. We have this, whether or not we want it, from in-utero until the day we die. We have this whether we can speak, have amnesia, are mentally damaged, get Alzheimer's, anything. Emotion is there, and it is simply non-negotiable.

Our Mental Instinct is trickier. It is paired with body instinct, and is housed in justification. Our mind is going to talk to us and tell us a story that makes sense. It *needs* to make sense to us. This is a psychological *need*. So, you feel scared? That is your Body Instinct. It's your Mental Instinct upon feeling that *to find a monster*. You are angry? Mental Instinct is there to *find a bad guy*. You are happy/in love? It's your Mental Instinct to promote things about whoever you are in love with that agree with your feeling, and downplay those things that do not.

So here's a scenario: In the ghetto, in the middle of the night, in an alley, we run across a tall and physically imposing man...and whether or not it is true, we are very unlikely to think of *how beautiful his shirt is*. However, when he gets home, his wife will notice the nice new shirt she bought him and think of how lovely it looks on him.

While we are crafting a story about his possible malice and danger to us, we are doing so to *justify our fear*. While she is loving on him, she will see the shirt as her gift, and his wearing it as a symbol of her love, and that will *justify her love*.

Both are just reacting to feelings and present experience with a **Mental Instinct**: something that justifies our feelings. Both of those lines of thinking are reactions, not creations. These instincts need to be treated as external reactions, things that are external to our being, and that go on with or without our permission and regardless of our wants, needs, and will.

I must be clear about something here. These thought reactions are not inaccurate, and they are necessary. They keep us alive and help us operate the machinery (physical and mental) we are charged with. *These reactions are not, and cannot be wrong to have.* They are non-negotiable, and outside of our control. They simply are. Once we accept that they are not us, and we go further to accept the reality of their effect on us, the conversation we have with ourselves can change.

Back to the playground we go.

Conversations Part 2

"So, what do I do now? I want to play and I need you guys, sorry I haven't been appreciative of your stuff"

"Well, if you're going to be nice, then you can take a look at what we like to play with, and learn the games we play."

"Well, all right, but why can't I just get you guys to play what I want you to?"

"Where did you get that…'want'."

"Well, I just liked something and wanted it."

"No, it wasn't that simple, and you didn't ask us. We are the 'want,' and the 'why.' You may have used us, but you weren't playing with us. So, it's pretty likely that **you saw** *someone else doing something in their playground that you assume made them happy, and then decided that it would make you happy.* You did this without asking us. You made a decision about yourself without asking us, so it was meaningless. That is why we didn't play with you."

"So, what do I do now?"

"Learn our games, learn our playground. Be kind to us."

The idea of "getting to know ourselves"? This is actually what it looks like, broken down into little bitty pieces and exposing the difficult aspects.

The reason we don't succeed in knowing ourselves is not that we lack the tools and capabilities. It is because this knowledge is not valued in our current society, for various devious reasons. I assume it will become important shortly, though. It is too large a component of a healthy reality, and we are getting a bit too smart to miss it.

When we are small children, we learn our bodies. We are humble before our inability to control our limbs, and the world around us. As the world gets bigger, and as our inner circle of reality changes, it begins including the whole of the planet (albeit slowly), and we get totally freaked out. We look to others as a result of this, to steady ourselves as the world, unlike our body, does NOT conform even remotely to our commands. When we look to others, we assume that because they look steady, that they have the things that they want. Why wouldn't they? We *want* steady, and they *look like* they have it. So *of course that's the goal.*

That is the prime moment when our Body Instinct and Mental Instinct work together to form the **Fatal Flaw** in our growth matrix. We are scared (Body Instinct upon seeing a large piece of reality we cannot control), so we look to something outside of ourselves, **assume its properties**, and imagine ourselves in its role (Mental Instinct upon recognizing our fear, needing to justify that our ideas on how to stop it are real). WE imagine that this is where safety and comfort lie.

Just to quickly note why this doesn't work, for the official record: 1) They are not us. 2) We are making an assumption based on little to no knowledge (as it is not us) about a person as a result of fear-based desperation. 3) We can't end "scared." It's eternally connected with this incarnation.

This is the moment when we stop working with our body, and **TRUST WHAT WE THINK IS GOING ON IN OTHER PEOPLE'S BODIES.**

We can't keep that up and get anywhere. We know that, because very simply, we haven't gotten anywhere in some time. That has to change, because at the speed with which we are changing the world through technology, we need more skills and understanding to manage ourselves. We need this in the same way that a boy coming out of puberty needs to get a handle on his body. This is because he is going from not being able to handle himself as a kid (whose biggest repercussions may have been breaking some dishes or losing a toy) to someone who has to control himself well enough to drive an automobile that has the power to kill him or others if he makes a minor mistake. That is where we are with technology.

So let's see how we can do that.

Conversations Part 3

"Learn your games, huh?"

"Yes. Learn us, and learn how we play."

"Well, all right then, who are you?"

"We are Feelings Guy, and Logic. Feelings Guy does exactly what his name suggests. He has feelings about external realities, including us. He does not need to be handled. He does this on his own. I (Logic) make what he feels make sense."

"All right, and what can I do?"

"You are the Observer and the idea man. You can organize and create, if you want to."

"Then why don't you guys listen to me if I'm the idea man?"

"***You're not the boss***. You get to have ideas. Then he gets to feel and I get to logically show how it makes sense. So, when you tell Feelings Guy not to love someone he loves, you aren't showing an idea. You are just being bossy. That makes Feelings Guy angry or sad. Then I have to come up with something that is believable for you."

"Can you give me an example?"

"Of course, I'm Logic. So, you remember that ex-girlfriend...the one who cheated on you and humiliated you?"

"Yes, I think she's still in the old memory banks."

"Remember when you told the Feelings Guy that he wasn't in love with her anymore, so it was cool to be friends with her?"

"Yes."

"Well, that didn't work, did it?"

"No, I ended up fighting with her and we had a terrible blow-up and said awful things that brought out the worst in both of us."

"Ah, yes, you do remember. What you don't remember is the feeling of resentment, which is what happens when you try to boss Feelings Guy around while ignoring the way he feels. He just waits to express it. Because we are both here, he has to have a reason. He has feelings, and simply waits for any excuse. The truth is that he was still very angry about being humiliated, and also very angry that he was bossed around and ignored. But what he wasn't angry about was the fact that she called you when she locked the keys out of her apartment and asked you to come get her. He just used that to explode and it was obviously inappropriate. But since you were not in contact with Feelings Guy, *you had no idea how ridiculous it was.* That is what happens when you boss him around and ignore him. He stays feeling the way he feels, adds on some anger, and then he waits for me to give him a reason to express himself that I can make sense of. And to be honest, I can make sense of just about anything. It's what I do. And as the Observer, you believe me. That is the case until you get to know me, and understand that I am not to be counted on for truth, just a Perspective that makes sense and allows Feelings Guy to express himself."

"Shit."

"I know, right? It's crazy. How do you think all the hypocrisy in the world happens?"

"I guess all that does certainly make more sense now. So what do I do, again?"

"Well, you're the Observer, so you've seen everything. And you're the idea man. You can use any of that Observation to imagine possibilities for the future. You can ask us what we think of any part of it, though I'll let you know that it's very important to look at us separately, and understand that what

I say is simply a result of what Feelings Guy feels. So you should really start with focusing on him. Ask him how he feels about things, and what he likes; then I will explain it, and that should lead you to more questions. When you two get comfortable with dealing with each other, then everything gets easier. He's still pretty pissed you ignored him for fifteen years after you guys were so close when we were young. There are plenty of techniques. This communication is called connecting with Intuition, because you don't need me for it. I'm really just a bridge, and if I'm not relegated to being a function of Feelings Guy, I can be your tool."

"Why do most people not do this?"

"Because the first step is to apologize, and humble yourself before something you thought you owned. And as you do that and we come out to share things with you, you realize what a bully you have been and that you cannot be a bully anymore. That causes Cognitive Dissonance. It is not your fault, but it causes guilt anyway. Then you are reminded every time it happens because Feelings Guy is right there to feel guilty on our behalf. Then I have to explain your guilt to you, while you just watch, and hopefully come up with new ideas quickly so we don't get bogged down by it."

"How can I trust that this is accurate, instead of some justification to confuse me?"

"That's easy. Since you have gotten to know Feelings Guy, you know that he isn't really engaged one way or the other right now. When he doesn't need me to justify how he feels by using everything at my disposal to do so, I am free to answer questions truthfully. So, if you ask me something and he doesn't need me to respond a certain way, you get as close to the truth as possible. When we are not emotionally activated, and needing to justify a state of being, we can work pretty efficiently and harmoniously."

"What if you don't know? You can't know everything."

"You're right, I can only use combinations of things you've seen, or can imagine. I make you two fit. That's all. If you are looking for answers and we don't have a specific need that has to be filled, I can use anything and everything I can get a hold of instead of JUST things connected with the emotion I'm trying to justify. I get a lot more to play with. This is self-aware imagination. You can have imagination and not be self-aware. But since we're talking about it, it's the self-aware type."

This is how we engage the fullness of our mental abilities: with humility and a focus on listening and cooperation. The magnitude of the difference between fully engaged mental processing, described at the close of this chapter, and the infantile relationship we were looking at in the beginning of the chapter, is gargantuan.

We are capable of forming this relationship, and we are also accountable for doing so. Taking this conversation to heart gives us Perspective, and that can make us powerfully influential.

PART 3: CALM ON THE BEACH OF QUIET EMOTION

There is information everywhere. There is experience everywhere. We take part in a manner proportional to our relationship with ourselves, not in proportion to the world around us. And like our ability to create can be clogged and knotted up by anger, fear and frustration, our ability to experience, relate to, and integrate the world around us is also subject to those forces. So...don't clench.

We think about "inhibition" as something that stops behaviors, but we rarely think about inhibition as that which stunts our ability to feel and experience the world around us. This is understanding what it means to be open-minded, and why mind-clearing exercises are so important to keep close by. The world is always expressing itself, as are we, but the internal noise of emotional rhetoric can drown out anything.

So let's imagine cigarette smoke, because that's what anger and fear are like. We have smell, sight, and taste, all affected by it. So imagine our lives, living with anger, as sitting in a room full of second-hand smoke. Our avocado wrap sandwich doesn't taste as good (and the fresh tomatoes are almost unnoticeable), we can barely notice the perfume on the sweet woman next to us, and our eyes sting a bit.

We get used to it though, not a big deal. I'm not asking what we do now. I'm describing what we did not twenty-five years ago in this country, when smoking was allowed basically everywhere. That's just what we did. Even if we didn't smoke, we had learned to handle and deal with the effects of second-hand smoke and what it did to our sensations. For a moment, get yourself in that space where you're used to something of that nature, and dealing with it like it's not a big thing.

Now, imagine being on a lone Caribbean island under a pure breeze skipping off the nearby ocean. Imagine how you feel everything. Imagine the taste of fresh fruit in a glistening bowl and a piña colada at your side. Now, imagine someone walking up beside you and blowing cigarette smoke in your face. Kinda vivid, huh? And awful. I feel like I'm choking and getting upset just thinking about it. Ewwwww.

Now instead of getting into anger and all its negatives, just stop for a second. Think about how all that yummy food, the smell of the beach, and the warm sunlight touching your skin feels now. It is all clogged. You cannot feel it anymore. Nothing tastes or smells as sweet, and your frustration is making it difficult to feel anything good about where you are (*or **anything** for that matter*).

This is an example of how **fragile** feeling good is, and how much is lost when we are "clogged" with negative emotion (*as well as how much the presence of negative emotions can affect a person previously enjoying a positive space*). We get used to this type of toxin because it is common, not because it is something we should get used to. And this environment is ours to affect and Influence, because the smoke is altering OUR abilities to take the world in.

This is where having the mental tools associated with clearing the mind can come into play. Whether it is meditation, music, walking/exercise, or going out into nature, these are important because the goal is not to become used to the smoke (or in our case used to the horrors and frustrations of the world that will continue to play out as long as we live), the goal is to **GET TO THE BEACH, AND STAY THERE**.

The **Beach of Quiet Emotion** is the place in our consciousness where all emotional, physical, and spiritual sensations are heightened. This is the place where our innate abilities to connect and form relationships with ourselves and the world through creative ideas takes place. This is the place where we are most likely to find love, joy, growth, health, and happiness. It's a fragile space, and it is vulnerable to even the smallest puff of smoke. The ease gives us heightened sensations, and those that are pleasurable are deeper and more resonant. But with that comes the fact that toxic sensations such as pain, anger, and fear are not only more vibrant, but more destructive to the peaceful mind then they could ever be to a toxified mind.

So, how do we stay there, and remain free of the effect of toxicity? First we make peace with the fact that there is no state of mind during this life that is free from the possibility of toxicity. There is no safety in that. Then we can go about forming our own personal manner with which we relate to taking on and dealing with the toxicity that we are presented with. The smoke inhalation example is a physical reality. Toxicity from anger and fear is also. We can take care of them the same way. We can become people who are *"in relation to,"* not *"in reaction to"* that which throws us off center and clouds the beauty.

The Adrenaline Drop

So, I ask her, as we come screeching to a halt: "Did you drop?"

"No, I caught it," she says.

This is what I ask my mate when we almost get in a car accident. They are rare because I'm like the best driver ever (seriously, I'm so good), but when they almost happen it is always a question of how close we came, and did we get "the drop."

"The drop" is the release of adrenaline. This is when our bodies react so quickly that panic engages our brain BEFORE our frontal lobes have a chance to assess the reality of the situation. Just so we're all very clear on who is responsible...his name is the Amygdala and he's a total jerk.

This is not just "getting scared." This is your brain flushing adrenaline into your muscles, and slamming your heart into full gear to pump it around your body. This is the fight or flight response, and we really don't need to do either with our seat belt on at a red light. So, the heart-pounding craziness of adrenaline is not only wasted on us, but everything we were thinking or talking about is gone. This is not just an interruption of what we were lending your attention to. This is having to calm down before we can even hope to get back to a normal state of mind.

So now the operating centers (frontal lobes) are engaged in the fact that there is nothing to fight, and nothing to flee from. But that has nothing to do with the PHYSICAL response of our bodies. They are jacked up, and uncomfortable. There is junk everywhere now that needs to be cleaned out. Adrenaline is not a leisure chemical; it is serious business. Now it's clogging up the normal processes of muscles, organs (were you digesting as the BMW changed lanes and swerved into you? Oops. Good luck with that stomachache.), and our mind, which is racing now to keep pace with our racing heart.

This is a physical response, just like we would have if someone actually blew smoke into our face on the beach. Our lungs would be full of something that didn't belong, the choke response would engage, and we'd have to get it out before we could go back to what we were doing.

Clenching is an emotional response to a situation that releases fear and anger into the mental reality. It changes the character of everything we are thinking, but has no "noticeable" physical effects. If we don't check with ourselves, we have no idea it has happened, and we continue to act in a way we think is normal. However, it is not normal; it is altered by an internal toxic response. And because we did not respond to an outside stimulus, but to our own internal reactions, these usually go unnoticed.

One of the reasons we respond with such ferocity to our emotional body is because we misidentify it as belonging to us. That…is silly. It is as silly as getting truly angry at someone for what they did in our dream. It was a dream, first of all. And beyond that, it was OUR dream. That is an obvious description, but what about one that is not so obvious?

In example one, we say "I am angry at you because in the dream I had last night you betrayed me!" That is our interpretation of our reality. It would be nonsense to implicate someone else in such a thing.

In the next example we say "I am angry at you because at the party you drove Jimmy home without telling me; you betrayed me." Well, that's a little less obvious, and has some circumstantial aspects to it. But, it is still *we* who are creating the betrayal. Might as well be a damn dream. This is not to say that we were not betrayed. We may well have been. But Jimmy may also have been hammered and needed to get home at a specific time and your friend driving him home saved his life and there was no way to tell you. That also may have happened. When you find out that there was an explanation, ***it is the same as finding out that the dream was only a dream***. The difference is that we naturally assume that our emotional reactions are based in reality. That is the assumption I like to call **The Raccoon Trap**.

The Raccoon Trap

The Raccoon Trap is a funny thing. It is an open block with a shiny ball bearing in the bottom, with spikes that lead down toward the ball at an angle.

The goal of the trap is to attract a raccoon through its natural curiosity and get it to grab the ball bearing at the bottom, trapping it. But trapping it, how? Not by injury, not by snare, ***just by confusion***.

The trap is set up so that ONLY the ball bearing, the subject of our focus (emotional reality) is stuck in the bottom of the trap. The raccoon (that's us) gets all excited and jabs its hand in to grab and retrieve the ball bearing, then cannot get his hand out! Why can't he get his hand out**? BECAUSE HE WILL NOT LET GO OF THE BALL BEARING**. His hand is not stuck; he is free. The object of his focus is not attached to him, and he can drop it and walk away at any moment. Yet, he does not.

What he does is *freak out*. He jumps and yelps and makes all kinds of noise, reacting to the assumption that he is trapped. He does this because he makes the false assumption that the thing stuck in the trap is part of his body. IF HE ONLY LET GO OF THE SHINY OBJECT OF HIS FOCUS HE WOULD BE FREE. Sounds kinda familiar, huh?

You're angry? You're sad? Really? You sure that's YOU? You sure it's not a physical response that you're attached to? You sure you can't just let go and walk away, rather than be trapped by the feelings and chemicals in your head?

Maybe you can't. Maybe they are too strong, and goodness knows I have had many an instance where they were, and we ALL do and WE ALL SHOULD. That is life. *But...it does not mean that the momentary emotion, no matter how powerful, is attached to our consciousness **in a way that cannot be separated***.

Byron Katie's work covers this, but picturing yourself as a raccoon might help you understand the full mechanism.

⟨∞⟩

Being "in relation to" these changes rather than "in reaction to" is the main component for being able to work with states of consciousness. Having a relationship with our reactions is what affords us courage, as it is the transmutation of the momentary fear reaction. Courage is not the lack of fear. *It is the fear reaction **alchemized** into positive, creative action.* And that is how we must "relate." I've found that the easiest manner for describing this, in order to convey the violence, skill, and speed that is necessary is citing Jiu-Jitsu.

In Jiu-Jitsu, the artist in combat uses the energy of his opponent against him. The expert watches as the aggressive energy comes toward him and reacts "in relation to" the energy to use it against his opponent. There are a few attitudes that should be mentioned. One is that of humility. You have an opponent that deserves respect; not only are his actions capable of injuring you, but they are the natural essence of his being right now. They are not for questioning, judging, or underestimating. We are powerful souls with powerful bodies, and the expressions of strong emotion that we are receiving from our bodies are supposed to be affective imprints on our souls.

The second attitude is that these aggressive moves are necessary to this combat art. There is no fight without an aggressor, and thus the role the "attack" plays is necessary and productive for the exercise. This can be used on any scale, in any manner. All energy is mutable. Every Perspective is changeable. The initial act is one of entropy, the second is one of refinement, the two creative forces of the Universe. Both expressions are part of the movement and music of reality and consciousness. Our emotive realities, in all their messy aspects, are the foundation for all creative graces in this world.

The third attitude is training. There is always a stronger opponent in the world of combat, and in correlation, every internal challenge we face from our reactive minds is a worthy adversary. Fear leads to courage. Anxiety leads to calm. Chaos leads to focus. Anger and fury lead to peace. Those are not reactions**, *those are relationships*.** Those are relationships defined by the transmutation from one type of energy that is toxic to creative thought and living, to a more refined type of energy that harnesses the emotional content of the human body and directs it with Grace across the expanse of conscious existence.

The last attitude is that of being fully open. Our attacker is our strength. ***Our own destructive emotions are the source of our power to refine and transmute reality***. The opponent in the combat arena must attack and we must be fully accepting of the energy coming at us in order to use it. If we shy away in fear from the oncoming aggressive and destructive energy, we will not be able to harness it. It is in the distinction between that which *is us* and that which *is attacking us* that we form this relationship. To do so we must be able to experience it fully without tightening up our reality in apprehensive fear.

We must be fully open.

Stasis, and the Urge to Leave the Beach of Quiet Emotion for the Smokehouse

Be open rather than closed. Be receptive and integrating rather than fixed and limited. This is a Lesson-Based Reality, and it is not going to take a moment off, ever. It's always going to be coming at us. There are always going to be new informative moments to learn from, positive and negative... and they are going to be engaging us daily, unendingly.

This is a difficult situation for a number of reasons, but one of the main reasons is that the External Mind craves stasis. Stasis seeks to diminish or nullify the incoming emotional activators. ***To fully utilize the power of our emotions we must consciously resist stasis***. We must do this in a way that does not raise our stress levels, as that would render us incapable of processing complicated information. There is a fragile balance we can achieve that allows the mind to function at an optimum level while suspending the need for stasis. The balance is achieved, like most things, through focused practice.

So let's go back to the beach. Let's discuss how we get there, and see how we get moved back and forth between the beach and a nearby Smokehouse. This will relate to our moving from clarity to toxicity throughout our lives. Before we go into this, please take a moment to think of a couple times in your life when you were calm and focused, and other times when you were buried in emotion and confusion. It is important to relate to these descriptions, and we are all capable.

On the Beach of Quiet Emotion there is a gigantic pitfall. It is the sensitivity to toxicity. The violence of experiencing a toxic moment on the Beach is so much greater than in the nearby Smokehouse. **The Smokehouse** is where most people stay. People who have trouble processing emotions call the Smokehouse home. We have all spent time there in our lives. The length of our stays and regularity of our presence there is what we want to work on, and limit. Depending on our family of origin, we are more or less given glimpses of both areas, but we are not connected to either in a deep or meaningful way. The extent to which we become emotionally and mentally toxified in our youth, of course, varies directly in relation to the quality of our life, safety, and environment. This is the "nurture" aspect of our experiential DNA.

Our childhood, however, does not determine anything completely. First, the environment we take in as children is only a glimpse. It can position us closer to one reality or another by giving us Vibrational examples that we can find and emulate in adulthood. But, it will never change the fact that

STAYING ON THE BEACH TAKES SKILL. *It takes skill because achieving stasis in a high-sensitivity area is rare*.

When I speak of stasis in this analogy, I am specifically describing what is lost when we have smoke blown in our face while on a clear and beauteous beachside. In comparison to the same experience whilst in an enclosed house filled with smokers, the smoke on the beach is much more noticeable, much more violent. So, when we have smoke blown in our face in the Smokehouse, it's not so unnerving. The mind is in stasis, and though it may be unpleasant to have smoke blown in our face, it's bearable, and to some extent, expected. It is not the shock and demoralizing assault that it is when you're relaxing in a beautiful and non-toxic space.

So, when we're sitting on our beach and something really toxic gets into our space (it's gonna happen; the world creates toxicity as a natural byproduct of growth), we notice the painful loss of clarity and clean air. How adept we are at handling this moment is *vital* to our lives. VITAL. It is vital because if we are not skilled at "handling and processing toxicity," we will not be able to suspend the need for stasis, and *our mind will lead us back to the smokehouse*. This is **Reflexing Out**.

Reflexing Out is when we are traumatized by the presence of something toxic in our internal or external environment, and we bail for a more toxic environment where the violence of the toxicity will be lessened. This is why when something bad happens, we escape so quickly. This is why bars get such good business. Escapism is directly related to how incapable we are of managing our emotions, and the frightening world around us. *When we have pain we cannot manage, we move to an area of narrowed sensation. That is why we are an addicted society*. We Reflex out, and go back to the Smokehouse.

If we are not skilled at processing the toxic smoke that occurs on the beach, we will not stay and fight. *We will get confused and leave.* This is not because we want toxicity in our lives, but because our need for stasis is greater than our ability to handle the vast difference between how healthy our surroundings are and how healthy we feel at the moment.

To make it clearer, the air quality on the beach is a 10. Our air quality was a 10, but we've been hit with smoke, and now we're at a 4, while in the midst of 10-quality air. That difference (6, for us math whizzes) needs to be fixed. **That is what stasis demands.** So if we cannot get it back up to 10 through emotional processing, we will simply change the quality of the air around us. We will go to the Smokehouse, where the air quality is a 5 (and the difference then will only be 1).

We can see examples of this in our lives. When we feel out of shape, we do not want to be surrounded by gorgeous people, even at the gym. We do not want to be recognized at the store if we have the flu. Heck, I don't even want to be in a clean house if I'm feeling sick; it reminds me of how "not right" I feel. This is not a difference in the world around us, but an example of how we are ill-equipped. The contrast around us maximizes differences when it is in our nature to want to blend in and disappear if we are uncomfortable.

This is related also to The Hangover Principle, obviously, in that *controlling failure* can be better than *working to attempt to process* emotion.

The helplessness we feel and the frustration we take on while trying to find stasis, along with the lack of certainty that we will have success, is often too much to take. That is the case **until we become acutely acclimated to the violent fluctuations of existing in a heightened state of sensitivity.**

Existential Philosophy, and the Steps for Managing Emotion on the Beach

As children, we get glimpses of what is to come. These can come from our environment, as well as from media and stories that depict other environments. But, no matter what we are shown as children, or how positive our surroundings are, when we leave our nests we get completely overwhelmed. This is the **Wound of Passage**. The incoming stress of building a life and having to manage foreign responsibilities (rent was really foreign to me, quite the insulting feeling) prompts our move to the Smokehouse. Too much toxicity from stress wipes us out, and it is much easier to find stasis in a more toxic arena. I was not a fan of my twenties. It was the "Well, I guess it made me who I am" decade.

Disillusionment, disappointment, depression, and despair. They confront us at the beginning of our adulthood, and they are the result of not being able to process pain, fear, loss, and stress. Our lives will all have a great moment of unmet expectations, where the ideals we had for ourselves are in contrast with our inner realities. At this point, the question that everyone has an opportunity to ask, and answer, is "WHAT DO WE DO NOW?" This question is the basis for Existential Philosophy. *Do we try to live? Or do we settle on stagnation and stasis?*

We face the task of having to overcome all the "D" words at some point in our lives. Then, on top of that, we have to slowly acclimate ourselves to the violent world of emotions, and train our minds to be able to handle living without stasis.

Wow. No wonder we rarely change. It's really difficult to improve our lives. It is demanding and challenging at every level. I never fault anyone who isn't up to it ...even though we really don't have much else to do during the approximately eighty years we get to hang out here.

Now we come to the crux of this chapter, and how all of this all relates. We will look at the process of dealing with toxicity. It can come from within us or from external sources. It can come from those who are close to us, our jobs, family, home, city, everything. It can also come from our memories, judgments of ourselves, and traumas of all types. So what do we need to do in order to process this stuff quickly and efficiently? *We need to not clench up with fear and we need to not freak out when it happens*. DON'T CLENCH. When we are out of stasis, we are VERY uncomfortable, and we cannot let it get to us. If we let it get to us, we will not be able to think clearly, and we will not be able to create our way out of whatever situation is frustrating us. We need to **create**, and we cannot do that if we are freaked out. Our mind will not perform the way we need it to if we don't find a way to become calm.

We create a pathway out of discomfort by altering our momentary Perspective. We **Zoom Out**. We remember the "You can't get there from here" aspect of not being able to control things, right? This is where it really matters, because we are freaked out and uncomfortable, and we cannot go straight back to The Beach of Quiet Emotion. We have to go to "calm down and manage yourself" first. Then we can find the Perspective that will clear our mind of its toxicity.

This is the process.

1) Accept the toxic moment without clenching, or Reflexing Out.

2) Calm yourself.

3) Focus your creative mind on finding a helpful Perspective.

4) Use the Perspective you've found to clear the air.

5) Use the strength of the toxic moment to turn the present situation into an opportunity for growth.

There is no other process that works effectively (escapes like drinking and repression don't work; those count as Smokehouse Techniques). We don't always win. None of us do. Not even with the most practice, best family, and best environment. Those things all add to the likelihood that we will be successful at stopping our toxic moments before they do damage or send us downward spiraling off to the Smokehouse. But this is a Lesson-Based Reality, so the only way to keep growing is to lose every once in a while (or more than likely, often). Then we get stronger, and we make the necessary changes to our reality when we recover.

The relationship we form with our internal matrix determines our level of engagement in our reality. It determines how much we feel, and it determines how present we can be for those around us. The difficulty in fostering this relationship is not to be understated. It is the challenge of living. Creating a space we trust for ourselves, and learning what Influences our ability to maintain that space for the good of ourselves and all around us, that…is priceless.

Chapter 11:

This chapter seeks to illuminate Intuition, and to validate its presence in our lives. I am looking to show that we already use it, albeit mindlessly, and without engaging. It is already a part of our lives, but it is capable of becoming a valuable tool.

There are a lot of Perspectives on Intuition. A high level of Intuition might even get labeled as a sixth sense. This is one of the more irresponsible aspects of our scientific community, for a couple of reasons. First, it makes it suspicious to gather information in this manner…this breeds doubt within any community, and doubt in the self. That is poisonous. Second, it is something demands thorough examination should one case exist. "We can't explain it" is not a good enough answer. In fact "We can't explain it," in the scientific community, is NEVER a good enough answer. *It should be a rallying cry for immediate action on a global scale*. We can explain the movements of planets and the life-rhythms of stars that are millions of light years away. Given that, "We can't explain it" is a huge red flag when it happens in our society.

I don't know anyone who hasn't experienced unexplainable

feelings about things that they were not in direct contact with. Still, the idea that Intuition plays a role in our reality has not demanded investigation on a major scale. Now, in 2013, there have been more than five popular TV shows that are based on intuitive characters. But even with the increased social acceptance, we are not seeing increased attention from the scientific community. This is a flat-world response. It is unacceptable.

To make a quick point about this violation of duty by the scientific community, let's remind ourselves of the Placebo Effect. This is something that is allowed for in all experiments. It has its own statistical set. It is simply the body healing itself with no outside chemical interaction. The healing is attributed to the BELIEF that effective medication was given. The body heals itself based on belief and there's no investigation of that phenomenon? Man, that's irresponsible. Then to top it off, after witnessing and recording the body's ability to heal, the medical community insults and dismisses any ideas that suggest the possibility of mental focus or will power healing the body. This is **rude**. It is not scientific, and it is the result of Cognitive Dissonance over an entire field of thought. It is the lack of scientific inquiry where phenomenon has presented itself. That is the antithesis of scientific exploration.

I am saying this because speaking of Intuition on a psychological and scientific basis runs into the "Science hasn't found it yet" argument, and I want to bypass that completely. The scientific paradigm in place has taken itself out of role of having an authoritative opinion by not inquiring on this matter to a satisfactory level. They don't get a say in it because they have violated their code. When these marvels of reality are met with curiosity and examination instead of dismissal, they can weigh in. Until then, as a species we need to be open to any theories on the matter with a logical or correlative foundation. 2000 years ago, in Greece, Eratosthenes not only figured out that the Earth was round, but correctly calculated the circumference. It was not that difficult for the entire populace to ignore obvious truths about the world around them for thousands of years. We are not different. So when I or anyone asks for a Perspective with an open mind, please attend graciously.

Rant over.

So, let's take a look at brain power, the subconscious mind, and Intuition.

The Subconscious Mind, Our Limitations, and Mind Expansion

We don't use ten percent of our brains; that's a myth. The truth, in my estimation, is that we use far, far less. And that is not the true crime. The true crime is that out of every 1000 actionable bits of information, only two or three go into our conscious mind. The other 997 go into the subconscious mind, and are stored permanently in the depth of our awesome, yet difficult-to-reach brains. Part of the last set of chapters was built around understanding how little control we have over our brain's abilities, and that Body Sovereignty acts beyond our scope of control by about a million light years. Now is the time to take a look at what we *can* do to *Influence* this world, the world of Intuition where the conscious mind has the capability to connect with and communicate with the subconscious mind, even if it is indirect, and limited. We want a larger presence here.

There are two things that the subconscious mind has that we need more access to in our conscious mind. We need its *heightened sensation*, and we need its *ability to recall pertinent information*. Intuition is simply tapping into those. It is a tool for connecting with those abilities. We may need to use more of our brain, though, so we should be ready for some extra intellect and sensitivity to be a side effect of drawing on such expansive areas of cognition.

The reason we don't naturally have access to these areas is not magic. There is a very basic fundamental reason that is imperative for survival. Right now, we are overwhelmed by large amounts of information. The body will do anything to remain in stasis, in safety. **We will not have access to anything we cannot handle**. We have to be ready, calm, and focused. But have no doubt about the goal. The goal is to push, as a species, for heightened brain function.

We know that this information is there, locked up, because it shows up in our psychologically determined reactions. It is the matrix within our behavioral reality. We calm to the sound of a beating heart because of time in the womb that we don't consciously remember, but that our body reacts to nonetheless. We react to songs we can't remember that were played when we were babies. We are, very truthfully, IMPRINTED by every single thing that has ever happened to us. Our subconscious mind has made correlations between our feelings and the characteristics of our specific surrounding environments. This relationship already exists in psychology, but it has not been developed. We can change that.

When we see the word "Imprinted" and understand it to be "Imprinted by." We must understand that it is "Imprinted with." Every piece of information that our subconscious holds onto is a tool meant to aid us in our lives. We must engage these strengths.

The thing our subconscious mind can do at all times is attend to the expression of the world. This is not limited, period. Our External Mind and our external realities are always expressing themselves. Always. And our subconscious mind is listening.

We have all experienced weird feelings without knowing why. We have all thought that something was about to happen and had no idea where the thought came from. Those are examples of the subconscious mind's heightened sensitivity to the world around us.

So now let's make a basic comparison between instinct and a computer motion tracker.

My Dad's Truck Story and the Motion Tracker

An aspect of major focus in this book is the demystification of mind expansion. It is not *extrasensory* or *superhuman* to do things we now consider extraordinary. In fact, we are already doing them all the time and not calling attention to it for one reason or another. There is an example from my dad's life I am going to use, not only because it is a solid example with easily correlative scenery, but because my dad is a statistician and completely opposed to any thinking not based in sound logical fact.

He was twenty-two, and on his way home from the University of Pennsylvania, driving through the outskirts of Philadelphia in the middle of the night. He came to an intersection where his sight was blocked, and stopped at a red light. There was little to no traffic anywhere in sight. He paused, drifting off as he does when he drives, and relaxed his eyes. The light turned green, and he resumed his ready-to-drive posture. But he just sat there. He did not go. He was kind of stunned at his refusal to step on the gas. But just as he had started to become aware of his reticence to move, a semi flew by at 60 mph, blasting through its red light, and scaring my dad to a near panic.

Many people have had such experiences. We hear of Guardian Angels protecting us, or miracles saving us. Fine, call it what you like. I am going to suggest a different theory, one that makes a tad more sense than the existence of a conscious invisible being following us around. I believe that symbol is a beautiful way to describe our own subconscious reality as it expresses itself to us.

I believe our subconscious mind has such heightened capabilities of experiencing and analyzing reality that from deep within my dad's mind it KNEW there was a truck coming, and it used what small Influence it had to make my father pause.

I plan on highlighting possible mechanisms for this, so let's talk about surveillance and motion trackers.

Imagine, if you will, the most advanced system for tracking movement that you can. Imagine that it can measure sound waves off of every surface, and can detect and analyze the movement of air around any given space. Imagine that this motion tracker does not use anything like visual analysis to track motion. Just Vibrations, air patterns, and sound waves. Pretty awesome machine, huh? Not too hard to imagine, is it? It can pick up the Vibrations of a moving truck humming along the road, the sound of the engine, and can quickly do the necessary computations to get the truck's size and speed. It could likely also, at some point, realize that the light was green, but that this oncoming truck was not slowing, tracking its movements along its current path at high speeds. That motion detector would know that my dad was going to get

T-boned and killed if he pulled forward into the intersection. It would know the truck couldn't stop in time, and it would tell my father to stay put until the maniacal driver went through the intersection.

That is not hard to imagine, is it?

Now, understand that our brain is categorically stronger than the most powerful computers ever made, and that they have tons of experience (in my dad's case, twenty-two years) in recording and managing billions of bits of information.

It's not a stretch to imagine that our subconscious mind is responsible for our instincts when we look at the world like that. It does want to survive, after all.

I've heard from so many people, after describing events of this type (I'm betting you have too, since it is pretty common), that there is "no logical explanation for what happened!" What? ***There is a totally logical explanation and I just said it***. If a computer can pick it up, a more powerful organic computer, that uses more sensors than a rigid monitoring system, *can definitely pick it up*. This is the **Subconscious Motion Tracker**.

I would like you to take a second here. I want you to think of the miraculous things in your world, and apply this type of logic to it. This doesn't make them any less amazing. This does not explain why the mechanism works the way it does, but it DEFINITELY proposes HOW the mechanism *could be working*.

The world is always expressing itself. This is the mechanism that describes how those expressions get relayed to our conscious mind.

We can understand our role as conscious beings better when we get our heads around how cognition turns into rapid cognition and precognition.

My mate and I were walking the other day. We were looking at power lines, and wondering why they looked so low, and I began to think about how many times we'd had that response just before power lines broke, or a tree fell over, etc. Instead of assuming it was chance, I understood that my mind was picking up information that is being fed into the vast area of my subconscious. So if the lines had snapped, instead of freaking out (*Oh My God I just thought about that happening and then it did!*), I would simply have known that there was an expression taking place, and that my mind was translating it into my consciousness. The wetness of the power line after the rain was likely making it hang low, and the tension on the metal brackets was expressing itself.

Reading expression is not new for the world. It has been performed and perfected by mentalists for ages. People are expressive beings. There are entire fields of study that analyze micro-movements and facial expressions. These are examples of relatively new fields of study becoming more mainstream (TV shows about it, books, etc.), but human beings have always had access to this as a talent. The description "reading people" has been around for as long as I can remember.

Is the "reading people" that family members use on each other different from the micro-movement detection techniques used by science now? No…of course not. This is why trained professionals are better lie detectors than polygraphs. It should also be noted that many people are excellent at this without any awareness of what they are doing. Some people are naturals at reading expressions and mannerisms. Some were forced to learn as a survival skill in their childhood. But everyone is capable of getting better at it. It is a "skill," not a "gift."

The reason we want to understand this mechanism better is so that we can remain as open as possible to the world around us. That allows us access to the world of experience and analysis that exists within our subconscious. If we are freaked out, confused, or unsettled, we are simply less capable of receiving and using information from these sources. We cannot validate a connection if we are freaked out. It's like flinching when someone is trying to kiss you. It kills the moment. *Not being ready to connect, kills connection.*

The chills we get when we pre-cog something or have synchronicities in our world should come as a joyous experience. It is not magic. It is a deeper experience in relationship with the world. It takes care to maintain, and effort to strengthen. But I will say that fostering this relationship is the fastest way to advancements in cognition that exists.

Getting to a state of being that can allow for these wonderful experiences is not as far off as it may seem. The following essay is a description of our most direct link to instinct.

Hunger: The Prime Example of Connection to Instinct

I want us to use more of our brain, and developing a healthy relationship with instinct is the most direct way I have found, *as it engages the subconscious mind.* We have been trained to keep most thoughts of Instinct outside of our "normal" everyday experiences. We can go ahead and let go of that. The distance between our everyday reality and creating a useful, healthy, and stable relationship with instinct is present all day. It is hunger.

I have spoken about instinct being acquisition of external expressions and internal realities. Well, this is one of the "internal reality" examples. This is the one that ALL OF US have experienced. It doesn't matter if we are the most conservative scientist or the most excessive hippie fruitloop (my apologies to most of my awesome family...I like fruitloops), we get hungry. *Because we all get hungry, we can all work on our connection to instinct in a direct way*. We can do this daily, we have plenty of opportunity. In fact, we cannot get away from it.

Our subconscious mind expresses the needs of our bodies directly to our brain. The fact that hunger is *common* hides its ability to become one of our body's most personally expansive properties. It is expansive, not because food is the key to everything in our world, but because listening to hunger and making good decisions for our body's nutrition is the exact same as making any other decision in our world. So...*the matrix of instincts that steers our eating habits can be used to steer much deeper emotional realities.*

For a couple years I wrote a daily menu and shared it with a large number of people in my environment online. This was greatly misunderstood. Many believed I was prescribing what I believed to be a healthy diet for everyone, others thought I was listing off what I was going to eat that day (they would often remark at the amount of food I took in, wondering how I could manage 7-10 meals a day). Those who looked forward to these posts liked to use the energy I put into thinking about food to get inspired about their own meals, something that can be very mundane. Often there were synchronicities in the eating patterns among those who were interested, and that could be exciting.

I was not trying to tell people what to eat, though. I was not divining the plan for food perfection for the day. I was sharing *how I dealt with my instinctual reality*, and hoping to inspire similar practices in others.

See, when we're hungry, our brain does something that exemplifies how the subconscious mind deals with everything in our world. We don't second-guess hunger, or judge it, or have serious psychological hang-ups with it (eating disorders have to do with control, not the actual *feeling* of hunger). So let's take a look at what we have to work with as adults that eat food.

Our subconscious minds, which direct our instinct, have not only experienced the taste of every meal we've ever had, but they have logged and categorized the after-effect of every chemical contained therein. That's a pretty large bank of knowledge.

Given the amount of knowledge our subconscious mind has about the needs of the body, and our history of taste-sensations and the correlating nourishment after-effects, does the body have the ability to direct hunger in a manner that is consistent with it speaking up for what it wants?

Could our instinct design it so that we become hungry for broccoli or steak if we need iron? Could it tell us we wanted orange juice if we needed vitamin C? Could it suggest fats and carbohydrates during the winter for weight gain? Could it lead us to water over other drinks if we are dehydrated, or to sugar if we are running out of energy?

Hasn't everyone experienced this? This is **Intuitive Hunger.**

I guess we can look at the possibilities of there being a connection and shake them off...or we could look at the example that led me to this line of examination: pregnant women.

Pregnant women are feeding a baby. They are providing the exact nourishment necessary for the creation of organs, tissues, and the skeletal system of a tiny person. What they intake is probably the most important of any person we could examine, and in correlation, they also have the most oddity-inspired hunger.

So...let's think of our pregnancies, the pregnancies of those we have known, and all the pregnancies in books, in movies, or on TV. They all contain food cravings. The hunger for specific food is almost violent, and it is totally accepted by our society as *"just something that happens."* We are taking the miracle of Instinct for granted when we think of it like that.

What is our subconscious mind doing to us when we're pregnant?

Our subconscious mind is realizing that nutrition is more important than usual. It is finding out what is in our food from stacks and stacks of memory banks, and then designing our cravings to meet the needs of a pregnant body and the developing body of the baby.

We don't marvel at the human machine often enough. We just don't.

So, how is our mind doing that? It's obviously turning up the volume of its wants and needs much louder than usual... enough so that it overrides habitual behavior and expected societal norms ("Ma'am, did you just order six sides of mashed potatoes covered in mustard?"). The mistake in our thinking is that we go about our lives like this is something that just happens, *rather than something we can use.*

This is the body at its best. We should be marveling at this daily, as well as learning everything we can about this process. Our body is overriding whatever our normal habits are, and using the well of experiences we have had, to come out with its desired effect. This is evolutionary genius. It is a system that functions powerfully enough to overtake any habitual action.

We can exercise faith in our instinct. It is always speaking. It may not be as loud for us as it is for a pregnant woman, but our body, like the world, never stops expressing. It needs to be validated and listened to for a relationship to form, and we are accountable for increasing the volume of its many helpful voices.

What I want to express is not just that we can and should engage this part of our bodily processes, but that we have a duty to do so. Only when engaging this part of ourselves, this instinctual reality, a goldmine of subconscious content, are we capable of actualizing faith in ourselves. **Faith**.

Faith: "the duty to act upon our trust in something." That is the definition. Faith is a meaningful word in my reality as it relates to behavior, as are the words "belief" and "doubt."

In the example above, the pregnant woman specifically, we see the easy relationship between her instinct-hunger and her actions. We see the whole of the act as an expression of trust. That is where our minds need to grow. We need to honor the expressions of the subconscious mind with as much Validation as possible. That is the forming of a relationship through trust. Our bodies are not trying to hurt us. They are not misinformed. They are smart, and they are never self-loathing, confused, distracted, or insidious. We need to act on and honor our trust in this area. That is how the relationship is formed.

The relationship is an important one, because it gives us something that we cannot have otherwise: an intellect free of all the crap that is making our lives difficult, and keeping our Perspectives limited.

Our connection to our body ensures that we have access to forming a relationship with our instinct. Within this infinite well of goodies we can find information that will aid us in every area of our life. Validating that relationship puts us in relationship with expanded manners of communication, and heightened sensitivity to the world around us. This creates a much richer experience, and our Resonance and Rapture grows exponentially as we shift our conscious mind into these vital areas.

PART 2: SUMMONING INTUITION

We need to validate our Intuition. We need to recognize and honor it. It is wisdom passed down through the code of a species, and it connects us with everything in ourselves that is life-affirming. It connects us to a well of information we cannot fathom, and supports us in ways that are vital to our joyous engagement in the world around us.

Through Intuition we can see Instinct, a manner of Commune heavily used by other beings on this planet. We should be humbled by its power, but more humbled by the fact that we have access to this font of livelihood.

Being Quiet and Understanding the Presence of Instinct

We are going to take a look at the animal kingdom. Instinct exists in all living things. The extent to which it guides behavior depends on the social structure and practices of the species being examined. For instance, sea turtles hatch, and are totally alone, knowing exactly what they need to do. That is powerful. That is an imprint, not just of an idea, but a *co-ordinated host of motivated behaviors that lead to a desired survival effect*. That is volition, muscle movement, and focus, designed for a purpose, **with no social instruction**. Impressive seems to be an understatement.

Looking around at others in the animal kingdom, we can see ritualized survival skills being transmitted in sparse social settings. So when we speak of instinct, before we confuse ourselves with genetic code and social construct in order to avoid the obvious and sublime power, let's just understand *that instinct is powerful enough to keep every species on the planet alive*...and adjusting to reality in real time.

There is not a species on the planet that does NOT use instinct to help itself survive and thrive. In fact, almost every species functions with instinct playing the primary role in behaviors. *Not us, though*. We have, through social training and the development of complex societies with expected behavior, taken a tool from our evolutionary toolbox, and buried it. That is why we must be quiet, so we can begin listening.

Being quiet has been mentioned in reference to understanding and validating conscious thought. We are not our mind. We are the Observer Consciousness that is listening to it chirp away. I have noted the importance of making this delineation in our Perspectives on the mind for many reasons. Most of the reasons have to do with deciphering motivation, engaging thought, crystallizing intent, and investing in mental and emotional reactions. This is not the case with instinct. With instinct, the reason we must recognize the mind as an external feature that we can Influence, is because the unending stream of NOISE that is the External Mind *buries* instinct-based Commune.

See, animals don't argue with their instinct, **because they don't have frontal lobes**, and thus do not have issues with incessant and trivial banter drowning out the useful material. We have frontal lobes, and as a result, we are the least-well-adapted species when it comes to heeding our instincts. We are the only animal capable of talking over our inborn internal guides, and instead of figuring out that we are doing this, and STOPPING ourselves, we have basically chosen to ignore it.

Without too much ranting about the abusive stance that religion and the medical community have taken toward na-ture (and its still-as-of-yet unclear ways of aiding us through means like instinct), I can say that it has not helped that our social paradigms have turned away from nature's means of attaining knowledge and making decisions, and insisted on being totally different from the so-called "beasts" of the ani-mal kingdom. We have frontal lobes. That's it. We're not that special. We give bears frontal lobes and they'll be building and managing coffee shops in months. Frontal lobes account for everything we have now…all of our planning and designs for building a better world, *except when it comes to incorpo-rating the other types of knowledge.* Namely, the kind that be-ings without frontal lobes use to move about their lives every day, all over the planet.

I don't know if that's fully clear. Having different brain hardware has made us ignore the very thing that keeps ev-ery other animal on the planet alive. That … is dumb. When we hear someone say "Oh, you know, it's just instinct," we should try replacing that sentence with "Oh, it's just the thing that keeps everything on the planet alive except us, we just don't care about it because we're, ya know, better."

It's powerful. It deserves our respect, and we need to form

a relationship with it. Its greatest enemy is now clear. That is our chattering mind, full of judgments and logic and plans and reactions that scream until everything else is drowned out. And it's not even us, it's just a damned nervous habit that comes with this particular style of brain. Goodness, we need to let go of it. We need to **Depersonalize the Mind.** Once we depersonalize it, once we become the Observer Consciousness, we have a better shot at being quiet when we need to.

Intuition has a voice. Instinct expresses itself to animals because they do not have the messy machinery that we have. They do not have anything in the way. On top of that, their lives depend on the information they receive in this manner. Their instincts are their best friends. But how do we form a relationship with our Intuition?

There are moments in life when we experience stillness. Sometimes we are capable of planning this. If we are skilled at managing our consciousness, we will likely have a pretty quiet mind regardless. But beyond seeking stillness, there are other ways of getting Intuition to speak up through the noise. And if we can get it to speak up, we can learn its voice. If we do that, then we can draw our Intuition forward, and even recognize it from within a busied mind.

Learning the Voice of Intuition by Asking Open-Ended Questions

The best answers to the dire questions I've asked in my life have always come from inside my head. Thing is, I didn't know *where* inside my head for a long time, and that made the answers less potent for my conscious mind. Something in me knew when every relationship I ever had would end. It knew that I was going to go bankrupt, become an alcoholic, drop out of school, get involved with my best friend's girl, all of it. Dangit (I do not like being predictable). Wish I had known then what I've been talking about this chapter. Oh well. Lesson-based realities will bite from time to time if we don't learn to take advice. We can bank on that.

Asking open-ended questions is an invitation to our subconscious mind. It is a call to Intuition. We have separated the Observer spirit from the External Mind, and learned how to manage our internal experiences through Conscious Validation. Now we have to motivate some of the most talented pieces of our orchestra to participate.

Let's imagine a first date. Imagine we are asking questions, trying to get to know someone. Imagine the way we did it when we were nervous or young or inexperienced (like we are as a species in regards to consciousness). We would ask a question, and try to relate to it quickly and miss half of it, cut our date off, talk too much, etc. *Messy.*

Now imagine we are older, calm, and patient. Imagine how we ask and then not only wait patiently for the answer, but do everything in our power to Influence the comfort of the situation. We want to connect, so we want an answer that is meaningful and intimate. We can picture how much easier it is to foster a new relationship working with that state of mind, can't we? Now let's transfer that level of attentiveness over to the subconscious mind, and ask our Intuition out on a date.

We can ask ourselves anything. We rarely do, because we do not understand the nature of our vast mind. Also, we do not know how close by the Subconscious Mind's treasures are located. They are right at our fingertips.

But...why would we ask ourselves questions? *Because we can get answers.* We can ask ourselves anything. We can do this at any time. If we can shut down our rational systems of responses, or at least filter them to a minimum, we will be able to get information.

So here's the exercise. Sit down with a pen and paper one day, and think up some questions you want the answers to. Some should be mundane, and some should be deep. Some basic, some extravagant. Whether it is how many children you want to have, what food you should try cooking, how you feel about your spouse or your coworkers, where you want to go on vacation, what house you'd most like to live in, what car you'd like to drive, who you'd want to be on your deathbed, etc. There are a lot of questions that can be asked. We know the answers to these questions...we think. BUT, if we ask them in a calm and creative mindset, we will be surprised at what answers come forth. I am surprised all the time.

So, after writing out the list of questions, put the list away until the next day. When you have a spare moment, one you would use to meditate or relax, take out the piece of paper, and ask yourself the questions. Write down the answers, no matter what they are. They may be nonsense. Usually at least some of them are. Some of them will also be right in line with expectations. But some will be new, and they will resonate. No matter what, just write them down. In doing so, you are affirming the voice of Intuition. You will then be more likely to recognize it when it presents itself to you.

The new answers, the ones that resonate, will alter your Perspective. This voice can change our conscious mind powerfully, and immediately. The answers themselves are not anywhere near as important as is *the willingness to change* that comes out of the exercise. In fact, when I practiced for some time, I asked the same questions because the answers were not what I was after. I was after the voice. I wanted to hear it.

Whether we think that any meaningful information can be gleaned from such an exercise does not matter. We're not doing it for the answers (of course, some may be very good). We are doing it to learn the voice. If we learn the voice, we can use it.

My mother asked me once, when I was in a bad relationship, "So what exactly are you going to do?" ... and I looked for the voice, and said, "I am going to try to drink myself to death over the next six months because I'm too scared to do anything else." Because of that my mom made the necessary arrangements to get me help after that period of time.

Our Intuition knows us. It knows the world. It is not always right, but creating a relationship with it allows us access to Perspectives we could not get anywhere else. That is invaluable.

We are creating a relationship, and we are creating familiarity when we do these exercises, and when we observe the different voices within our consciousness. This can give us strength. It may not seem like something that could seriously impact our decision making, or become part of the complex matrix that drives our decisions from moment to moment, but **we must remember how truly fragile our mental makeup is**, and how *desperately* we seek *stability* in times of confusion.

I am going to discuss a few ways in which stimulating a connection between Intuition and the conscious mind can work, based on the idea of tapping the subconscious mind.

Giving the Subconscious Mind a Voice: Numbers and the Japanese Businessman

There is a story about a Japanese businessman who swallows his deals. Literally. He has amassed a large fortune through making choice investments at critical times and taking or refusing deals in the process. But he has not had to stress in the same way the average businessman has. He has exported some of that tension to a more manageable location. He summons his Intuition to handle his final answers.

When this man gets close to a deal, he arranges a lunch with a prospective partner and tells them that he will listen fully to their proposal, and then let it settle for 24 hours. He goes to the restaurant and meets the person pitching the idea, and orders the same meal every time.

After hearing the proposal, he goes home and relaxes, having given himself no extra stressors for that day. He is waiting. He is waiting for his stomach to talk to him. He was eating during the proposal's pitch, and if he gets an upset stomach, he will REFUSE the deal. If his stomach shows no distress, he takes the deal.

This sounds magic, and fantastical, but it is not. He has developed this technique by observing himself, and habituating into a situation where he has become capable of tapping directly into a larger well of information than a conscious mind ever could. He started by noticing how his stomach would respond when he was close to decisions, and then he simply ran with the idea.

We all have moments like this. We do. We get nauseous, we get dizzy, we get angry, we get **activated** when something is not going correctly. But we are rarely being observant enough, or focusing enough to begin to wield the true power of this information.

I used to get parking tickets when my subconscious was trying to tell me something. We get descriptive feelings so commonly that "I've got a bad feeling about this" is a movie cliché. We have packed this away in the "I have no idea what to do with this" compartment of our brain, but now we can get it out and play with it. This is our subconscious mind coming to help us, and if we create a healthy relationship with it, we may be able to count on it to do some heavy lifting for us.

How could it do any heavy lifting? Well, besides the Japanese businessman getting good advice on his future exploits (he was a successful businessman), he also did not have to stress out about his deals. He didn't spend hours and hours in painful deliberation. He let his subconscious free him of all that worry.

The truth is that this story is not about him being a successful businessman. It is about the relationship he formed with his subconscious mind, and how that relationship helped his life.

We have clues set up all over our realities. We are always looking for reminders and triggers that can keep us one step ahead, and external Validation to keep us calm and focused on our current plan of action. There are so many tasks that show no results, so many futures that we cannot control or contend with, and so much chaos overwhelming us at any given moment, that anything we can use to not be forced to shrink back in terror from the world around us is vital. Anything that can help us with our lives, in any way, is a tool we must learn to use.

I like to use the clock. Not an actual time, in my case, but the numbers on digital clocks. It does not matter if the clock is set to the actual time. I have found a way to use the clock to speak directly to my subconscious mind.

There were people in my life many years back that would get all gooey over seeing 11:11 on the clock—they thought it was either good luck or some kind of omen. It was all very confusing to me, at first, but instead of getting fussy, I decided to try to *use* it.

So I tried to focus on feeling "even," and having 11:11 show up to me at those moments. And I realized that if I was "in the zone" mentally, I was more likely to pick out that moment to look at a clock. But that was not the extent of my experiment. I would look and see 11:10 sometimes, or 11:12. I started thinking of how I viewed life and growth as a spiral pattern, and figured that 11:10 was "just before being in the zone" and that 11:12 was "just finishing being in the zone."

That gave me more than just Validation. It gave me a Perspective to measure with my conscious mind. I would have to check with the clock, and then with how I felt, to see if the combination was accurate.

Remember the mechanism here. My brain is taking in every aspect of my sight. It can see the clock at all times, no matter whether I take the time in consciously or not. So if my Subconscious Mind wants to get me a message like "Hey, something's about to start," "all is perfect," or "yes that just finished, you can have closure on that moment" ...my mind will wait until the right moment, and urge me to look in the direction of the clock. It's not magic. It's the science of a vast and unexplored mind that we know next to nothing about.

I realized later that I just wanted to use the clock for Validation that everything was progressing as it should, and saw 12:34 as my new number. But then I realized that I wanted the option to get reaffirmed more than twice a day, and made it "___:34." As a result I saw that number everywhere. No matter what hour it was, it was always ":34" when I needed some support or Validation. I still see it now, and it makes me happy every time. Of course I also get happy when I see the time that correlates to my birthday.

I am not saying "Numbers have meanings!" I am not saying that. I am not saying they don't have meanings, either. They may, and there are many codes and studies of numerology that many intelligent people ascribe to. I simply do not have much interest in that. That's all. But what we can see is that my relationship with an experience can affect my mood, my consciousness, and the overall way I go about my life. Now THAT is impressive. There have actually been times that I was losing my mind, and I looked at the clock and it was 6:34, and I calmed down. *That is a tool that is as powerful as a drug, without the feeling of using a crutch.* Wow. For a fella with PTSD that is not a tool I am going to ignore, regardless of what anyone thinks of it (including me).

In baseball, it's not about whether or not the rally caps work. It's about how we feel when we're wearing them. That is the **Creation of External Validation**.

Intuition is a tool. It is larger than our consciousness, and connected to everything in ways we do not, and likely never will, fully understand. It is used heavily by every species on the planet except us, because we are too confused and distracted. It does not have to be like this anymore.

We can accept its presence when it shows itself, and we can listen for its many voices when we still our manic minds. We can summon it, stimulate it, and validate it. We can use it to glean information, learn about ourselves and the world around us. We can lean on it for support and Validation by asking for clues to our reality, and we would be doing no more than following the advice of Carlos Castaneda's Don Juan in the "Agreements from the world around you" chapter of *The Journey to Ixtlan*.

I have enough comfort in the science involved to not worry about how this type of Commune can take place, but even if I didn't, and I was conflicted about the mechanism, I would still use it, because it works. Baby turtles get to the ocean, and they don't stress about trying to figure out how they knew to do so. We are too fragile, staying on the Beach of Quiet Emotion is too hard, and the world is too chaotic for us to ignore a tool as useful as this.

Section 2

Chapter 12:

Creation Versus Reaction

PART 1: FEAR AS A WEED IN THE GARDEN

I don't know if there is a real way to set this section apart. Most of the Perspectives I have been discussing (and that's what they are, Perspectives) are going to be used for the purpose of creation. Everything that has been mentioned is a way to see ourselves, our reality, and our power (ability to Influence, not control). The rest of the book, for the most part, will be about managing those expressions.

To take a look at it, we have the following: allowing ourselves to be human, allowing a picture of the universe that makes us a part of it, allowing accountability, allowing ourselves to listen, allowing patience, allowing ourselves to parent and step into our divine energy, allowing our physical and experiential genes to play their role in our reality, allowing the loss of any idea of control, allowing ourselves to try without expectation or need for success, and allowing the expression of our instinct and the world around us.

There is a reason that *allowing* is a big deal. I'm betting most of us have been told in a very specific manner to allow things to happen. To relax. To be patient. Why? What about those things tie together to form an attitude? If we are going to be involved in our life, we are going to be creative, or reactive. Those two attitudes dominate our responses.

Life is something that expresses itself every moment, and we are going to either *react to it*, or *create with it*. There is no third option, and one of those two options is more beneficial than the other. I covered this in the "Don't Clench" section, where I described the Beach of Quiet Emotion as the optimal landing place. But I have not yet described the antithesis in detail. That is the **Garden Overrun with Weeds**. This description is so prevalent in the world I am writing from (USA, 2013), that even the slightest positive changes in our management of consciousness will change everything, and likely very quickly.

The Presence of Fear as a Weed, and the Parable of the Boy

We are all bountiful creatures full of the capacities for creation, imagination, and connection with all other consciousnesses (this includes EVERYTHING) in the Universe. We are capable of individuated and shared creation (as we have been divided into subjective sets of individuation), then thrown together in the hopes of achieving something magnificent. Synergy of Commune is the method by which we are capable of this. We are much like a garden, capable of producing flowers to set an example of beauty, or food to nourish the world and our fellow living things. But this is not all the life that dwells on our plot of enriched land. We also have things that spring up through us as *reactions* to life, *existing in correlation with the presence of an external reality that is out of our control.*

This is *fear*, and ***it is a weed***.

Fear is a reaction. It is not unnatural, or evil. It just is. It is also contagious, active, and very influential over our behaviors, Perspectives, attitudes, and actions. It is the primary survival trait of all living things. **It is a byproduct of life.** It is a weed in a glorious garden, and that is how it starts. Where it ends up is something we must exercise Influence over.

Let's look at the example we are very often afforded here, and that is of a beautiful Garden Overrun with Weeds. The goal of the weeds is not malicious... in fact it is the opposite. It is protective. The job of the weeds is to protect us from things we cannot control. Because we cannot control certain aspects of reality, those aspects are threats to our creations as well as our identity. These uncontrollable properties are loosed on everyone and everything around us. They are *contained as a possibility* in every experience. They are supposed to be there.

There was a very good reason for us to develop this method of protection. The need for a fear-based matrix to dominate our personality has only dwindled down to being part of Vestigial Psychology in nature over the past 100 years (it still exists in third-world countries). We were scared because we were in danger. Fear kept us on our toes, and though it kept us from making a lot of meaningful relationships and connections, it was still pretty beneficial given that survival is a prime directive and scarcity did in fact exist. "Did." *Past tense.*

The natural fear we develop through consciousness is part of us. However, it is of absolutely no use to us. Each fear, were it to be looked at as a single weed, growing simply because it was afforded a space, is nothing by itself. Each fear is manageable. There is no need to hide from them, ignore them, or stifle them. **There is also no reason to let them continue**

feeding on our nourishing energy. They are fed by our active imagination of things we do not want, and they are given power by our ability to rationally justify those possibilities. For the most part, as conscious beings, we allow this habit to flourish simply because we are distracted. We have no idea how powerfully destructive such a habit is.

"Fear leads to anger. Anger leads to aggression. Aggression leads to suffering." - Yoda

The Parable of a Man I Know:

So the boy is born to parents in a time when passing down fear is commonplace and expected. He may or may not be sensitive; it matters not, for the weeds that grow around the nourishing fruits born of his creative heart and mind soon cover and protect his beautiful garden, now overrun.

The battle for dominance is over before adulthood, and all experience shows him that he is being attacked. Everything presses on his outside barriers. The people he loves, the sun, the rain, all of the world slamming into the barrier of brambles and thorns surrounding his garden with reckless abandon trying to destroy the living wall surrounding him. He reinforces the growth to ensure protection, feeds the weeds with thoughts of being attacked and fighting back. His barrier grows strong.

As he gets close to others, he feels safe because his weeds are giant and powerful. He spreads onto others' gardens, stifling their growth so that they are protected. If those he is close to are not appreciative of his offerings, or if his gaze is drawn in other directions, he simply leaves his growth and moves on, *the gift of protection existing as **the invasion of the rich soil of others,** and the subsequent scarring that occurs.*

He can see only the inside of his barrier and the riches of his garden from where he dwells. So all communication that comes to him, all the essences of others must reflect his beautiful garden or the strength of his weeds, or *he cannot hear them*. **His ability to listen to the world becomes completely dependent on the world's ability to deliver only exactly what he sees.**

His garden is beautiful, and beyond reproach. When his weeds are questioned, he simply does not understand. They are a part of his garden, and a part of the beauty. He cannot experience the question as anything but an attack on the weeds, not knowing that he and he alone can see his garden, because it is walled off from the rest of the world. He nourishes nothing but himself with his garden. The weeds of fear and protection that he believes to be a part of his garden (*rather than an infestation of poison drowning out all possibilities of experience*), become his identity to the rest of the world, as he becomes the ruin of creation, connection, and love. He is the classic narcissist, and we are a society that is hell-bent on his creation.

Weeds are a reaction. They are the objective correlative of fear. They grow up and out, and when supported (as they often are) they form more sophisticated structures to separate our nourishing and creative soil from the outside world.

The issue is not their presence. Their presence is a necessary part of life, because as we nourish and create more life around us, we create more objects of care...more connections to be protected. The issue is our relationship to them, ***our attachment to our reactions.***

The tough thing about our reactions is that we identify with them. We do this because they are in our mind, and as I have discussed plenty, our mind is simply not us. So as we experience fear it is vital that we identify it, and isolate it. Once we isolate it, we can decide whether or not we want to feed it. Since this is a good analogy, I'm going to stay right within it. As a weed grows up next to other creations of nourishment and beauty (veggies and flowers) it needs to be isolated, blocked from getting the water and plant food that is going to the healthy lives that we are trying to cultivate. So, we put a bag over it. This draws back to the section on **Conscious Validation**, and specifically the notes on "thoughts to be altered" and "thoughts to be ignored." Have you heard the parable about the wolf? Which wolf wins between the light wolf and the dark wolf? *The one you feed.* Same here.

We can take small steps in our lives to single out our fear-based thoughts, and use Conscious Validation to limit or stifle their growth within our daily news feed.

What happens if we do not ignore and separate these thoughts? They get the same food everything else does. They get our mental attention, and they grow stable. They get support from our minds. They get stories, and identities. But, unlike the beautiful and nourishing growths, they are impervious to attack. ***Our fears cannot be attacked, without being replaced by more fear***.

They can be suffocated, but the more complex their foundations and intricate their connections, the more difficult a task that is. Fear turns into anger, and with tending, it turns into **Justified Righteousness**: a filter, nearly impenetrable, that colors every bit of honest information and renders us incapable of taking in new information, or effecting change where it is needed.

⟳⟲

Blame and Accountability-Shifting

I'm going to deal with the most common ways of tending to our weeds. Our history, and the government. They are one and the same, honestly, in the spirit of blame. *"Something bigger than us is responsible for our happiness, or lack thereof, and we are powerless to affect it."* At its most accurate, though, the sentence would be seen as *"Something large is having an effect on the world in a manner that makes it difficult for us to adequately Influence our reality and come out with our desired results."*

There is a reason that words and descriptions matter, because the first quotation is inaccurate, and has no viable option for motion. It is stagnant. It also describes us as powerless. "I'M NOT MOVING UNTIL IT CHANGES!" On the playground, this is the ill-tempered kid getting all pissy and taking his basketball home. Now no one can play.

The second shows frustration and some form of respect for external realities that have an effect on our day-to-day lives. This is true. *Things are big, and they affect us.* Also, the word "difficult" is accurate, but it most importantly implies that it is *not impossible* to change, and just may take some work and focus. This is true. The world that we are a part of is big, and we have to learn to manage our relationship to it.

"Government is corrupt, and our history is to blame for our problems now." Let's take a look at this. By "history" we can be speaking of any trauma or abuse, from within the family, environment, or act of God. Government is symbolic for any external structure that is seen to stifle the individual.

The problem is not that these things exist (newsflash, they exist), the problem is that we feed them, and allow them to grow thick bonds in our realities to the point where we identify with them as being a part of our garden. *We mistake them for our creations, instead of what they are, which is **petty criticism and complaint***. We shift our power and accountability from our ability to create and nourish…to our ability to react and protect. The problem with making weeds a part of our garden is that anyone who wants to touch us has to deal with the brambles. Anything loving that we produce has to somehow be reachable through these nasty barriers.

I'm going to stop right here for a second and make note of the fact that this description is the reason interpersonal relationships (especially romantic relationships) have such a low success rate. In order to get to someone's beauty you are going to have to reach through their fear, and somehow convince them to suffocate their brambles and weeds, without having them think you are attacking them. Good friggin' luck.

So a statement we hear a lot, "I finally opened up to them," is actually "I finally stopped attacking them as they were trying to enjoy my nourishing creative self."

That is how much of a role the weeds play in our lives. We all have seriously overgrown gardens. Learning to get at them a bit, learning to starve out fear as it is born, and allowing others to infiltrate our defenses and love on us, is key to our evolution. This is not just psychological evolution, but the evolution of health, growth, power, technology, and society that is involved here. This is because Synergy of Commune is actualized only when someone can get through the weeds and engage our creative nourishing mind.

So, the main thing to do, to assess the existence of a weed-rich garden full of obstacles and brambles, is to translate. We have to do this for ourselves, of course, because we are covered (most of us) in the same weeds we see on others when we try to reach them. Being gentle in this process is vital to unlocking the nourishing gardens underneath.

Here are three translations in action.

"Other things are big." (I am small, *I am vulnerable*. I do not have control.)

"Evil exists." (Bad things happen. *I am vulnerable*.)

"I was hurt." (I have been affected negatively by the world. *I am vulnerable*.)

All of our ideas about how the world is "not a good place" have to do with these three things (all connected by our vulnerability), and can be reduced down to them in seconds. We do not have control, bad things happen, and we have been hurt. While all of these things are true, THEY ARE NOT THE ONLY THINGS THAT ARE TRUE. They are just the only things we hear if we don't get to the root of the righteous anger we have so intricately woven over ourselves.

Criticism is not creation. Justification of criticism leads to stagnation, escapism, and separation.

The breakdowns above are **Base Fears**. They are the ones we get to after going through all of our justifications and finding the root of what bothers us. What we use to cover up the fears that are motivating us is nothing but a script. The stories woven together to justify our righteousness and our Perspectives laden with anger can be dismantled through investigation. Once we make a habit of discrediting these scripts that keep us in states of anger and fear, we no longer have to struggle to figure out its validity. We simply suffocate the voice, and pull it out like the weed it is. We pull it out because we have become engaged in a habit of not wasting our time.

If we go through painstaking deliberations over a situation, and find that they are invalid, we dismiss them and go on about our day. However, if we go through our deliberations and find that our fears and descriptions of reality ARE valid, we have to make a decision before we can go about our day. In the face of overwhelming odds and no certainty of safety or success, we have to choose to keep going. And then we go on about our day, relatively exhausted from the struggle.

Either way, we go on about our day, one way is just destructive to creative energy and vitality. That is wasting time. We are going to choose life, or we are going to choose fear. **The validity of the fear will not change the answer for us**, so we can skip the drama.

But the drama reinforces the weeds! The drama keeps our belly-up powerlessness-charade on the air! It keeps us safe from having our ideas rejected. Let me say that again. The whole mess of fears and distraction-dramas accomplishes one thing. It keeps us safe from ever having to feel rejected. That is success in *accountability-shifting* and *loss of power*.

If we are unhappy, the world around us makes a great scapegoat, *because it is imperfect*. Our histories make great scapegoats also, *because they include pain*. So whenever we use these non-creative systems for the purpose of excusing ourselves from life (and we all will, as fear is a natural byproduct of life, and justification is a natural survival trait), we must check for new weeds, pull up what we can, and go on about our day. Vigilance here will reward all of us.

Tapestries of Mature Fear

We are looking for our external systems as tapestries of mature fear. So let's look at one area. Conversations can veer into this realm pretty easily.

"People will never be free as long as they bow to a corrupt government," "People are sheep," "This or that political party is wrong," "The elites of the world control everything," "Money is evil," "Corporations run the country," "We are all slaves!"

This is used as righteous criticism. It is used to divide people. It is the imposing father figure keeping the car keys from us even though we've been SO GOOD and we got STRAIGHT A'S! It has always made me want to ask,

"What is this expectation of the world being a fair and just place, and what planet did we get it from?"

Many have this attitude. It is poisonous. It assumes that reality is something we can approve of or not, with a justified foundation. We could as easily be disgusted with the fact that we don't have five thumbs.

Now there are a lot of people who at least raise their voices in protest to say "Well what are you doing about it?" ...in response to which most people cite some plight or another of being against some paradigm, agenda, or system. Some may even have ideas about how things should change, like "We should use the barter system and do away with money," or "We should put all the corrupt politicians in jail." And they say this without realizing that this is not a solution. It is in fact, almost totally meaningless. That is because *it is not a creation*.

A wise man once said that we mustn't fight the current system, but make a new one that renders the old one obsolete. That was Buckminster Fuller, actually, and he was right.

This is true in every area of struggle, no matter the size. Creating an enemy just reinforces the weeds. It strengthens the barrier of fear. Creating a new and glorious reality requires that we strengthen ourselves, and starve out systems shaped by fear.

This is the first step of any quandary that is societal/global. We must take the opportunities we have to starve the old the system, while creating a strong world and family to be the example of what systems should look like. That is how we can create new structures within the most complex matrix.

This is where the breakdown occurs. We are generally stagnant when staring this opportunity in the face. We are stagnant because the purpose of the intricate weeds is not to display a plan or an idea. They serve to justify our anger and our withdrawal from engaging in reality, and *we NEED to justify anger*, and withdrawing from reality. Without justification, those actions cause Cognitive Dissonance. The weeds provide an excuse.

But we can learn a secret. The secret is this: We can change the world without being angry at all. In fact, it will be easier to change the world if we are not angry at it. *We cannot create when we're angry*, we can only react. We cannot build a new system...we can only fight the old one, over and over and over forever (think of any country in constant revolution).

In fact, the only thing that anger about social issues can do for us is give us an excuse to be a crappy parent to the world around us (from close family to the world in general). But we'll be safe from rejection, because we do not need creative ideas to be critical. We just need a mouth or an internet connection. Complaint is really lazy and unsexy. And this whole **Citizen Inferiority Complex** is sad.

The section above was for weeds grown and justified through fear of the large outside world that is constantly attacking us. This next section will focus on our attachment to our own history of trauma.

I simply had to split these up, as they are worthy of sections unto themselves. The idea stays the same, though, in that everything in our reality wants to reinforce our fear, and our protection of ourselves, so that we are constantly led away from engaging with the world. It is in our survivalist psychology to not want to evolve in this way, and that is why it has taken so long to do so, and why seductive fear-based authority has such a hold on the globe.

Everything in our DNA wants to justify our desire to run and hide. Everything in our history is capable of supporting that. This is why any movement to a more open reality is a huge step for all of mankind.

Attachment to Trauma

Our attachment to trauma is valid. Whether real or imagined, its effect on us is real and justifiable, as we are fragile beings. Some scars are physical, and remind us every time we look in the mirror. Others are more subtle. Sounds and smells can trigger panic, and that is very real also. What we do with those traumatic triggers, and how we manage that relationship, is different for everyone.

So think about yours right now. I think about my brother's cancer and my bouts with addiction and PTSD, anxiety and panic attacks and the lot. Then I think about my friends and family members, and all of their triggers that I am privy to.

I find that most women have been abused sexually. I find that almost everyone has seen some awful sight, and been deeply affected by it. Many have experienced the death of a loved one and not gotten over it. I find that a lot of people have done something horrible for which they cannot forgive themselves (yes, that counts too). Many people have had horrible physical pain or sickness (crippling anxiety is very prevalent now, as is PTSD). I'd say, of the people I have come across, 95% fall into one of these categories.

How we all manage our reactions to these experiences is a mixed bag. *To whatever extent we identify ourselves with whatever has happened, we tend the weeds and become withdrawn.* To make this point more clear, to whatever extent I am disabled with Bipolar 2 and PTSD with a brother afflicted by cancer, I AM LESS Vito and more weeds. Those Influences are real. They have a serious affect, one that is chemical and has measurable effects. They need to be managed. They are powerful. ***But...so am I...and so are you.***

It's really easy though, withdrawing. It's really easy to allow the *"fact"* of the illness or trauma become intermingled with our *need to justify fear,* allowing it to stabilize. We reinforce the bonds with our actions and words, as well as our silent consent (**if we are looking for actual slavery in our society, this is where it is**).

I want to take a moment to give respect to those who manage affliction and chronic disease. This is not meant in any way to challenge or blame; my only agenda is to support. I know too many people afflicted chronically, and much of my energy goes to discovering moments of peace for anyone currently engaged in such a struggle. I stay involved here.

There are other life experiences that we identify with, especially in relationships (romantic mostly, but it can also be family, job, social groups, etc.). We have been hurt. Let's see a show of hands for all the folks who have never been hurt...anyone? Anyone? Now this can range from being sexually abused by a family member to having been stood up for prom, or teased in the middle school cafeteria.

How can I compare teasing/shaming to incestuous rape? Not lightly. I do it because both are moments that we have to get over (some are easier than others, obviously). *Neither is a part of us. They are not our identity*. But they affect us deeply. I have seen people lose themselves in any trauma, and have seen people get over any trauma.

The difference between the people who get over these brutalities and those that do not is the only aspect we are dealing with. That is our focus. Whether horrific or the seemingly common, the people who get past trauma are the ones who *do not make it a part of who they are*. They do not feed the weeds. They do not create an identity that includes something awful that *happened to them*. This is not easy. The pull of shame, and the habit of internalizing it, is dominant.

My brother has a ton of funny stories about how doctors looked at him after his first couple of bouts with cancer, because he was a prototype NFL QB physically (at 6 '4" 230 lbs.). He was strong and vital. He would fill out the intake form and check off "cancer, surgery, blah, blah, etc." ... and then check "healthy" at the end, because that was how he felt. It was also how he looked. Doctors were always stunned. The incongruence was equal (I imagine) to watching Babe Ruth down a pitcher of beer in the dugout before hitting a homerun.

I have heard "Oh I had no idea you had PTSD, or anxiety issues!" I have heard people say to those I know, "Oh I had no idea you were abused!" ...rightly so. The reason they did not "get the idea" was that **we were not wearing it.**

It's a difference like the difference between tattooing something on your skin versus wearing a jacket just as long as it's cold. The difference is dealing with an external reality versus making it a permanent part of who you are, and showing it off.

For the record, not telling people about something that happened to us is NOT keeping it to ourselves. It is expressing *"holding a secret."* Huge difference. If we think we are not burdening the world because something is a secret, we are grossly mistaken. The world is unburdened only if WE are unburdened; the burden expresses itself like every other load-bearing structure in the world does if it is carrying more weight than it was designed to.

The reason all of this matters so much is that the world needs YOU. It does not need your anger, your sickness, your shame, or *what you believe you should be showing us*. It needs your presence, your joy, and your engagement.

You are not what happened to you. Though it may be true, *it is not genuine*, and it is not your Identity.

Genuine. It is different from true. It is a goal. It can become a habit. It is many things, but mainly, *it is heroic*. The world needs heroes. I'll finish this chapter with heroes, because we are going to need them for next chapter.

We need them because this scenario is at play in our world.

*

VICTIM OR HERO?

The more people you love, the more people you will lose (to death or rejection).

The more engaged and vulnerable you are, the more you will get hurt.

The more you invest of yourself, the more of your energy and time you will lose.

The more you trust, the more you will be disappointed.

*

We are going to fail. The more things we try, the more often we are going to fail. Being genuine is accepting and understanding failure when it occurs. Being **Heroic** is *changing our relationship with failure*, so that deeply painful losses become the exalted foundations for our creation of future growth and health. We have to do this, so that we do not stop trying.

This is not easy. This means accountability. This means losing things we care about. This does not mean pulling out before the pain. This means not walling off to the world.

This is not to be confused with exalting pain. This is not to be confused with identifying with our sacrifice and seeing ourselves through those lenses. That is martyrdom, and it is a system of power and control we play with ourselves from time to time. It is not genuine, or heroic. It is a system of protection, an example of weeds. It keeps us separate, divided.

This is when the Lesson-Based Reality has to be accepted, and incorporated into our soft voices, as we urge ourselves to patience and deep breaths when they are necessary. This is when focusing on the "Now" becomes a battle we need to learn within ourselves. We need to learn this moment, and this dance, so that we can keep our reactive minds and bodies at bay.

And that is why the word "Genuine" is perfect. ***It is perfect because our reactions are a lie***. They are a story we are making up to keep us protected from the outside world. Whether the story is true or false does not matter, *its goal is a lie.* Its goal is to remove our souls from the world. That goal is contrary to saying "Yes" to life. It is incongruous with drawing breath, and incongruous with the blessed fulfillment of existence.

PART 2: COMMUNITY IN CREATION VERSUS COMMUNITY IN REACTION

I have been an avid psychology fan since I was about ten years old, when I was introduced to Family Systems Therapy and the description "Dysfunctional Family." I loved that description. Over the years, though, I realized that the term doesn't fit. Dysfunctional Families do exactly what they are not supposed to do. They function. They not only function, they *maintain functionality from generation to generation.* They maintain stasis. They maintain roles. This is perfect for an unchanging paradigm and social system. Unfortunately, we do not live in an unchanging world.

A world that is constantly changing creates a need for any social system, be it familial or cultural, to be dynamic. We need to be able to accept new information, and adjust our attitudes and practices accordingly. We also need to do so with as little as possible fear and reactivity, because however large their role in our process, the more difficult adjusting is going to be with their presence.

People have lost their families, livelihoods, and even been incarcerated over the last fifty years, in progressive countries, for the color of their skin or their sexual preferences. That is insane. It is barbaric. It is telling someone, with a straight face "Hey, you're not allowed to be who you are." It's unreal. How can we say such things as a society, with no realization of how morally wrong it is? Because our view of the world is solid, based on accepted roles, and based on our reactions to expectations being met, or not being met. Ewww.

Why is society like this? Very simply…over thousands of years we moved from caves to cities. We moved from rubbing sticks together to lighters and electricity. We went from thinking the world was flat to landing on the moon. The things we did changed a TON, but the survival instincts that allowed us to survive in caves for 100,000 years or so did not disappear in the 2,000 years it took us to become technically proficient. Until now, we have not had a global connection. The internet should, in time, end every nonsensical and unnecessarily cruel aspect of societal living. But I see no reason not to speed it up whenever possible.

How does society's fear express itself? Let's take a study on apes to make the point.

The Apes, the Ladder, and the Banana

There was a study by Stephenson in 1967 that made a point about how fear- based realities are spread needlessly from generation to generation, and how social groups followed cues from each other rather than using repeated experimentation.

Five apes were placed in an observation room. There was also a ladder that led upward toward a banana that hung from the ceiling. The apes were hungry, and so quickly one ape made for the ladder to get after the banana.

Upon getting a step up onto the ladder the research team sprayed the apes with freezing cold water…and the ape climbing the ladder had to get down. Once off the ladder, the assault of freezing cold water stopped.

Another ape, not having made the connection, made a break for the banana. Again, by the second rung of the ladder the spray of freezing water began, and making the connection, the apes all rushed toward him to pull him off the ladder in case he had not made the connection; once on the ground, the water stopped.

Now for the fun part. One ape was rotated out, and a new ape that had not experienced the water spray was rotated in. He saw the banana and went for the ladder, at which point the other four apes in the room grabbed him and beat him away from the ladder, knowing that it would cause the water spray. This is society at work, folks. It was a success: the water did not need to be sprayed. The apes were one step ahead of their torment.

Another new ape was rotated in...same thing happened. He went for the banana and was violently stopped by the other four. They did this three more times, until every ape in the room was a "new" ape, *apes that had never been sprayed with the water*.

Now, upon the final ape entering, we had four apes *that had never been sprayed* beating the ape going for the banana. They were beating down a member of their own species for wanting something, and for trying something, though there was no longer any danger.

So the situation is a social construct, because the guardianship of the banana ladder is learned, not just through pain, **but by example**. It is the same way families teach roles in "Dysfunctional Families," because *expectation fulfillment equals safety* for us more-evolved-than-ape types.

So as we look through the titles in a Dysfunctional Family System we see the addict, the emotional wreck, the clown, the abuser, the obsessive-compulsive, the surrogate spouse, the sick child, etc. We also see allegiance to the system's continuation. No one "just stops" performing their role, because the threat of establishing an identity is too scary, as it endangers EVERYONE IN THE SYSTEM when one person breaks out. That is why it is so very difficult to leave a system and establish a new and healthy one. You have to first break out of your role. Then you have to face the horrific encounter with a family that has been betrayed by your unwillingness to perform the role you did not want. Then you have to deal with the guilt of the fear and pain you caused simply by honoring your own wants. Then you have to leave that whole mess with whatever shreds of relationships that are still intact, and create something positive and loving *without ever having had an example for it.*

That is why it is so difficult to change society. We have to be the ape that does the following...after sitting with hunger long enough, he moves toward the ladder, and climbing up really fast, snatches the banana and satisfies his hunger with no consequences. Now he has to look around at the other apes. Can you imagine the rushes of fury and confusion this causes amongst the rest of the apes? THEY ARE PISSED! WHY DOES HE GET THE BANANA? WHY WERE WE GUARDING IT THIS WHOLE TIME? WHY WAS I WASTING MY TIME? Cognitive Dissonance, anyone?

The shame and confusion alone are difficult to ignore, even just imagining apes being studied in a far-off lab. We can see it and feel it in our minds, can't we? Now imagine it's not a banana, but a family. And imagine the object is allowing joy and individuation, and that it can destroy and shame the family's entire way of life.

This is why our society has roles. Not because there is danger, but because we lack courage. We lack the courage to go for the banana, and we lack the courage to face the aftermath. The aftermath is an unprecedented mess that almost no one can bear. It is time for us to begin bearing it, though. We just need help. We need to know it can work from seeing examples, and we need to not do it alone. We need to learn how to manage a hot stove.

How to Deal with a Hot Stove, Lesson-Based Reality-Style

"Don't touch a hot stove." That was the example that was used with me when I was young when it came to taking advice about doing something harmful. It seems pretty prevalent in society, the hot-stove message. There is always a point in our lives when we are too young to fully understand the consequences of our actions, and have a choice to make that authority figures will weigh in on. We can choose to listen to authority, or risk the possibility of learning through pain. The upside to learning through pain is that the understanding is much deeper. The downside is…well…the pain. And the pain is a tad more powerful than we like to admit.

Most clichés and teaching tools are too short. "Don't touch a hot stove" is a single-serving example. It gives us no idea how to move forward in our existence. It falls far short of the goal, which is learning to engage a risky reality we cannot control so that we can use it as a tool.

I don't know about you, but I've been burned by a stove. *I still use stoves to cook food.* It's actually a pretty important part of my life. But, the cliché doesn't explain that part: "After being burned, it is time to slowly, over the course of your life, get yourself used to the stove as well as over the injury of being burned since there is a ton of nourishment that is related to the stove." I have not seen that part attached to the cliché.

Kids are great for where we get into trouble with this. I'm sure if you have kids, or are close to kids, you know how violent their avoidance reactions can be. Not only do most children burned by the stove not touch the stove again, but they may not even go into the kitchen. They may not be comfortable seeing frying pans or pots lying around and get all anxious and weirded out watching their food spooned onto their plate from one. They may lose their appetite altogether.

We move about as people understanding that "Parenting" ensures that most grown adults--mind you, "most"--can handle stoves, and pans, and kitchen equipment. However, as soon as we compare such hot-stove lessons to the vital issues facing adolescents and adults, everything gets a tad murky.

If we deal with a hot stove as a child, and we are comforted in our searing pain by our parents, and given the basic truth of heat and burns so that we can continue learning about the kitchen. Whereas if we get a broken heart as a sixteen-year-old, we may be told truths about the world of relationships that change our behaviors permanently. Depending on our parents, the comforting teachings can be much worse than the basic truth, but the truth is bad enough. The truth about relationships is that they all end, and cause pain. The greater the relationship, the higher the capacity for causing pain. That's not much of a ringing endorsement for continuing to engage in the experience.

Thing is, unlike food, we don't have to try love again. We don't have to be vulnerable or sincere again. We do not have to force ourselves to learn.

For instance, if we were going to get married, wouldn't it be great if we had already gone through all the random insanity? Wouldn't it be nice if we knew we could, with confidence, protect the person we love and ourselves from pain and move toward the greatest good at all times? That would only take *having been through everything already*.

Something tells me that is unlikely.

So what does this all point to? The issue at hand is that pain occurs, and that we learn to deal with it when we need to. Our society shows us that when problems *less abstract than psychology* affect us, we are likely to get the help we need. But when emotion and psychology are prevalent in the issue, we are given little to none of the help we need. We walk away from the hot stove in pain and confusion, and *no one forces us back to it*.

I have mentioned how important parenting is. That is self-parenting, and the parenting of the world (adults specifically). This section is the main reason. The most important things in our lives are the loving connections we make with our environment, and each of those connections makes us vulnerable to injury. Every connection is risk. ***Every vital and resonant aspect of our reality is a hot stove***.

We think about getting burned, how furious we get at the pain, as well as the humiliation and sense of betrayal that accompanies the fury. However, we do not correlate that experience with emotional pain. Broken hearts, for instance, are culturally understood and accepted. We understand that it is courageous to recover, and continuing to love is a good thing. But we are not held accountable for how truly available we are making ourselves. No one knows how hard we are trying. We can simply connect only fingertip deep...and no one will stop us. We find someone who will not go near a frying pan, or walk into a kitchen, and that person will kinda stick out as being odd. However, this world is littered with people who will simply not emotionally engage themselves or another person, **WHICH IS THE MOST IMPORTANT AND VITAL PART OF OUR EXISTENCE**, and it does not raise any red flags. That is because it is common, not because it is not a big deal. Commonality keeps the focus of society off of curing itself through teaching. We are that scared, collectively, of having to face up to our pain, and risk our hearts. We'd rather not even discuss teaching it, because facing it is so painful. That sounds like an addict who has refused to accept that they have a problem, and it is a global addiction to escapism. It might be time for an intervention.

It is okay, you know. It hurts, and I don't blame us for running from pain, and humiliation, and fear, and withdrawing into the smallest parts of ourselves. But it doesn't work for life. It doesn't work on every level, from individual, to familial, to societal, to global.

So what's the big deal? What does it matter that we get freaked out and don't engage? What does it matter that we set up static roles to play so that we are not vulnerable? It has helped us survive for thousands of years. I am honestly thankful for it having been a part of our story.

The big deal is that while the species is safe from momentary pain and discomfort, the species will become stagnant. As soon as survival is not the most pressing need, growth and happiness become more valuable to our reality than anything else. Rigid roles and non-engagement do not allow for individuation and expression. Living in a challenging and engaging reality is healthy. We are no longer in caves, and our technological reality offers us many frontiers for exploration and experimentation. But we, as a society, *are still living in caves psychologically*. It may seem harsh to give such a critique, but the system of stasis we have created to survive is now out of sync with our reality. Being out of sync is nothing to joke about, and it is not a small thing. Being out of sync creates unnecessary conflict on every level. As our world gets more and more connected, this becomes more of a problem.

So here are a couple examples of how static roles and dysfunctional social groups impact our world. The significance is more easily shown by comparing like situations from the micro level to the macro level.

Static versus Dynamic: Working from the Micro to the Macro

We have within us a view of ourselves that meets our expectations of what we are. We have expectations of this view of ourselves that keep us at peace in our minds. Confusion about ourselves is pretty tough to manage, and can be destructive to our reality. We like to keep that at a minimum. Families have expectations of what members are playing which roles. Society has a view of how its resources and its members should function. All of these are in place for safety and convenience. But we have to be able to affect and Influence these realities based on new information as it comes in, and we have to understand that we are not always the author of this information, and that it may clash with our expectations.

So let's look at some problems.

Here's the version of non-inclusivity on the micro: we do not include our own thought realities because they clash with pre-conceived notions. This is the singular-self version.

We are growing, and have expectations of ourselves as an adult. We are male, let's say, and have planned on getting married and having children. This is our expectation. It could have come from a million places, but this is not important. It is what it is. We then run into a very attractive man and have serious sexual feelings for him. Now we have a situation that is incongruent with our picture. We did not plan to have sexual feelings for a man, and coming with that brings up questions of marriage, children, etc. that need to be dealt with. This is not something that was accounted for, and its presence is violent.

We are looking at something basic and joyous (sexual attraction), and seeing that in a static system it is violent and possibly destructive. That is a real issue. Changing plans to allow for new realities and information should not be *that devastating*. It doesn't have to be. Very simply, someone who was living within a fluid and dynamic mind frame, besides not attaching too strongly to visions of the future, would simply say "Hey that guy is hot, I dig that. That's certainly a new feeling. Guess I have to leave open some doors for that."

Doesn't that sound a lot better than "I can't be gay! What will my parents say? How will I ever get married? What about kids? I WANT kids! How is any of this ever going to be all right?!"

Those are two different reactions to the same piece of information: One in a dynamic system that looks appropriate and calm, and one in a static system that looks like a chicken fighting itself to the death. In a dynamic space, the thought and physical reaction-want is honored as reality. It is non-threatening. The soul includes it without violence. In the second the thought it creates turmoil, and may very well be rejected because it does not fit in with expectations. One *creates with the reality* presented. The other *reacts to the reality* as if it is an enemy.

These are not equal results. One makes the world more loving, the other does not. One leads to expanded expression while the other leads to repression.

As we move from the micro to the macro, there is a "next step." No need to go global and societal yet, because our issues in this realm express themselves first and foremost in our primary relationships. This is generally our immediate family.

So we have a child. We have a family. We have, let's say, a religion in the house. There are numerous ways of expressing an example of this nature, but politics and religion are the most divisive things in the world, so let's stick to these. We have a child that has no interest in church, and to the depths of their soul cannot believe in a biblical God. In fact the child stops there, without labeling themselves atheist or agnostic, simply because the whole genre is beyond worrying about.

They decide to get married, maybe even to an atheist, and because it is not in an agreed-upon church and a Catholic ceremony, most of the family does not attend, creating a rift... creating animosity. This is a defining line for where support ends, and rejection begins.

We have a loving situation. We have a gathering as meaningful as marriage with honorable people involved, and they are rejected for being honest about something important to their identity. We have them being rejected for having integrity. They are rejected because they refused to lie.

In the end, at the very least we have a *"black sheep"* of the family as a result. This term, which was initiated into culture *for the purpose of showing individuality as an evil,* is perfect for most situations of this nature.

Instead of integrating a family member's expressions, and honoring their unique experience, a "thing" is honored. A set of expectations based on an idea of how things should be is exalted over a living person. The family member is rejected, and cast as a pariah. This can happen with anything. Whether it is sexual preference, following in the family business, going to college, whatever the expectation...many times it is not this obvious. Many times it is "not being sick"...or not being affected by manufactured drama between parents, or being strong. It can be being good at math. Anything that is outside the system can be the blemish on the stasis and a threat to the family's stability. It calls their reactive self-images into question the same way grabbing the banana does.

Asking for what we want, if it occurs outside the lines of a reactive family setting, is bad enough. If you happen to get what you want, and are happy, when the rest of the family is not, creates serious turmoil. This is why an addict getting healthy puts pressure on many families. It is also why people trying to manage their addiction, and leaving an official 12-step program, is trying on the members of that group.

How we mess up our **Primary Relationships** or try to express ourselves through them is kind of where our society is getting stuck now, although it is getting better. We're working here, but we need to get better at a lot of things that are not that complicated before we will be successful.

The problem with this issue is that since we do not know how to begin to manage ourselves, we act out our frustrations on all of society. This may seem like a social critique, but it is simply an opportunity. It is a Perspective to show a concrete manner for turning consciousness into action, and turning singular internal realities into larger global change.

A quick note about the section above is that it is the state of mind allowing the self to want, and expressing our true natures to those close to us, changes society over time. In the South of the United States fifty years ago, being friends with or having an attraction to an African-American man or woman was not accepted. Very simply, *people who embraced their desires refused to lie to themselves and those around them* for long enough that society had to adapt. People were willing to listen to their hearts, and act in defiance of family roles, and the result was often violent. Many families suffered because they refused change. But not all of them. The families that allowed change, and adjusted to the realities they were being presented with, *became the examples* of how other families could manage themselves in a confusing world. Their examples of happiness, specifically, opened the door for all of society to slowly change.

It generally takes a generation. Adults with belief judgments about "how things should be" are likely to cling to them like life rafts in the roaring rapids (when in fact they are on the shore flailing like idiots, and in no danger), which is why they are generally not the ones doing the changing. Even adults that are in full mental alignment with the changes still hold vestigial psychology close by, even though it goes unused and unvalidated. Children do not have those issues. They see joy, and they imprint it wherever it is. So after a generation grows the old views simply die off with the affected consciousnesses. People who are stuck are less vital anyway, and they stick out like sore thumbs, so their cardboard cut-out realities are not that difficult to discard. That is how society changes. Someone steps up and does something new, and is happy. The rest of the dominoes fall over however long a time span it takes, and then the world has a whole new focus on the issue.

So let's talk cars. Or we can talk global energy, in general. The industries we have in place for creating energy, from heating our homes to fueling our transportation are mostly built on coal, natural gas, and oil. These would be fine if they were getting the job done efficiently and without negative byproducts. But they're not. The problem is that these resources are limited, their use damages the balance of nature, and in order to procure them there is much risk of toxifying the planet. That's not okay. If only there were a solution. Oh, yeah, one has been around for sixty years (it has actually been around since before the Earth)--it's called the SUN. Turning sunlight into energy has been around for a while. So long, in fact, that you'd think we could have made an entire switch to a limitless, free source of power by now. It was discovered two hundred years ago, was turned into something usable through silicon cells in the '50s, and legislation was put into effect in the '70s to harness the energy for the power grids. And then it stopped.

This is the stalling point, and we have been sitting here for thirty-five years, by my count. The reason that this is different from the more micro scales of role expectation is that is does not have to do with personal love or deep desire. It has to do with an abstract concept that some of us attach to more than others, but it is not something strong enough to overthrow the dominant paradigm.

We think that the greed and power-hungry nature of the people who rule the industrial complex is something magical, but it's not. *It's the same father energy in the static family* and the *same rigid expectations* we dealt with in the first two sections. There is only one paradigm. It is stasis through fear. Is it more complex on a societal level that involves infrastructure and complex monetary systems? Of course it is. But that's not why it hasn't changed.

This may not be exactly clear, so understand that when a father in the '60s had a righteous daughter fighting for equality and rights for African-Americans in the South, it was cool. The father could understand her passion and enjoyed the spark she showed. He wasn't being engaged, though--not until she brought home her new boyfriend. Then he was engaged, and forced to deal with his reactions. Then he was moved off his spot, and the dance of becoming dynamic on this issue had to take place.

Someone has to bring solar energy home to meet the folks. I do not know exactly how this happens, but I can envision a few ways. A country has enough scientific breakthroughs and financial support to arrange an entire community around it, such that all energy sources of the community and transportation are now based on electricity gathered from the sun. This has to be a recognized community. They have to express their presence to the rest of the world. They will have become passionate about this change in the way that inter-racial teenagers falling in love were passionate. There would need to be a high passion for it, and not much standing against it.

Then the dominoes will fall.

Other cultures across the planet will look at the one doing fine with photovoltaic energy and say "Hey, why can't we do that?"

They will say that in the same way a person with rigid self-expectations looks at a joyous person who makes major changes with new information about themselves and says "How are they happy when they just changed everything?"

They will say it in the same way that someone looked at a happy mixed-race, or LGBT couple and said "Hey, how come they get to enjoy those types of attractions and relationships and I did not?"

This is the **Romeo and Juliet Moment** for society.

Then we get permission. We get permission from the only person who can ever tell us no. Ourselves.

This is *Community in Creation* on one side and *Community in Reaction* on the other. Non-inclusivity and rejection...division...these are not things that are in sync with our technology anymore, and our social lives are so tied in with technology that I sincerely doubt we can ignore the facets of consciousness that deal with harmony and role fluidity without seriously bad consequences. On the flipside of that totally-over-the-top warning, I have to say that the whole point of describing this is to show how easy it has become, through the very technology that puts us at risk, to find examples of how things work well. We can then use those examples to create with each other, on behalf of each other.

The accidental goal of technology was to connect everyone. Get us all up close and personal. Social media has allowed us to make every breath public record, and allowed everyone to comment on and judge everything that everyone does. Wow. I don't know if anyone saw this coming 30 years ago, but it is literally like 200 kids arriving at a heated popularity contest in middle school after being alone in the woods for their whole lives and barely being able to read or write. It is a colossal debacle. It really is. But as we all get involved in the up-close-and-too-personal world that sits before us, it is a LOT easier to identify moments and actions that had previously unnoticed. There is too much information about the world to hide from any of it. There are also too many mirrors reflecting our behavior to pretend that we cannot see it.

The generation coming of age now doesn't know it, but they are the **Overload Generation**: a generation whose prime function it is to bear out the fruits of a global social test of immersion. The term used in psychology to handle experiences that are scary through overwhelming the subject is "flooding." The result of this flooding is exposure. Through social media we are exposed to ideas, and other people's views of them. The well of insight we are drawing from is global. Parents are not here to describe the world to us, just give us their version among many other versions. This bodes well for growth. In the past, parents were the be-all end-all of presenting reality. They are simply a piece now. The extent to which they are loving and trustworthy gives them a proportional amount of Influence over the child, or student, or friend. But before, if they were not loving, they were the only voice within earshot (besides a lucky teacher here or there, or coach), whereas now they can easily be drowned out by other voices that can win trust and love: voices that are endearing to the listener.

We live in a time when people get to pick who they shall be parented by. We get to live in a time where becoming a good example no longer falls on deaf ears. "If you want to change the world, change yourself." –Gandhi. It may not be obvious, but in looking at moving from the micro to the macro in cases of dysfunction, and describing the search for role fluidity and dynamic Perspectives, we just laid it all out. I have been working at this idea for many years, and have not seen it as clearly as I do right this second, and I love that.

We find a reaction, a new want, a yearning, or a realization of care in our reactions and hearts for something that exists external to us. We find something that engages our joy that is surprising and new. We want Romeo seeing Juliet for the first time. We want to figure out that we love something. Then we want to be free to express that want, that reality and joy that brings us to life. Wanting, joy, desire…these things are a part of who we are. They are creations.

So how does saying yes to our wants, and creating a new reality with their present change anything on any other level? We want to express it, and we *then become an example of expression* in doing so. We change the world because, especially now, everyone sees our desires. They see how we go about dealing with them, and they see our courage. ***This is not a movie, this is not fiction, and there are no filters***.

This is social media. We have a global Audience. We have a "friends list." We have worlds upon worlds of effect and the inclusion of all realities. So when we decide to step outside our blood family, we are not alone. When we take a stand for our love of the environment, or any other such noble cause, we are not alone.

And the best part is that kindness, love, and hope get a ton of airtime, because they are the most precious and valuable (and attractive) things in the world. So when we act lovingly, when we become dynamic and deal with our reactions, when we get the support and love of our Audiences, we affect their ability to engage lovingly. All the stories intertwine, in real time, and the ability to maneuver through the stasis of history that we encounter in friction through every new movement is getting less and less like trudging through mud and more like being on a Slip 'N Slide.

We make waves by loving and trusting and changing. We make noise. We make noise in a way that inspires, and we get support. We get support, we inspire others, and the spiral of change and joy starts accelerating. ***This is expression creating Reality.*** This is our integrated wants changing the world.

I do not believe that we know we are doing this right this second. But we are. So when you think about your actions in your everyday reality, please think of the Resonance it has with everyone, and everything, everywhere.

PART 3: CREATION VERSUS REACTION: STEPPING INTO YOUR POWER

*

When we call reality real, or we call it illusion, we are dangerously wrong. It is neither. It is art. Art that is a correlative of ourselves and that shares and determines our dimension with us.

*

So, how much time do you spend worrying?

It's a pretty valid question. It is usually met with "a lot" or "not too much." It is a natural part of thought processes to manage incoming fears and deal with their validity by imagining them playing out in a multitude of scenarios. That sounds about right, yeah?

The extent to which we develop the plot of these worries depends on many things, like our attachment to the outcome of certain parts of our lives (job, Primary Relationships), and the level of tending we've done to the "weeds" in that area.

It's much easier for us to imagine everything with a new relationship will go wrong when it's happened a couple times. And since most relationships end in a breakup, we are not going to be hard-pressed to find evidence to support our imagination.

That's not very powerful of us, though. It's all right, not something we need to beat ourselves up about, but we can do better. We can do more than look at the scripts of previous movies *and make the exact same movie.* Evidence will always tell us things are going to be the same. It's rare that evidence will tell us things are going to be different. That's because evidence doesn't come from "hasn't happened yet" or "surprise." Evidence doesn't come from "one in a million." It usually comes from "Give me the most common example." But extraordinary things happen daily. That evidence merely doesn't get the same airplay naturally within our mental framework. We have to take a couple steps to get that message involved in our everyday thought, so let's begin.

Let's look at one way to create a new story.

The Missing Ear Buds

This morning I took my boy to the bus stop, which is a slight bit away from the house, and we realized upon reaching our destination that he had forgotten the ear buds for his electronic assistant (this is what I call any device these days that connects us to…well…everything). This was not a good thing. There was not enough time to go back for them and they were a vital part of his day.

I do things like this all the time. I forget stuff. Sour cream for the fajitas, ice cream for dessert. These are things in my day *that cannot be rectified.* They are, as my father once lessoned me, "irreconcilable losses."

I also know that when they occur, no matter how small the issue, there is a period of mourning. I let him have that for his ear buds. After a couple minutes (after he has grieved for the loss), it is time to look at options in a serious manner.

We call this a "teachable moment." Although, in reality, it is an explanation moment, because we are hardly the authority on how to handle loss. No one is an authority on that. That is because all losses are personal to the consciousness experiencing them.

We take a breath together, and hopefully we can look at this situation in a way that improves it. In my head I come up with a million ideas (albeit mostly silly ones), so he can create a better day for himself. I start making a real effort to do this, because the ability to create a really crappy day is SO EASY to come by. That is just *allowing our previous experience to write our future for us*.

"I'm not going to be able to do _____"...and "____ is going to be boring"... can take the lead at any moment if we do not speak over them. So I say to him, "Create a new day. Make a day where you didn't need them, or a day when you were engaged with cool stuff so that you didn't have a spare moment to use them. You know how to do this, dude; work with it."

He does know how to do this. He's good at it, too. He has been trained by his mother from a young age. When he was feeling sickly, she would tell him, "Well, you have to go to school, and going to school sick is awful. So you might as well create yourself feeling better as fast as you can."

This is not a reaction. Reactions are specific, and almost always dismissive. Being dismissive is disrespectful of the Now. We do not want to dismiss anything; doing so creates repression and resentment. The ear buds are gone. We do not win points by lying to ourselves and saying that they don't weigh heavily on us or that they don't matter. We get ourselves in the right Perspective by creating. Instead of telling ourselves that our mistake is unimportant, or that our worry is not valid, we address the future.

The ear buds provide entertainment and joy. So let's get at that directly. He must now look to all the possible things on the bus and at school that are going to fill for moments when he would have been using his ear buds. He can get to ideas like this pretty easily. My ideas, which I keep to myself because they are silly, are still effective as they are creative. My ideas were "Someone is going to lend him their ear buds," "There is going to be a great philosophical discussion on the bus that will make ear buds unnecessary," "He will think of ideas that will govern his future life in untold ways because of what he hears on the bus." That was the stuff that I came up with in the three minutes we had to try to generate a better day for him. My bet is that he came up with better ideas.

But the likelihood of these ideas is not the issue. The issue is engaging the possibility of unforeseen futures. These are futures NOT based on your past experience or your expectations. This is true art. This is a consciousness in action.

Maybe when we see it with an eleven-year-old it's easier to say he is "stepping into his power." **Stepping into Your Power** is simply becoming creatively engaged in your reality as an "attitude." It has to be consistent. Looking at my stepson in that moment, watching him address his consciousness and get himself together, I thought, *That was a very adult moment for him. He's totally growing up.* Stepping into Your Power is becoming an adult.

I have mentioned that becoming an adult is a never-ending process, and that is why we need to continue to parent ourselves and others. This is not only because there are so many Perspectives from which to manage ourselves, but because being creative in the face of loss is very difficult.

I want to make a very clear distinction here. As adults, we look at what he did, and we do not see the moment as we should. We can easily blow the situation off and not teach, but just react. This is a real mistake because *we are letting ourselves off the hook for some serious growth opportunities*. My first instinct in every situation where my boys are greeted with a loss or frustration is to minimize its importance. This is a reaction my brain comes up with immediately to decrease my empathic pain, and it makes total sense to me. It is a mistake to follow through on, though. So let's look at what I almost did.

Val's ear buds...here's the story that didn't happen. I, in my experience and wisdom, know that having ear buds is truthfully not a very big deal. It is a small part of a long day, a day whose focus should be on less-frivolous things. So what I want to do is tell him that, and drive that nail home. *The reason that he should not be upset is because what he is upset about is not important.* I see the truth in this, as evidenced by many years of experience, and I simply go at it hard. "For goodness' sake--it's not a big deal; just deal with it, dude. It's a small part of your day and you shouldn't be that engaged with entertainment during school anyway." Those are, even from where I sit now, valid and accurate points. They don't work, though. And they're mean, to boot, as they are dismissive of his loss.

Those are reactions from a consciousness that has had the experience in question, some loss of joy on a small scale, and lived through it without much damage. The reason it is a big deal to not dismiss it using that type of Perspective is this: NOT EVERY EXPERIENCE IS LIKE THAT. Those were ear buds, and instead of learning how to be creative and focus on the future, *he would have learned how to be dismissive*. That's fine if the issue is ear buds, not so fine if you lose a child in a tragic accident. Some experiences do not have "dismiss" as an option.

The fact that we have not experienced something, when we are children, makes it VERY POWERFUL. This gives us an opportunity we rarely take as parents because it takes energy, and forces us to engage. *It gives us the opportunity to teach how to create while still in a state of seemingly overwhelming loss*. It is easy as an adult not to lose your mind over little stuff. That is because of experience. Experience creates a threshold for losses which can be dismissed. But as adults there are still experiences that cross that threshold, and because of our inability to create, and our attachment to being dismissive of loss, we STILL HAVE A REALLY HARD TIME BEING CREATIVE. *We have a hard time stepping into our power*.

Catch a fish for someone, feed them for a day. Teach them how to fish, feed them for a lifetime. Get someone over loss by being dismissive of the loss…take away their pain for a day. Teach them to create through their overwhelming momentary sensation… *take away their ability to be crippled by pain* **for a lifetime**.

This has been a description of a breakthrough reaction, due to a loss of some sort. This can come with having been given bad news of any kind, or coming to any realization of loss. But this is not the only type of worry we can confront to work toward a more prosperous reality. In fact, I'd likely say that as far as time spent in types of worry, that last example, while powerful, is not the main type of debilitating worry we need to remedy.

Worrying: The Never-Ending Scarcity of Time and the Limits of Goods and Experiences

We are not our worries. By that, I simply mean we are not the endless-chatter-reactions to our imagination of the future as it relates to realities which we do or do not want. This is a rhetoric that takes place in our mind. It is powerful and consuming. It is also habitual...and totally malleable.

The endless-chatter-reactions are a narrative. They exist to reinforce our reality. They consist of all the thoughts in the section on Father's Day and Conscious Validation, along with thousands of other thought-minutiae that weave their way through our mind daily. These are here as a byproduct of wants. They are necessarily connected (this is why in Zen Buddhism they do not address a management issue as it relates to thought; they simply do away with wants altogether- -*they are that impossible to separate*). They serve as a manner of locating and managing our wants within an ever-changing external reality. They are also our manner of protecting what we believe we are already in possession of. It is a lot like sonar going off in every direction at once, determining the theoretical distances between our exact spot in the world and the satisfaction of all our wants, as well as the location of possible threats to the things we possess now. The mind gets involved in mapping toward our wants and threat identification and assessment. That is not a bad thing by any stretch, and if it were used properly and in moderation, could be a very useful tool.

The issue with this type of narrative is that it becomes a habitual thing, a narrative that recognizes the distance between us and the things we want, as well as a deep rooted NEED to find threats. That makes it, from a Vibrational standpoint, *more like a complaint than a plan*. That might not be so bad, but then you have to hook that into the system of "wants"...and realize that it is limitless and infinite (which is glorious), while time and resources are finite. Another aspect within the narrative on the system of wants is that we truly control so little of the external reality we are engaged in that "planning" is just another word for "thought-out frustration and eventual failure," and the idea of protecting what we already have becomes a fool's errand. So there are always going to be justifiable worries. Oops. That can't be good.

So, why is that bad? It is bad because it mentally and emotionally wears us down. It is bad because when we are engaged in this type of narrative too much we are not creating new opportunities. We can only write such a narrative with past experience and past emotional realities. It is bad because when we are worried about protecting something, we cannot experience and enjoy it fully. It is bad because when we are seeing the distance between ourselves and an object of want, we cannot connect with it confidently. I have not covered the Law of Attraction in this book yet, but screaming "How am I ever going to be able to afford that?" and being able to actually afford it are pretty far apart, aren't they? Also all the focus going toward what is lacking, and identifying incoming threats, *keeps us from engaging what is present, and being gracious.* That is why I describe it as an activity akin to complaint.

This is what is meant, when people speak of not being Present in our lives. We are not Stepping into Our Power.

"Life, it's the thing that happens when you're busy making other plans." - Lennon

Two hundred thousand years is a long time. Genetic instinct is powerful. We are not supposed to be good at disabling this system. We have been out of caves for 25,000-50,000 years, and have pretty much been in charge of the planet for the last 5,000. Our technology over the past 250 years has basically doubled the amount of the previous 100,000, and most of that has come in the past 50 years. We have not focused on evolving our relationship with consciousness, and there is no one that should have taught us this. **It is new**. There is no one to blame for the fact that we, as a species, have not yet stepped into other ways of dealing with the world around us. It has not been available. Our frontal lobes have been busied with protecting ourselves, and have no habit to slide into. This has to be done manually.

We can use Conscious Validation, become aware of our Pivot Points, try to stay on the Beach of Quiet Emotion, etc. But we need to form a relationship with how our mind engages with the realities we are presented with. Stepping into Your Power is not just something to do. *It is something we are becoming as a society*. It is a step in the evolutionary process that is going to be determined by behavior within the social systems already in place. It is basically an **Insurgence of Consciousness**. We are all going to start trying to do this. I am not saying "we should," I am saying "we are going to." It is the logical next step. Once it is a goal that is common to have, or in vogue, like "being awake," or "being centered," we will start to see how the motivation to address our consciousness changes everything.

When our alarm goes off in the morning we can hit the snooze button, and this is no different. Whenever we are subversively engaging in worry, we can catch ourselves listening to the narrative. We can catch ourselves believing it. We can hear ourselves painting scenarios of things that haven't happened yet: worrying about money, and bills, and rejection. We can worry about how to pay a bill that came in the mail even though we've never been late paying. We can worry about things going wrong that have never ever gone wrong. It is our nature to attach a fear scenario to any object of thought. *We just don't have to keep doing it.*

We have to know that it is coming. We have to understand that it is here to protect us. Then we need to form a relationship with it, so we can get to being creatively engaged in our world. We must do this so that we can be present, so that we can enjoy our lives, and be gracious. We will then make adjustments that can cut through the system of weeds sheltering us from the experience of life.

This is not always easy. Sometimes the world comes at us, and not reacting seems impossible. We do not like getting hit, that is why we spend so much time worrying about whether or not we are going to be attacked. We do not like invasion, and we do not like pain. But not only are they things that come with the incarnation here, they are things that come within our closest relationships.

Every good person is going to hurt someone they care about. It's going to happen. Everyone is going to be hurt by the people closest to them, and more than a few times in all likelihood. Fostering a healthy relationship means being vulnerable, so how do we deal with the seemingly oxymoronic needs of the body? We need to feel safe, and we need to be close to people through vulnerability. How do we do this?

We learn to create with incoming attacks, rather than just reacting. This is upper level stuff, but it is something we all need. I've seen many work this skill at some level in their lives.

Stepping into the Punches, Creating through Reactions, Interpersonal Alchemy

The world is going to keep coming at us. But how do we respect it, and create with it, while it is attacking us? It's not easy, certainly, but it is possible. The best example of this difficulty occurs with Primary Relationships that have faltered, or become abusive. This means that there are people we are tied to and habitually reacting to…whom we cannot leave. They are going to be at our party in one way or another, just like the world is going to be hosting it in one way or another.

So let's look tense situations where attacking can be easily identified. When it comes to parents, and ex-spouses with whom we share a child, we simply have our whole lives to either work into a healthy Perspective or not. It can happen with coworkers we are stuck with, or bad roommates, but it is less obviously a permanent tie to our lives in those cases (I still suggest using this). We can, at any moment, decide to create through attacks, and not continue living in reaction to the person whom we are tied to.

We can forget reason, forget logic, forget everything that has happened, and take a step back. We can look at these people in our lives in a different way. We can look at these people like needy children, and see ourselves as the parent. This is the truth. If we have a high capacity to love and understand, and we wish for their well-being more than they do, *we are the parents of the situation*.

Can we see it like that? That is the first step. They are not in control of themselves. They are violent specifically to we who are trying to help them. This is because they are scared out of their damn minds and feel comfortable only when they hurt people. It is the only time they feel powerful, and thus the only time they feel safe. That pretty much describes the worst sides of any person.

So that Perspective of parenthood is Step One…Step Two is more intense.

We have to take our reactions to their harmful actions and our reactions to our own frustration, and red flag it, *because we need to reprogram our responses*. Each time a conflict-moment comes up we have to see ourselves as the parent: powerful, giving, patient, loving, and helping a violent child to calm down.

We have to take those reactions--reactions we have had for years, in all likelihood, bless them--and move past them into a "creative" stance. We must do this so that whenever we get hurt or frustrated we can see it as a teachable moment, just like with my son and his ear buds. And in our moment of clenching up in pain, we must expand into creation. We must give our divine parenting self to the moment, and fearlessly walk into the mouth of the fire-breathing dragon.

It doesn't matter much what action we take when in creation, because if we give ourselves to it, it will demolish anything in its path. It will throw a wrench into the system that this relationship has been operating under for however long it has.

It sounds ambiguous, so I'll be specific. Imagine them doing their thing, whether it is coming into your space and yelling at you, belittling you, or being hurtful and abusive. In the middle of this violence, relax, and offer something. Offer something that changes the story from the one you've been having for years, to one that has not been written yet.

"Thank you for _____." Fill in the blank with anything, and be sincere. There are always things to be thankful for, and gratitude dismantles negativity. Anything that will change the script, and keep us from rewriting the same story, is what we want. We will be capable of finding it if we are acting in creation with the moment.

Being able to do that, in times of stress, will change relationships. Everything will change. Be creative instead of reactive. Be an active parent.

This ability to take relationships and change them is **Interpersonal Alchemy**. It is the means by which we can improve any situation, and have an Influence on a world that can be truly challenging. The act of taking the hurt that comes at us, and changing our Perspective to that of loving parent rather than injured and struggling angel, is the moment we have taken the world and turned it into a story we are co-authoring. And when we say "We are all gods," that is what we mean. This is how we become divine.

When I look at the power we can have in our world through Influence when we engage in creating, rather than reacting, it is stunning to me. I wish I could be so on top of my consciousness that I succeeded every time an opportunity presented itself.

This is how we do it, though. This is how the Romeo and Juliet moment happens. This is how we learn to cook on a hot stove, and overcome our wounds. This is how Parenting our World happens. This is how we become less attached to our reactions, our histories, our traumas, and the stories that our past wants us to continue writing unconsciously. This is how we change the world.

Chapter 13:

On the Law of Attraction: Enjoyment, Gratitude, and Presence

Be here now. If you have had some time in the ever-expanding psychologically versed culture that expresses itself through social media, you have probably come across the idea of "Being Present" at one point or another. Like most suggestions about complex psychological and subjective states of mind, it falls short of describing what it needs to in a full and accurate way. Gratitude is "being present in thanks or appreciation." **Being Present** is the ability to consciously engage and validate our reality, or exert Influence on the world around us. Having gratitude is the type of presence we are going to analyze in this chapter, as it relates to creating a healthy relationship with the world around us.

Having gratitude is an action. We can say "I am thankful for___," and "I am grateful for ____," however, it is not a complete expression to simply vocalize the words. The fullness of what gratitude means gets lost because *we assume we have already done something* when we have simply vocalized. We assume this in the same way that my boys assume that "brush your teeth" means "Sit on the couch not moving for another five minutes." They think that because they nodded and said okay, that they had fulfilled the request, even though their actions were lacking. *They were lacking Presence in brushing their teeth.* It creates Cognitive Dissonance to confront the fact that we do not under-stand these terms, and that we do not fulfill their character of **Healthy Expression**. We do not confront the fact that we miss these opportuni-ties, because it happens so often that it's truly depressing. We mustn't be discouraged, though. Even the smallest attempts to fulfill and em-body gratitude change everything in our world.

The Law of Attraction is pretty in-vogue right now, so I will simply gloss over a couple ideas about its nature that I believe are missed. In this chapter I am going to describe the **Fulfillment of Gratitude**. This is "liv-ing in consistent enjoyment of what we have been matched with." This, when accomplished, is **Completing the Circuit** of the Law of Attraction.

I wrote this section three years before this book--figured I'd leave it as close to the original work as I could.

Cake Eating!

Ever wondered why manifestation was a finicky little trickster? I have wondered why since the first time I heard Abraham Hicks when I was about eleven. I knew that some people were simply better at it than others, and recently I have realized why. So now I will share it with you, free of charge, unless you have a lot of money, in which case I don't know why you haven't paid me already.

Dream, delight in the dream, and allow the dream. Be gracious for it when you get it...NOT ENOUGH. I realized one word has been missing from the process to make it a complete exchange:

"The last prerequisite for manifestation is that you VALIDATE the exchange and connection by ENJOYING the manifestation."

Allow, be gracious, sure...that's a start. But the next example will show you why that's simply not enough for universal discourse to occur and intervene for the fulfillment of your yummy requests. It is the husband and wife drama...the wife's birthday.

Wife is craving a chocolate birthday cake, homemade, and she mentions it enough so that the husband realizes she really would love it as a gift.

The husband gets all the ingredients, and works with his dearest love to make and deliver the cake, which is presented on the birthday at the appropriate moment.

The wife thanks him profusely and showers him with affection. But...*she refrains from eating the cake.*

A week goes by and she doesn't touch it, and the husband ends up throwing it out.

She asked for the cake, she allowed the cake, and she was grateful for the cake...but...she didn't eat it.

Assume you're the husband. Next time she asks for something, are you as motivated to fulfill her request? I'm not. I wanted to see her face light up when she tasted it, and I'm disappointed that I did not get to have that experience. I don't want to be upset about it, but I am. In this situation, a piece of the exchange was missing. Because of that, *the exchange was not validated.*

Now, *we are all the wife in this situation.* The husband's role is being played by the Universe. We need to eat the cake. Otherwise, in the same way the husband feels dejected, the Universe does not get its Vibration matched.

What the world wants from us is the **Vitality Gasp** of enjoyment. That is the fulfillment of the cycle. The world doesn't want a thank-you card. I say the world, rather than the Universe, because ALL conscious beings respond to the Vitality Gasp. A baby laughing, a lion roaring, a wolf howling, love at first sight, the jump from the ledge into the ocean, deep sexual satisfaction, triumph, any mind-blowing experience, the first bite of a delicious piece of cake...these are what we ALL live for.

Those who enjoy life the most, in my experience, seem to have their dreams fulfilled at ease, without worry. And when their dreams are fulfilled, they love up on them.

Most of us have a wish fulfilled and don't stop to enjoy it before moving on to the next want.

This is why manifestation is an inconsistent thing. It's as if the universe has to trust that we're on the same side. We rarely have enough self-knowledge to know what we want, and when we do, our society has an issue with things being easy.

We can let the idea of "work" and "earning" fly right out the window. This takes time and practice, like everything else. The only thing we have to do to deserve the delicious cake... IS EAT IT AND LOVE IT! We must *be Present in a state of gratitude through enjoyment.*

This traverses into every area of our lives, though and we must understand the underlying sentiment. WE CHOSE TO BE HERE, in this body, at this time, in our situations. We are alive. We have been delivered this existence in the same way our storied wife has been delivered cake. I am not saying that happiness is necessitated, but AWARENESS and RESONANCE and EXPERIENCE certainly are.

Along with manifesting items, we manifest into the broadening of our reality by taking it all in...and saying GIVE

MEEEE MMMOOORREEEEE. We must do that without halting the process by saying "OHH, ITT'SS TOO MUCH!" It backs off when we clench up. We know this.

If it gets to be too much to handle, then we smile and flow the best we can. We do what we need to get through, and *life will keep sending LIFE our way.* The more we enjoy our world that we chose to be in, the more those feelings will resonate and create expansive possibilities for us. We are not just "spiritual beings having a human experience." We are spiritual beings that made a deal to be human, promising our best effort at fully embodying these physical forms. Now it is our job to show up. Our presence in our world is how we show gratitude for our lives.

So live. Enjoy your life. Enjoy the fruits of your labor, and dismiss worry as often as you can. The manifestations you receive, the lessons you learn, take them and use them. When you feel like you have gotten to a place where you are at peace...BE AT PEACE. It validates your journey, until the next one is needed.

There are a couple good conversations within this essay I wrote years ago about how to keep as close to the Law of Attraction as possible. Feeling like we deserve something is often an issue that people have with the LOA, and for good reason.

We all deserve exactly what we can use and fully experience. That is the prerequisite for many blessings.

The other good point to take a look at is the Fulfillment of Gratitude aspect. It's relatively vague, and unfortunately, upon further investigation, it stays pretty vague. Vague is its nature. There are no guidelines for it, and there is no way to guarantee its affect. D'oh.

How much do we have to enjoy something? How long? How do we know when we're done? How do we know it worked? I can answer these ...

As much as we can enjoy it, as long and as often as we can for as long as we can remember it, we're not ever done, and we don't ever know for sure if it worked. So we at least don't have the pressure of ever having to address or worry about those questions. That saves time.

The reason that these two aspects have been highlighted here is that they are necessarily connected to each other. The Fulfillment of Gratitude occurs when we become deserving of the reality we have been gifted with. That is the Completion of the Circuit of the LOA.

Lots of big words and very little concrete description above, huh? Let's fix that.

Presence.

The Universe wants us creative. It wants us present. It does not want us worrying. Worry is the burden of having frontal lobes unfortunately, and leveling our consciousness up has some unwanted byproducts (just...like...everything... worth...having...does). When we worry, we are shutting down to gratitude and expansion and enjoyment and blah blah...etc. We are not taking in the experiences outside of us that are cosmically expansive. We are just experiencing the repetitive things going on in our head.

Let me repeat that (I'm being bossy). We are not taking in new information, just playing old recordings in our head. It's a skipping record. *Everyone worries the same way; **no one creates*** *the same way*. It's the difference between growling and singing. Growls all sound the same, *every singing voice is unique.*

If the Universe is a flowing river of energy, worrying is tensing up to try to stand still in the center and blocking the water's flow. It is discordant.

Now is the time to take a look at the **"On to the Next Problem Mentality."** As a college student, working full time with a full-time band, I was very, very busy. I got used to constantly looking at upcoming responsibilities and quickly prioritizing which one needed my attention in the direst way.

From waking up in the morning...opening my eyes (I'm exhausted, have to go to school)...getting up late (now I have to rush, gotta take everything I need for the whole day)...getting out the door late (now I have to speed and risk getting a ticket, or being late because of Southern California traffic)... getting to class late, disheveled and hungry (great, now I can't relax because I rushed and I can't focus)...changing clothes in my car and driving to work from school (great, how am I going to do my homework at midnight when I get home from work, and when am I going to design the flyer for my upcoming show?)...then working at a fast-paced sushi bar for six hours (great, now I'm exhausted). At no point during this day was I ever at peace. At no moment was I ever fully present, either. I ended up crashing this life into the side of a small mountain, dropping out of school, and going bankrupt.

I figured I'd be able to relax without anywhere near as much on my plate. But that was not the case. The mentality on display here is not simply due to circumstance. **It is a habit of adulthood.** Worrying through our realities is the norm, and that status quo has to be changed. The good news...is that it can be changed.

Ever worried about paying a bill? As in "Goodness, how am I going to get that paid and still have enough money for food? I wish there were a way to get everything done and pay that bill!"

Did it get paid? It did, right? But then there was another bill, huh?

Bills are the easiest place to see the On To the Next Problem Mentality. Focusing on paying that bill was two weeks of worry. Then we derived ZERO pleasure or relief from paying. Wow. *We just replaced the object of worry with another object of worry.*

You may be asking "What are we supposed to appreciate? It's a bill." We are supposed to take a moment **to appreciate the success in achieving a goal**, and to allow the peace of mind that should accompany it to make us relax for a minute or two. We should ALSO use that Perspective to see that the next bill will likely get paid, even if we cannot figure out how at the moment, and that worrying (stopping the flow of the Universe and our creative nature) is probably not the best course of action. It is not a habit we want to *validate*.

The peace of mind from achieving a goal is a form of gratitude. We underestimate its value by a gross margin. The effect of doing this is brutal for our mental states, as well as our ability to keep connecting with our reality.

What we do when we do not allow ourselves this peace of mind, is validate our relationship with the presence of worry. We also validate the lack of appreciation we have for our own efforts, highlighting our unforgiving expectations of ourselves. We validate *"taking ourselves for granted."* That is a nasty group of effects.

So, here's a solid example: me right now. I'm pacing around in my tiny apartment, getting all fussy about the fact that I cannot come up with the next section of this chapter. I am worrying. I am worried that I am missing the understanding necessary to express this point of view clearly, and that I may just simply have bitten off more than I can chew. I am worried that this task is too large for me. In fact, the entire book I'm dedicating a ton of time to, may be beyond my abilities.

Now I want to take a look at the brutal implications of such a destructive line of thinking.

I have to *ignore and discount* a lot of information to have that opinion. To validate that Perspective, I have to invalidate or dismiss a lot of others. I also have to be disrespectful of all the previous versions of me that got the job done. I have to do that to justify worrying myself into a non-creative space for over an hour (then, of course, I figured out what to write).

So let's see how much I have to dismiss to justify my "worries." I have to first off, dismiss the 250 pages I've already written. Along with that, I have to dismiss my positive opinion of those pages. I have to discount the knowledge and experience that led to their being created. I also have to forget that I've felt this way like 100 times during the writing of this book and pulled through each time. That's already a lot. But wait, there's more!

I have to forget that I'm a writer, which is the fulfillment of a childhood dream, now manifested in my adult life. I have to ignore that I got what I wanted, and that I love this part of my life. I also have to disrespect all the compliments and support I have from all of my friends and family. These are also vital parts of my life that I wished for and received.

I also have to ignore all the tools I have at my disposal, tools I have gathered tirelessly over the years to help me through moments of frustration.

WOW. That is a serious list of destruction that has to take place for me to justify being in a crappy, worried space. *Then the result of my doing so is my inability to create.*

If I did this to another person, it would be a brutal insult to their entire existence. It is psychological assault. I am not going to get into the psychology of self-esteem, because it doesn't matter with respect to our goals. What matters is changing this habit.

The habit is our relationship to worry. No matter how many chapters I write, I am capable of doing this to myself. No matter how much we accomplish, we *can* immediately start worrying over the next thing we have yet to do.

There is a reason we want to minimize our worry. Besides the fact that it is ungracious, it pulls us away from the world. It is akin to complaint. It is a rejection of our self-confidence and our hopeful possibilities.

This brings us to the Disappearing Vito.

The Disappearing Vito

I mentioned before that the Universe wants us present. We speak about being present in our Now moments. This, however, is not described to satisfaction. It does not mean just "paying attention" ...it means bringing our entire selves to wherever we happen to be, so that we can fully participate. **Participation** gets its own chapter later.

The person I am when I am calm contains all of my hopes, gratitude, and love. I have full contact with the *Vito that I identify with*.

This is akin to driving a car and being able to fully pay attention. We have all of our tools and the qualities we need for the task at hand. I used the driving analogy in a previous chapter to express how rarely we are sober within our mind.

But let's say that I am stressed, or upset, or worried. Those are states of being that are incompatible with gratitude, and creation. This means that the Vito that I identify with is NOT HERE when they are present. He has disappeared. All the things that make me who I am have dissolved, *and the things that make me exactly like every other worried person* are present in my place.

This happens to everyone. We are unstable, reactive beings. When we are not at peace and in creativity, we become a token for a type of person, rather than an individual expressing unique glory.

In the same way that the Garden Overrun with Weeds looks like weeds to everyone on the outside, when we are worried we can express only worry...not selfhood. There is nothing about worry that is an expression of our divine being.

That is the disappearing Vito. Vito is gone when not living in gratitude. A nameless, worried, human animal takes his place. I am no longer present.

So, let's think of all the awesome things we've been gifted. This is where we start working with the Law of Attraction accountably. We use the joy we've had...to stop worrying. This is where "becoming deserving" and the Fulfillment of Gratitude connect.

So what do we have to be grateful for? Well, the answer is very simple. **Everything**. Everything has a Perspective that can be loaded with gratitude and enjoyment. How can we express that? We get involved in validating the Perspectives that generate thoughts.

Getting ourselves involved with these motivational forces is an aspect of being present. Being Present for our world, and our blessings, is a vital part of the Fulfillment of Gratitude. If we are not present because we are worried, or scattered, or stressed, then we are not capable of integrating joyous experiences. If we are not capable of integrating them, we are undeserving. From a Vibrational standpoint, this keeps us from Completing the Circuit of the Law Of Attraction.

The Circuit of the Law of Attraction is completed when we incorporate the experiences of our history into our present moment, and use them to express ourselves more abundantly.

Our history includes only two possible realities: things that were joyous or pleasant, that we can remember and be in Commune with; or things that were not so pleasant, which taught us and gave us valuable Perspectives having gone through them. Blessings and Lessons.

In understanding this, it means that right this second, we are either in the former or the latter. One is an expression of joy; one is an expression of personal power. Both are glorious. Both are healthy. That is what we have to be grateful for, and how we can be present in enjoyment for every state of being.

"Happiness is a choice" versus "You might be able to do something with that."

I am going to spend a moment addressing the "Happiness is a choice" grenade. Yes, grenade. It is a grenade because it is true...but it is awful. Just like grenades.

I was a waiter in 2005 when my brother went in for a huge surgery. I was waiting tables during the day shift, and though I was lumbering a bit due to worry and frustration, I was still a good server and a kind person to my customers.

During the shift I waited on a small group of haughty New Age kiddos, likely around my age (tweny-six). They were eye-balling me, which I've noticed is a common trait among people who are cocky in the New Age field. I was a bit behind on my service and apologized for it, and mentioned that I was not at my best today, to which the ring-leader of the group stated: "Happiness is a choice."

This was, of course, not the right time for that. So as I was bussing his table and in mid-stride, I responded back to him "Yeah, you're right, but it's not an equal choice. See my brother is having surgery right this second and my mind is with him...so while it may be a choice, it is not the same choice that you are making while sitting here in the sun enjoying gourmet pizza. But thanks."

See, it was a choice I had. It definitely was. But it was between me, myself, and I. I was not using my history to make my present moment better, and it was affecting not only me, but other people. I was not present. I was accountable for that.

But there is a reason that it is not a good idea to toss that idea at someone who needs it. It is because the present state of being they were advising from was simply nowhere near the battle I was having. So, no matter how right they were, all day long, they were wrong. They are wrong in the same way that the man in the suit walking past a homeless man and saying "Get a job" is wrong.

So, hence the title "You might want do something with that." What I did after the young man made a swipe at my attitude, besides enjoy my own with a tad at his expense, was take his advice. That's funny, isn't it?

So I was walking away thinking of how unequal all situations are, and how no one can really tell anyone else that they should be able to handle what they are going through, I started thinking of all the different times my brother had been in the same situation, and that each time I had gotten stronger. As a result, I immediately got stronger.

See, part of who I am is the suffering I've been through. It is my experience, and I have always integrated it as fully as possible. This means that the power I had attained from my experiences was augmenting right then, while pacing the restaurant carrying sodas and taking orders from people who were absolutely oblivious to my reality. They were oblivious to the amount of creation that had to take place before every smile, and every kind word I spoke. I had become present.

So, to finish this up, I am going to make a very direct suggestion. Never say "Happiness is a choice." Not to yourself, and DEFINITELY not to anyone else. It is never an equal choice, and you are likely in no place to deliver the message. Even if you have been through a situation that seems exactly the same, I can assure you that it is not. Everyone, and every situation, is different.

But this does not mean you cannot ask someone to be more present. This does not mean that you have to let someone in an awful space just sit there expressing it. It is not healthy for anyone, most of all for the person expressing it. We have to have a way to at least nudge people toward their power, grandeur, and gratitude.

So when someone is in the middle of struggling...say the true thing. "There might be something you can do with that."

During any hard moment, whether I am suffering, frustrated, out of my mind, or worried ... It's likely that I can do *something*. Hmmm. Should I think of the joys of my life? Should I be grateful? Should I get a larger Perspective of whatever I'm going through and envision its majesty as a whole experience of incarnation? Certainly sounds like whatever joys I had manifested in my world, from family on down to miniscule successes and accomplishments, could be used to get out of a discordant space, and get aligned back with my gracious and vibrant self.

Certainly seems like I *could* do that. I'm pretty sure we all can.

So what does applying our history do for us? It engages our entire being. It takes our experiences, our Resonance, and our Rapture and brings it to the forefront. That is living in gratitude, rather than experiencing just a moment or two of gratitude. That is a huge difference. All the times we wished and intended for certain joys or certain circumstances and they were fulfilled, we are able to use them in concert with the present moment to complete a circuit. The joyous wanting intention is completed not by the receiving of the article or object in question, but by the Resonance and continued power of the feeling of that satisfaction. That satisfaction lasts as long as you keep it alive in your heart.

How much gratitude is enough? It has to be enough to change you...not once, but every time you tap into it. It is not the fish that satisfied your hunger, it is the knowledge of fishing that can remove your fear of hunger forever.

Chapter 14:

Vaya Con Dios: Healthy Expression

Valuation. Some things are better than others. Some thoughts you have, some actions people take, some political stances, religious doctrines, etc. ...some things are better than others. They are.

When we are learning about different cultures, people, religions, schools of thought, and so on, we are generally taught to at least *try* to approach everything from a relativist stance. This means "adjust for the fact that it is foreign, and know that it is a good idea to someone else for a reason." As a result, we get used to not consciously judging (we judge all the time, it is an unconscious reality that we are either aware of or not). We also get used to having a solid defense against being judged, or subjecting ourselves to certain types of criticism. We also get used to not ever valuating others' actions (which can really help us if we are looking for excuses to keep an abuser close, and most of us are).

This is not to say that we do not criticize ourselves, we do it ennnndlessly. But we criticize ourselves in an unconstructive manner, and one not attached to the actual value of life, which *can* be named.

Baby Bird Busy Being Born

There are many types of motivational energy. There are many reactions, emotions, and volitions that can create behaviors. The descriptive words, like rage, excitement, fury, depression, bereavement, anxiety, etc. can be traced back through the emotional cores of the mental matrix down to only a few base emotions—in fact, I believe, only two. Love and fear.

Both love and fear are natural. Both are necessary, meaningful, and unavoidable aspects of life. But...they are not equal. Just ask the baby bird.

Picture yourself warm, cozy, and safe, having all the nourishment you need. Now imagine that in order to leave that environment, you will have to do something violent and put yourself wholly in harm's way.

That is what we all do to be alive, and I can tell you something for sure: FEAR is not what makes a baby bird break out of its shell. It is passion, and passion is a form that love takes. Passion is risking safety to have experiences.

Whether one believes, like me, that our soul matrix energy risks everything to incarnate for heightened sensation and the friction of subjective experience within a large grid of consciousness, or you believe that some God caused it, or that it's all just chance, **FEAR is DEFINITELY not the reason for the existence of the Universe**.

The baby bird agrees.

So when I speak to anyone (including myself) of risking, trying, and experiencing, and then I mention all the possible negative outcomes that are necessarily connected to such endeavors...know that I am speaking to a baby bird in its comfort zone, and pleading with it to break open its shell. Because, he not busy being born…is busy dying.

The Universe is expanding, time is unfolding, and the chorus of **Creation, Entropy, and Refinement** is playing to countless new dimensions as consciousness experiences it and resonates with it. That is the flow of the Universe, and the flow of life. So…go with God.

"Vaya con Dios." I remember hearing it in old Westerns when I was young. It always sounded way better than "Good luck," or "Have a nice day," so it stuck with me. I learned later that it meant "Go with God." That gave me some pause, because I always figured it was a religious thing, as I could not yet see beyond my own interpretations of how I believed the world worked. But I came to love the phrase, because if divine energy is anything for certain, it is flow from one place to another, like a baby bird out of its shell, and the flow of life to create more life.

The mixture of Love, Risk, and Passion seems to be the space where a term in language is vacant. It is "birth energy," "life force," and "MORE!" mixed in to one. I am not satisfied with any one term in any language for this description. While they are not defined by an exact word, they all fall under the description of "Going with God."

If we look back to Chapter 2, where I outlined a belief in specific incarnations as "Course Curriculum" for soul energies to experience reality subjectively, I touched on the idea that the fullness of experience was the purpose for existence. This is where the existence of divine energy in the Universe, and our behaviors and thoughts in our three- dimensional reality, meet up. Resonance and Rapture.

If we are opened from love, embracing risk and passion and

creativity, we are going with the flow of Universal Energy. If we are in closed from fear, expressing ourselves through anger, resentment, bitterness, and worry, we are fighting Universal Energy. Open...or closed.

The former description is what I call **Healthy Expression**. Healthy Expression is open.

Waveform Harmony in a Discordant World

The world is always expressing itself. We are always expressing ourselves. I have discussed the orchestra of the mind, and that conducting it is truly a feat. It is a feat to be able to tune into the different parts of consciousness, and attempt to get the best music out of the system as a whole after learning the intricacies of each instrument. It is not easy. The result of our abilities in this area, every second of our lives, creates our moment to moment reality. That reality has a quality. It is described by emotional catch words like "happy," "sad," "tired," "stressed," and the ever-present "fine." But the intricacies of our reality create an expression that sounds off throughout the world. This is what we are accountable for, *whether we like it or not.*

This whole phenomenon ends up being like music. We are expressing waveform. ***We are Frequency Delivery Systems for the planet***. We never stop expressing.

I spoke last chapter about how, when we are in a reactive or frightened space, we are all the same. Worried is worried. Frightened is frightened. Angry is angry. That is a single set of frequencies. I have mentioned that, in contrast, when we are calm and joyous, we are all uniquely expressive. That is representative of many different frequencies.

So, let's think about ourselves in healthy expression. We are producing a unique frequency that is positive and creative. I equate this to playing music. We are playing harmonious notes with the world around us. There are millions upon millions of combinations of musical expression, as there are millions upon millions of results from creative moods.

When we are playing music, we can get in tune or touch with the world around us. We can alter the sounds, and mix our moods and behaviors to suit situations in a creative manner. A great example is going out on a date one on one, where two happy people are simply grinding through music until they find harmony in their language, and they start making music out of the situation. It is representative of Synergy of Commune.

But Synergy of Commune can work with the globe as a whole. We have to be expressing, and we have to be focused on engaging with our surroundings. So why is this not as easy as it sounds? Why is the world so discordant? It is because, as a species, we are rarely in a good mood. It is rare. And the mood we are in normally poses a serious problem. We are **White Noise** in the orchestra.

When we look back at the Garden Overrun with Weeds, we see how much fear-presence is a part of our expression matrix. This means it is very rare that we are expressing health. Of course, we mistakenly think that if we are not expressing health we can just withdraw, and not be creating or expressing anything. Nope. We are ALWAYS EXPRESSING. If we are upset and hiding, we are expressing that. If we are in a state of worry, or resentment, we are expressing that. We are expressing our entire reality every second. So the result of being in a bad mood (which is natural and unavoidable) is like white noise in the orchestra of the world surrounding you. It is mind-numbing, irritating, and violent. It also drowns out the sound of anyone that is playing music, and expressing health. This matters. A lot.

I am one of the happiest and most peaceful people I've met. I have not always been this happy, but I have always worked on trying to be. If I look objectively at my frequency delivery...on a good day I make out 50/50. That is crazy high. I am expressing genuine presence 50% of the time, and the other 50% I am white noise. I don't know anyone who for sure tops that amount (in my immediate life). The Dalai Lama tops it; he's probably around 80/20. But he doesn't have to do anything but be happy. He doesn't have to wake up early and drive his kids to school, or go to work, or pay bills, or compromise his soul to make ends meet. So comparing anyone to him is really silly. The hardest thing about life is trying to be fully present and divine *while in the midst of a storm of stressors.*

To get to this 50% I have a ton of tools (from bouts with panic attacks for a decade), and very few real stressors. So...I have plenty of help to get to my 50%. AND EVEN THEN, IT IS **JUST** 50%. And in that 50%, there are streaks of days and weeks where I am all white noise with almost no break.

So please understand: we are not shooting for a perfect score. We are not shooting for "most" of the time. We are shooting for moments. ***We are shooting for "more" moments today than yesterday.*** That has been my goal for seven years. That is how long I've actually been trying to express health to the world.

If we were to look down at a group of adults, say walking the streets of New York, or in a mall. If we were to tag these people that were expressing health with their own unique and expressive symbol, we would not be tagging very many. Maybe 1%, by my estimation. The rest would show as hooded figures (that's my symbol for featurelessness of not expressing health). If you were to go to a seven-year-old's birthday party at a skating rink an hour into the party after everyone was comfortable, and look at them, you would get mostly unique and healthy expressions. The weight of adult responsibility and knowledge of the world as a whole is the prime factor for stress and fear.

So what do we do, knowing this is the situation? The world is predominantly white noise. Everyone is affected by it, and everyone is a part of it. What do we do? There is an answer, of course.

We get ourselves expressing health, and making music. We listen hard for others making music, and support them when we find them. We help relieve the stressors that push people into White Noise. We teach and validate Healthy Expression.

I have so much hope for the world. I have seen so much gained in this area, and such major changes as a result of those gains.

We understand in a common-sense way that our moods affect the world. We know they are physical and palpable things. We know when someone is in a bad mood, and we know that everyone's moods affect each other. I have basically taken an entire chapter to explain the obvious fact that our moods matter. This is because we are coming to level of time and focus that will allow us to engage in accountability for our moods.

I remember my first "aha" moment with mood. I was reading Castaneda (*Journey to Ixtlan*), and Don Juan jumped down Carlos' throat about his crappy attitude. He said basically, "This could be the last moment of your life and you are wasting it on this whiny mood." That was in the "Death as an advisor" chapter.

So I understand why we have not been accountable before, and not walked into an arena that forced us to confront our moods in a committed manner. It is REALLY difficult to lose all day. It is demoralizing. Our moods subjugate us and enslave us, and to enter into a relationship with our own personal plantation owner looks demeaning and awful. But it is the most empowering thing we can ever do. I can make that promise.

Going about our day with the understanding that everything we do and feel matters is a daunting way to live. But if we take a second and look at it, we may realize how much of our own power we allow to surface when we approach life in this manner. "I AM SO POWERFUL THAT MY MOODS AFFECT THE WORLD!" Say it out loud for me, right now, would you please?

That's a pretty nice thing for us to say, and it is fully accurate. It's heavy, though, because after we understand this, every time we get our butts kicked by reality and get moved off our spot, we are accountable for our frequency's output. We are also the only ones who are capable of bringing it back into alignment with Creation Energy. This was described in the section on The Beach of Quiet Emotion, where the smoke from a cigarette needs to be cleared due its drastic discordant affect. All of that responsibility for behavior and involvement falls on us.

⊂⟩⟨⊃

You can see them, and they can see you

We are asked to face our demons. We are asked by those who love us. We are asked by society. And we ask ourselves... because only we can protect others from the demons within us.

Seems like it's not such a task. It is, though. Once we begin to travel within the world of self-awareness, we are confronted with an issue. We must be able to act and remain calm when faced with our own failures. The things we cannot control within ourselves, the reactions and frustrations and worries that damage our peace of mind and threaten our environment through our mood...those are the demons. *And once we become aware of them, our accountability for their existence is painful.*

In more than a few superhero mythos stories (as well as in accounts of sorcery), the power you attain becomes the object that attracts your enemy. This is true in many ways, but I will just deal with the one that comes with the awareness of healthy expression.

With the mythos of demons and devils, those who walk among us and Influenced our actions, the way to enter the battlefield was to get in touch with our ability to see these intruding demons. But, as it is said, when we can see them, they can see us. *We become vulnerable to the power of the level of reality we are engaging.* This is a story, but the analogy it is making is for everyone. The more of our reality we wish to engage, the more we will be confronted with.

So when we are looking into Healthy Expression, we have to be aware that "unhealthy expression" is the contra-indicated reality that we do NOT want. Whenever we engage, rather than withdraw, we have to come to be at peace with the dualism that we are presented with. The richness of this dualism and the discernments we make within our chaos-of-moments is the main staple of an experiential consciousness. *It is in this realm of confusion that we live our way into the answers we feel we were destined to find*. This is where we get Resonance, and Rapture. This is where each of us becomes a knight in shining armor.

Some expressions are better than others. Some are with the flow of life, and some are not. We are going to be presented with our failures if we invest ourselves and try. If we participate in the mess we are going to be made aware of *our mess*. Those messes, along with our fears, are the demons we are now going to be able to see, and the demons we are going to be vulnerable to.

This sounds kinda sexy, honestly. It sounds like it fits the terms "warrior" or "master" or "dragon." And in truth, this IS the case. But the romanticism we may feel now gives way to humiliation in practice. It gives way because it is not a fire-breathing dragon that we must slay, but a basket full of unfolded laundry. It is not we who must stand in the fire without blinking an eye, but we who must sit in traffic in Southern California without descending into road rage. It is we who must make peace with having burned dinner, not vanquishing our enemies. And it is not the devil we must cast out, but our own self- nullifying critique of our shortcomings throughout an average day.

I can't control it, it's not my fault, but only I can make it better.

Most of this chapter has been centered on how to manage reactions, as well as descriptions and evaluations of expressions. But as of yet I have not said much about being proactive in this area. Being proactive here is one thing we can do to make life really beautiful.

We are taught most of our lives how to react, and attempt to control, but we are so rarely given information on how to be creative and proactive within our consciousness. We ARE given techniques when it comes to the arts. We are given scales on the piano, tracing and freehand drawing, color mixing, etc., when it comes to creative "productions." But there is something within us that is an invisible product. It is *imagination*, and our understanding of the power of this tool is Neanderthal-ish.

We are artists of being alive, artists of consciousness, but unlike arts with visible "products," we are rarely in touch with our epiphanic creations. Artists are taught that they can take a picture in their head and make it appear on a canvas or drawing, musicians take a sound and create it on a recording. But as healthy expressive people we are not trained to take our love for the world and MAKE…THAT…REAL. This basic reality is the source of all healing practices.

Imagination

Think of something. Connect with it. Validate the connection with your conscious mind. And finally…have an emotional reaction. That is imagination. That is breathing life into your thoughts. That is the practice that turns the imprint of artistry in our creative minds into a dazzling glory on the canvas of the world.

Those four steps change everything. If you have used prayer, or focus, or intention, then this is not news to you. It may be the first time you've seen it written out, but it should not be a surprise by any means.

The generation of thought, in my humble opinion, is miraculous. I have no idea where it comes from. I know we get to take part in it, and that is enough for us to use it as a tool. It can be a tool, because everything we think of has a signature. There is a physical manifestation to every thought, and within that manifestation lies Influence. The beautiful thing about this Influence is that its power is not limited to our subjective reality.

My uncle, an MD and energetic healer, tried explaining the power of imagination to my mother. She is a therapist, and for all intents and purposes, one of the most powerful healers I have been near. She, however, does not see herself as such. After a group healing session he thanked her for doing the heavy lifting with a certain client of his. She told him that she didn't actually do anything, to which he responded, "Of course you did." She took care to tell my uncle that all she did was imagine the person feeling better and being stronger. That was all she did. He told her the truth: "That is all that anyone can do, and all that needs to be done. That is what healing is."

There is not an extra part. The amount of faith we have in our imagination varies from person to person. That faith is a powerful aspect of the impact our creativity has on the world around us. But the nuts-and-bolts of healing intention is simply the use of our creativity to summon an image of what we want in our imaginations, and our conscious connection to it.

Think of it. Connect with it. Validate the connection with your conscious mind. And finally, have an emotional reaction. That is imagination. That is the process. *That is our Healthy Expression changing the fabric of reality every second.* We can take part any time.

The example I am going to share on this is present in my reality right now (which is consistently the case as I've been writing this book). My boy is sick. He has the flu. So, how do we go about Healthy Expression here? This is where it matters. This is also where we can really get ourselves motivated because seeing our children in distress is beyond unnerving. So, any time something like this happens, it presents a great opportunity for exercise and growth.

My stepson went to school on Thursday, and was kinda tired and out of it. So be it. I got a call from the school nurse at 10:30 explaining that I had to come get him because he had a 102 fever. Now is when the monitoring starts.

My reactive-self felt angry and guilty because I hadn't noticed the fever, or seen it coming. I also felt powerless and afraid because I believe (whether or not it's true, I do believe it) that his immune system is something I should be able to have some effect on, and I had failed. That was my reaction. That…is worry. That is NOT Healthy Expression. That is creating the examples of anger and frustration and releasing them into the world so that they multiply. No. Not doing it. So I stopped myself, and using Conscious Validation I slowly eliminated them from my thought field.

What filled the space instead, was a picture. This is what I do. I picture my son's body fighting bacteria, and the active matrix of his immune system working seamlessly and efficiently to raise his core temperature and cook out the bacteria. I imagine the waves of bacteria crumbling before a mighty army of white blood cells. I imagine his body burning through the invading adversary, and being in the grip of the battle until it is finished. Then I picture him healthy and happy, doing the things he does when he is healthy and happy. That is the picture I create, and the picture I connect with. I validate its existence consciously, and that gives me a feeling of power and joy. That joy rings loud and clear. *It is the punctuation on my creation.* It is Healthy Expression. I share this vision with him when I pick him up from school, and tell him what the plan is. He sees my calm and powerful emotion, and he responds in kind. He does not worry. He knows his body is battling. He knows he is strong. He has no doubts, or worries. Now there are two of us engaged consciously in a matching vision of reality.

But we do not stop at the two of us. I let his father and mother know. Later his brother gets in on it also. We all capture around this idea. We are all involved and invested in our imagination of his soon-to-be-healthy reality. We are all confident in the power of our imagination. He sees this, and it makes him confident. It makes him unafraid. It makes him strong. It supports his immune system and releases his stress. That is how imagination heals human beings.

The description above is specific. Our stories are specific. How we find our way into expressing with the flow of our healthiest manifestations of reality doesn't matter. It matters that we do it, and that we make a habit out of it.

There are more things going on in my life than my boy having the flu. There are MANY more things in the world on my **List of Great Concerns** than my boy having the flu. Each one of them can be a part of our creative matrix of expression. With each one (as with all things), we can be reactive to their existence, or creative in concert with them. One is Healthy Expression, the other is worry. Worry does not make us strong. It does not make us feel alive. And while one may argue in vain that positive thinking and creative imagination are a waste of time, they are not the harbinger of doubt, fear, and confusion that worry becomes as it passes through our consciousness into our reality. Thinking positively can't hurt us. Worry does.

Each item on my List of Great Concerns, an evolving list of aspects of reality that I am invested in changing, can be a subject of my imagination. This can happen at any time. No matter how large or small we believe our power to be (I believe I am pretty powerful), there is no denying that our imagination and our connection to its creations Influence the world. At the very least, *they make US stronger.* They make us more vital as human beings. That in itself is enough to warrant making them a daily priority.

Engaging in imagination in concert with our daily activities is what I call **World Painting**. I love doing it. It is a beginning step into Transmutation, and it simply beautifies our thought processes. It is a gracious and joyous practice. And, like gratitude, it is very difficult (impossible) to employ while experiencing worry or complaint. It makes us powerful. Participation comes with power. Being an active participant in the experience of our world, running through our individuated consciousness, makes us co-creators with the forces of life all around us.

World Painting

It's a big canvas we have to work with. It's a big world. It is overwhelming to hold a Perspective of relationship with it. It is overwhelming, and empowering, to live in the understanding that we affect all of it every second we are drawing breath.

World Painting is a mixture of meditation, creative expression, imagination, and prayer all working together in harmony with the ocean of reality. It is a conscious effort at first. It is not natural for us, a small consciousness in a huge world, to assume a relationship with everything we come into contact with.

Being taught that control is a goal, and that we have limitations does not help the actualization of World Painting. It's akin to being taught how to dance in specific manner to specific music. Knowing how to dance to a particular tune is lovely; *thinking there is ever a good reason not to dance is not so lovely*. We cannot control everything, though, just like we cannot always choose the music. Many refrain from dancing to foreign music. This is one of many things to unlearn as we move into this new heightened state of engagement with our world. We dance here, we don't get wrapped up in whether the music is what we're used to, or what we have been taught. No matter what we have been used to, it cannot stop us from creating a new habit, and the new habit we create will go further toward unlearning stolid habits than anything else will. So let's create some new habits.

World Painting, as an expression, is the pinnacle of every day habit. My best days are littered with this behavior (it is a behavior, like meditation). There is always room for more of it. It is joyously addictive. It is healthy to engage in it, and it is healthy for the subjects of our engagement.

World Painting consists of taking the canvas of our reality, and upgrading it in our mind. This is not limited to anything. It just has to sit well with us once we've thought it. For instance, if we think about upgrading our life by injuring someone we dislike, I can guarantee that we will receive a very quick visceral negative reaction. I always do. That is immediate karma, and pretty much all of us have it built in.

There is a good chance that the subject matters may give us pause. For instance you may be wondering to yourself "What kind of situations can we use this with?"

The answer is "All of them."

Everything from managing our internal energy through visualization, to thinking about a promotion a friend may get, to wanting our favorite band to do their first album since 2005... all situations can get painted. They are all canvas, and it is our place to engage them, and give them the loving attention of our care and imagination.

On my good days I do much more of this than on other days. It takes my patience, joy, focus, and confidence to participate in this. If I am not doing so well, it's unlikely that I am going to engage in it much. Those days are bummers for me.

One of the most basic forms of imagination I use deals with visualizing myself. When I am engaged in upgrading my idea of myself, I generate an energetic picture as well as a physical construct. Any feeling I have is visual, and I have those two pictures to work with when I think of myself. On an energetic level (and this is an example of what I do, *not to be confused with* what everyone should do), I picture energy flowing in from the top of my chakra set through the roof of my skull and energy flowing up and in through my feet. I picture that energy meeting and forming a tornado-like swirling pattern and circulating like a storm through my whole body. That is what I look like when I feel good. I reinforce the visual throughout the day, and if I begin not to feel so good, I take a few moments and focus on visualizing it very clearly.

I can also picture my body. I can picture every system in my body. It is true that I have pre-med knowledge of the human body, and that helps here, but anyone can get on one of

those fancy internet machines and look up a couple of pictures of what their body looks like. It's not rocket science, just
Biology 101. So, during the day along with my energetic visualization, I can reinforce my healthy feelings of well-being by
seeing the processes of my healthy body in my imagination.
I usually do this after eating, when exercising, while waking
up, while driving, and just about any other time I can snag a
few seconds to engage the process of living on a second to
second basis. Our involuntary muscles and organs are busy
with this activity all day, we might as well lend a few moments of conscious brain power toward it.

If you were to address only your own physical and energetic conditioning with this practice, you could busy yourself
with it all of your waking hours. So, ask yourself, "How often
do I engage in visualizing my own health, if ever?"

This principle should be attached to meditation. As soon
as the mind becomes clear, and it can begin to recognize
individual incoming thoughts, the next practice should be to
imagine the *healthiest version of these thoughts*. In this manner, any moment of stillness can become a fertile environment for expression. Then, it becomes a habit.

But, it is not limited to the self. In fact...it is not limited
at all.

It is vital that we understand that World Painting is an every-mo-
ment option. It is also vital to know that we do not get to take part in
choosing what comes into our reality, but we nonetheless bear the
gifts and injuries of how we deal with what comes into our realities.
There is nothing we cannot improve.

Life...Is Tips

I was a waiter and bartender for a long time. I learned a lot about myself by watching how I maneuvered through a restaurant during a shift. On any given night I would be dealt a pretty variable amount of groups of people. How I managed those specific interactions determined how my night would end up.

We are presented customers, *we do not choose them*. We have a basic job to fulfill, and that is the minimum. Take orders, bring food and drink, and refrain from being a downer. That is the minimum. But...I was working for tips.

Working for tips is an awesome example, because it is a *blind errand*. For those of you in the service industry, you know, as well as I do, that a portion of customers are not going to change from their fixed amount of tip-output no matter what you do. Sometimes this number will be a high percentage, sometimes small. But we don't know who those people are beforehand, just like we do not know which areas of our lives will yield dividends when we put our energy into them with our imagination.

This is a synopsis of investment and hope that plays out at our neighborhood diner every night. *Every incoming bit of information* we draw to us for processing, and *every reality we are confronted with* on a daily basis gives us the same opportunity. We can do the bare minimum, or we can try to do more. Using imagination to improve our world in real time as it comes at us from a million directions is trying for more. I like doing that.

We get a lot placed in front of us during an average day. As a waiter, I have everything from parties of ten for birthdays, first dates, foreigners, first-timers, old unhappy couples, finicky eaters, know-it-alls, people in a dreadful hurry, people who waited too long, groups with multiple kids drinking fifteen sodas, people exhausted from a long day, people totally relaxed after an awesome day, newlyweds, etc. And they all have one thing in common: ***They are people I can affect***.

Their day was bad? I can make it good. Their day was good? I can make it better. First date? I can allow them every opportunity for intimacy. Birthday? I can make it memorable (I'm not telling you the things I've done to make it memorable). Parents being annoyed by their kids? I can take the attention away and take the pressure off. I can do something to make life better at *every* table.

But does it guarantee me a better tip? Nope. It does not. Just like putting effort into our imagination does not guarantee the outcome we are storyboarding in our head. But for the important question: "Does it improve my tip count over the length of my job?" Yes. It does. *Does engaging as much of your reality as possible pay dividends in effects for the betterment of the world?* **YES**. I know it does, and *you* know it does.

Can we do it for everyone? Nope. We are not always in possession of the necessary tools. Can we do it all the time? Nope. We are not always at 100%, for reasons that we cannot control. But we can focus on doing it as much as possible. And if we focus on it, the things that distract us from being able to perform in this capacity do, over time, *disintegrate into non-factors*.

This was my job. It made sense to me to take every situation and improve it. I looked afterwards at my family, and saw that they were no different. I looked at the grocery store clerks, the cop that pulled me over, the other drivers on the road with me, the other parents at the Little League game, and everyone else I ran into during the day, and I saw that they were the same as my customers. Then I looked at ideas and world events, like politics, oil spills, pollution, anger, war, resentment, poverty, starvation, and bullying on all levels of society, and saw that they could be improved in the same way.

They all come in and sit down at our restaurant. We have a basic relationship to fulfill in regard to them, **but we can do so much more than the minimum**. Even if we get stiffed, the byproduct is the knowledge that we did our best, and the confidence that comes with it. That confidence is priceless. But we will not always get stiffed. Even in the most long-term and global goals, if we are patient, we will see improvement everywhere.

Using imagination to create new worlds and realities for all situations, and expressing the positive emotion running through us when we do, is the actualization of Hope. This is how we do it.

There is a better expression. It takes our focus, and participation. It takes a willingness to engage.

We have to tell ourselves it's not a big deal. We have to tell ourselves it doesn't matter, because we are too sensitive to our own failures, and lack the Perspective that is needed. We have to tell ourselves that we do not have power, because otherwise we incriminate ourselves for everything in the world we haven't done. Each time we consciously notice what we could be doing, it brings the pang of failure for every time we missed in recent memory (*especially if things are not going so well).* This means that engaging in the first step of this behavior gets us burned a little.

But it is a big deal. We do care. We are powerful. And it does matter. We have to be strong enough to face the fact that we are powerful, but not all-powerful. The focus we use and the experience we draw on are limited. That is the nature of subjective consciousness in the Universe.

So why should we work through the pain of failure, to use our imagination, which is not guaranteed to work? When it doesn't work, we feel humiliated. When we miss, we feel regret and guilt, and when we look out at the amassing infinite world imposing on our finite attention, we feel duly overwhelmed. Why do it?

The drop of water says it matters.

The Monk Meditating and the Water: A 70% Story

An often quoted, yet seldom-appreciated experiment is that of Dr. Masuro Emoto, who found a way to get images of water molecules after a freezing process. The water is put into a situation, and then frozen. Then it is observed. The water that is presented with loving calm meditation produces a marvelous- looking, intricate structure. It is glorious to behold. The water that is put into an environment with negative emotions (anger, violence)…crystallizes in an asymmetrical manner. It seems kind of like sludge in comparison to the "work of art" that was in the positive meditative environment. In fact, the water engaged with anger has the same visual qualities as water that was physically polluted.

The only difference in the experiment was the thought content of the people in close proximity. That is the mental mood of the room where the water was in the freezing process.

This experiment can start a TON of unnecessary arguments. A TON. It starts a ton because we are not in the mood to deal with the magnitude of our power here, so let's just skip all the extrapolations from this for right this second, and ask ourselves a question.

You are given a choice between the two waters, and you have to drink a gallon. Which one are you going to choose?

Now extrapolate. You get to choose the water that is running through your whole body...which water do you choose?

You get to choose the water that is filling the rivers and oceans...which do you choose?

Did you pick the magnificent-looking water? Do you think there's a chance that the loving focused meditative environment MAY have had something to do with that? If so, do you believe that there is a chance such mental focus could do that to things *besides* water? Maybe?

Do you think it is worth trying? Do you think it is worth focusing on? Do you think it is worth *prioritizing*?

I do.

So this is the deal, ***the canvas of the world is not going to paint itself***. It's not. The music of harmony in the world is not going to come into alignment unless everyone picks up their instrument. The art that gets onto a canvas, and the music on the recording do not appear spontaneously. They are first brought into existence in the mind of the creator. This is where it happens. We use our knowledge of the medium to bring it to life.

The world does not get healed, or changed, without us investing our time and imagination. We use our knowledge of our world (or a person, or a specific thing), and our picture of how we want it to be, and we BREATHE LIFE INTO IT. This is not a crazy, ambiguous spell. This is "think of it, connect with it, validate the connection, and have an emotional reaction." Four steps.

Chapter 15:

Discernments in Expression: Discipline and Remorse

Not all expressions are equal. In the same way we have differentiated between types of expressions, we are going to look at how we connect to goals for ourselves and others. This occurs through judgment. We are going to do this because some manners of going about this are synonymous with health and growth (discernment), and some are not (reaction).

Many of our habits for trying to improve ourselves and the world around us involve a huge amount of unnecessary violence, and as a result, very little positive effect. The ways in which we take in and assess the world around us, as well as the means with which we attempt to make improvements, are available for in-depth analysis and great insight. From this insight, changes can be made, and Perspectives can be utilized or discarded as necessary.

But we first have to understand that the way we look at any situation--those that include us, or those that do not--naturally comes to us from one point of view. We also have to understand that one point of view on anything is *never* enough. Ever.

The reason it is not enough is that *one Perspective is simply not representative of the reality of any situation,* even though one Perspective may be completely correct or accurate. This is not an "everyone is right" moment. This is a "that doesn't matter" moment. A one-Perspective take doesn't matter, because it is not a creative idea. It is simply a reaction opinion. And reactions, whether right or wrong, are not useful. They do not keep a dynamic world moving in the right direction, and are thus, useless.

I am going to examine a few practices we take part in from more than a few angles. This is not just to point out what things work and what things do not, but to take us through our exposed consciousness as it relates to these daily activities. The practice I want to push *entails identifying poles within a focus*, something that is helpful vs. something that is utterly unhelpful, to be exact. I am using these practices because they are the ones I believe are the best examples, and they are also the ones that could use our focus the most.

We will deal with Discipline and Remorse. The poles are "restriction" and "expression" for Discipline. The poles are "regret-shame-guilt" and "imprint usage" for Remorse.

The Refinement of the Gray

One of the biggest issues in addressing Perspectives is that we think there is a spot to land, a "right spot," rather than a bunch of spots to land with different aspects of our consciousness. The truth is that in every situation we are given the black and white poles, without ever being able to hit one or the other cleanly. We land sort of "all over the place" and try to come up with something black or white because it creates less Cognitive Dissonance to do so. Very specifically, we are going to hit BOTH poles in every situation we encounter, and then we get to try to adjust from that reaction to create something more positive than what we started with.

I call this practice **The Refinement of the Gray**. It is about slowly making adjustments in the gray-scaled reality of the world. This is necessary. It is necessary because *our reactions, while capable of being Influenced over time,* **will never be fully under our control**. Thinking they are under our control will lead us directly to regret, guilt, and shame. That will take us right out of the game before the description of the rules has even been laid out. This is not about bossing our responses around. It is about allowing the totality of our responses to come forward, then using Conscious Validation to sift through them, and finally validating a response that weights the many reactions we had *in accordance with our soul's Resonance*. This is about working with our reactions and making them stronger.

In practice, **this means that we are going to combine reactions, and refine them into an expression**. This is very close to an overall day of Conscious Validation, where we sculpt a total reality out of many uncontrollable processes and some very reasonable intentions.

When we are looking at our history, we can all think of a moment where we made a mistake and something bad happened as a result (if you cannot, please take your unicorn and go). Having this in our past can make us stronger, or weaker, *depending solely on what we do with the event*. If we beat ourselves up about the event in question, and feel guilty about it, we are simply incurring damage for something that happened. It does not do anything else. However, if we dispassionately assess the situation, and feel the depth of the moment in question without distracting ourselves with some judgment about it, we can use it to Influence future decisions in a positive way.

So, we got too drunk and were awful hung over. If we think of getting too drunk and beat ourselves up, we will feel bad. That's it. And odds are, when presented with a situation where we may overdo it again, we will be more likely to drink like that again as a result. That is the outline for the creation of a negative spiral. Those are really destructive, and all too common.

But...if we simply note how we felt when we were hung over, and we do not have any guilt or shame, we will be more likely to say to ourselves "Hey, I do not want to feel like that; I remember it clearly, and it was very unpleasant." We will be more likely to not have bad consequences again. Our recall of the event will be tied to a calm consciousness, one that can prepare us for situations in advance, and make it more likely for us to choose more wisely. This means that, in this one section, our life will have gotten better from experience.

That is an improvement. That is what we are after: taking our experiences and turning them into useful Influences. Guilt and shame...not useful Influences. They create more destructive behavior.

But we cannot control how we respond. So we are going to get a mix. This is why the gray of our reactions must be refined. *What we do with the mix, over the course of our lives, will go a long way toward creating our quality of life.* We are going to get guilt and shame alongside being able to put ourselves empathically in our history. We are going to have to open the flood gates, and sift through the incoming reality for the best possible information, and do the best we can with what we find.

This means, that as we trace back over our past to help us Influence our future decisions, we have to allow our guilt to present itself, and do our best to eliminate it from the process of creating a new future. This happens in the poles of every **Situation of Discernment**. A Situation of Discernment is an opportunity. It is a moment when we are capable of using ideals to create a reality that is more of what we want in our world, and less of what we don't, *while knowing that ALL are going to be present*. Every moment of discernment contains all possibilities, and a cacophony of feelings screaming to be heard. We must be calm and focused, to gain Influence here. We must express our discipline.

Discernment is a form of Discipline, and having Healthy Discipline makes us a powerful player in our own consciousness, rather than a victim. Here, the idea is that we want to use Expression Discipline, rather than **Restrictive Discipline**. Being restrictive is crippling. Its Influence is negative and chaotic. It is disharmonious.

Expression Discipline is based in creation, and hope. Its aim is to use focus and attention to bring about a future made up of characteristics we want. It is going to the gym because we enjoy working toward a strong healthy body, rather than because there is something wrong with the one we have. It is looking upon a past mistake with the hope of learning from our mistake rather than incurring pain from guilt. It is doing homework or studying to ingrain the information and integrate knowledge, making ourselves more powerful, rather than just doing it to get it done and out of the way. It is telling the truth because we want to be accountable, rather than for fear of punishment getting caught in a lie. It is discipline that leads to morality, and integrity. It creates the adult we are constantly becoming throughout our lives, and does so in a way we can be engaged with, and proud of. I will spend much more time on the negative, as it is more prevalent in our world.

Restriction Discipline is critical and non-creative. It is no different from using fear of punishment as a motivation for good behavior. Does it work in simplistic momentary ways? Yes...it does. "I'm so stupid for eating that; I have to eat better!" "I take such crappy care of myself; I need to work out!" "I need to stop choosing to be around people who treat me badly!" "I really need to stop thinking so negatively!" "I can't believe how stupid I was to make that mistake; I won't do that again!" ...they all lead to "I will stop behaving badly because I am so angry at myself!"

It doesn't work. When we do this, we haven't actually given ourselves any usable Influence. We've just smacked a puppy for peeing on the rug. That's it. Except that when dealing with consciousness, the task was not like potty training, it was to use cognitive matrices mixed with experiences gathered over our entire lifetime to improve our ability to make informed decisions on the fly...which is more like asking the puppy to do calculus.

We are going to get the restrictive reactions, but if we Refine the Gray, we can begin moving more toward expressing Discipline, and being creative.

Expressions of Discipline Versus Restriction and Critique

Discipline is a form of self-love. Eating healthy, exercising, and tending to the mind and body are simply good things. Tending the consciousness is what we are looking at this chapter, because in the same way the activities above improve our physical and chemical realities with our body, tending our consciousness improves the relationships we have with every aspect of our world.

This is important because we want to learn from our mistakes so we can make less of them. It is important because we want to take good advice and be able to use it, rather than having the knowledge we attain never turn to usable wisdom.

So how do we relate to our mistakes? Do we relate to them in a manner that makes us focus on solutions, or do we relate to them in a way that cripples us due to negative emotional overload? In general, everyone experiences a bit of both, and that is why we have to focus on the reactions and practices we want to be influencing our behaviors. This is not easy.

It is easy to judge ourselves harshly. And it seems like it works *because we can FEEL it*. The harshness of the judgment can really get our attention. But it doesn't work a lick. Yelling at ourselves about not exercising is as close to the planning and carrying out of exercise as drinking a fifth of vodka is. I mean that literally. The energy we need to pursue and follow through on discipline is sapped by the emotion caused by our negative critique.

This is tricky. It is tricky, because when we are looking at a mistake emotionally, we have the small picture. In the small picture we see restriction and criticism work. We see it work because we are devaluing our state of mind at the time, and focusing only on an outside goal. We see it work because we assume we will recognize the situation and be flooded by the same feeling, and that it will motivate us. But no two situations are the same because WE are never coming at them with the same Perspective or state of mind. There is another reason that this behavior line-up does not work.

Although we see ourselves possibly behaving in a specific manner as a result of negative reinforcement, we do not see that our overall health and happiness suffer when we go about attending to goals by beating ourselves up. We lose in this manner by focusing on a goal that is a means, like *"going to the gym,"* and **giving up our end of happiness and health to get it done.**

I want to reiterate this. If we are going to the gym to become a healthy and happy person, but we use shame and guilt to motivate ourselves to get there, we are undermining our big-picture goal. Keeping focused on our overall goals of joy and health demand that we treat ourselves in a specific manner when dedicating ourselves to improving our lives. It is incongruent to use cruelty with ourselves to improve our health and happiness.

Being able to prioritize within our consciousness is a huge task, and it takes constant focus.

The reason that the focus behind a behavior matters when it comes to expressing discipline is that basically every human being walking the planet has the ability to self-sabotage, and to be self-destructive. We can control self- sabotage, so it makes us feel powerful. That is a tough temptation (see Chapter 6). But we cannot allow these practices to keep their traction.

Making ourselves feel bad about mistakes lessens our ability to incorporate usable wisdom from them. *Making ourselves feel bad about mistakes lessens our ability to incorporate usable wisdom from them.* True story. Taking on a habit of making ourselves feel bad cripples our ability to learn from any of our mistakes. This is because we do not imprint information during moments of guilt and shame; we imprint emotion.

Wonder why you keep making the same mistakes over and over? Because you are too busy feeling bad about your mistake to learn from it.

I have a perfect example from my youth when I was riding a bike. I went over a jump and busted my leg up. Furious and humiliated, I got up and went over the jump again, and busted even worse. I didn't realize why I had fallen the first time, because I was too angry and emotional. So I just went and made the exact same mistake and fell again.

Learning, like creation, is incompatible with negative emotion.

It takes discipline to learn from mistakes. We have to resist the temptation to fall prey to our own emotions in a moment of failure, and concentrate on imprinting the external lessons. This is very hard because our internal world is in pain. The moment of failure is a crushing loss. It is brutal and unforgiving, leaving us without an obvious recourse. But in every moment of loss, the bounty of the moment is still fresh, and the wisdom of how those mistakes were made is close enough to imprint.

I remember when I was young and playing baseball, I was up to bat at the end of the game in a clutch situation. It was a 3-2 count, bases loaded, two outs. I froze. I looked at strike 3 and the game was over. I exploded into tears and lurched my way back to the dugout in shame. We are not going to be able to control our reactions all the time, but luckily, *our first reaction is not the only reaction we get to have.* When I got back to the dugout I relaxed, and I looked around at everyone present as they were busying themselves with picking up the equipment. I thought to myself "Wow, this is how it feels to blow it." And I stopped beating myself up. I still felt horribly sad, and the tears were still flowing, but I was fortunate enough to have the presence of mind to go back to the pitch. I used the emotion I was feeling to imprint my memory of the pitch, *rather than the memory of feeling horrible*. I remembered vividly my mistakes. I was aware (I was ten, but still aware). I realized first, that I was hoping he threw a bad pitch. I was hoping for a way out of the pressure without having to swing. I remembered that. I remembered seeing the ball come out of his hand and within a hundredth of a second I knew it was a strike, and realized that I had decided beforehand that I was too scared to swing. *I was too scared to look foolish swinging at a bad pitch to even try*. I used the wealth of feeling to imprint my memory of the specifics of the failure, not my own dissatisfaction with myself. I Refined the Gray, and focused on the helpful reactions. I was in five more of these situations before my Little League career came to an end… and four out of five times, we won on my swing. The other time I was out in the field and failed to recognize the situation as being the same. It is very difficult to see situations as the same, even if they occur during a baseball game at the end when you have to make a play. During life the situations are *ALWAYS different*.

We have so little time and so much experience to sift through during these moments that any negative emotion we are experiencing is going to make it nearly impossible to take in the moment in a way that lets it imprint.

This is Discipline. All of our disciplines in this life are in place to make us stronger, and wiser. They are the difference between us using and wasting moments. They are the difference between experience being a tool for the future, and it being a handicap.

Remorse is an area where these theories and practices can really be broken down and analyzed effectively, because remorse is in the past. We have so many angles from which to address our past that milking it for information and strength is a well we can visit often for improving our abilities. On the flipside of that, if our goal is to cripple ourselves, then we have an equally vast well of experience to dip into for negative emotional memory.

All of these tools are powerful, and depending on how we feel after engaging in these practices, we can know to what extent we are using them responsibly and effectively.

The Tools of Remorse: Guilt and Shame versus Imprint Usage

Using our history to affect our future decisions is part of our behavioral matrix. It is not something that can be chosen or avoided, just worked with. Sometimes we can control and plan our missions into our memory banks as they regard our future, and sometimes we are thrown carelessly at memories and have to deal with them, the same as inclement weather. The more we go at this practice on purpose, in a controlled manner, the easier it is to manage the moments of inclement weather when they arise.

One of the reasons that this well of information is so bountiful is because we get to play Observer for ourselves in another Perspective. Whatever Perspective of ours made what turned out to be a mistake was doing what it thought was best.

The next section will be on Judgment, **Healthy Judgment**, and this will take us deeply through how we view other people and their realities, but the main crux of this will be that through Psychological Determinism, we can understand that everyone did the best they could, and made the best and only decision they could, given their environmental information at the moment. If we can use this when we look at ourselves in our own past, we can take a good shot at removing harmful mental reactions while we're trying to learn.

So let's look at a situation that that is one we have likely all been through in one way or another, but that is serious enough for us to remember deeply. Betrayal. I have betrayed people. The first clear moment I remember betraying anyone, I was five years old. I told a secret and ruined something for someone (my friend got an ATV for his birthday). I am pretty sure we've all said something we shouldn't have, but it is really a sting when you get older and you truly break someone's trust or heart. So let's get to one of those moments.

When I was fourteen my friend told me something about the boy she liked (a friend of mine) that was not for his ears. It was juicy, though. So…I told him. That was my first time losing a friend, and it wasn't via mean message or a text. It was a horribly upset phone call from a girl who had trusted me, and whom I had betrayed.

It was really painful. She was really hurt and exposed and humiliated, and I had caused it. It was a mess. She and I were both hurt, I felt terrible from every side of it, and our friendship was honestly over. This is a perfect moment to look at for a learning experience, because it was a failure at every level, with irreparable loss as an added bonus.

Given that this was many years ago, I have had plenty of opportunities to go back and get my **Remorse Perspective** all tuned up. Let's see what types of reactions I had, which were not healthy:

Guilt: "Oh my God, I ruined everything!"

Shame: "I am a terrible friend; I deserve to be alone."

Frustration: "I wish I could just beat myself up and change what I did."

These examples are all painful, so naturally my ego began to get defensive, and followed with…

Anger at her: "Why did she have to react like that; why can't she forgive me!"

Dismissal of the betrayal: "It isn't really that big of a deal!"

Those are all acts of violence. They are inaccurate and they do NOTHING. Nothing. They are also the natural and first reactions we are going to have, so it is important to get to know them intimately as we make mistakes throughout our lives. They do not change. We blame and beat up ourselves, and then we blame people outside of us, and then we try to dismiss the reality entirely. That is a mechanism that we can go ahead and get comfy with. What happens AFTER all that junk recycles through our brains is where we make our imprints. Those are creative, and they incorporate the experience into something we can use.

Here they are; notice the difference.

"I got really excited about being liked by my male friend and betrayed my female friend as a result. I needed the attention and it made me feel like a big shot to tell a secret. I also was getting some revenge because I did not get the type of romantic attention from her that I wanted, and exposing what she said to me in confidence was the only way I could hurt her. I resented her for liking my friend and not me."

Wow. Those help, don't they? I can look at that set of observations and really imprint some wisdom. The notes on resentment, and using secrets to gain favor with friends—wow, that is real usable data I have found in that situation. Look at how powerful those motivating factors were! I need to really look out for those realities being present in the future if I want to *not make the same mistake again*.

Was there anything in the first set of reactions that was helpful? No. The emotion present allows us to imprint, but the first conversation was crippling and harmful. This is the difference between guilt- and shame-based Perspective, and empathic imprint Perspective. One tells us "We don't deserve good friends and we are awful" or "The other person is to blame for our pain because they overreacted to our transgression," while the second tells us "Hey, watch out for being resentful of female friends that do not return your affection; you might do something to attack them."

The first set is an attack. The second set is protective of myself and loved ones. Refining the totality of reactions down to a validated response was vital.

It doesn't get much clearer than that. The difference is profound. Now I didn't get all of that when I was fourteen. But I knew there was *something to get* about the situation beyond how I felt and my initial reactions. There is a web of information to be woven from all of our experiences, and learning to gravitate toward creating those webs is priceless.

Expression Discipline can help us in any moment when our mental boundaries are pushed, and it can help us when making changes in the fabric of our lives. It can place us securely in a respectful student's chair when we need to learn a lesson, in the artist's loft when we need to create a new Perspective for ourselves, and it can give us confidence going forward and making adjustments in any area of our lives. It helps us sift through an overwhelming amount of internal re-action information, caused by an endless sea of external information.

The way we go about judging, appraising, and valuating the world we are co-creating is vital to our ability to engage deeply and achieve the results we are looking for. It is how we slowly change our habitu-ated reactions and restrictions into personal art...how we develop integrity through our commitment to the quality of our presence. It does this by taking the avalanche of reactions we have about the whole of our world, discerning among them, and creating an elegant response-habit. Discernment is how we make ourselves Potent in a chaotic world that overwhelms us.

Chapter 16:

Expressions in Discernment: Healthy Judgment

The world comes at us really fast. Even if our External Mind was quiet (good luck with that), the external reality we are all taking part in gives us so little time to exercise our Consciousness. We are continuously forced into responses and analysis in real time at full speed.

We are constantly judging everything. This is not a good or bad thing; it just is. Forming a relationship with this aspect of Consciousness is a matter of some importance, though. Doing so changes our intake. It can change our level of understanding and empathy. It changes our relationships to people and ideas everywhere. It changes our level of internal peace and gives us more Influence over our internal compasses, especially where ethics and morals are concerned. Also, it relieves fear. This is because *the more active we are in the world that is coming at us, the less like a victim we will feel.* The more engaged we are with everything, the less likely we are to see anything or anyone as an enemy. The fewer enemies we have, the better everything in our world will be.

The types of Judgment for this chapter are Judgment-of-others (where the poles are "Damnation-dismissal-critique" and "empathy-relationship); Judgment of incoming facts or ideas (the poles at "face value" and "in-depth"); and Judgment of how we need to be relating to another person or situation (the poles there are "on our terms for our sake: entangled" and "on their terms for their sake: parenting").

In the end there will be a tale of two tools. We will either be relating with reality, or upon finding that it clashes with us in some way, attempting to beat it or ourselves into submission. The way we have to look at all of this is through the eyes of Psychological Determinism. There is no place in our psyche that this idea may matter more, than how it can guide our judgments of ourselves, other people, and the world around us. It removes enemies, internal and external.

It removes them, because to fully engage with our world, *we must aspire to fully embody it.*

Walking a Mile in Their Shoes

"Never judge a man until you've walked a mile in his shoes." I am pretty sure this is a common enough cliché that it shouldn't be a surprise to read it. And I would lay money that most reading this understand it the way I did when I was a youngster. Namely: "We can't make an informed decision about whether someone was right or wrong to do something without being in the spot they were in when they made it." But that is not the extent of the Perspective that is needed… not by a long shot. Psychological Determinism applied, this cliché gets really deep.

The "spot they were in" is the key. The spot everyone is in when they make any decision is a culmination of their entire set of experiences, their present chemical balance or lack thereof, and their genetic makeup. So the "spot they were in" is not something that we can ever surely have. There is one thing that we can know, though: that whatever action they took was determined by those factors in question...*the ones that made that spot theirs.*

The factors that led to any action made that action the best option available to that person. If we begin to examine in this way we can, over time, become engaged in a level of empathy we rarely see. But it takes effort...effort in a direction that is uncomfortable. It takes a level of effort that does not just put us in the situation where someone made a decision. ***It puts us in the mind that has THAT DECISION as the BEST OPTION.***

That is what "walking a mile in someone's shoes" is all about.

This is an easy road to take when it comes to looking at a teenager who vandalized a piece of your property, or someone who called in sick to work because of a hangover. We can feel it...maybe we have even done it. The urge is memorable as a sensation, and though we may not have acted on it, we can likely empathize with it. That's the easy stuff, though. It gets difficult real quick, and it has to, because we cannot be dismissive of people's behaviors. Being dismissive, or damning someone's behavior, gives us zero chance to learn from it in any way.

So let's get to the hard stuff. How about child abuse? How about torture? How about killing? How about rape? Ouch.

My most challenging one has been people in positions of power molesting kids. That's a really tough one for me to process without damning or dismissing. But it really does us no good to dismiss it, and it's the coward's way out. So, we have to assume that whoever committed such brutal crimes was acting in the same way everyone else was...just using what they had (or lacked) to make the best decision possible. I said it was going to be difficult.

What does this mean I have to do, exactly? This means I have to step outside my comfort zone *quite a distance*. I have to 1) imagine that my depth of attraction for adult women is now focused on children; and 2) imagine that the power of that attraction, and the urges involved are strong enough to overpower my sense of duty to protect children from harm.

The second one is difficult, and in order to get it done, 3) I may have to spin reality on its head and say "It is in some way in their best interest," or "It's not that harmful."

That's a long way from Kansas, Toto. Goodness. I'm editing this chapter for the first time and my stomach is getting tight just reading this.

I'm going to take a moment here to allow for some catch-up. I just went from a basic cliché to telling everyone to imagine being a child molester. That's what happened.

Why would I do that?

Because...**that is empathy**. And empathy is really, really important. It can also be really, really uncomfortable. That is why we do not do it often. We can go ahead and dismiss entire groups of living things, ideas, and places in ourselves rather than be uncomfortable. However, it is destructive to the world to do so.

The truth about this whole exercise though, *is that we are all capable of empathizing with anything*. We don't, for a huge number of reasons that all boil down to fear...as if seeing through someone else's eyes will turn us into them in an irreparable way, like the same way we turn into apple trees after eating apples (that doesn't actually happen).

So when I look at the distance I must travel in my mind to take on the Perspective I mentioned above, *it looks huge*. It is not, though. It is not even unnatural. 2400 years ago adult/children relationships were not uncommon, from priestesses in Africa to young boys in Sparta. To the eyes I have now, lodged fully in this culture, that is a truly foreign and frightening prospect. But at one time in history, it was totally normal.

Then I realize that people would marry off their daughters at twelve and thirteen not even a hundred years ago, and that Jerry Lee Lewis married his thirteen-year-old cousin sixty years ago.

All of a sudden, the distance I realize I have to travel is *something made up*. They are the result of societal changes, not genetic changes or attributes of our species. And thus, it is something I can likely disengage if I put some effort into it.

This will not change my sexual orientation. It will not change who I am attracted to. It will not make me something other than what I am. **It WILL change the amount of the world I can allow without becoming defensive against it or violent toward it**. It will simply allow me to integrate the Perspectives of others, and in doing so, I will understand them, myself, and everything a little better. It will enable me to *allow the presence of things that are confusing or uncomfortable* to me. It creates space for difference among living consciousness. Being able to empathize with others is synonymous with the ability to love them. It is the embodiment of peace.

I've made a habit of asking myself tough questions about my motivations, and I have found that I am capable of a lot of questionable behaviors, given certain situations. But because I have done this imaginative mapping of my possible reactions, it is unlikely that anyone will have to fear me.

It is really difficult to fault anyone for their urges (even if they seem monstrous) once we have made a habit of working to find the monsters lurking inside of us. The ability to love ourselves and others more deeply is a direct result of this practice.

Sociology, when taught correctly, teaches us to view a different culture through a Perspective other than our own. It does this for a very specific purpose. We cannot be in reaction to a reality and fully understand it, or our relationship to it. It takes college- level adult students effort to make this happen for themselves, and most of the time it is a mere "suspension of ethical Validations" rather than a "full immersion into the mindset of the culture."

As a society that attempts to limit value judgments on people, we have gotten accustomed to at least attempting that style of empathic reality assessment. But the true student of human beings does not stop there. The true student takes the chapter on the cannibals in Africa, and realizes that were he born there, he would likely have a very different menu to enjoy. He travels to societies where strange gods are worshipped and odd or illogical rituals are performed as a foundation for cultural experience, and he incorporates the Perspectives that led to their presence and continued practice. He learns because he does not lose himself in reaction.

This student may also be able to go back in time to the era of human sacrifice, and see it as the honor that the willing tributes saw it as. He will come out with a greater understanding of death, sacrifice, and suicide if he does. He may go back to 140 years ago in this country when men could own other men. He could go back over 140 years of racism and get into the heads of people who were the examples of prejudice, and he may learn through feeling the fear that existed on both sides. He may LEARN through feeling their FEAR. Their fear of things that were different…and their fear of losing control or power.

The reason that sociology professors (and history, and psychology) preach that you must use relativistic sight when appraising and learning another culture is that you simply cannot learn ANYTHING if you are busy freaking out in reaction to it. You cannot learn when you are *judging*. It is a reaction that shuts out evidence, shuts out connection, and completely handicaps our ability to engage with the whole of reality, *including the vast reality within ourselves*.

Every human mind is another culture, and the world is a sociology class with a very large syllabus. Being judgmental and reactive about how we see other participants in the grand mosaic keeps us at a distance from reality. Worse than that, it keeps our motivations and the knowledge of our desires hidden from us as well.

The mind is incapable of rectifying the Cognitive Dissonance that is created from our damning of others. It is incapable. Whatever we are habitually criticizing becomes an arena where we are blind to ourselves.

This is the Shadow. The shadow is not evil, or dark (it can have those aspects, but they are not necessarily tied), it is simply the blind spot created by the public picture of ourselves that we face outward.

For instance, sexuality is not evil. But that often lurks in the Shadow, especially if we are members of a repressed or judgmental culture growing up. Being homosexual is not evil. But some factions of our cultures have seen it as so, and this blinds anyone in that culture to whether or not they may be sexually attracted to people of their gender. That's not evil, just hidden from them by their own habitual judgments.

I wrote a Perspective on the Shadow a while back. It was meant to highlight why we have to manage our fear of our urges. It is meant to show how we can work with all of our desires, even though we all have many that are not fit for sharing the world with others in respect and equality. It allows us to give all of our desires a voice, and if they have a voice, they are not repressed. If they are not repressed, then they cannot catch us off guard and express themselves negatively on the world around us.

What I want to describe here is **The Mold**. The Mold is a set of ideas based on the same factors that go into Psychological Determinism. In this case, they create an ideal of how things or people should be, rather than behavior in situations (as Psychological Determinism does). We all have The Mold, and none of us have direct access to its vaults. It is the part in our matrix of Psychological Determinism that leads us into judgment.

The characteristics of The Mold make it an outstanding resource for ongoing self-analysis, and a great place to practice engaging in Consciousness. First, we did not make our Mold. Second, we can only find out about our Mold through our reactions, *specifically our criticism or rejection of anything*. Third, The Mold does not have to be logical, or accurate. Fourth, it is the cause of Cognitive Dissonance, the very thing that blinds us to ourselves and separates us from others. It also paralyzes us in action.

The Mold is very important, very influential, and very harmful if not addressed. It is our problem.

The Mold...and the First Step of Every 12 Step Program

The first step is admitting we have a problem. We do. The ocean of evaluations we make during the day is beyond us. The sources of our opinions on every little detail and their accompanying reactions are simply out of our sphere of control. Having a certain picture of the world that reality must adhere to creates a

multitude of problems. These problems occur when our expectations of how things should be in the world (including within us)
are not being met by reality. Why does the Mold exist? Its existence is part of creating comfort in stasis. It is not a bad thing to
have, but it's a bad thing for us not to know we have.

When the Mold is not matched by reality, there is a reaction. The reaction consists of an emotional component in
the body and a declarative component within the mind. The
declarative component has two parts. It can be described by
simple judgment statements. These two things are linked.

1) That thing is not the way it should be.

2) That thing is "not me." I am not an example of that thing.

Unfortunately, neither of those things is helpful, and in all
likelihood, they are also inaccurate. To compound the problems created by this, once we have had this coupled reaction,
we are incapable of dealing with whatever caused it.

If we are conscious of this occurring, and have the presence of mind to engage it, we can get a glimpse of the Mold,
and possibly make changes to it. We first have to address
the thinking that puts anything outside of our reality. So let's
change the statements in the same way we would using
Conscious Validation.

The two statements of reaction should actually be:

1) That happened, and I want to reject it because it is different from my expectations.

2) I would have done the same thing if I were them at the
moment they did it.

That is a healthy reaction…not a problem-creator. That is
what we're after. If we can get to this in-the-moment, we can

begin to empathize. Then we can take a couple stabs at deriving purpose, or motive from the behavior that set us off. Being set off in this way is a blessing because it leads directly to self-awareness… *if we take the necessary action.*

"Everything that irritates us about others can lead us to understanding of ourselves."--Jung

If we engage in this, we prepare ourselves for something important. We prepare ourselves for the moment when our own life and action do not fit the Mold. The first step is admitting we have a problem. The problem is not reality, though; the problem is the Mold. Reality does not have a problem. We do.

The same passionate response that leads to the rejection of unwelcome realities outside of us *leads to guilt and shame within us* when our behaviors and traits do not fit the Mold. That is unhealthy, and it is the kind of unconscious expression that we are trying to minimize until it is gone. **When we experience Cognitive Dissonance, we need to be able to perform this maneuver.** We need to be able to take a moment, and validate the observed reality. In doing this we can look at our motives, and we may be able to find valuable information. We will also be able to change the Mold. We cannot change what is in it, but we can change its size, and add new Influences. Every time we allow a reality that we initially rejected, the Mold gets bigger, more tolerant, and the opinions within it get less powerful. This is transmutation. This integrates realities that do not fit, by utilizing empathy.

Looking at the idea of the Mold is fun. It's a psychological exercise. Books have been written in and around the ideas associated

with it. The trick with the Mold is that getting stuck on its nature is very seductive, and also *a total waste of time*. The Mold has a use. That is where we want to focus. The reason we want to focus there is that the Mold is a concrete matrix of reactions. It is something we deal with all day, and we need to engage it. Trying to conceptualize it makes it abstract, and *it is not abstract*. It is like muscle memory, not a theory. Trying to figure out what it is would be like trying to learn to hit a baseball by playing a video game. Moving our fingers on a joystick is NOT moving a bat through the strike zone.

When we begin to understand that conceptualizing is not the goal, the familiarity with how The Mold functions becomes the focus. This is because it does not contain answers about us or descriptions of what we are, just reactions… *reactions that we did not author*.

These reactions are an expression. They are an expression of fear based on discomfort: the discomfort that occurs when something is not okay. **The discomfort exists only because The Mold is limited**. We, however, are not limited. The discomfort and fear belong to The Mold. The fear does not need to be ours. We can let it fall away by addressing it whenever possible. This is not an easy thing to do, and it is not always possible…but it is worth it. Nothing is more empowering to our human soul than to be fully engaged with the many forces that motivate us and shape our outlook on the world.

When we have these reactions, these judgments about the world around us, we are being given information. *We need to **use** it.*

My Mom's First Marriage

When we talk about shadow work it includes a lot of questions: questions we must ask ourselves, and the courage to allow honest answers. That courage comes from having released the habit of engaging in damning judgment. The acceptance of honest answers allows us to use the information we get to provide safeguards and love within our behavioral matrix.

My mother's first marriage lasted about eighteen months. She was nineteen years old, and though extremely intelligent, was not aware of many elements driving her life. Her Mold included judgments that hid her true wants and desires from her in some areas.

She was not in love with her husband. She didn't know this at the time. She had assumed she loved him, everything fit into the Mold of starting a family in the early '60s. So, what happened to change this? What was the mechanism?

In this case, it was dreams. She had dreams every night. They were pretty much the same every night. My brother was a few months old, there was no abuse in the house, money was in order, and my mother was having the strangest dream.

Every night, my mother would dream of brutally murdering her husband. Every night. It took some time to get to the next step. It took six months, actually. She brutally killed her husband every night for six months before she even asked: "Why am I dreaming of killing my husband? Am I unhappy?"

Her Mold *did not include having made a mistake* with who she married (this is realllly common). So no questions had been asked up until this point. Her Mold also did not put any value on her happiness, *so the fact that she was unhappy had not registered* (again, really common). She was also not allowed to go against what her father wanted (he had stopped her from going on dates while she and her husband were engaged). No red flags went up. That is how powerful the Mold is. It keeps us from asking questions we are unprepared to answer with Cognitive Dissonance. **IT WILL NOT LET YOU ASK A QUESTION IF THE ANSWER SCARES YOU**.

This is the same for sexual repression in religious families (in fact, for any repression). The repression of the genuine self, or the inner child, or the id, all falls under the category of "Things that can be found only through relating to and understanding the Mold." Notice I said "through" relating to the Mold, not "by." The answers are not in the Mold. ***The answers are evidenced by the Mold's reactions to everything we see in the world.***

The Mold stops us from understanding things, from including things in our mental framework that make us uncomfortable. It keeps everything outside that fits that description. Unfortunately, our inner world, as well as the world outside of us, makes us pretty uncomfortable.

The Mold keeps us comfortable. This has value. In order to do this, it tells us lies. "That cannot happen to us." "I am not like them." "I do not feel that way." "I would never be in that situation." Pretty common. How do we bypass it? We ask questions. We ask ourselves questions that make us uncomfortable and we get used to trying to answer honestly.

In the section before, I described a maneuver that one could perform. The maneuver was moving our Perspective from one of denouncing something someone did as "bad," to seeing it as "the best option they had at the time." Why does this connect? Because if it was "the best option they had at the time," then that means it could happen to us. The Mold will not let you think that. That is very uncomfortable: Cognitive Dissonance in full effect. It causes great stress. But we all have, at some point growing into adulthood, performed this move plenty of times. And if we do it often, the Mold gets malleable.

In order to see ourselves as an adult, the mold has to get malleable. I didn't realize it at the time, but that is why all teenagers are less rigid than adults. They are engaged in overhauling their Mold every day because they have to rewrite the "adult" section as they learn more about it. This is because the child-version of the adult section is grossly inaccurate.

Think of it. When did you learn the most about yourself? During the stages of adolescence, leading to adulthood, the Mold is at its weakest, because the standard of comfort is totally gone. The rushing chemicals and changes in desire in the body are so whacked that its grip loses a ton of strength. To go along with the inner turmoil, we as teenagers also had the incoming stresses of having to deal with taking care of ourselves in an adult world that is getting bigger and more real by the second.

But after that awkward six or so years, things mellow out, *and this is when our ability to make changes in the Mold gets cut short unless we tend to it consistently.* Adulthood is stressful, and keeping comfortable becomes more of a priority.

There is only one way to be comfortable and work with the mold simultaneously: forming a relationship through consistent engagement. It has to be something that we do on a daily basis for the Mold to lose its rigidity. Our mind wants the Mold safe and stable. If we are afraid of being uncomfortable, the Mold will happily take over for our internal compass and cut off our ability to empathize.

The focus of this chapter is on creating a practice. The practice is Healthy Judgment. This is a type of judgment that comes through the Mold's limited nature, and ultimately ends up expanding the Mold.

The Steps of Healthy Judgment

Healthy Judgment: Have the Judgment, Heal the judgment, Find what scares you, Ask questions, and Take on a new and empowered Perspective. Repeat. Five Steps.

Judgment is an expression. It is a thought or set of thoughts that originates in us, and Influences us. We want this expression healthy. In order to have this expression healthy, we have to engage our consciousness as often as possible with the operation that renders judgment harmless. This operation also leads to knowledge and ease in future situations.

1) Have the judgment.

You cannot help but have it. It is going to be there, whether it is a judgment about someone's appearance, someone's actions, or a state of affairs that is present in the world.

"Political Corruption and corporate greed are destroying the planet!"

"Bullies are awful!"

"Oh my lord that person is so_____ (fill it in, mine is "frustrating")!"

This is the "**That is BAD, I REJECT that**" section. I have these reactions. I have them every day. My body reacts viscerally to realities I am presented with. That is step one. It's going to happen. Allow it to be heard…then step in.

2) Heal the judgment.

"The people who control the money believe they are doing the right thing with it."

"Bullies are acting out, likely from being abused or neglected by parental figures. Their behavior creates a balance

for them by filling some need. If I had been mistreated I would
likely have been a bully too."

"That is too bad. I want this person to have certain ideas
and values and they do not. I want to be able to communicate
my ideas to them and it is not working."

This is the "**There is a reason things are the way they are...
allow it**" section. This is same as changing thoughts in the
Conscious Validation section. But these are not just thoughts.
We are defending ourselves from realities that freak us out. So
integrating them as "possibilities" in our world helps us get to
the next step.

3) Find what scares you.

"I'm scared that my family will not have their needs met
as a result of others' greed, which is destroying the planet in a
multitude of different ways."

"I am scared that the cycle of abuse and acting out will
reach my family and friends, and the perpetuation of violence
will continue unabated."

"I am afraid that I will not be able to have the impact I
want on the world around me, and will be subjected to things
I do not want as a result."

This is the "**It's gonna get me**" section. This is what all rejection reactions end up boiling down to. If it makes us react,
it is because we are scared of what we reacted to and its possible impact on our lives. That is why we have reactions. They
are defending us. The emotional/visceral component provides
us with motivation to logically justify the reactions and make
declarative statements.

Judgments end up as a defensive stance against reality.
And in defense (assuming attack from anything different) it

becomes violent. That is the nature of judgment. Thus our shadow becomes the bearer and cause of our violence toward other living things. It does not have to be this way.

4)   Ask uncomfortable questions.

If I were in their shoes, what would make me want to hoard my money like that? *"Why is it not enough that I have all of this wealth? Why do I have to make sure others do not have enough to live comfortably? I must be deathly scared of them. If they are empowered, or not struggling, I am in danger."*

If I was a bully, what would I be getting out of it? *"Why does making someone else feel bad make me feel good? My life must be so far out of control, that being able to enforce my will on anyone or anything gives me moments of peace that override any feeling of wrong doing. Being able to make someone afraid of me like I am afraid gives me the power I lack."*

Why am I not being understood? *"Why can this person not understand my point of view? Hmmm. It's likely that they have different values and experiences, so I cannot be clear with what I am saying from my own Perspective."*

This is the "**What would make that a good idea? Why is that my best option? Oh…that's why.**" section. I do not think we can always find answers to what is motivating a situation. But there is always a reason, and we have to try as often as possible if we want anything in our world to change. Everyone is doing the best they can, and putting ourselves in their place can give us insight into what values they have, and what tools they are using. *This is where "feeling empowered" is born.*

5)   Take on a new empowered perspective.

"The wealthy do not feel safe being involved in the economy. They do not feel safe with the rest of the world being

comfortable. I believe we should focus on making them feel safe. We should let them know that we are not their enemy and that being involved in the whole global economy will end up being a good thing for them."

"Bullies do not feel safe, and need to enforce their will on others. They need others to be frightened of them like they are frightened. So we should focus on helping them with their fears, and removing whatever fear they inflict on their victims so it is no longer a source of power for them to behave in that manner."

"They cannot understand me from my point of view, so I need to more fully understand their point of view. So I must keep changing the Perspective I am coming from, as not to frighten them, and to keep trying to understand their values and focus."

This is the "**Empowered Perspective**" section. This is not just a reaction anymore. ***It is a reaction with an action and focus built into it***. This is like a counter-block in karate. The reaction includes habit and muscle memory functioning together to create an entire new way of reacting to a situation. One that is not violent, and elegant.

You can do this.

This is only a light foray into the power of Perspective...something I will finish this book up with. It is something we can all do and it can change our world. The peace we have been searching for in the world can wash over us in minutes, and the example we set will wash over the world at lightning speed.

Chapter 17:

Blessings in Expression

PART 1: ANGER AND FORGIVENESS

We give some of our expressions a special place in our mind. We try to give them "feeling" status, because they are so important that we do not want to have to be responsible for defining them, defending them, or attending to them. Love is a mystery everyone is capable of experiencing, and the most important aspects of one's life will largely revolve around it. Forgiveness is the thing that we all want given to us when we make mistakes, and it is a healthy and powerful thing to give to another for their transgressions. Confidence is something people just have, *supposedly*. Being able to be of service, or aid to others, either through official licensing (doctors, therapists, teachers) or through another type of care facilitation (family, friend) makes us feel powerful and needed on top of any worthy benefits that it provides to our loved ones or society. Feeling helpful is beneficial.

However, *none of these are feelings*. They are *wants*. They are a way we want to see ourselves, an identification we seek to match. **We want to be the kind of people who do these things**. In the ways we are not attaining the goals of these feelings…we are blind. This is because The Mold, as it relates to how we want to see ourselves, does not allow self-analysis if we are falling short.

None of these ideas (love, forgiveness, being helpful, or confidence) is a feeling. They are intentions behind actions. *Our actions either fulfill or do not fulfill a want.* Our love…it is a *want.* Your love for your child is a *want.* It is a want of closeness and health and many other things, **things that can all be defined, and analyzed.** Our forgiveness is a *want.* It is a want of being able to feel safe and comfortable, and a want of being able to grant freedom from guilt. Our being helpful is the want to feel needed in the world, and to foster parenthood with another. Our confidence is a want of ability and sanctuary in selfhood.

But all of these are expressions of *intentions.* And the ability to express our intentions, the ability to make our wants viable, depends on our abilities to behave in harmony with these wants. That may be something that takes a ton of experience, focus, fearlessness, or intelligence. **But it is certain that it takes something.** It takes something.

Because of that, being able to express these glorious wants is a blessing. We have either worked for it, or been gifted it. But it is a blessing, if we have it.

Forgiveness…Original Injury and Then Some

Forgiveness is not a decision we make. Forgiveness is a feeling that occurs when we have successfully gotten ourselves free of the pain and resentment associated with a transgression. If we have not been successful in getting ourselves emotionally healthy and clear, then the issue is not forgiven *regardless of what we say or do.*

What we can do, as far as making a decision, is decide whether or not we want to be a forgiving person. We can decide what our attitude toward forgiveness is, and focus on doing the things that are necessary to improve our chances at being successful with it.

The basis for this complex reality is that *forgiveness is a state of being*, and we simply cannot control those. We cannot control our reactions, and we cannot control how our body feels about certain people or situations. Thinking that we CAN control these things leads to a couple of major issues within the realm of forgiveness.

The first issue is that we think we have forgiven something when we haven't, and our resentment causes us to unconsciously (or consciously) act out vengefully toward the person or situation. This happens all the time in every type of relationship and it is sooooooo destructive.

The second issue is that there is actually a ton we can do to improve our ability to forgive, and thinking it is a decision we can make prevents us from giving any attention to improving our skills with it. As in "Because we think we can choose it whenever we want to, *we do not do the necessary work it takes to attain the ability.*"

The analogy I love to mention, the one I use in my life, is the Relationship House analogy.

The **Relationship House** is the objective correlative of the relationship between two people. It is symbolic for the bridge between them. It has a structure, and is outside the identity of either person in the relationship. When we are dealing with a transgression, what we are dealing with is damage to that symbolic house.

If there is a breach of trust, or a cruelty by intention **or** carelessness, the house gets damaged. The level of the damage is not up for discussion. It can only be accurately appraised, or not. The fair amount of damage for the transgression is something we all like to talk about, but it is a total waste of time. *What we think is fair has nothing to do with the actual damage done.*

This description also works for relationships with ideas or groups of people, like police officers, our body, the government, doctors, etc. We have expectations and systems of trust for our relationships with everything in our world.

So how strong is our house? How good are we at repairing it? How well do we understand the structure? Can we see clearly what has been damaged?

These are all questions that need to be asked consistently to ensure that we have the highest likelihood for success when trying to allow ourselves to forgive.

This brings us to what our purposes are. The purpose, of course, is to be on the Beach of Quiet Emotion when it comes to our relationship with anything. I do not want to be getting angry with my world. Any area of my life that I have not been able to fully forgive can make me angry, and get me off the Beach. I do not want that. Neither do you.

Having a forgiving attitude is an important thing in life. It is important because we have related expectations and trust with everything. I have expectations of traffic lights, and dogs, and gravity, and on and on. We are going to get injured, though, and every pain comes with a feeling of betrayal. A transgression. Either we were actually injured by an outside force that did something unexpected, or we realized that our picture of the world was wrong, and were betrayed **by that picture we had created**. In both cases, an attitude of forgiveness is vital for our purposes. It is difficult, because our expectations are formed in childhood, and are amended only through either pain or epiphany. Mostly pain...d'oh.

This exercise focuses on what I call **Original Injury**. It is when our expectations of relationships or groups of people are inaccurate, and we feel betrayed as a result.

Think of how you felt about the following groups and ideas as a child.

1. Police officers.

2. Doctors.

3. Lawmakers.

I can tell you that my picture of police officers did not include their getting frustrated and beating people. I can tell you that Serpico was a really frightening eye-opener. I can tell you that the first time I got a gun stuck in my face during a routine traffic stop I was pretty surprised.

I can also say that having doctors not listen to my symptoms was surprising. I was also surprised when I was injured once (baseball bat to the mouth) that a doctor took it as an opportunity to try to make $30,000 by bracketing my mouth for a year. I didn't even think that he might be in it for the money. Scared me to death when we called my orthodontist, and he called the man in question a "butcher." Nothing actually needed to be done with my mouth. Wow. My ideas about doctors changed drastically, and it freaked me out. To this day, I am STILL involved with this type of betrayal. My PTSD, in large part, stems from my fear of and anger toward the medical community. I am STILL trying to forgive these transgressions.

I was also really stunned the first time I realized that the president could lie. I remembered thinking our government

was "the good guys." That did not last long either. Many people are very hurt when they find out that politicians and the
government are not always the good guys. This is disenfran-
chisement. I was not too hurt by this. I was raised by a family
who is sure that the government killed JFK. I was still upset to
learn of corruption at all levels of government as I grew, but I
didn't get my heart broken.

Now, think about people that have bitterness toward these
groups. They have not forgiven the initial transgression. *They
have not adjusted their picture of reality to include the way
things are*, and thus their anger is a fixation for them. We are
incapable of forming new pictures, or reacting to new information when we are angry. When we are angry at a "group,"
we will become emotionally aroused and fixated in anger by
every instance of the reality. It requires work and focus to adjust for this presence within us. This matters.

So when I think about the groups above, I can think of
how I feel when I see any cop car's lights go on. I can see how
I feel when I visit a new doctor. I can see how I feel when I
hear about new legislature. Anxiety is almost always my first
reaction.

In the first example, I have gotten pretty used to responding to my reactions with "They are not after me, and they are
doing their job, it's a good thing." In the last example I can
adjust with a "Wait and see what the bill says, or what the
lawmaker is going after" before I get all bent out of shape.
With doctors, I have not yet forgiven them fully, so I actually
have to have someone else talk me through it. I can take any
evaluation and turn it into a fear.

The issue with this is that it leads me to act out. First, I
simply avoid them like the plague. I do not EVER want to go to

the doctor. Then when I do HAVE to go, they get the absolute worst side of me. I am angry, impatient, and less than truthful. I have not been able to fix this on my own. Because I know this, I will not go to the doctor alone. Ever. I need someone there translating me back into reality, and speaking for me on most occasions. This is serious, and I take it seriously.

I'm looking forward to a day when I have forgiven the entire practice to the point where I am not immediately convicting every new doctor of some awful offense before meeting them. *The world deserves a better version of me than that*. It will take time, just like the child in The Little Albert conditioning experiment had to be fully unconditioned *years afterwards*, so that he was not crippled by his fear. It will take my time and focus, but my attitude of wanting to live in a state of forgiveness is consistently helping me resolve this issue.

We are going to move around a good amount with this concept, because it is vital to be able to lend our attention to the specifics of many cases where our intentions are not being met by our behaviors.

I have dealt with group ideal Original Injuries. Now I am going to move on to Interpersonal Original Injury.

Original Injury and Interpersonal Relationships

When it comes to even the most pedestrian aspect of these Original Injuries, we are going to get tossed off our Beach of Quiet Emotion. We are not going to be able to think clearly, or trust, or engage our effort in trying to make the world better where they are concerned. This is a big deal, but not as big a deal as our inability to forgive is when it comes to interpersonal relationships. So instead of looking at titled people, let's look at interpersonal relationships, and what expectations and injuries we have there.

Think about the pictures you had of these as a child.

1. Close friends.

2. Lovers.

3. Your parents.

4. Bosses and employees.

Take a moment please. This is an exercise. I'll share what mine were now.

My picture of friends did not include them seducing my girlfriend and having an affair in my house when I was at work. It did not include lies. It did not include being robbed. It did not include being wrong about who my friends actually were.

My picture of being a lover in a relationship did not include screaming fights. It did not include lies, it did not include resentment. It did not include having entire weeks of not being kind to one another. It did not include a lot that is included in the average relationship. It did not include what happens to people when things go wrong, and they do not know how to fix them.

My picture of my parents was that of powerful people who were known for their integrity. It did not include fallibility or weakness. It did not allow room for their humanity at all really.

My picture of bosses and employees did not include favoritism. It did not include usury. It did not include my expendability. It did not allow room for them to operate with my existence as a piece of their business. But that is what it is. And that's all right. My ideas of coworkers did not include people trying to sabotage and undermine me, but that happens sometimes, too.

I have experience with all of these types of people. Even my parents have changed identities for me many times over the course of my life. Everyone will have many friends and lovers, and in all likelihood many bosses and coworkers. And since everyone changes all the time, people will experience their own parents in many ways. If we have not forgiven these ideals for not being accurate, *we will be carrying resentment around with us for everyone who embodies those roles*.

If we do not heal our first broken heart from our Original Injury in every area, we will be carrying violence with us into every relationship that is similar. Every Original Injury is a broken heart centered on an idea, not a person. We are not just afraid of the friend that hurt us, we are afraid of "friends" …just as we are not just afraid of the police officer who harassed us, we are afraid of "cops." This becomes more of a disaster when we have the pain in a romantic relationship, because that pain tends to be more intimate and humiliating. It is more of a betrayal because of the power of the feeling involved. But it is our idea of what the world should be, based on fairy tale-ish ideas we develop unconsciously as children.

As children we do not allow for a lot of reality, because it is beyond our capacity to think abstractly during the ages we are forming role solidity. It is not our fault. We cannot think of our parents as "people," we cannot think of couples as "having problems," and we can't imagine bosses sabotaging their employees (even to the detriment of their business). None of those realities are black and white. We don't have the capacity to take on those realities because they would cause stress beyond our coping mechanisms. We simply do not have the experience necessary, or the ability to manage these abstract concepts...and that is okay.

What we need to be able to do is understand that we are going to get injured by the simple presentation of reality in our interpersonal relationships throughout our lives. Because of that, *we must develop a means of coping with and recovering from injury in these areas.*

I see a ton of ability. I see a ton of focus and Perspective that can be engaged and managed, and it makes me happy. I hope it has that effect on everyone. Beyond the external realities where forgiveness needs to have its intentions matched for a more smooth, less anger-laden Consciousness, our internal realities and the surprises that confront us throughout our lives need attention.

Original Injury: Body Betrayal and Other Internal Realities.

To recover from Original Injury with ideas and situations outside of us is difficult, but not as difficult as those that occur internally.

Now the final section.

1. Our body
2. Our mind

Everyone gets to watch their body fail them. Some have this experience earlier than others, but we all have it. I watched my brother's body betray him at twenty-two. It gave him cancer and almost killed him. But the damage done to his body, while serious, was nothing in comparison to the damage done to his mind. The fear was unreal. He could no longer trust his body.

Everyone gets sick, and everyone gets the wear and tear of aging. Our bones break and weaken, and our strength fails. *Conceptually*, we understand that this leads to the final break-down, as these bodies' lifespan run their course. But we begin to understand this in a more than conceptual way at some point in our lives, and *this is a brutal moment*. It feels wrong. And it stings even more because conceptually we knew it was coming, so the violence of our realization is humiliating on top of everything else.

Our mind is trickier to deal with. Some can go their entire lives under the assumption that what is going on between their ears is totally theirs. But there are many of us who have the hidden blessing of being betrayed by our mind. This gives us an amazing wealth of Perspective if we can get past the anger and frustration of it.

No one told me my mind could bail on me. I did not expect that my mind could bail on me. But in the throes of my first panic attack I learned that my expectations for the inner workings of my mind were not based on reality. Chemical fluctuations inside my head were capable of conducting a symphony of destruction at any given moment. The uncontrollable panic and fear was a betrayal of the worst kind, and my bitterness and confusion over this betrayal led me into many evasive actions during the years I was not being correctly medicated for it. I could go from feeling normal to crying and shaking on the floor in a matter of ten minutes. And what's worse, I could not bring myself out of it. In these panicked states, my mind was not fully available to me (and I don't know if it would have helped had it been). This was a brutal new relationship I had to begin to work with. I had to accept and forgive my mind. I had to understand that I could go into a panic attack for no particular reason (and I definitely had triggers, also), and that once I was in one I could not bring myself out. I had to know this, and try not to be afraid of it because being afraid led to stress, and that led to panic attacks. Cycle, anyone?

So now not only was my mind my enemy, but knowing that my mind was my enemy made it even more powerful an enemy? *The thing that I use to solve problems goes away at the exact second I need to solve a problem, and knowing this makes it MORE likely that I'm going to have a problem!?* Holy cow, what a crappy thing to find out.

But this is what we all truly need to accept. This is why Psychological Determinism is so hard to allow. It acknowledges the largeness of the power of the physical/chemical/environmental mind in relation to the itty-bitty consciousness that works in cooperation with it. The tool we use to manage our interface with the world can totally betray us. The fury over this is the reason that many people do not want to validate the realities of people with mental issues. This is because, in doing so, they have to admit that something inside of them, something they count on, can be lying to them about the world. They have to admit that the tools they count on may not always be there. They have to admit that they are not completely safe and in charge inside their own mind. I don't blame anyone who stiffens in protest to this fact. It is a truly intimate betrayal.

So when we are faced with this reality, we must try to forgive so that we can work with it. If we disrespect, dismiss, and deny it, we will unable to Influence the resulting situations. **We will be unable to form a new and accurate relationship with our primary tool for interfacing with the whole of reality**. We do not want that.

We have to allow the Original Injury of *"realizing that we are not in control"* in order to pursue a new relationship with ourselves...a relationship that includes our patience and observation, as well as our humility before the majestic complexities occurring within us. Because if we remain in a state of resentment about the nature of our mind, we will never truly trust it, or its glorious abilities. And we need to trust our mind in order to use it.

So I have described forgiveness, and talked about the importance of healing Original Injury, but I have not mentioned how to go about healing. The resentment or grudge we "carry" is unlike most concepts of consciousness in that it is not momentary, but a permanent companion within the consciousness. This gives it qualities that *increase our ability to engage it*. We can set aside moments to take peeks at **Held Anger** within us. This is basically resentment, but being able to be aware of it and engage it makes it mutable over time. And it is in this engaging that we can find and validate expressions of forgiveness within us.

Unpacking Held Anger and Conscious Validation for Fostering the Expression of Forgiveness. Oh … and a Box of Bees.

The difference between Held Anger and Resentment is that Held Anger is something that is not actively influencing your world. We can have Held Anger and Resentment over the same issue, but they are not the same thing. We cannot deal with Resentment: it is a force…a motivation. We can deal with Held Anger, because it is the compartmentalized set of experiences from a painful situation.

When we finish with an experience that was painful, it is rare that we've dealt with its fullness, or subtleties. We wrap it up tight, like a suitcase after a vacation, and push it into the closet that stores our painful memories as soon as we can, because without doing so we cannot go on with our daily lives. This compartmentalization is a survival trait, and one that is unhealthy only if we do not understand it. We need to focus on understanding it, and using it to foster our expressions and our relationship with our intimate histories.

I like to think of these painful memories that get wrapped up like a suitcase, and engaging them as Unpacking. So, we have to take an experience and look at every messy detail. We get better at this over time if we do it correctly. However, performing this correctly is very difficult, and since the mechanism that works has not gotten a foothold in our society, most get frustrated before they can get the hang of it. I'm happy I was able to stumble upon it, and even happier I was aware of its full nature as I began to use it and grow with it over time.

So, let's do the story.

My first real girlfriend and I were really mature for sixteen-year-olds. She was my first love, and we had a messy break-up. Not mean or violent, just messy. While we may have been mature, we were not experienced, and were pretty clumsy as a result. We had been together in one way or another for about eight months, and I was moving to California. We knew about this, but did not exactly know how to let the relation-ship run its course. So...we kinda crashed it.

The situation we were in was one where I was choosing to leave over staying with her. We depended on each other a ton, so she was nervous about not being able to be independent again when I left. I felt guilty for leaving. I was trying to con-trol the situation so that I could leave peacefully, *and became so fixated on deciding how I wanted it to go that I stopped paying attention to how she was doing.* This is all pretty stan-dard stuff. Nothing fancy or out of the ordinary here.

So, she ended the relationship. I wasn't exactly clear on it. Both of us stumbled a lot over the next few weeks. We both acted out and hurt each other in a few ways. I was hurt, jeal-ous, and ended up humiliated as a result of my clumsiness. I felt betrayed.

Then...I moved to California. I had to take the entire situ-ation, with no real resolution and with a TON of hurt feelings, wrap it up, and stow it in my emotional closet. Then I learned the art of **Unpacking**.

Every few days, when things were mellow enough, I would go back to the situation and re-experience it. I would think about specific times and how I felt, and watch myself re-act to facts as they came to light. I would feel it all again. And I would be viciously angry. But...I didn't want to be angry. So each time I went through and experienced the situation, *I*

focused on whichever part I could forgive. So, it would be a moment at a time.

So the first time, I dealt with the fact that she was leaning toward one of my friends…and I was angry. I thought of a night at a party, and then another party the following week, and many moments during those evenings were sources of pain. I was angry at him, and her, for the roles they played in my pain. But they were just living and doing the best they could…*and I knew that*. So I noticed one time I was rehashing it, and I wasn't angry at him anymore. I really focused on that feeling. It was tangible, and I believe everyone has felt it. It is like a pressure valve has been released, and instead of anger, it like a gigantic sigh coming from deep in the body. **I LOVE that feeling**. That is the body Expressing Forgiveness. The freedom of that moment is what I focused on, and I imprinted it. Next time I went back into those memories, I was not angry at him, and I had the feeling again, but with something different. I was not angry at her for that specific transgression.

There were twenty days and about fifty moments that stung me in that situation. Over the course of about four months I unpacked and dealt with almost all of them. The feelings were released, and as they were released I would Consciously Validate that my anger was leaving. I would imprint forgiveness and understanding. The moment when I was crying in an orange tree because I was heartbroken changed to a feeling of peace. The moment when I brought her stuff to her at her work changed from righteous anger and pain to peace. Each time it took me allowing the pain and anger from memories I could not change, and it HURT EVERY TIME. But each time I could find something that would release. I would find something that didn't bother me, and I would focus on the feeling of having *freedom from anger*. That was what I would imprint each time. And then I became confident that I could do this with any situation. I was right.

This is what **Fostering the Expression of Forgiveness** is about. It is about being committed to Unpacking painful experience and *allowing our natural ability to understand and forgive to express itself through us*. We have to be at peace and vulnerable (we're not going to be able to feel forgiveness for someone or a situation if we're feeling violence toward them)...and we have to be willing to experience pain.

This is not an easy thing to commit to. Besides the fact that we have to be in a good space to have success, it is really like opening a box of bumblebees. The bees that are still too full of emotion will sting us. The bees that are truly happy to be out of the box will fly away and go on about their lives. This means that every time we engage in this we are going to get hurt until there are no more bees in the box. But it means that every time we open the box, we will get stung less. And it is the only way to *empty the box completely*. And until we empty the box completely, its weight will be affecting our lives through resentment.

We work with the Held Anger from our Original Injuries, and from the many injuries we incur along the way. We work with them because to be able to hold loving intention, forgiving intention, or to help anyone, we must be willing to engage and dispel our anger as it relates to the world. If we are pent-up and resentful about anything in our histories, that will forever express through our actions.

Being capable of Fostering the Expression of Forgiveness is not an easy achievement. It involves our willingness to experience pain in exchange for something that is not obviously harm to us or anyone else. It is not an obvious harm. It is a subtle and deep one. But we have plausible deniability for its consequences in our world, and only we know whether or not we are engaging the depths of soul Commune in these areas.

So I am asking. This chapter, through all three sections, I am asking that we meet our intentions with fierce engagement as it relates to the essential expressions we are here to create.

PART 2: LOVE

Love, *as a feeling*, is subjectively powerful, and objectively trivial. If we have the ability to express that feeling healthily, **it is objectively powerful**. Being able to express it healthily is honoring it, and that is pivotal for our lives. That ability will be the creative force in the construction of whatever beauty exists in our world. That is the ability that will allow us to fall asleep more easily as we grow old. That is the ability that we will find as a foundation for peace on our deathbeds.

Love, as a Feeling, Is Objectively Trivial

Love is not an action. Love is not a behavior. Love is something inside of us that needs to be translated into the world, and that translation is vital. That translation is the birthing process that either brings the love we feel into the world, or twists and perverts it into something unusable, or destructive. So as I am going to focus on the translation for the rest of the chapter, let's take a look at how pivotal it is now.

Newborn babies love their mothers. Unadulterated joy washes over them at the sound or sight of their mother. They are very capable of receiving love, and this a glorious skill to have (one that we undervalue). But they are not capable of translating their love in any other way. This is not a judgment on their ability to feel love; it is *pointing out a limitation on their ability to show love.*

In truth, we are all limited in our ability to show love. How limited we are determines whether we are capable of loving anything at all. Many people are so inept at translating love that their innermost feelings are never honored through their actions, and thus never manifest in reality.

We have a way in our society of missing the mark when it comes to the judgment of love. This is to protect ourselves from self-judgment, and Cognitive Dissonance. It makes sense. So when we look at people's behaviors, we judge their feelings. We judge the amount of love someone feels by how they behave, rather than looking for the actual cause of the behavior. This is because we do not want to confront the fact that we can feel great love for someone, and act in a totally unloving manner toward them. *That is not an incongruent reality, and that fact is frightening.*

"How can they love someone and _____" (Insert questionable behavior here).

We pose questions that we assume cannot be answered. How can a person love someone and beat them? How can a person love someone and betray them? How can a person love someone and undermine their health and growth? How can a person feel one way and act in a manner that seems contrary? Easy. **Feelings *do not* create behaviors**. They can Influence them, but they do not create them.

So this is the situation. **A person can love math and fail a math test**. The feeling does not create behavior. There is no substitute for study and practice. But at least with school subjects like math, we know what we are studying, and that studying is important. When it comes to human beings, we do not know how to study, what to study, or even THAT WE NEED TO BE STUDYING. Goodness.

A good description to cap this idea is man's best friend. My dog loves me. It is a true thing. His ability to love me is not limited by his feelings. His ability to love me is limited only by his understanding of the world around him.

If this is a tough one for you to picture, take your picture of a loving dog and give him thumbs and increase his intelligence tenfold. Give him the ability to read. Now think of how much more awesome the world around him is. Think of all the extra chores that get done around the house. Think of the amount of care this pooch would put into everything, and how tirelessly he would work to keep in the light of your affection. The dog that killed and dragged a raccoon onto your porch would totally do the dishes forever.

So why do we dance around the idea of feeling love as if it were this holy thing that determined the quality of behaviors?

The first reason is because we do not want to face the consequences of realizing that our deepest feelings are inconsequential when it comes to our behavior. We want to be able to say "I love them so much that I am going to _____" (insert truly awful idea here), and have our feeling be the justification for the perceived quality of the action. Stalking is the obvious one that comes to mind.

The second reason we do not want to face this is because *it means we are never done working*. We always have to keep learning about the world, and the people we care about. The pressure of keeping up with this reality is so daunting that we'd rather just pretend the whole situation didn't exist.

I don't blame anyone for wanting this reality to go away. I want it to go away. So here's my wish...it is this wish that crystallized this issue for me when I was looking at it as I was growing up.

What do I really want?

I want the feeling of love that I carry within me to create the exact right behavior in every situation. I want this to be instinctual and last forever. I also do not want the possibility of error, because the feeling I have contains no error, so neither should the behavior that it generates. I also do not want it to ever come into conflict with any other feelings in myself or others.

THAT IS WHAT I WANT. I do not want to have to negotiate this want. And I want it so badly that I am willing to pretend it is true. That is my reality, and to this day I have to struggle to honor my love for things through the process of living and learning.

Live and learn. We get better at most everything as we get older. Learning how to love people is a really difficult and taxing job. It is frustrating. It is frustrating because we are continually learning more about the nature of health, the nature of our environment, and the world around us. It is even more frustrating because the living objects of our love are constantly changing in every possible way.

We are truly ill-equipped to manage this situation. Even those of us who deeply devote ourselves to our favorite human beings and have extensive knowledge of health, psychology, nutrition, and the lot of existence are, more often than not, totally lost.

Here is another situation where *having an accurate picture of the inherent difficulty of a task gives us direction* in our focus. The Perspective matters. Seeing ourselves as naturals in translating the feeling of love into an expression cripples us. It cripples us because we take it personally when our efforts are failures. It cripples us because we do not know that a constant state of learning and evolving is necessary to honor the love we feel. We cannot prepare if we truly believe we are already masters. **Knowing we are never ready is a priceless motivation**. It makes us ask questions, and makes us patient observers as we await answers.

So, say it with me: *"The love I feel is perfect. It is glorious and divine. My ability to honor that love through action is limited by my knowledge and focus. My great feeling of love deserves my unending effort."*

Asking the Right Questions...Prepping to Teach Classes

How does love manifest? Let's say someone loves music--what expectations do you have about them given that fact?

What type of music do they like? How many albums do they own? Have they studied music? Can they play music? Which musicians are their favorites? How do they use music to make their lives better? How does their experience of music change the world and make it more abundantly musical? How often do they engage with music, by playing or listening?

We have some expectations here. If someone says they

love movies or art, we have expectations there as well. We expect that certain behaviors have been born of the feelings they declare they have. We expect that they are engaging the object of their love.

But when someone says they love someone, which is a huge, life-changing reality in someone's world...we do not ask the right questions.

"Oh, you love your husband? So you've studied psychology and nutrition, right? What's his blood type? How does his history motivate him on a daily basis? How is his body aging? How has he changed recently? How does he scare you? How does he make you feel more alive? What are you looking forward to for him as far as his emotional growth goes? What projects make him feel alive, and how are you helping him to achieve his goals in those areas? In what ways do you strengthen yourself as to add to the health of his environment?"

Ever heard those questions asked before? They are asking if you are engaged with the object of your love. If you love someone, I want you to be able to answer EVERY question above in detail. In fact, what I want is exact. It is the same that I want for myself. I want to be able to teach an entire class on everyone I love. Now it may be true that I can give only a two-hour lecture on my grandfather, but I better be able to give you a full semester on my wife and kids.

It might seem like I'm asking too much, but it is not me that is asking it. Love asks to be honored. It asks to be manifest in reality. The feelings we have demand an avenue for expression. My love demands it. So does yours. And for the glory of life love bestows on us, this is not asking much.

So how do we prepare ourselves to teach a class on a human being?

There are really only three big things to focus on. First, it is vitally important that we learn the mechanisms that all human beings share. We all have bodies. We all have minds. We all have histories and genetics and experiences that shape our Perspectives and inner realities. The way that all of these things affect us can vary slightly from person to person as all of those have variables built into them. But understanding of the human body, mind, and experiences that form the matrix of life are the core concepts, and learning those is our ability to learn the people we love. No matter where we apply this knowledge, it is helpful. It is never a waste of time or energy (especially since we are one of the people we apply it to). This includes zeroing in on specific traits within medicine and psychology that our loved ones present to us. Do they have allergies? What is their astrological sign? What is their ethnicity? What can we learn about them by the subsets of groups they are included in? That was the first part.

The second is observing the person. This is difficult only if we don't actually love them. If we love a human being, field of study, idea, etc. …it is in our nature to engage our focused attention in that direction, and observe the manifestations of that which we love. Really, the second part is "Paying Attention to something we love." It's pretty simple, but it does demand that we focus when we are distracted, and that we care to find changes in the object of our love. That gets difficult, and is demanding. We are engaged with someone we love in an intimate way and change is frightening. As fathers and mothers, we may not want to see our children growing up. As husbands and wives we do not want to see love fading, or attention fixing in other areas. This is normal. We fear change. Hopefully we get used to it before it stops us from being able to see changes in the ones we love that are closest to us. Hopefully.

The third is our keeping ourselves in good, conscious shape. We are not capable of learning anything about anyone if we are not operating from a healthy focus. We are not capable of observing clearly and openly. We are not capable of gaining wisdom on the human condition, or applying it to our observations, if we are not happy and stable. If we are operating from fearful Perspectives, or are worn down by stress or illness, we are not going to be able to keep up with the subject matter. We will not be able to keep up, because we will not be Present.

"Some blessings come with prerequisites." – Steven Jackson, NFL running back.

We want to have the ability to love in a way that honors our feelings. But my description of love is in a chapter with the title of "blessings of expression" because there are prerequisites that must be met before we are capable of really engaging in loving behavior and focus.

I mentioned previously that when learning someone we had to be in good mental and emotional shape. This is true. If we are not in good shape we cannot be Present, and we cannot love anyone if we are not Present. If we are not Present we may as well hit the mute button during a music session, because there is nothing to transmit the expression outward. If we are Present, we can express love, anger, joy, violence, and everything we feel within us…if we are not Present, we can express only absence.

So what do we get when we are Present? What benefits do being Present and engaging our loves afford us? What happens when we know someone well enough to teach a class in them?

Learning and understanding someone makes us feel safe, and that makes us capable of more love. When I mentioned that we cannot express love when we are not Present, it means that whatever makes us stressed, frightened, and angry is capable of denying our love its outlet. Since there are major issues we all face as conscious beings (like rejection, confusion, and shock) it is very easy for us to be much closer to fear, rather than a place of safety when it comes to those closest to us. The truth is that this fear is totally justified, because the people we love and are vulnerable with will always have the greatest ability to hurt us. Learning others can ease the distress we feel that is caused by this fact.

When I love someone, I am watching everything they do. I react to their existence, and empathize. This means that I am vulnerable to hurt when they hurt, and feel rejected by their wants, needs, and attention. This causes a constant state of distress, but it is one that we can learn to live with over time. If we learn to live with it, we can also learn to lessen it, and thrive in its presence. I want to show some ways that learning and engaging our loved ones ease our own levels of stress and fear, and allow us to move fully engage the ones we love.

How We Ease Stress and Fear for the Purpose of Heightened Engagement

I know a lot about the people I love. I know a lot about people in general also. This allows me a blessing that is so joyful for me that there are many times when I can barely contain myself as a soul-body compilation. It allows me the ability to love bountifully.

There are things I know about everyone in my world that helps me with them, and so I'm going to cover examples. These are not esoteric examples, and every one of us does this naturally to some extent. This is because it is not just an aid in loving, but a survival mechanism that we can tap into...one of the rare occasions a survival trait can be used to thrive in this world.

Here are some examples of how knowledge helps people I know relieve stress, feel safe, and give love. I will present those along with descriptions of what NOT having that information would look like. When I mention what not having the knowledge entails, it may look like I'm being dramatic...but while subtle ways we improve our world may seem tedious and trivial at times, they are crucially important.

Situation 1

My nephew has issues with gluten and sugar. He gets beyond cranky. He gets out of control and violent if his chemistry is not in balance, and he is very sensitive to this balance.

The knowledge we have: My sister-in-law knows how gluten and sugar work with the body. And over time she has become very attentive to even the most minor changes in his physiology throughout the day. She pays attention to him, and can watch the fluctuations of his mood with enough focus to feed him what he needs, without feeding him what he doesn't need...all throughout the day.

The result: My nephew is a well-behaved kid. He trusts the people around him, and the world, to meet his needs. He is less prone to acting out, and rarely has melt downs. When he gets close to having one, my sister-in-law can react with the proper food and attention to make it less painful for him. That's the primary result. The secondary result is for my sis-in-law. Instead of being confused and frightened all the time about my nephew's mood swings, she can relax and just provide him with what he needs when he needs it. This makes the entire household run more smoothly, and it can serve as a "healthy family example" for anyone who needs one and has similar circumstances.

The result for a family that had not addressed, or found out about the gluten issues: The violence would not have abated at a young age and the acting out would have gotten worse. The family would all be tense, as there are four children, and my sis-in-law and brother would be in a constant state of worry over my nephew's erratic moods and destructive behavior. It is unlikely that he would be able to attend school, and the strain on the family as a whole would be gigantic, removing the likelihood that the other children get their needs met. The stress on the household would also likely manifest physically with illness for everyone in the house. It would be very difficult for anyone to visit, or extremely stressful if they did.

That was just *understanding a gluten sensitivity*. But how many of us do the necessary research to help those we love? Many of us do, and either cannot find the correct answers, or do not have access to the right resources when we do find the correct answers. Then, on top of finding the information, it takes tireless effort and focus...effort and focus that must be followed up by training my nephew to be as mindful of himself as we are of him. **The whole of that endeavor is an expression of love**.

Situation 2

My boy is twelve. That in itself is an issue. Puberty is an insane time for boys and girls, where their actions are bigger and bear more consequence than before, at a time when they have the least amount of control over their actions and impulses. My boy is loud, prone to wild mood swings, violent with his brother, forgetful of important things, and over-reactive. Puberty is like being on drugs, and knowing you're under the Influence of an odd chemical reality eases a lot of the fear and stress related with it.

The knowledge we have: I know that his mind is expanding and hungry. I know that he is hugely frustrated by everything everywhere, and has no idea how to control or even relate to his ever-changing emotional matrix. I know that his levels of stress directly relate to how he will grow emotionally during this period. I know that our responses as parents can give him stability and boundaries, which he needs during this process. I also know that my reactions to his behavior need to be really tempered by my understanding of where he is. I tell him all the time that he is building more neural pathways than he ever will again, and that requires that a chemical imbalance be in place. It is normal that he feels uncomfortable, because that means he is imprinting new concepts that he will use the rest of his life

The result: We get a young man who is capable of asking for time alone. We get a young man who makes mistakes, and has consequences, but does not live in fear. His ease and comfort make him capable of allowing himself to go through frustrating cycles and learn to process emotions without reining in his nature due to fear of what those expressions will cause in the world around him. He feels understood, and listened to. He does not feel alone because we can mirror back to him what he is feeling, and validate his growth. His behavior is mellow. And due to all of those factors, this growth period is not violent, or alienating for him. Haven't been able to do much about the clumsy or forgetful part yet, though.

The result for a family that does not know about adolescent psychology: The child becomes increasing frightened and stressed because his mood fluctuations are taken very seriously, and he becomes afraid of his expressions. He begins to withdraw and act out. He seeks help, seeks feeling understood and safe, and finds a frustrated parenting unit who are perplexed by his irrational and ever-changing behavior. He lives scared. He does not act on his instincts, and begins to not trust himself. He begins to feel alone. Thus, he begins to keep his internal reality under lock and key. He represses his emotions because they scare him and those around him. He and his parents lose touch. He has the choice of disappearing completely within himself or finding ways to ask for help. These ways get more attention the more destructive they are. The child spends years trying to understand himself, searching to feel known and loved by those around him. He becomes resentful and disengaged.

This is just puberty. While people and expressions vary, we can all do more to treat this time period as the crazed author of the future adult that it is. Patience and calm reactions to the many changes within the previously stable mind of a child are essential for their development.

Situation 3

My mate is a Gemini. Now I have never been a huge fan of astrology. From a scientific perspective I am not sure how gravity functions to create personality traits in fetal tissue. Now I can take my skepticism and walk with it as long as I want, but I am ignoring a possible tool if I do so, and I know it. So…I became familiar with what it means to share my life with a Gemini.

The knowledge that understanding a Gemini affords me: I know that she can hold two opposing viewpoints and experience untold amounts of stress as a result. She can draw from these opposing viewpoints at any moment, and switch back and forth on every single thing in our lives. She can want a combination of things incompatible with reality. That is normal for a Gemini. For me, her focus looks like steering two cars at once and randomly choosing which roadway she is reacting to. That is what it looks like to me, *but that is NOT what she sees*. So she'll be steering on a mountain road in one Perspective and on a drag strip in the other, and I don't know what's going to happen when she gets to a turn. All judgments about this aside, this is scary for me. I cannot believe that it works, because I CAN'T WORK IT. But it's not my business to make it work; it's my business to let her work it. That is where my responsibility can end. I don't have to be stressed out. The only way she can find out which landscape she wants is by steering in both until she has to pick one. Until then I treat both as real, because they are, even if to me they look incompatible. She is expertly working schemata that I have absolutely no ability to even witness.

The result of my knowledge: I can watch her bounce around within the same Perspective in ways I cannot wrap my mind around. I can relax. And when I'm relaxed, she'll find out what she wants faster, and with less stress.

The result of NOT having that knowledge: I get nervous. It makes her nervous. I get into cycles of fear each time she is making a decision, and it makes me sensitive. She begins to feel guilty about the way she thinks and makes decisions. She starts to hide it from me, or feel nervous tension every time it occurs, and this exacerbates the problem and makes her much more likely to make bad decisions due to the discomfort. Worst case scenario is that she feels so uncomfortable she becomes resentful, and leaves the relationship.

These are all examples of Perspectives we undertake to make life more awesome for the people around us. We undertake these Perspectives out of respect for our loved one's experience. Respect lies in the non-dismissal of whatever their reality entails. If their realities lie outside of our sphere of understanding and control, we work outside of our comfort zone, rather than dismiss part of who someone is to make them fit into a container we understand.

We live a life filled with sound bites of people "not getting" this. "Why can't she just be happy!" "Why can't he stop drinking?" "Why can't they get over it!" "Why can't they control it!" "Why don't they understand!" "Why doesn't he let his emotions out!" "Why is she like this when she's hormonal; she knows it's coming!" "Why does it always have to be a fight!" "Why doesn't she make up her damn mind!" "Oh My God they make me so crazy!"

Those are all the same question: "WHY DOESN'T THIS PERSON FIT INTO MY PICTURE OF WHAT REALITY SHOULD BE LIKE FOR THEM." Yeah. It's not their problem, it's ours. If we want to see ourselves as loving another person, it's best to get those questions, translate them, and transmute them into what they are. *They are ALL a call to action.* They are the call to MORE FULLY UNDERSTAND THE PERSON WE LOVE.

We do not have to become part of a cycle of rejection with them. We do not have to get freaked out and reject their situation…have them feel rejected and pull away. Knowledge about the ones we love makes us unlikely to be frightened and defensive about their way of relating to the world around them. Knowledge can help us avoid situations that damage our relationships. Each human being is an entire culture, with a language, a science, and a history. Being a good student is a vital prerequisite for learning how to love anyone.

Study and focus into areas of our loved ones' lives can and will yield results that are pivotal to the survival of any relationship, and our overall ability to thrive in the world. Understanding the realities and motivations of people we love creates a *LARGER SHARED REALITY* between the two parties involved. That sounds like Synergy of Commune to me. That brings us to the final and most important aspect of loving. Knowing, understanding, and loving the self.

This is not the proverbial "know thyself" of philosophical ambiguity…this is a "know thyself" that relates to how we are capable of loving ourselves or something/someone else. It ends up being nearly the same course material, but with a different applied focus. The focus is different, because *we* are teaching the class in *ourselves* to someone else. How well can we teach THAT class to another person as it relates to our relationship with them?

This is not "How well do you know yourself?" …this is "How well can you explain yourself to each unique person in your life?" It is, of course, not just about sharing our hearts and minds with those we love. It is about protecting others.

For anyone we love and are close to, we have the ability to hurt them more intimately and deeply than anyone else. We have heightened opportunity. They are the audience that will get any excess violence that we need to express. They will be the beneficiaries of any unmanaged aggression. We also need to focus on teaching others how to understand our language. Misunderstandings are powerful and all too common, as is our ability to take everything personally. None of that is helpful.

The more we know about ourselves and can share with others, the more likely we are to be able to skirt around the many landmines that can present themselves in everyday situations. The more comfortable we get with maneuvering these hazards in concert with another person (Synergy of Commune), the more of ourselves we can share. That means more of our pain can be healed, and more of our joy expanded.

Knowing the Vito and Teaching the Vito: Protection and Enrichment

I have been pretty good my whole life about not making myself more complex than I have to be. It's very rare that I force people to figure things out, and there is not much that lies beneath the surface. There is a lot, and I have a tendency to overshare more than an over-caffeinated drunk, but it is pretty straightforward stuff.

I have PTSD. I am bipolar. I have six years of college under my belt, and twenty years of organized study that I carry around with me. I love football. I am well-versed in many areas of life, and excited about sharing ideas and connections in those areas. I have been an addict and a drunk. I have been an adrenaline junkie. I was a musician, and care a ton about music. I am very tuned to visual Intuition. I am VERY sensitive. I am an ambivert (super social one minute, an introvert the next). I can have debilitating panic attacks that can be

brought on by anything. I need seven hours sleep uninter-
rupted, or I am not going to be myself and will have to find a
way to adjust during the day (due to being bipolar, and to the
meds I take for sleep). I am compulsive. I frustrate easily.

That is what Vito looks like on paper for the most part.
That is the outline of the class I am going to teach on myself.

The class changes for every person I am teaching. That is
my job. My job as a Vito (and your job as a You) is to adjust
the class to the **Audience** I am addressing. The content changes, the length of the class changes, and my language changes.
My mate, my children, my coworkers, my friends, my clients
...they all get different voices tailored to their learning styles,
and content appropriate to the growth of *our* relationship.
Explaining ourselves is not just about us and what we want to
express about ourselves. It is about everyone, because *growth*
is about everyone.

It is more difficult than I have stated here. It seems like
"finding the right voice" to speak with someone shouldn't be
that hard. But it is really hard. It is especially hard if it is a sensitive issue. It is difficult if we fear rejection, or are in danger.
It is difficult if we are asking for help. Those moments are the
ones we need clarity of communication the most, and they
are the most difficult to navigate successfully.

I had ten psychologists. Ten. I did not get the complete
and accurate diagnosis until the tenth. It took me five to get
the bipolar diagnosis, then another five to get to PTSD. Now
I can sit here and blame psychologists all day for not being
able to diagnose me...but the truth is that I did not express
who I was in a manner that would allow them to understand
what I was experiencing. That is my job. My job is to express
myself in a way that "specific others" can understand.

Now what does this have to do with Love and prerequisites? I can tell you that if I had never gotten myself across correctly to my tenth psychologist, I would not be where I am. Not close. I would still have been dealing with the issue of mental instability. I was not capable of safely loving anyone, or *protecting others from my instability*. I needed help. And in order to get help, I had to be able to communicate with someone that could help me.

The difficulty is obvious with a psychologist, as they are strangers, and have to build an entire profile of my life based on what I tell them. But the difficulty is everywhere, and it is imperative that we do not get too frustrated, because we cannot ever give up on communicating our experience. My mother had to live with me through some rough years. I was drinking heavily and having panic attacks daily.

I remember that I had tried to explain the feelings that led to drinking on a daily basis for five years. We had to have talked about it hundreds of times. She said she understood my description, but then she would ask questions that led me to believe she did not. *So I did not give up.* After five years I found an analogy that described the combination of a panic attack, energy overload, and its physical component in the necessary manner to get my point across.

Not only did that breakthrough give me peace and satisfaction, which was a huge weight lifted, it provided her and me both with means of protecting each other. Her focus had always been to try to help me control a panic attack. That is not only impossible, but painful. When someone is trying to "reason" you out of a panic attack, it is insulting, frustrating, and infuriating...and they do not mean to be. So when I finally got myself across fully, *she stopped accidentally hurting* me. When I am in a bad panic attack, which happened daily for years, I am in awful physical pain. But the pain is REALLY difficult to express in words. So she would tell me that I was safe, and show me that my surroundings were secure. She did that because she could not see or understand how the pain was manifesting and affecting me. The fact that she couldn't understand the pain made me feel less safe. It made me angry. It frustrated me. It hurt my feelings. And all of those things together made the panic worse.

I was a grease fire. She could use only her tools and knowledge of my situation. Until I broke through the gap in our communication she would simply see that I was on fire, and douse me with water. But I was a grease fire. So every day she made it worse by accident, because I could only say "I'm on fire!" really loud. At this point she would toss water on me, making the fire worse. I was doing my best and she was doing her best. ***It wasn't good enough.***

That is a frustrating thing, beyond what I could ever explain. It doesn't seem like it should be that hard, or that it could be that hard. But it is. She was my mother, a therapist, and we had lived together for twenty years of my life. AND IT STILL TOOK ME FIVE YEARS TO EXPLAIN. Wow. It's humbling.

So we can see how teaching the class on Vito is going to be different in every exercise. It is also never to be underestimated. It's rather important that I know it backwards and forwards. It has been much more of a focus for me because I am over-reactive. My bipolar disorder and PTSD, panic attacks, etc. ...they have been a part of my life for a long time. I consider myself lucky to have been gifted with some extra challenges in the area of consciousness, because it has afforded me the necessary forced attention that lead to everything I am trying to get across in this book.

Being very intimate with myself and learning the manner in which I can best explain myself to others has been irreplaceable for my relationship with my mate. I have spoken about how I teach myself to strangers, and how I teach myself to family. This is how I go about continuing to teach in my **Primary Relationship**.

The issue with our Primary Relationship that gets us into trouble, and why I believe getting involved and engaged with teaching a class in ourselves, is that we have to be vulnerable. It exists to an extent with everyone...the ability to be vulnerable and become healthy, powerful, and achieve synergy. The opportunity exists with everyone, but the necessity to do so does not exist...neither does the pressure or risk associated with it.

"Are you okay?" I have heard that question a million times from my mate and my boys. They know that being out and about can rile me up, and get me flustered. They also know that if it gets bad I will be a wreck for an entire day, or longer. That is no fun for anyone and can severely injure our plans. Over time, being able to use that question to protect things from getting out of hand has made me able to do things I never could have done otherwise. When my mate or my boys ask me if I'm okay...when I answer, I have to be right. I cannot love them if I am not stable, and they cannot keep me from becoming unstable unless they know exactly where I am. This means that I have to have constant clear observation of where my emotions are, and be able to give an immediate account of it.

Answers to this question range from "happy and mellow" to "totally messed up," and everything in between. When I am answering my kids, if things aren't going so well, I am very careful to also say "but it's a matter of time, and you don't have to do anything. I'll just wait it out." I try to share as much as possible with my boys without burdening them. I have been asked this question while driving us home, and upon my answer "Umm, I don't know exactly how I am," we stopped the car, and my mate took the wheel so I could mellow in the passenger's seat. Sometimes she asks while I'm driving and I say "Not so good, but the driving is helping me and I'm focused and safe." If I am not safe, or am not sure if I am safe to drive, I tell her. **That is really embarrassing**. It's really not fun for me to admit that I have, for no apparent reason, lost the level of consciousness I require to drive a car safely. But I love her, and not telling her is putting her at risk. That is unacceptable.

In order for me to put those I love in the best position possible for joy and health, I have to know where I am and what it means for them. I can tell my kids I'm not doing well, am crazy angry, or panicked, and that validates what they saw that made them ask the question. Then I know enough to absolve them of guilt, blame, and responsibility. That is how I protect them.

I can tell my mate that I am about to lose it, or have gotten flustered by something or someone, and trust that she will not resent me, use it against me, or ruin her day trying to help me. She will ask me what level of attention I need for help, and I almost always know how much it is. "*I've got this one,*" "*I want to try to get this one, but I may miss,*" "*Need help when you get a second,*" and "*Need you right now*" are statements that determine actions in my household. They are taken seriously.

She wouldn't be able to help if I didn't know where I was. And if she can't help me, then I will spiral down and out, and have a "lost day." That means she has a lost day, and the boys have a lost day.

I know myself, and my moods, and my world, and thus can protect those I love from anything about myself that I cannot always control. My life would not work if I could not do that effectively.

The rough part of explaining this is that the average person without PTSD and anxiety disorders has no idea that this applies to them too…and just as much. We all get weirded out, and scared, and have over-reactions to things. Everyone can get crushed by stress or confusion or anger. While my panic attacks are awful and horrific, the average road rage exchange is not exactly a picnic. "Mommy, why were you screaming at that lady in the other car?" Funny…kind of.

My panic attacks keep me from doing normal things, but others' frustrations make them yell and scream at people they love, drink until they have fully escaped consciousness, and unleash loads of transferred rage onto everyone close to them. *We do these things because we do not know ourselves well enough to figure out how to decompress and heal ourselves throughout the day, as well as because we refrain from asking for, and getting help from those around us*. So who pays? Our loved ones do.

My panic attacks are a gift. Because of them I learned to manage my entire consciousness. I made friends with the forces that motivate my behavior. Everyone can. Everyone can take their relationship with their reactions and emotions seriously, and engage the things about themselves that are volatile, frightened, defensive, or aggressive. Then we can work in concert with those who love us to slowly alleviate their Influence. That is how we truly love.

Telling the person we love (and want to always impress) where we are weak and what we are scared of is epically difficult. There are descriptions of "relationship distress cycles" that could fill up an entire book. I will leave it at saying what should be obvious. While it is risky, and often leads to humiliation and pain, we have to do our best to know our weaknesses, and *allow ourselves to be known in all our rich human vulnerability*. We will not be happy if we do not. We will not feel known if we do not. We will not thrive if we do not. We will not be able to express ourselves if we do not. We will not fully exist if we do not. **I cannot be loved if all of "I" does not present itself**. I cannot be loved unless I show up, and teach those I love to see me. It is the only way they can protect me, and the only way I will ever feel known.

The payoff for this risk is superhuman strength. The power that flows from allowing this risk, and the influence it has over the health and glory of our lives, is priceless.

This is why we do it. We do it because pain, sadness, weakness, and fear shared are halved…and because joy and love shared are doubled. This is because love, when we present ourselves vulnerably, is shared…it has honor. That is an honor that can be expressed throughout society, and heal and empower anyone who wishes to genuinely partake in it. In the next chapter we will look at helping others, and how this ability to teach classes on ourselves, and our ability to be vulnerable, changes the nature of all relationships.

You cannot teach a class on yourself without self-love. That is a love for yourself that is larger than what things you dislike about yourself. This means that if you pile up all of the things about yourself that make you cringe and confront yourself with them simultaneously…you will still like what you see overall, and be at peace in the discomfort. That is the threshold, and it is not an easy business to succeed in.

The saying "You have to love yourself before you can truly love another" is accurate. It has holes, it is vague and incomplete, but it is accurate. In order to see it fully, we have to buy into the word "truly," and its genuine nature with all of its implications. Anything we do not love about ourselves is not going to get hidden behind you as you step closer to another. It is going to be between you, preventing you from loving fully. Always.

In 12 step programs, where people are fighting for their lives and livelihoods, Step 4 is based on listing and then looking at all of our transgressions. Writing out our mistakes is harrowing enough; being faced with the fact that we were the person who committed the acts is pretty damning. But while we all have fourth steps to write out, there is no motivation to do so if an addiction is not destroying our lives. I have not heard a non-addict say "Yeah I just wrote out my fourth step, because I thought 'Ya know, it's a good idea for everyone to do.'"

Much of the next section of the book will be dedicated to the idea that existence demands rehabilitation. Thus, twelve step programs become more obviously necessary for everyone in wanting to live full and healthy lives. But why does the average, non-addict person have to face this stuff?

The Result of not looking with self-love: Inability to share love. Why self-love is a prerequisite.

The main issue with self-love being a key piece to being able to love another person has to do with equality. However we speak about equality as a society, or as people when discussing politics simply doesn't matter. It is *theory*. Theory is cute and all, and it is where we present ideas that we like, but it has little to do with our behavioral-motivational matrix.

The truth is that we know exactly what we are scared of, and how much of ourselves we are able to present to the world around us. We know what we are not sharing. We know that we are hiding things. And besides the fact that we are expressing "hiding" when we do this, rather than whatever else we believe we are doing, *we are making equality impossible.*

There may be a moment here where you think "Yes, but I keep things from my kids, and I love them fully and consider them equals." *They are not equals.* They are kids. They are not supposed to be equal and no amount of saying how you feel about them will make them have adult experiences and cognitive matrices capable of understanding the fullness of your adult reality.

I love expression. Everything is always expressing itself. So how does not having self-love express itself by making equality impossible?

1. **We don't look at ourselves**. Being frightened to see and allow our internal realities is difficult, and if we are not too fond of ourselves, we simply will not look into areas we are uncomfortable with, and as a result we will not learn. When we do not learn about ourselves, we cannot protect others or get help from others.

This means we know we have not looked, and will not feel equal to someone who we believe has. If we believe they have not looked, then that doesn't make them equal; it just puts a different amount of imagination into the inequality. Whether we secretly believe we are doing more or less in this area leads to many realities, *but equality is not one of them.*

2. **We feel like a liar**. We know we are not being truthful about everything. We know that the person who loves us loves who they think we are, and even if that is not the case and they do totally know us, *we will never believe they love who we truly are.*

3. **We Disable the person who loves us**. "Wow, that person is *dumb* to love me; they don't know how awful I am." That is one expression. "Wow, that person loves me even though they know I am awful; what a *sucker*." "Wow, that person loves me; they must be totally *blind* to all my awful qualities." **When we cannot love ourselves, WE HAVE TO INVENT A DISABILITY FOR SOMEONE WHO DOES.**

4. **We resent the person who loves us**. "Why do they have to see me so incorrectly? I think I am awful, why do they have to make me feel bad by loving me even though I am so unlovable? What, do they think they are better than me, are they pitying me? Who the hell do they think they are to take pity on me? It makes me so angry that I love someone who is too disabled to see what a scum I am."

5. **We become the swine**. "Do not cast your pearls to swine, lest they trample them underfoot, and *turn on you.*"

If we are not presenting ourselves fully, or we are bereft of self-love in the face of someone actually loving us, we will turn on them. This is where "people pushing others away" happens. *"I am awful, and you are stupid that you don't know or don't care, so now I'm going to really show you how awful I am, so that I can see the look of fear and disgust on your face that echoes how I feel about myself."*

How many times in a relationship have we gone way overboard and screamed "Now you can see what I'm *REALLY* like." What's even worse is when the other person does not validate us by looking back at us with the same eyes we use when we look inward at the self we have not fully accepted.

6. **We run**. When someone can accept us, when we do not, the shame is overwhelming. If we have the strength to not turn on those who love us, we will run until our legs fall off and our entire world burns.

I want to be very clear about something. This still happens when you have self-love. All of these scenarios play out during even the best relationships with the healthiest people, because we do not love "aspects" of ourselves. But it does not get to the pure violence of the later stages of this *because we love ourselves more than we dislike whatever has come up.* So no matter how overwhelming something we have to deal with at the moment feels, our reaction to it will not drive us from engaging and asking for help. And there is nothing two people + love cannot conquer.

That's the toughest thing about not giving 100 percent of ourselves, or hiding bits and pieces that we don't like. We are incapable of feeling deserving. If we do not feel deserving, we will violently repel anything beyond what little love we believe we deserve…because we are defending ourselves from it. It is too painful to bear the shame of being loved when we do not have self-love. We will defend ourselves against it.

We are not capable of loving fully until we are capable of loving ourselves. We may be able to give love, and we may be able to have moments of it, but we will not be able to share it. Love is meant to be shared. It belongs to the world. It is the goal of Synergy of Commune. We want to create a world more capable of producing loving realities.

Love is shared. Self-love allows loving action to flow unhindered. While this is obvious with interpersonal relationships, it is not as obvious when we look at our relationship to society and the world around us.

In the same way we would push another away when they get to close to areas of our realities that make us uncomfortable, we will also push the world away. We will push money and abundance away. We will defend ourselves from everything we do not think we deserve. We will aggressively and pre-emptively be violent to the world around us.

However, if we pull off the prerequisites for being able to love, then we are blessed. We are blessed with an ability to participate in the world with those we love, and honor the feelings we have for them. We are blessed with the ability to present ourselves and be known, to share closeness. We are blessed with knowing that we are expressing that which we believe to be most dear to our heart and in a way that others can rightfully see. We are blessed standing in the sunlight of our own glory.

And beyond those truths, we become the blessing we are capable of being to ourselves, our reality, and the world. Then that ability to love becomes a motivational Influence on the world itself. This is because love, all love, is shared.

PART 3: CONSCIOUS ASSISTANCE

This section is interesting. It has been hours at the computer and I cannot figure out how to start it. It is much more of a warning than the past two sections of this chapter. Love and Forgiveness are specific parts of our world where simply embracing a role of larger responsibility is needed. This section has to do with helping others, and **Being of Conscious Assistance**. Being of Conscious Assistance has to do with our ability to function in a multitude of roles across our life. It is not a focused idea that can yield an obvious ideal to strive toward; rather it is a list of warnings as to how NOT to behave. In other words, you know for sure when you do Love and Forgiveness correctly. You can feel it and it is reflected back to you. In the arena of helping others, Being of Conscious Assistance *can only let you know when you're doing it wrong*.

"Our prime purpose in life is to help others. And if you can't help them, at least don't hurt them." – Dalai Lama. This is way more difficult than it sounds, and we often end up hurting others because of the way we enlist ourselves to help.

We make a lot of assumptions. We assume that being able to love is a feeling, and that forgiving is a decision. We also assume that we are capable of helping others through effort whether we are actually qualified or not. This is because we are taught to believe that effort = work = help. This is not the case. Effort is simply energy expended. Energy expended needs to be tailored to a situation through our consciousness. For this we have to know ourselves and our abilities, as well as have a deep understanding of whatever situation we are trying to affect.

The main problem is our *assumption that we are grown up enough to be helping anyone do anything*. I am NOT saying that helping others, or directing others is something we should not think we can do, but rather the following: "We need to be diligent about asking what and why we are helping or teaching someone, so that we do not simply assume that we have any business doing something we shouldn't." We need to assume we are kids in the kitchen.

Kids in the Kitchen

Kids can't cook. It is hilarious watching them try. They do not have the manual dexterity, or patience, or sense of timing or measurement necessary to get through a meal. They crack me up. They cannot read directions and follow them. They are not supposed to be able to, though. They're kids.

They think they are helping, though. They don't notice that it takes an adult twice as long and five times the energy to manage them so that they do not destroy dinner. They will feel like they helped, and have a sense of satisfaction. This is a good thing for children to get a chance to do. It helps their confidence.

Now let's look at adults trying to manage their lives. Not that different.

The difference between children helping their parents cook, and adults advising themselves or others on major issues in life, is that there are no parents around to make sure the adults don't set fire to everything. The parts of adult life that matter the most--psychology, motivation, consciousness, spirituality, human anatomy, and relationships--we have only rudimentary knowledge in these areas and *no supervision.*

I am going to mention just really quickly, that none of the above is taught in-depth in high school. We have an entire scholastic career until the age of eighteen, and the study of our minds, relationships, and spirituality (meaning of life) is not a focus. Is that a joke? I was studying psychology, myth, comparative religion, and nutritional biology before I was out of middle school.

For instance, until Kinsey (and later Masters and Johnson) dealt with the world of sexual relationships we did not have sex education courses in this country. That was only sixty years ago. Until then adults had to guess, and knowledge was handed down from parents to children, *and was wildly inaccurate*. That is where we are with psychology, motivation, and spirituality now. It is a primitive and incomplete knowledge. It is unacceptable. **We have about the same concept of our bodies and minds as a five-year-old has of a kitchen.**

So we have the analogy. Our ability to help with issues that concern "how to live" are akin to that of a child's ability to cook dinner.

We can look at our skills, and we can do some things pretty well. This is why we get all confused, just like a child would. We see that we can program a computer, or build a house, or teach mathematics, and our confidence grows. But these skills are just single skills only partially related to the whole of the endeavor of living, in the same way knowing how to pour a half cup of milk, or break an egg, *is only partially related to making fried chicken*. And that is usually where our "expertise" ends.

Thing is, without a parent present, a child is unlikely to have success. Remember the chapter on Society Parenting? That is what we are trying to do. We are trying to collectively create a parent-body that can aid us in our "**Kitchen of How to Live**." These would not be rules. These would only be tools, along with Perspectives on how to create tools in new situations.

Rules in our Kitchen of How to Live are what religion has given us, along with some meager tools. Religion, at least in the forms it has taken now, applies rules because they are easy to understand, but the rules are in place for ONLY ONE TYPE OF MEAL. They are in place to meet the needs of an unchanging society and are thus useless when the meal changes from fried chicken to spaghetti and meatballs. The absurdity of using the directions for fried chicken to make spaghetti and meatballs is exactly like applying the ethics and science of a two-or-more-thousand-year-old religious text to our present-day society. In such a situation, you can make use only of the symbolic aspects that transfer to all situations.

Ideals like faith, love, gratitude, and reverence, kinda transfer to every area of our lives. Having a clean workspace, the proper set of cookware, and knowledge of kitchen appliances will always be of use. But our lives are an ever-changing meal and the ingredients we have to work with are not only different all the time. They are not under our control. So, one set of directions is not going to get it done. Two is not going to get it done. In fact, 100 sets of directions won't get it done.

No matter how many sets of directions we have, it cannot cover the whole of existence. So what exactly should we be focusing on? Intimacy. How well do we know our kitchen? How well do we know our meats and veggies? How well do we understand food and flavor combinations? How well do we know the ways in which ingredients react to one another? How well-equipped is our kitchen with appliances? Because the difference between how capable we are on average (*a child in a kitchen trying to read instructions*), and how capable we could be over time with focus and attention (*a master chef that can take any ingredients and perform alchemy to turn them into a magical dining experience*), is the difference between two worlds. One world is nourished and thriving; the other is frustrated and struggling to survive.

Certainty of rules in religion keeps us from intimacy, curiosity, engagement, understanding, adjustment, etc. Certainty of order and rules in relationships keeps us from learning individual people in our lives. We are children who want directions …what we need to do is learn our kitchen.

This is not the fault of religion, though, and it is not the fault of social norms. They are simply the extravagant expression of our inner desire for certainty, whose elusive nature I have covered over and again in this work.

There are many reasons that humility and reverence are pivotal in this life. The reason that I want to focus here is that these two attitudes are necessary for allowing new information in, and allowing our view of the world to change with the new expressions of the world.

Everything is expressing itself. Everything is a language. Everyone is a culture. Our humility before the grandeur of existence is what allows us to learn. It allows us to engage in attempting to translate the majestic mysteries that exist all around us.

There is a good deal of what I am going to be talking about that would fit within the chapter on parenting. This alludes to the parenting of all, by all. It references our ability to learn, and our ability to teach everyone through our actions and attitudes. But this chapter will be looking at subtle differences in expression across a wide field of human experience and expectation. In the section on parenting we focused on our need to understand our ability to Influence. This section will focus on our need for humility and restraint, showing that their presence in our behavioral matrix is essential for being of aid to the world. We need humility and restraint because those attitudes allow us pause to ask vital questions about our role in any relationship, at any moment.

It takes a good deal of learning before we can help anyone with anything. It is a long journey to get to the point where we can successfully help ourselves. We have not been trained, and we are frightened. We are frightened of admitting how truly lost we are, in the same way that doctors were frightened of admitting that germs might exist, 150 years ago. It puts our illusory authority at risk. **DISCOVERY CAUSES COGNITIVE DISSONANCE IF HUMILITY IS NOT PRESENT**. So when I speak of humility, I am speaking of life-altering information, *and our amazing ability to ignore it.*

Realizing how ill-equipped we are to understand and utilize the most significant aspects of reality is the first step to being able to manage and improve our world. There is a life event that many of us have had that is a great analogy for this.

Learning to Drive: the Humbling Reality

I remember thinking that learning to drive was about learning how to steer and shift. I was pretty stunned when that was less than 5% of actual driving, and that *"paying attention to all off the other cars on the road"* was actually 65%, and learning *"how not to die when something crazy happened"* made up the rest.

I learned to operate a car on a farm with a long dirt road, empty of traffic. I was focused on steering between the lines, and shifting smoothly. What I could learn in a day made me confident and joyous about my future freedoms.

I remember how it felt to finally get on the road. I remember the difference. It was violent. It was humbling. The multiplicity of moving parts, the rules, the speed at which things occurred, and the realization that mistakes were permanent were not the only things that humbled me. My inability to have foreseen such a drastic change in focus, and such a violent rush of fear, completely stunned me.

How did I not realize that I would have to worry about every other driver on the road? How did I not get that driving was an idiotically optimistic attempt to move in concert with the rest of society in metal death machines? And how did I not know that I would have such fear of every other person on the road? How? Because such fear does not serve us. It is overwhelming, and takes a ton of energy and focus to overcome.

But we all want to be able to drive (at least in American culture)…so we are motivated. There are a ton of rule books, teachers, classes, and tests to make sure we can come to a great sense of skill and confidence within this reality. Also, the people who teach us, have for the most part, mastered the skill of operating a vehicle in a city setting. **This is not the case with managing consciousness, or our mental states**.

Another aspect of this is that our effort is not enough to keep us safe. It is not enough to keep the others on the road safe, and it is not enough for us to be able to ensure the safety of anyone we are teaching. *Our effort does not guarantee success.* Steering safely in my lane did not mean I did not have to worry about an accident.

So, as soon as I realized this, I became hungry. I became hungry for the ability to learn every weakness I had. I became hungry for learning how to translate the environment of traffic, and all of the many personalities of the road, into the best matrix for determining my behavior while behind the wheel. I learned to look into cars and read the expressions on drivers' faces. I learned to watch for tendencies in specific cities and settings. I've learned to drive more carefully when it is hot out, and manage the environment of the car as far as noise and distractions as they are determining factors of my safety, and everyone else's safety.

This is why you are reading this book. You want to learn. You want to understand the rules of the road in a vast and unpredictable world that exists internally and externally. I do too. Honestly, I have reread this book since I started writing it.

We want to help the world. We want our expressions to improve life. We want experience and Resonance. We want Rapture, and we want to share it. We want to help others. We feel good when we help others. We feel worthy and powerful. It is natural upon giving the gift of improving someone's experience that we feel joy, because we have had our lives affected in this way, and we know how much respect and gravitas comes with it. We know it because of how we felt toward those who have done the same for us.

It is a true bounty, being helpful. It brings joy and power and life to everyone on all sides of the exchange. Being of service can change our life focus and retrieve us from truly dark times.

We can get into trouble with it, though, and that is why it is a blessing and privilege, not a right. It requires more than our simple effort. It involves our engaging in the full relationship that contains us, those we wish to help, and the subject matter being dealt with.

Who Are We to Try to Help? The Psychologist's Dilemma and Checklist

We really have to ask ourselves questions all the time. We have to keep a running dialogue going with ourselves, because if we do not, we can do a lot of damage. So the thing we need to ask, every time, is: "Who are we to try to help?"

I ask myself this all the time, now. People have been coming to me for advice since my freshman year of high school. I did not start asking myself this question then. In fact, I don't know that I started asking until I was close to thirty years old. I had to watch the effects of all of my actions for a long time before I decided to engage the safety mechanisms I now use to keep myself and others healthy.

See, I want to answer EVERYTHING. I want to be a "Helper." I wanted my relationship to everyone in the world to be one where I was aiding someone else in getting healthier and smarter and becoming more alive. This is not a bad thing to want. I still do want it. But now I understand this want, and how seductive it can be.

I realized, when I was about nineteen or twenty, that I answered every question asked me. Whether it was about science or philosophy or religion or math or literature...didn't matter, I answered it. However, I realized that knowing the answer to the question was not necessary for me to give a response. I would answer whether or not I knew anything about what I was talking about. I'm not saying that I was sometimes wrong. I'm saying that I would be asked a question like "Why is the sky blue?"...and I would think to myself "*I don't really know that, **but I'm going to answer anyway**.*" I responded with "The sky is blue because the water is reflected back to it from the sunlight, and it's all blue because the Earth's surface is 70% water." Sounds good, doesn't it? I made it up.

Why did I do that? Because it felt really good to give an answer. It feels really good to be the holder of great truths and meaningful information. A large part of my self-esteem was connected to it, so I served that need like a slave, and ignored my Observer's voice. Unfortunately, while falsely knowing why the sky is blue does not have calamitous effects, the questions we are commonly faced with in this society have life-changing consequences. And when it comes to these types of questions, we, as a society, are even more likely to offer a response without checking ourselves.

So this brings us to the Psychologist's Dilemma. I have had good psychologists, and not-so-good psychologists. But I do not envy their task, for it is truly daunting to take on a human being and give your energy to understanding and helping their mental reality.

How can a psychologist have an impersonal, unequal relationship with a patient, and hope to help them in any way? Friendships are based on reciprocity. Friendships are based on equality. How does someone help someone who is not a friend to them? Why do we think this is possible?

There is certainly an entire profession that deals with this, but why on Earth do we think we can help anyone with their innermost realities? We may be able to, certainly. But we need to definitely ask ourselves questions as psychologists (*which we all play at one point or another*). These are the same questions we ask about our ability to guide or advise anyone on anything.

This is the **Psychologist's Checklist**:

1) Do we know anything about the situation? Do we have experience in real life? Have we ever gone through anything similar? Is there a standard successful way to go about it that has been developed over time?

2) Do we care about the people involved? Are we connected? Do we empathize with their situation? Can we see ourselves in their place, thinking as they are thinking and behaving as they have to get to where they are?

3) Do we understand the consequences of what our advice could be? Do we understand the gravity of the situation before us?

4) Can the situation be communicated between the two parties? Can they trust one another to get close enough to the reality of the problem that the other can translate it into their language?

5) Are we hung up on any aspect of the situation? Does it contain aspects that make us emotionally unstable? Does it make us uncomfortable? Can we trust our advice is unhindered by our own emotional involvement, or is there a Conflict of Interest based on our need to avoid Cognitive Dissonance?

6) Is there someone that can advise on this situation better than we can?

7) Are we willing to let the person we are helping know if we fall short on this list?

Can we ask ourselves these questions? Are we capable of letting our love for the world and the people in it create for us a moment of reflection before we cast our opinion, educated or not, into the creative matrices of other people's lives?

We have to be able to ask these questions, and answer them honestly. Like it or not, we are ALL PSYCHOLOGISTS. And as psychologists, we face the Psychologist's Dilemma.

I spoke at length about learning other people well enough to teach a class on them, and I spoke of understanding the rules of the road in driving. To understand the magnitude of difficulty involved in helping someone else with their life, it would be akin to giving lessons on how to drive…but it would be an odd vehicle you have never driven, and in a country you have never visited. That is how hard it is to help a stranger with their life. To the extent that we could teach a class in someone, we become more capable of helping, assuming we understand the subject matter (health and happiness).

That was the Psychologist's Dilemma. I'm going to separate that and the Addict Dilemma.

The Addict Dilemma

The Addict Dilemma is closely related to the Psychologist's Dilemma, but focuses on one small aspect that is so common that it needs its own section. This book is about understanding relationships, and addictions are simply relationships…they can be with anything.

When I was an addict, I told psychologist after psychologist, "I'll quit drinking for my future wife, not for you." The Addict Dilemma is what we have as humans performing as psychologists. Whenever we are helping someone with a chronic issue, whether it is chemical (alcohol, cigarettes, drugs), dietary (bad food, lack of exercise), behavioral (bad friends, bad choices, unhealthy relationships), or otherwise, we need to understand that we are trying to do something very specific. We are trying to remove something from someone's world. But we need to know, deeply, that what we are removing is not just a symptom of a larger problem, but the person's TOOL FOR MANAGING THAT PROBLEM.

Addictions are tools. They are very crappy, destructive tools. But they are tools, nonetheless. The most obvious tools are escape drugs. Whether it is alcohol or heroin, escaping reality is the goal. So, if you have a person that has a real aversion to reality, the drug is not the problem. The drug is a solution-symptom. It is a tool that person is using to deal with the aversion to reality. It is how they are winning their battle, or at least not losing it. When we go about trying to help an addict, or anyone with a chronic problem, *we are trying to take a tool away from them.* Our society does not see it like that, and as a result, we are dreadfully bad at healing addiction.

We need to understand as Societal Parents, that **the removal of an unhealthy tool does not equal the presence of a healthy one**. There needs to be a healthy tool in place before the removal of the unhealthy one will do anything positive. Unfortunately, as helpers, we don't get to decide what that tool is. The addict does not usually get to decide either. The presence of a healing tool can be worked toward, but not controlled or guaranteed, just like everything else.

So, when we are trying to help an addict, or someone in a bad relationship of any kind, we have to understand that we are trying to pull their crutch out from under them. This is why they lash out and resent us. We have to know that is going to happen. It's a part of the process. We also have to know that the root issue is going to be a much larger and more immediate problem than the addiction was. We have to be VERY careful because with this because the risks are life-threatening when dealing with addiction.

The **Addict Checklist** has fewer questions.

1) Do we know what the prime cause for the addiction is? (Because it becomes a more pressing issue as soon as the tool is gone.)

2) Are there any other tools this person can try to use? (Because they are going to need a tool, and if one isn't there, they are either going to go back to their addiction, or lose a much larger battle with their problem.)

3) Is it safe for this person to be without any tool? Are we willing to bet our lives on it? (Because we are betting their life on it.)

I have been this guy. I was waiting for something and drinking to escape until I found it, because I could not cope without it. I was waiting for someone who could calm me, and make reality not hurt so bad. I knew that I was waiting for that, and so I didn't mess around with trying to stop drinking. I was too comfortable with suicide to trust myself without my tool.

To be clear, I had successfully been sober for a year at one point, but it was the worst year of my life, and was much more likely to end in suicide than drinking was, so...I started back up.

I had a lot of psychologists tell me I had to stop. I had a lot of psychiatrists tell me I had to stop. Not a single one of them offered me a tool in its place. Not one.

Our duty in helping others is to *"at least not hurt them."* But that is what we do with addicts. **We remove their crutch and walk away as they fall face first, and act like we did something noble**. It's irresponsible and ugly.

I had a therapist whom one of my colleagues knew. He had successfully, through many years of coaxing, gotten her husband sober. He had severe bipolar disorder and PTSD, like I did. He got sober to be with his wife and daughter, because his doctor told him it was the only way. He made it without that tool for six months. Then he had a breakdown. Then he ran away and lived in the streets. Then he committed suicide. Being with his wife and daughter didn't happen. Creating a widow and orphan did.

When people are in bad relationships with anything, or anyone, we want to help them get out of the bad relationship. *However, that does not equal getting into a good relationship.* The removal of a bad habit is not the same as creating a good one, and as friends and cohabitants on this planet we need to understand that our role in helping others is to help them create healthy realities in their world. **When healthy realities are created, unhealthy issues naturally subside.**

The addict checklist is how we protect others from our irresponsible desires to help them.

We can see that knowing ourselves and those we want to help is difficult enough, but what about the subject matter? The subject matter is usually joy, ease, calm, satisfaction, hope, and other positive feeling experiences. Do we have those? If we do not, how on EARTH could we know anything about what it takes to get them?

Also, if we are happy now, have we ever been where the coun-selee in question is? Have we been unhappy in the way that they are, and then became happy through the use of some method that can be transferred or taught?

Who are we to help? What is the deciding factor between me-chanically being able to understand a situation and ways of guiding someone through it, and actually being able to help the person heal their world? Easy … Love, Respect, Humility, and Knowledge of our innate Equality.

Love for the person, and knowledge of their struggle.

Respect for their individuality of experience and the character of their reality.

Humility before the magnitude of the soul's journey and the pow-er of guiding another soul through any aspect of this world.

Knowledge that we all have the need to be guided, and continu-ously rely on the support of those around us. Thus, Knowledge that a person's difficulty in any area of life should not allow us to feed off our ideas of our superiority. We have these feelings and judgments as we grow, but they need to be habituated *out* of our behavioral matrix.

The Relationship Mold and The Master's Conundrum

This book is about forming relationships with every aspect of our consciousness. The last issue to keep in mind when guiding someone in an area of their life…is the Influence of *our* Perspective of the relationship.

This means that once we have met all of the other condi-tions that we set for ourselves we have one last feature to pay attention to. This feature is vague, and to even describe it is going to take engagement on your part.

The **Relationship Mold** is the set view you have of every relationship in your life. It has a character and quality that is based on perceived value. It collects evidence about the nature of every relationship and builds a narrative through which our view of the relationship makes sense.

So the fact that I took out the garbage and washed the dishes is something that makes me feel powerful and safe in my role as "keeper of the house," as it relates to my mate. And there is a part of me that keeps track of everything that she does, so that I feel good about what we are each contributing. This is not a validated practice in my consciousness, just something that happens.

The fact that I taught my cousin algebra is something I have not only with my cousin, but with her mother, my aunt, and the rest of the maternal side of my family. **Why did I catalog it?**

I couldn't help doing it. It performs a function as a survival mechanism. As a result of being ashamed of myself for drinking heavily, as well as numerous other life failures, I was always afraid of being attacked. It did not matter that the attacks almost always came from my own imagination. So I actually held "teaching my cousin algebra" as a tool to use in my mind so that I was capable of defending myself should I feel the need to do so (the attacks would generally come from me). It let me feel as though I had performed my familial duties and should be regarded with respect. My production justified my existence.

So, take a moment and think of five relationships you have. Close friends, mates, co-workers. *Think about who is ahead right now.* This is something we do unconsciously, and we want to understand its presence as far as it gives us self-knowledge, and the ability to counteract its influence on us.

We need to feel safe in relationships, and this can undermine who we want to be to other people, as our need to feel safe and powerful will always overcome our desire to guide others if there is a conflict of interest and we are ignorant of it.

We can't heal someone if we want them sick. We can't teach someone if we want them ignorant. We can't free someone we want under our control. **We can't help someone grow strong whom we need to be weak.**

This means it is very important to be very clear with ourselves about how we see and feel about every relationship we have. It is important because "help" and "sabotage" *are easily switched.* The location of sabotage occurs in codependent relationships for the most part, yes, but *every relationship has some codependent qualities.* Every. Single. One.

If we ignore the parts of ourselves that identify our worth with how much another person needs us in a specific way, we will be likely to sabotage their growth efforts to ensure their continued need for us.

The Master's Conundrum is a description of the nature of guiding others, and the psychological aspects that create a balance for the sharing of knowledge. When one shares wisdom, techniques, or tools, they are sharing POWER. When we catch a fish for a man, we are not teaching him, and thus our status as "source of food" is not threatened. When we teach a man to fish, he no longer needs us for that reason. We have given something away, and *there is no amount of money that can make that balance equal.* Knowledge, like experience, is permanent.

So what we do as teachers and guides is use the Relationship Mold to bolster our sense of self-worth. We do this by becoming the "authors of another person's future success."

Even then, however, we are in a bind. Because when someone has our skills and understanding, then they can take our role as teacher also. *Every bit of knowledge and ability we share with others is a risk.* Every time we make another person more independent, the less powerful we become in comparison.

This is a conundrum, but as long as we keep in mind that our overall focus is to slowly make the entire world around us more powerful, and identify with that **Long-Term Life Goal**, we will not be tempted to clam up and hoard our resources. If "making the world around us stronger" is not our goal, *we really shouldn't be teaching anyone.*

Humility serves us well. Our knowledge and power slowly fade into other people over time, and we bow before the shifting of power from one generation to the next, forever into the future.

One way to see this process in its pure form is sibling rivalry. Each child perceives his value to his parents through the role of what he can accomplish. The older child gains accolades from authoring the younger sibling's learning wherever possible, or from withholding teaching in areas where he feels less secure.

This is a clear thing in the case of siblings, and it is powerful. It is self-valuation based on a comparison of one's abilities to another's. The idea that such valuation does not occur into and through adulthood is simply inaccurate. This is why the Master's Conundrum ends very simply with the creation of a stable and effective Long-Term Life Goal as it regards sharing knowledge and abilities that equate to power, and self-valuation. Whatever momentary Validation and power we get from authoring someone else's power and growth, it is not a dominant motivator next to our devotion to a held ideal. Thus it is never a real threat to alter our behavior to the point where sabotage could come into effect.

So the Master's Conundrum is seeing the growth our actions have led to, and while being joyous, actively disengaging from the authorship of another person's strength.

We are looking at levels of care when in a position of power. We are looking at our capacity to express our knowledge and share the wealth of our experience. It takes more than the effort we have likely been putting in for some time. However, the effort is not a bad thing; we need the effort. It just needs to be channeled into protecting the validity of our Long-Term Life Goals through a devotion to expressing ourselves carefully and healthily.

Using the checklists in this chapter will get us almost all the way there, but there is one more aspect. We have to allow people to change. We have to allow dynamism in our Relationship Molds.

Long-Term Life Goals and Dynamic Allowances

When we guide others, we are in a position of power. When engaging in relationships of this type *we must have a dynamic attachment to our Relationship Molds.* No matter how small or seemingly trivial the guidance we are giving seems…aid of any kind changes someone's life permanently. We play down this fact because it is quite a load to carry when showing someone how to screw in a light bulb. But the load only gets lighter by carrying it, not by ignoring it.

Parenting adolescents highlights the need for an outlook on the world that includes rapid and uncomfortable change. When I say "allows dynamic growth" it sounds very soft and fluffy. But what it actually is entails allowing a child we raised to enter into adulthood in the "barely prepared" manner we all have. At some random time between 7th-9th grade we have to deal with the movement from childhood toys and games as conversation centerpieces to sex and drugs and politics and world events. Ouch. Every time we blush in embarrassment it shows how unnatural it is to be totally okay with changes in the people we love.

Let me say that again. Change is natural, but it is **TOTALLY UNNATURAL** for us to be okay with it.

This is why we need a Long-Term life Goal about allowing dynamic change. It has to trump momentary discomforts. For it to be able to do that, we have to be able to recognize momentary discomfort, and not underestimate its power.

Case in point: In many religious circles that have repressed sexual views, it is more likely that sexual education is going to be lightly discussed, if it is discussed at all. The result of being Influenced by that discomfort? Elevated teen pregnancy and STD transmissions. That is a direct cause and effect. Are you uncomfortable with a part of the world? Yes? If you let that discomfort influence your guidance, then your children and those that depend on your guidance will suffer.

In the chapter on love, we talked about knowing ourselves in order to protect others. This is an extension of that. We want to be wholly involved when we give aid to another. In allowing change and fostering growth we can embody the divine through our genuine presence. It is "Vaya con Dios" coming right through us and out into the world.

The presence of the Relationship Mold makes it important that we exercise our ability to use the Psychologist's Checklist, and the Addict Checklist. The Master's Conundrum must also be present so that we may form a **Held Ideal** in the form of a Long-Term Life Goal as it regards being of service to others. Held Ideals are easily referenced purposes within our matrix of consciousness. ***Being in a position of power should always inspire us to seek humility for balance***. These are the ways we make sure that we are capable of honoring that.

The reason that this is so important, besides the "do no harm" oath we take in our hearts, is that we want to "share" knowledge, not "use" knowledge. The difference is that if we are using knowledge to improve our standing in the Relationship Mold, we are less likely to be cautious of possible consequences. Teachers that disseminate information regardless of the consequences have no business teaching, and that is exactly where we do not want to be.

Where we want to be...is sharing knowledge. Our knowledge was sourced elsewhere. It was a gift. This gift is not to be lorded over others or used as currency in power, but passed along throughout the growing and expanding world we co-create. Synergy of Commune exists outside of the demands of the Relationship Mold, and while this mold is always present, we can put our hearts into limiting its ability to motivate our actions.

We want to share. Joy shared is joy doubled. Pain shared is pain halved. Love is shared. In fact, love is the manner in which "Sharing" takes place. Being able to share and being able to help are blessings...because they demand that we engage and invest in our ever-changing reality. This is how we share.

Chapter 18:

Blessing of Connection: Source Plug-In Chapter

Much of this book deals with relationships. This is because every-thing in our lives is a relationship. How we relate to what's around us does more to determine our world than any single idea or focus we can develop. This chapter centers on how *we relate to energy*.

It takes knowing ourselves to form a relationship with the energy around us. Being in the zone, flowing, connected, or Present may be ways we have described a healthy relationship to energy. Let's call it **Source Plug-In** here. It is a connection we have with Resonance. We may slip in and out of being in healthy spaces without having formed this relationship, but it is not something we can fully take advantage of, or *share*, until we are capable of knowing ourselves in the Present moment.

It is not a simple thing to produce, mind you. The vaguest sugges-tion I have ever heard was "Get to know yourself." I couldn't figure it at first, but my confusion slowly began to form a question: "WHO gets to know WHAT...HOW?"

I like answering questions. "Who?" ...The being watching our lives that is not Influenced by our momentary reactions, but rather by the whole of our subconscious world and genetics...that is the *Who*. "What?" The manner in which the body and mind co-create a fluid reality, full of wants, and opinions about the world, through a myriad of expressions, is the *what*. "How?" You **pay attention** without fear, while limiting judgment about what you see. You **integrate the information** without a conclusion about who you think it makes you out to be. You **identify** with the picture the attention and integration has created for you in spite of any reactions you may have to it. This creates a Perspective. This is what you think, what you do, *and for all intents and purposes, this is who you are.*

So, the "Who gets to know What, How" becomes *"The Observer Consciousness gets to know the nature of the body and mind's co-created identity through paying attention without judgment."* That certainly is a mouthful.

When we are capable of creating this identity with a peaceful mind, even just for seconds, we are aligning with source energy. This alignment creates a sense of peace and hope that serve as strength for our overwhelmed souls. **This is being plugged in.** This is the goal of all of our inquiries, internal and external. Getting to know ourselves is the means to a glorious end, and by exercising this ability moment to moment we produce the effect we are searching for. *It is the only way to consciously experience ourselves.* It is the Resonance we seek.

I touched on connecting to this part of life in the opening chapter of this book. The Source Plug-In is Experience, Resonance, and Rapture within a moment. It is a habit of experiencing energy through Presence. It is what we are searching for, and if we are thorough and committed, it is what we are blessed to find. Being engaged in the fluid definition of who we are allows us unimaginable powers of Influence through Healthy Expression.

Finding a Way to Plug In

There is an ability we have, one that every major teacher in the course of human history has spoken of. It is one that we shy away from.

We must engage existence. We must have the Experience if we are looking for Resonance and Rapture.

We are a part of the whole of the Universe, and we must live the life we have in an engaged manner to play our role. Our role is small, to our eyes...and that is because of our Perspective.

We think that size matters. *We think that the size of our experience when compared to the whole of the Universe is small*. We think this to such an extent that we either run from our smallness toward a grandiose authority, or withdraw completely to avoid being overwhelmed and subsumed. But we are not small, not unimportant. The Universe will not and cannot overtake our individuality.

But we are scared nonetheless, and seek distraction. We obstruct ourselves by looking for rules and certainty, wanting to find a "way" of engaging the Universal Energy around us *without being vulnerable to its size*.

Our fear gives rise to trying to find things to put between ourselves and this bountiful energy...between ourselves and Source. This is not just money, toys, addictions, and religion. This is ideas.

This generation has been on a quest to form a relationship to energy. The reason we are struggling is because we are trying to find a manner of connecting to this energy that does not involve risk or vulnerability. We are searching outside of ourselves, rather than getting to know ourselves in the way described at the beginning of this chapter. This is why we still seek authority. We do not trust ourselves, and are averse to the natural presence of pain and risk in life.

Anything external that we want to use will put us further away from our Source Plug-In. This does not mean that ritual or spiritual books lead us away from our heart; it simply means that as long as we NEED them to get to our heart, we are still separate from it. The answer is right here, in the moment of self-knowledge, in all our flawed perfection. We are whole.

It is not easy. It is overwhelming. It is an abyss of energy, and when we look into it, it looks right back into us. However, *it is ours*.

Our Source energy is divine instinct. We do not need priests, or angels, or channels, or peace, or serenity, or meditation, or specific foods or practices, or any idea to get between us and where we want to be. We do not need anyone. It is consciousness of the self, engaging its full reality in real time. Everyone I have known, in every walk of life, profession, and level of spiritual focus is capable of doing this. *There is no prerequisite for this work, **and this work is the only pre-requisite for joy**. Every idea, and Perspective of the world we have, either helps or hinders this project.* We are capable, all of us. Our lives are filled with moments that pull us toward or away from this connection.

There are a lot of ideas that we welcome that can become barriers to this blessing. This includes Truth. This includes Justice. This includes religion. This includes New-Agey philosophy. This includes logic, fairness, equality, and even kindness. Our duty is Being Present. If our reality conflicts with an idea we are holding (that is expectation), it is *that idea that will separate us from Source*. We are the divine mess of presence, and are afforded a direct uplink WITHIN our humanity. ***Within the mess, and only within the mess, we are directly connected.***

This section is not meant to be anti-religious. It is an incitement to honor the Ascended Masters, specifically Christ and the Buddha, by "following" them as they asked, instead of "worshipping" idols and systems built by other men. They pointed at their chests and spoke of the kingdom of heaven.

We are the vitality of creative energy desperately trying to engage itself. We can, at any moment, drop everything and plug ourselves in. There will be people around us, and ideas we hold that will allow this to happen easily. We must honor those ideas and people that come to support this endeavor, and dismiss those that do not. This connection is a priority. This connects our soul to the Universal Heart...through our own heart.

This relationship, the one we form to our own well of energy through our heart, is the most important connection we will make in our lives. Being able to achieve this and tap into it as often as possible makes us alive in a way nothing else does. It is a connection that wakes us up. It is a connection that makes us Present. It is a feeling that becomes motivation for all of our present and future behaviors and decisions.

When we become Present for this feeling, it can be overwhelming and frightening. If we learn to manage it, we can share the motivation and joy with the rest of the world. We can become a fountain.

Managing the Incoming Energy: Striving for an Energy Bounty

I remember being young and being very interested in spiritual matters. My mom and brother were both very wise and well-read. They could explain things very well. I went to my brother most often, especially when dealing with high school social issues, and I would periodically get frustrated with him because of how our conversations would tie in a knot...or what I perceived as a knot.

We would be getting along on an issue, how to behave accountably and appropriately, and it would lead into him saying, "Well that's what I did, but I don't know what will be best for you." It would make me uncomfortable. So I would push: "Well, that's the right thing to do, so I'll just do that." And he would say, "That's not what we're talking about; we're talking about what you are going to do, not what is right. There is not a right way." And I would say, "Of course there is!" To which he would insist, "No. Every situation is different, and that may not be the right thing to do when it comes to be your turn."

So, being my stubborn self, I figured he was just being a jerk and forcing me to not feel confident with black and white answers. So I thought, *Fine, I guess; I'll play, but we all know there's a right answer.* There is a right answer. Of course there is. His point was not that there is no right answer. His point was "**You can never get your right answer from anywhere but your own heart, and every time you try to get it from me I am going to deny you.**" What an awesome teacher.

I thought that we were talking about answers. But we were talking about how he and he alone found answers. We were talking about Experience and Resonance. He had developed a way of relating to the world through himself, and was showing me how to do the same. He was teaching me how to find Resonance with my life. When we look at a system, something that contains our answers all wrapped up in a neat bow (and I could have sworn one existed), we are living "in reaction to" life. X happens, and we stop, and look into our pre-set bag, and pull out *"response for X."*

The worst thing about it is that it is dishonest. It's like plagiarizing a poem to get an A on a paper. Ewww. I wanted it when I was young, and you can bet part of me still wants it now when things get difficult. I want to go into my parenting rule book and use all the things I decided were correct when I had imagined them. Oops.

I remember being young and tapping in. I remember how overwhelming it was. I remember being inspired and freaked out, because it, like everything beautiful in this world, is totally uncontrollable. The amount of energy coming through is not manageable. *We may succeed in managing ourselves,* but the energy coming is not within our power to control.

I used anything I could find. I used tools and crutches to help manage myself with my connection the best I could. I used the teachings of trusted authors and trusted people. I knew that living examples were the best, but there were few available, and they were rarely stable.

This is not the case anymore. **We are in the world of living examples now.** I stay plugged in, and my mate stays plugged in. We get burned and pull away at times, *because it is still a lot.* I don't think we're supposed to be able to handle all of it all the time (especially given modern challenges). She and I are lucky because as we have learned to function as a circuit, not just a connection. This may be the true purpose of family units, and we may be coming into an era that stresses this type of energetic bond over bloodlines. The overflow of our particular circuit allows others access to healthy overflow if they are capable of reaching for it. That is because our energy is reflected inward...*as an example of how energy should be for every individuated soul*. The energy comes through us, and after she and I have **fully embodied** our energy, we have a natural overflow that goes into the grid of energy around us to be used if need be.

When we have formed a relationship with energy *that is self-sustaining* and includes this type of surplus, people can plug into the energy if they need to, and not drain us. For someone to drain us, we would have to unplug and turn our attention elsewhere. We would have to be distracted, or otherwise moved off our spot on the Beach of Quiet Emotion. This is why this is a worthy goal, and why this chapter comes directly after Being of Conscious Assistance. This is how we assist others energetically. For us to be drained, we must engage in self- doubt, anger, fear, or wishing ill on another. We have to unplug from our energy source. Otherwise our expressions of love and connection simply overcome anything negative in our path, and spill out over everyone in our surroundings. That is an **Energy Bounty**.

Being plugged in is epic. It is nourishing. But, I haven't exactly said what it is, have I? I was kind of sneaky about that, I think. The cheap answer is that it is "different for everyone," but I have more specific descriptions than that.

Here they are: Joyous imagination...The ability to manage our Perspectives...The ability to find meaning in whatever situations we are involved in ("feeling our path")... The ability to manage reactions in real time, validating healthy ones and ignoring ones that do not serve us...Being in a creative relationship with the world around us...The ability to be healthy; and express health...The ability to detoxify physically and emotionally from our encounters with the world without removing our engaged, spiritual self...The ability to embody a role of parenting with the people we come in contact with...The ability to nurture whatever community we are a part of through our continuous attention and behavior...The ability to love ourselves and others.

Things like humility, kindness, honesty, industriousness, patience...all of these things flow naturally from one who is plugged in. A person who is plugged in has rough moments, but they serve as valuable lessons for them and everyone around them. This is because of their vulnerable acceptance of the world on its terms. No experience is wasted. All experiences can lead to Resonance and Rapture when we are plugged in. All of us can be that person.

The previous paragraphs were a description of a healthy spiritual being engaged in life. That is what being plugged in creates. It looks different for everyone, and it's very likely that everyone would explain it differently. It's also not really anyone's place to look at how they plug themselves in and use that to analyze someone else's manner of doing so.

This blessed connection is a relationship with a very large version of ourselves, not "bigger or better," but more; *a version of ourselves that "encompasses" the other versions*. Who I am at this very minute is a part of me, expressing itself through my fully engaged and nourishing energy. I mean that I am sitting at a laptop writing these words and thinking about football, and the love of my life is eight feet away from me...but I am fully engaged and connected to everything I love about myself, the world, and my creative abilities at the same time. I will drive home later, and I will be focused on that in the same way I am focused on this now.

The business of this reality is to engage. We draw on reality for our ideas, for our nourishment, and for our energy. We do this constantly. It feeds the subconscious mind that supplies our Intuition. For a long time I thought there was a way to remove the negatives from this aspect of reality...to make the manner in which we contacted the world clean and without injury. But that ends up leading to sterility, and breeding a negative and judgmental attitude. It fails at creation, and in worrying to make our sources of energy "pure" (as if there were such a thing), we simply starve. So, let's look at ourselves as we are in our messy wholeness, so we can **create *through*** the toxic aspects of reality.

Energy Vampires and the Power Grid Analogy

We are all vampires (interesting start, no?). All of us. Energy vampires sucking the marrow of life from everything around us. We all need energy.

This is why our Source Plug-In is so vital. This is why it matters to take all extensions, all ideas, and all the justifiable clutter we put between ourselves and direct experience of divine energy through our divine mess, and place them neatly in the garbage.

I have thought about energy vampirism since I was a teenager, since before it was common practice to identify it.

But I kept coming across problems that my ego wanted to ignore. My ego wanted to ignore it *because I liked calling people vampires*. I think everyone likes it, or we wouldn't do it. Demonizing people, rather than analyzing actions, is more satisfying to a struggling consciousness. But I am observant, and I observed a few things that made me start to look at this story we are telling ourselves.

1) I could not be drained if I was in a good place. I noticed this before I realized that there was a Source Plug-In.

2) Everyone I knew, at one point or another, has drained me when I wasn't in a good place. This means that everyone is capable of draining me, and everyone is capable of being a vampire.

3) When I deeply engage with anyone, I can and am sharing my energy with them. And if I am not in a good space, I am likely draining them as well.

So when I am calling someone an energy vampire, I have no idea what I'm actually saying. I don't think anyone does, so let's create a new way of seeing this. I think we can find a way that makes us accountable for being drained by others. I also think we can find a way that explains how we can function together to keep the energy flowing, rather than running out. I think that we can do all of this without denying anyone access to energy or demeaning them for their hunger.

The motivational energy that we are all hungry for is sourced within us, and all around us. We are going to be accessing it whether we are conscious of doing so or not. We are just unlikely to use the energy wisely or appreciate it if we are unconscious of it.

We want to be conscious. We want others to be conscious. Tapping into our connection to Source energy is not always easy, and it is different for everyone. But how we perceive what is going on *when we connect matters, because we do not want to be drained, and we do want to help others connect.*

Photovoltaic Energy and the Power Grid of Consciousness

We all drink energy from everything around us, just like houses pull energy from the power grid. Since we are always drawing power form those around us, it is necessary to think of ourselves as a grid of flowing energy.

So, what happens when we put solar panels on our property? The electric company starts paying us. That is an Energy Bounty.

Whenever engaged with or in close proximity to another human being, we are tapping into their energy. This is the Source energy grid. We share power through connection.

When engaged, we draw energy from whatever/whomever we are engaged with. This is not unlike what a house does with its local power grid. However, when we are plugged in to our Source (engaging our own energy), it is as if we have solar generators going on our property, and can give energy back to the local grid.

The quality of our connection to the solar generators (based on how direct and open our connection to Source is) determines whether we are giving energy to the system, or taking it from the system. We want to be giving more than we are taking.

Energy vampires are not vampires because they come to take energy. Everyone takes energy. EVERYONE. *That is the nature of a shared conscious experience*. The difference is that when someone is not plugged in, they are giving a finite amount (or nothing) during the Commune. Everyone uses a ton of energy, and if they are not honoring their Source Plug-In (or specifically ignoring it), then they are going to leave the system having taken more energy than they put in.

This is not an evil thing and it can be fixed through appropriate relating. I have gotten to a point for myself where finding myself wanting energetically from being drained is really rare. This is a good place to be. It means that I am focused on my connection, and the quality of the connections of those around me, and we make a really nice, healthy, strong community of consciousness.

But have no doubts: we are all drinking up each other's energy with every engagement. *WE ALL TAKE.*

The problem is not the taking. The problem is the not creating our own energy by being plugged in. The problem occurs when we are not connected to our Source energy. Those that have not yet developed their connection to Source, and those that have emotional garbage in the way, cannot be genuinely Present. They lack Resonance. These people will consistently run low on energy. This describes almost everyone, honestly (how popular are energy drinks?). These folks will always gravitate toward people who are connected. They will use these electric "Hot Spots" to get their energy needs met, like a vampire going to a blood bank. Fear of self-empowerment, and *the accountability that follows*, is what makes the average person refuse their own connection and drink only from others. We have all done this. None of us have to do this anymore.

When energy changes hands, it becomes more valuable; so does everything shared in the Universe. We all have access…and we can all generate an Energy Bounty through conscious sharing.

The teaching-active aspect of this analogy is that the solar panels we use to maintain the integrity of our connection are not private… they are public. Understanding how we allow others in our community to access our energy can be something we refine and make glorious.

When people come to us, and share in our energy, they are basically parking a motor home in the lot next to an entire field of solar panels. If they are tapped in, they do not have to tap in through us, even if they are "energy-needy." We do not have to allow them direct access to us. Our job is to manage our energy in such a way that we plug them in for themselves. There are solar panels all over the property, and every person comes with a plug. We do this for our children. *As focused parents of the world, we are capable of doing it for everyone.*

The main reason for doing this is that we do not want to be anyone's moderator for Source energy. They may want to plug into us directly, but that does not help them. They need to plug into their own Source. Then there can be a shared experience. That has value.

I don't know if I've made this clear. When someone comes to engage us, and we are plugged in to Source, there is not an energy exchange between the two parties until they are plugged into their own Source. Their connection may be weak, it may be fragile and cut out intermittently, but it has to be there for Commune to take place. This is one reason I believe the majority of therapy fails. The reason is that most therapists let the person who needs the energy plug directly into them. It's a nice boost, but nothing is "shared," *and so no energy is created*. This is not bad every time, but it should not be the standard. For most, it is all they know.

So when we are in an energy Commune situation (no matter the length or depth of the engagement), if we are to explore a Commune and someone wants to plug in, we have to plug them into their Source first. If we do not do this, it is not a share, and *we are depriving them of their own part of the Commune*. They do not get to have a full experience without being self-engaged.

We want everyone to have their own experiences, and their own Resonance. We do not want to mediate Source for anyone. We don't want to be the reason that anyone is separate.

The energy contained in having confidence in our ability to Influence our world for the better, and protect the lives and well-being of those around us, IS HOPE. **And Hope is energy**. Hope, like belief, determines our behaviors and reactions. But Hope ALONE inspires our physical engagement with Reality. Hope is the answer when the question is "How do we say YES to life?" It is this energy, drawn from our own heart's connection to the whole of existence that demands we engage and invest in everything we can reach.

We get to tap into the confidence that life and the Universe has in itself. Only then does the risk of engaging an overwhelming and unpredictable world make sense.

Chapter 19

Law of Attraction: The Nature of Belief

Our consciousness is not a computer. It is not a machine. It cannot be programmed, and we are not in control. This is troublesome.

Belief is a defining tool of consciousness. Belief is what we hold the character of reality to be, and our behaviors are the evidence for it. Beliefs grow and change as we age, and if we are lucky they get refined as well. Every action we take contains belief. Every movement. Belief *is not* an object within consciousness. ***It is the word for describing how our consciousness relates to the world around us***. It is a map of expectations that we would be paralyzed without. But there is no reason to worry about going without it, for it cannot be separated from consciousness.

Every person, place, thing, or idea in our reality contains a system of belief within the mind. There is no "Absence of Belief" ...nor is there "Suspension of Belief." Belief is not a muscle and there is no act of willpower that can erase its presence. All beliefs can be verified by evidence. **Beliefs cannot be verified by declarative statements**.

What we each believe is a set of opinions (not facts) about everything. The way we relate to our version of "everything" shows us what we believe. What we tell ourselves we believe, and what we tell others we believe, may or may not be accurate. What our behavior shows us that we believe is ALWAYS accurate.

Beliefs are physical things. They are manifest in connection with every thought we have, and they are powerful. They are creative. It is beyond important for us to have access to the creative aspect of beliefs, and it is equally important for us to be able to Influence our beliefs throughout this life. This is because we hold beliefs about ourselves, who we are, and what we are capable of doing. Our identity is a belief. To be able to make changes in our identity *we need to be able to have a hand in the creation and maintenance of our beliefs.*

To be able to take stock in the idea that beliefs are physical things, and that ideas and Perspectives are powerful, we do not have to look very far, or in an outlandish area of science. The placebo effect takes this entire issue and shines a lovely bright light on it.

The Placebo Effect

I just checked an essay I wrote on the placebo effect five years ago. I don't have different thoughts on it now than I did then. I will say that the language I am going to use will contain many fewer F-bombs, as I am simply not as angry a dude as I was five years ago. So let's take a closer look at this aspect of science that is documented in every chemical experiment in our medical field.

The placebo effect is the name of an occurrence within a control group. The control group is the group in an experiment that does not receive the treatment being tested. So, if there are forty people being given anti-headache pills, twenty of them will be getting pills that do not contain the active ingredient being tested. Twenty people receive the headache relief pill, and twenty receive a "sugar pill." It has to look and taste like medicine, but contain no active chemicals that could relieve a headache.

In a perfect chemical world, the twenty people who took the real pill would all have headache relief, and the twenty who did not would not feel the effects of headache relief. But that is not what happens. Not only are the twenty people not healed by the test-chemical (almost no chemical has ever been 100% effective), but the control group experiences pain relief without ever receiving the chemical. The people who have this response are officially the placebo group. They respond the best way possible to the treatment, without ever actually receiving it.

The placebo effect goes anywhere between 10-90% of the control group normally, and averages out to about 35%. So, one out of three people receiving a fake treatment has a positive physical response to a chemical that is not present. That is considered normal.

This does not seem huge when dealing with a headache. But it is present in treatments dealing with every ailment from mood disorders to cancer. Every chemical trial has a placebo group.

The placebo effect is used to describe people who responded positively to treatment in a control group where the treatment was not given. However, that is not a description. That is just a name. *It is a name for a phenomenon in which the belief in the power of an expected treatment creates a chemical reality within the body equal to or greater than the actual chemical being tested in the test group*. The belief in the power of an expected treatment creates a chemical reality in the body.

We have likely been hearing of this effect for some time. It has been marginalized by the medical community, just like most aspects of our consciousness' power. We need to hear the meaning through the marginalization. We must translate

"30% of the control group for the headache pill had head-ache relief" into "**30% of the people given fake treatments believed in the treatment enough that their brain created a chemical reality that ended their headache.**"

We don't even need to extrapolate from that information to get that "belief is physically creative." You could spend your life studying science using just that bit of information and likely wind up with whole new fields of study. But my focus is what belief means for consciousness. So I am going to focus on a subtlety here.

Many who see the sentence "30 % of the people believed in the treatment enough that their headaches went away" and think that those people healed themselves. **They did not.** Their BELIEF healed them, and they are not in control of that. If a kid in jeans handed them a pill and said it was headache medicine, it is unlikely that their ability to believe in the treat-ment would be equivalent. *It is the belief, not the holder of the belief that is activating the process of creation.*

This process, of course, exists in many areas of the medi-cal field, and its history can be searched online extensively if one so chooses. Since it seems like an indictment of the medi-cal community, I will say exactly what I think about science's role in the dismissal of the creative power of consciousness as it relates to the placebo effect. This is basically a restatement of my take on the responsibility of the medical community from another chapter.

Whenever science witnesses and records data, and finds a correlative between certain actions and the improving of our world, it is the duty of the scientific community to ex-haustively investigate the mechanism of that correlation. So if the correlation is between "belief that someone is receiving treatment" and "successful treatment," with no other active factors, then investigations into the power of belief are demanded. If no such exhaustive efforts were successfully made in fleshing out the correlation by the scientific community, then they have simply resigned their authority to inform on the subject in question. It is unscientific to ignore the correlation. *It is unscientific to ignore anything.*

We should be talking about how Influence can be brought into the equation, since we want to be able to use it. Not all situations are equal, though. We will see soon, with our ability to Influence our own beliefs, *that confidence-inspiring behaviors* matter a great deal within the realm of creating reality through belief.

In the case of the headache pill, I'm betting that if you pictured the situation you saw guys in lab coats giving people pills one on one and telling them what to expect. That's a pretty fair expectation on my part, because the situation is a generic one. And the more generic a situation is, the more powerful it has the potential to be.

So, assume you are the patient and you are being given a headache pill. You may know that there is a control group, true, but you are reading cues from the doctor, and trust him implicitly. He is likely given a double blind in the experiment so he also believes that he is giving you the real pill. *So let's flesh this out by changing the situation.* Let's say he comes in wearing jeans. Let's say the pill he gives you looks like a gummy bear. How do you feel now? Are you less likely to believe that he is giving you a pain remedy for your aching head? I certainly am.

This is the **quality of the convincing agent** in the scenario. He has to be reputable. He also has to offer a tool that looks the part.

How about we change it again, so we can get a look at more of the moving parts? Let's say he has the whole doctor thing going on, and everything presents itself in a believable and professional way that matches your expectations. But let's say that when he gives you the pill, he tells you it is intended to grow back your amputated arm. How much do you believe him now? I do not believe him, and my reaction would likely be laughing in his face.

The **nature of the claim** being made by the convincing agent is rather important too.

There can be accompanying evidence, though. If the doctor in the last scenario had a waiting room full of guys you knew as amputees that had grown their arms back, you would certainly take him more seriously, but it might not be enough to make you actually believe in something that incredible.

The point though is that **accompanying evidence** is an Influence.

So, the quality of the convincing agent, the nature of the claim being made, and all accompanying evidence is what we have going into the placebo effect to make it work. We can see that our great teachers could inspire us to new heights through their belief in us. Those are also the exact things we need to do to Influence ourselves into superior growth and health.

Having a relationship with our beliefs is powerful. It is also very difficult. Beliefs are fragile, and new evidence can be irreparably damaging. For instance, if you believe the world is a good place...watch the news for a while, and that feeling will go away. The convincing agent is always working. He never takes a day off. We have to use Conscious Validation to sift through all the new accompanying evidence. The Nature of Claims that we have to deal with come from all sides, and like the Convincing Agent, they never take a day off either.

I get evidence all day long that makes my brain echo to me how good a person I am and how bad a person I am. It speaks on the Nature of the World, also (everything from being an awful place to it being an amazing place). It has always done this. In fact, when I was nineteen I wrote two songs simultaneously, "The Argument for Universal Sterilization," and "The Argument against Universal Sterilization." I could easily put myself into both songs. The Convincing Agent was reality. The accompanying evidence was everywhere for both, and the Nature of the Claim was not that outlandish given the evidence.

As I took those Perspectives on, though, I realized something. *I was also a Convincing Agent, and I could do a lot with the accompanying evidence*. I could use my own voice to Influence my beliefs about the way things were and the way I thought things could and should be. This is where the Law of Attraction begins.

The Tone of Belief Within Statements in the LOA

The Law of Attraction is about expressing desire. It is about creating a Vibration for a desire. That creates a reality where that desire can be fulfilled. Expression, however, is much more complex than we believe. It takes much more effort to Influence our expressions than we commonly understand.

Because we cannot control belief, we cannot control our expressions of desire. What we are seeking is the **Harmony of Intent**. This occurs when our emotionally active expressions match our beliefs. Here is a list of what we need to achieve this.

1) Belief in the Desire. We have to really want it, not just think we want it.

2) Belief in our worthiness of the Desire. We have to believe we should have it and we CAN USE it.

3) Belief in the existence of the Desire. The Desire has to be possible in our mind. The Desire to fly is fine, but we don't actually believe it exists for humans, so it is ineligible.

4) The ability to say what we want, rather than what we do not want. The emotional content is Present whether we do want, or do NOT want something. **The Harmony of Intent occurs WITH something**, *so the energy gathers around the **object of our focus***. Any noun is affirmed to the volume of our emotion.

Having all four of those in line with our expressions creates a Tone around an object. It becomes the Vibration we seek in the Law of Attraction. Having 3/4, or 1/4, or like many cases, 0/4 creates a confused tone, an inaccurate tone, or if you have an issue with #4, the opposite tone. But we can't control our beliefs, and the only way to find out about them for sure is to voice them accurately (internally counts), and observe our internal reactions closely *without argument*.

This is not as difficult as it sounds. So let's do some example exercises. I'm going to say some things out loud, you do the same. I'll tell you the reactions I had; you listen for yours. Deal?

"I want happiness." I get a pang of guilt for a second for the mistakes I've made, but it does not turn into a feeling. I'm clear on this one. Tone is clear.

"I am a great cook." I hear: "Yeah kinda, but you can't bake or follow a recipe." Now I can refine and combat this, but first I have to hear it. I have learned to bake, and though I rarely follow recipes, it's likely that I could. But the tone is muddled, so this needs a restatement with an asterisk. **I can think of what my protest is, discount it, and repeat the statement.** *"Even though I am not yet a good baker, I am a great cook."* That is a clear affirmation.

"I can do anything I set my mind to." Bull. I could never be a pro basketball player. I am never going to fly. I am never running for president or becoming a lawyer. I could not do those things. This one I would have to refine, because this is just a lie. And when we broadcast a lie, internally or externally, we do NOT BROADCAST THE WANT, **JUST THE TONE OF LYING**.

This is why when someone says "I really want to be happy, but I just can't leave my spouse," we don't translate what they said into what they wanted us to hear. We just hear their **Tone of Expression** in our head and likely mutter "bullshit" internally.

So, we can refine this desire expression. *"I can do anything I set my mind to, within reason that I really want to do... that I believe is physically possible."*

Yes, we have to change that statement so much that it barely has any meaning left, but it is better than saying something that we SIMPLY DON'T BELIEVE. The reason we can lie to ourselves so often is because we have not been taught how to catch ourselves. THIS IS HOW. We can learn this right now.

One of my favorite quirks about the Law of Attraction and Belief deals with winning the lottery. Besides the mess of having the lottery cross over the Vibration-attraction of a lot of people, we don't always believe in the want. I have been in-fluencing my belief in how much money I could win playing the lottery for some time, but I'll tell you a secret: "I do not believe that it is possible for me to win 1 million or more dol-lars." I don't believe it. Even if I say "I want to win a million dollars on the lottery," I don't believe it.

Funny thing? I have a number. It's $250,000. I could win that. I want it, and I believe it. That is HILARIOUS TO ME. Why 250,000 and not a million? I have no idea.

I do know this, though…the number is up to $250,000 from about $5000. So ask yourself how much you believe you could win, use, deserve to win, want, whatever. Feel what the number really is. (As I am editing the book, now the number is up to $650,000.)

The above description is just regarding money. It is not happiness or worthiness…just a dollar amount. It makes a good example, though, because we can watch our reactions (which serve as the evidence of our beliefs) and know that they change over time.

One of the things that affect our beliefs over time, and needs management, is the world of incoming information. If we are open to information (strongly suggested*) it makes beliefs more difficult to maintain without stress and effort.

The belief that I am a good husband may run into the information that I've forgotten my anniversary. Yelling at our kids may come into conflict with our belief that we are good parents. We have to babysit these reactions and work through them because our ability to func-tion is enhanced if we believe we are good people. We have more energy, are more productive, and have more clarity of thought.

We have to manage our beliefs with the information we have, and value it accordingly. To showcase an example where belief changes over time, I will get into something we do with our boy. We get good parking spots.

My boy and the Parking Spot

My boy is nine years old now. When he was seven we were focused on manifesting joyous luck at every turn. So when we pulled into the mall on a crowded day, we would say, "You guys manifesting a parking spot for us?" And the two boys would say, "Yes."

It worked almost every time. My older boy started switching, so they wouldn't be working on the same thing. So, when I asked if they were working on a parking spot, my youngest would say, "Of course. You know it," and the older would say, "I'm working on it not being crowded." Thus, the younger one became the parking spot creator.

He was seven. *There is nothing in his world that tells him that he cannot have an effect on the parking spot we end up getting.* He doesn't have to stretch his mind around a world of facts that contradict the likelihood of his focus determining what spots are available when we pull in to park. He is young. He does not have to battle the information of the world just yet. If I'm good at my job as a parent, his battles will be small and easily won as he continues to grow.

As a note, we pulled up in front of the Smithsonian in DC on a Saturday and a metered spot fifty feet from the entrance was open. Almost every time we go into a crowded lot, even if he is not with us, we think of him, and a spot opens up. We then thank him, whether or not he's there. This is a much different thing for me and his mother to have faith in, **but we can manage the information we have.**

If I were seven years old, I would just figure I was "doing it." But, as a 35-year- old man, I do not have that luxury. I simply don't believe that he rings some bell in the Manifestational Universe and someone gets the idea to evacuate an awesome spot (*I cannot control my belief*). But, I DO have a lot of information about the world. So...I USE it.

The correlative is that we simply get better parking than anyone I have ever met. We can count on it if we need to. It is consistent. That is the evidence I have. But I need the active mechanism to be able to consistently hold this belief, *because the claim being made is rather unbelievable.* This is where I can exercise my Influence.

So, I use what I have. I have a knowledge that distance does not exist when it comes to Vibrational reality. My boy can be tapped in to where we are going, and hold a perfect tone of belief that creates timing that gets worked out during the trip there. He vibrates the feeling of getting a great parking spot, and it syncs up with the creation of that availability, and that timing becomes a part of the way we drive subconsciously.

I don't know if that is accurate. I don't really care if that is accurate. I think it is, but I'm not going to go out of my mind because I cannot prove it. Just like the placebo effect. It could just be a "sugar pill" I am feeding myself. It does not matter. **I'm going to use it. It is a TOOL.**

The tool works because I do not have a need for certainty. My world does not hinge on the absolute accuracy of this correlation. I have enough evidence to know it could be possible, and that is enough for me to continue with my state of belief.

When I first noticed the correlation, the consistent open parking spots, I felt physically uncomfortable. I could not really believe it. That is when I was moved to find an explanation. I thought about it and found the way I mentioned above. That got me close enough to what I believed was possible for me to be able to use that belief to make decisions. I drive to the closest spots first, instead of playing Mr. Conservative Parking Lot Guy and circling toward a more likely spot. Because I believe in my boy, the closest spots are the likeliest. It changes my behavior.

His tone is clear when he expresses his desire, and so is mine. Mine just takes a bit more elbow grease.

This example concerns parking spots. But being fortunate is a powerful ally wherever we can find it, and *believing in that fortune dispels stress*. A lesser amount of stress makes us more potent as creative and productive adults. When it comes to getting the bills paid, or succeeding at work, or getting a job, or healing from an illness…belief matters. It creates **Healthy Confidence**. Healthy Confidence is a positive relationship between our mind, our beliefs, and the evidence we can present to ourselves at a given time about our abilities.

This is about influencing belief, and our ability to collect and use evidence that will aid us in forming the beliefs we think will best serve us in our daily lives. My boy is young. It does not take him much to hold a belief. We are older, and are faced with a reality that makes belief tougher to sustain.

Healthy Confidence is an amazing tool. Besides being the positive relationship between our mind and our beliefs, it is a manner in which we approach tasks. It is the difference between dealing with a problem, and finding a solution. It is also the difference between overcoming a crisis, and developing opportunities. It is an ability to harness the necessary Perspectives to achieve a state of being that will form a foundation. That foundation is the belief that will dominate our behavior while we are holding it.

There isn't anything quite so powerful for our focus, abilities, and overall well-being as Healthy Confidence. It necessarily involves our engagement and participation in our world through our belief in our own power. It is an attitude that forms the foundation for our ability to Influence everything we come in contact with, and every reality we are experiencing.

Are we sick? We can make ourselves better. Are we healthy? We can keep ourselves healthy. Are we angry? We can experience it, and change it. Are we sad? Same thing. Are we tired? We can increase our energy. Do we have a want? We are worthy of it. Do we have a goal? We can achieve it. Do we have something we want to be able to do? We can do it.

But it doesn't stop with us.

Are the people around us treating us like we want to be treated? We can have an effect on that. Is our job satisfying? Is our boss appreciative? Are our co-workers kind and fun? Is our family kind and committed to growing into a healthier unit? Is our neighborhood safe and friendly? We can have an effect on it all.

Is the world different than we want it to be? We can make it more like we want it to be. Does someone need protecting? We can help protect them. Does an idea need more support? We can garner support. Is a situation problematic? We can find a solution.

What about oil spills? What about global warming? What about politicians and war? What about starvation? What about inequality?

What about natural disasters? It's pretty far out to believe we can Influence those. But I do. That is how powerful our focus is. That is how powerful and creative belief is.

We can use Healthy Confidence to Participate in every aspect of reality. *Anything we can engage we can improve.* Every thought and every morsel of consciousness is creative, and every moment spent in creation to engage or change anything has an effect. Everything we believe we can affect, we can affect.

So how do we foster this ability to provide a foundation for belief in our power? We have to realize that *this is what becoming empowered means.* It means we participate in everything.

Creating Healthy Confidence

Healthy Confidence revolves around creating a good convincing agent that we trust, expanding our ability to make claims about the world, and highlighting the accompanying evidence that our life has generated through creation or discipline.

The paragraphs in the previous section show us that we can participate in many areas we may have thought we had no power in. This allows us to Influence them. We still need to have confidence in our voice (our convincing agent), but we can track down evidence to support our claims. **There is always evidence.** And the ready availability of evidence now is much different than at any other time in history.

Belief is important.

There have been times during human history where limited evidence has pushed us to extreme actions and rituals.

The rituals reinforced belief, and belief kept us calm in an unpredictable world.

Without getting too specific about which cultures did what, we know that some cultures engaged in human sacrifice in attempts to beseech the gods for a good harvest the following crop season. We also know that Native American cultures did rain dances in times of drought.

Now, take a moment and think to yourself. How insane were those practices? For most of my life I believed human sacrifice insane, while rain dances I always thought were kinda cool. As I learned more about meteorology, rain dances seemed sillier (new information messing up belief). But in truth, what is truly insane is NOT ENGAGING THE WORLD.

In both cases, people were using correlative evidence to try to Influence their world. They had no conflicting evidence that they had to deal with. As a result, I can surely say that they had three advantages over we who are engrossed in the scientific stasis and certainty of the world.

1) There is no way they had less of an effect over their environment than we do.

2) Their engagement with the world made them calm, and empowered them in their relationship with the world around them.

When I look at our society now, I can certainly say that I view the dominant-and-technically-avoidant group of humans as the savages we have typically made other cultures out to be in order to justify wiping them out and taking their land. Politics aside, what we need to take from this human history is the importance of belief, and using it to engage the world around us.

So how does that get us to Healthy Confidence? How do we use the evidence we have now to get to the idea that we can Influence everything we engage? How does our life produce the evidence we need to continue believing? There are only two parts to this.

1) Theory

2) Validation

My theory is that my boy can sense and tap into energetic signatures coming from the parking lots we frequent and that our confidence in his ability as a family enhances his ability. The Validation is continuously getting the best parking spots. That is one example built from a simple theory relating to a small fortunate part of our lives as a family.

Another theory is that the placebo effect's presence means that our belief in a treatment can succeed in healing an ailment. The Validation is when believe, and then get better.

Another theory is that we can use Conscious Validation to alter our reactions to the world over time. The theory states that if we dismiss thoughts of anger and resentment, they will be less likely to flourish during later events. The Validation occurs when we change over time due to our Conscious Validation.

A theory is that belief in ourselves makes us more attractive to employers. Validation is when we get the job.

These are all beliefs. They ALL serve a purpose as tools. Healthy Confidence is a collection of these tools, and the ability to craft more tools as reality demands.

So we have talked about the nature of belief, how important it is, how it can be Influenced, and the Healthy Confidence it leads to. I want to take just a moment to talk about where we must check and balance our beliefs with new information. Belief exists for every part of our world, and because it is such a strong building block, we can be resistant to new information. This is because new information means work, and risk. The work is utilizing all our information and *allowing conflicting evidence to exist within us until it can be resolved*. The risk is the distress created by the evidence, and the possibility of losing certainty.

Overcoming the Addiction to Unwavering Authority/ Certainty

I had started writing this section on the pitfalls and dangers of belief. But I realized it is not belief that creates this issue at all. It is an addiction to authority--an addiction to the safety and certainty that comes with holding unwavering belief. That is the issue, *the lack of fluidity in belief*, not the beliefs themselves.

All authority should be held in a state of uncertainty. Our beliefs should be as consciously malleable as possible. It is not possible to control the beliefs themselves, but conscious attention can definitely limit their danger. This will allow us to let information in, and integrate it as best we can. That is living in a state of respect with the world around us. The highest authority is the evidence and reality presented to us at the given moment, and that is where our focus should be.

In order to possess a healthy mechanism for allowing new evidence into our reality, we have to be willing to do a few things that are uncomfortable. The first thing we have to be willing to do is examine and investigate information honestly, even if it seems to conflict with our ideas. The second thing we have to be able to do is manage the distress that comes from the uncertainty of not having enough information to hold steady in a belief. The third and final thing we must be able to do is allow our beliefs to change with new information.

One of the places we see major problems with this is when ideas and beliefs are connected unnecessarily. I'm talking about religious and scientific texts for the most part. If one aspect of the Qur'an, Bible, or Grey's Anatomy is found to conflict with incoming evidence, we naturally think we have to throw away the entire tool (in these examples, books).

We do not have to throw the Bible away because dinosaurs exist. We just have to throw away the idea of the Bible being an exact historical text. That's it. We don't have to throw away entire theories on physics because super-positioning exists at the quantum level. We just have to make room for it.

We do not have to feel like we are losing a part of ourselves because we were wrong about something. That is what makes people get defensive, and then aggressive about ideas. Galileo is not a fan of that aggression; neither is Simmelweisz.

What we have to do to respect the world around us *is not dismiss information*. The easiest way to make sure this is not a problem for us is to make sure that we are comfortable with questioning authority…in ourselves, others, and text. Over time we learn to be comfortable with the way we process information, but that doesn't keep us on our toes. We must continue searching for any incoming information that would really make us uncomfortable. That is how we keep ourselves in a fluid relationship with our beliefs, and keep a healthy respect for the world around us.

The healthy respect for the world around us can also be seen as we turn our attention inward, toward the tone of our expressions. We have to be willing to acknowledge and allow doubt. Doubt can exist on a topic, in a mood, or as a Perspective. Doubt can exist temporarily, or can be necessarily connected to a subject. And this is why the tone of belief deserves the same attention as incoming information from the outside world. Our tone can be assessed only by someone with intimate knowledge of it (it can be assessed by another person if they know you well enough, or are gifted readers, but that's high-end intimacy and knowledge. In general it is our job to do the assessment).

The goal of assessing and acknowledging doubt is to eliminate it over time. We cannot eliminate all of it, for we are not in control. Also, doubt does offer us information about ourselves that has value. There is no need to eliminate the doubt, just our habit of excessive doubting of ourselves and the realities we want to be a part of.

The realities we want to be a part of, and engage, are what affirmations are for. We affirm our Perspectives of ourselves and the world through expressions, whether vocalized or internal. But we must be aware of their tone.

Too often while growing up I watched as people engaged in affirmative vocalizations, and saw zero belief in what they were saying. "I am beautiful the way I am." "I do not need the approval of others." "I am special and important." "I love my body." "I love being me." "I am worthy of love." Goodness. If we don't believe what we are saying, WE MUST NOT SAY IT. We are validating a lie when we do, and that adds guilt. That guilt becomes a cycle. It becomes a secret relationship we have with all affirmations, and creates a habit of lying in the mind and body.

"All I have to do is say something positive and look like I'm trying to feel better...then I don't actually have to do the work and risk the failure and pain." **THAT IS WHAT IS BEING VALIDATED WHEN WE DO NOT BELIEVE OUR AFFIRMATIONS.**

I stayed far away from affirmations for most of my life. I began to use one many years ago, and you have read that one already. Experience, Resonance, Rapture (repeat). Of course it is more of a directive than a self-affirming statement. It is my affirmation for the relationship I want my consciousness to have with the world. It is a Long-Term Life Goal too.

However, pretty recently I did find an affirmation that I really cannot find fault with. It has many safeguards built into it for the creation of a tone of belief. I will share this with you. Please use it. I was already very aware of myself and my tones of belief, and it has helped me immensely when assessing my expressions for belief and tone quality. It helps because it sets a standard feeling for belief that we can reference at any time. So we can express an affirmation or mantra...and then express THIS affirmation, and see if they have an equal tone of belief.

The Affirmation is "**PAID IN FULL.**"

Paid in Full

Finding a bulletproof mantra is not easy. Not as in "It'll take some time"... more like "twenty years of trying to find one and failing." The idea behind mantras is that they are meant to grind us into a Perspective that we can use as a tool. But our moods and Perspectives change, and thus our connection to our mantras always changes. That makes it difficult to gauge the continued power of our mantras over time, as well as leaving us with mantras whose meanings have changed, and are not creating the expression we want them to. Affirmations generally stop affirming what they are meant to over time, and when they stop affirming what they were intended to, they begin to affirm frustration. That is a problem.

Just to show a quick example, I had a mantra I tried out in AA. "I release this distress to my higher power." Any time I was craving a drink and needed to get some confidence in my ability and relief from the pressure, I would call on that mantra. I used "My future self" as my higher power: the version of me that had gotten through everything already and was looking back confidently at me. This, for the record, is a good higher power to draw on. However, it did not alleviate the distress very much. Also, when I fell off the wagon I started really doubting my future self. At this point, the affirmation stopped meaning what it meant. So, instead of "I release this distress to my higher power" meaning exactly what it said, it began to mean "I do not believe anything is going to help me and I'm really pissed off about where I am right now. I want out." After a while, there wasn't an ounce of me that got relief from the statement, and it simply made me more and more angry and frustrated because there was zero positive effect. That made me frustrated. Then the statement that was supposed to be synonymous with relief became synonymous with frustration. Oops. That's not so good.

Other areas where issues arose with expression were more about being specific and understanding belief. For instance, I was expressing the want for an espresso-brown Jetta Sportswagon. I even pictured it parked outside my apartment. I was specific. I want a Sportswagon, and I want it right out front. Well...the car showed up the next day. But it wasn't mine. It was just going to the store that day and happened to park in my spot. The issue here is that I said "in my spot," and that's the way the Vibration was answered. I did not believe that "in my spot" meant "mine," because my knowledge of finances prevented me from believing I could have it be mine that quickly. But I believed it could be parked in my spot that quickly, so that's the response I got.

Another spot is always money. I want to see more money! I want my cards down to zero! Yep. I saw more money going onto my credit card bills and my bank account going to zero. Because that's how I believe it works. Oops again. Using affirmations and mantras in the Law of Attraction is frustrating, but it's because we do not keep at it and record it long enough to figure out all the subtleties that make it the powerful tool it is. It is also frustrating because we do not know that we need to Influence our beliefs in order to have a more functional way of expressing our desires.

So, I found "Paid in Full." It works for bills and credit cards. It works for incoming money. It works for the love we receive, and our many blessings. It works for how we are treated. It works for that because "paid" can mean "gifted" on one hand, but it can also mean "anything received" from the world. It works with our ever-changing self-worth, because "full" is an idea that is naturally malleable. So if we believe we deserve 1,000,000 awesome points, then that's what we'll be expressing. If we believe we deserve 10, we will be expressing that at that time also.

The beauty of the expression is that in a field that is focused on matching Vibrations, it is built on a matching principle. Paid in Full is a description of being matched. Our internal effort matches with an external result.

One of the best things about Paid in Full is that it gives

us freedom from expectation. It takes the value judgment out of our hands. It also takes the method of payment out of our hands. For instance, I have a painting I did that I love. I have it for sale for $135. "Paid in Full," for that piece, was not "money received." It was "the fact that I got to keep it up on my bedroom wall for a year" because no one bought it. That was how "paid" expressed itself.

Paid in Full allows the meaning, the payment, the fullness, all to be determined by things more giving and constant than our critical and battling mind. I have never said "Paid in Full" the same way twice. It has never expressed itself the same way twice. It never needs to. The world does not have to fit into the expectations that I could set and abuse through other, more specifically detailed mantras. But that is not the only thing Paid in Full has done.

Paid in Full has allowed me a baseline for my tone of belief in expression. No matter what affirmation, desire, or focus I express, I can always take the feeling I have, the tone of the expression, and lay it beside my expression of Paid in Full. I can do this because I always believe it, so the tone is always consistent. While my mood and Perspective may change over any other expression, it does not change with Paid in Full.

So, enjoy the tool. Share it with those who are looking to create consistent relationships with their expressions of desire.

The holy reality of much of our life is found in the explanation of belief. It is a great tool, one that we need and cannot live without. It is also a tool we cannot control, and must form a relationship with in order to Influence. It can be a danger if ignored, leading to disrespect of the world and cutting connections with reality and other people short. It exists, and has power whether or not we engage in tapping into that power with our intention and focus. We cannot stop breathing. We cannot stop believing. We can use it unconsciously, or we can form a relationship with it that makes us more alive and more powerful.

Belief exists. It has a tone quality. It has expression. There is evidence for it that we must be aware of. It can be Influenced. It can lead to Healthy Confidence, a relationship with our abilities to improve the world around us through our engagement with it. It can lead to creation, through affirmations, mantras, and expressions of desire. We want to take part in the world that can be created by our confidence. We want to be able to be Present with our power and abilities in this way. We want to use this tool to **Participate**.

Chapter 20:

Participation

I want everyone to Participate. Whatever our beliefs on the purpose of life, or the process of living, we have to be Present and engaged to take part.

Try. I know it hurts...do it anyway.

Loving is difficult to learn. Helping others is difficult to learn. Forgiving is difficult to learn. All of them can lead to deep emotional pain. None of them are guaranteed to work.

Expressing yourself makes you vulnerable. Engaging with reality means you will run into problems. Investing in people or ideas means you will be disappointed. None of these are guaranteed to work, either.

Trying to make changes in your world is difficult. It takes focus, energy, and engagement. Trying to make changes in your mind demands the same: focus, energy, and engagement. None of these are guaranteed to work.

Everything is difficult. Everything takes our presence and energy. Nothing is guaranteed, and if we fail it hurts every time.

So that's the situation. I remember when I slowly came to see how powerfully Present this was in my fear-based Perspectives, but how rarely I even gave it a name in my joyous Perspectives. But it is accurate, and not managing the power of this truth gets us into a ton of trouble.

I like looking at this idea every day. I like to engage the fact that everything we care about is difficult, and success is never guaranteed. I think everyone should. We need to wear THIS fact on our sleeves rather than whatever individual hurt we have to shield ourselves from connecting and communicating. We all have those. But this is the true injury. Trying and failing, and getting hurt.

We must transcend the habit of keeping our specific injury as our focus, because it prevents us from engaging. If I am nursing and hiding MY BROKEN HEART, I am separate. I am alone, and *I am not capable of being helped*. The pain of my situation is not halved, and while I am disconnected, no joy can be doubled either. If we are focused on OUR COLLECTIVE BROKEN HEART, the one that is created EVERY TIME WE TRY AND FAIL, ***then we are always sharing***.

We are connected to each other in our vulnerability to the world. We see only the vulnerability, though...we do not see the strength. The strength is in understanding that anyone who shows up is either injured, or gonna be injured. We are asking everyone to make themselves available to pain. We are asking a lot. *That can bind us together in a familial way if we recognize it as our collective strength*. We can focus on the fact that every time someone offers their engaged presence they have done something for all of us.

Change: Pain and Frustration

Expansion: Pain and Frustration

Connection: Pain and Frustration

Engaging: Pain and Frustration

Investing: Pain and Frustration

That's the truth. I *can* guarantee all of those. This is the baseline for all experience here. The more of your heart and mind you put into your life, the more it hurts.

I want you to do it anyway.

So why do we need to Participate again? I would love to tell you "because it's worth it" (it certainly is sometimes). I don't know that for sure, though. It has been for me, but it was close. Besides, grounding the worth of participation in reward is still valuing the bounty of our experience below some random expectation for how the world is supposed to respond to us. That is a continuation of the **Paralytic Mechanics** that get us all confused over how things are supposed to work. We do not want to continue with practices and ideas that validate the confusion.

Paralytic Mechanics are systems we use to keep ourselves as safe as possible. There is no true safety, but there are ways that are safer. Unfortunately, those "safer" ways are based on non-engagement. There is always a reason to pull away from life. Always. There is always a reason not to try. It hurts. There is also no guarantee that it is not going to continue hurting every second. The reason to engage, also, does not get better. It is consistent throughout our lives.

Life is like a stove that is always likely to burn us...*that we must nonetheless continue trying to touch*. One thing we forget when recoiling from life due to the searing pain, is that not trying to touch the stove does not save us from pain. It saves us from "immediate" pain only. The deep, long-lasting pain is less obvious. It gets expressed on deathbeds. "I should have worked less, spent more time with my family, valued people over things, taken more vacations, and had more experiences." Those are the big five. They all say the same thing. *"I SHOULD HAVE ENGAGED MORE."* That is a pain that is far worse, and far different from the immediate pain of engaging. It is the pain of "wasted time and missed opportunity." There is nothing as brutal as that in all the Universe. I mean that. The Universe.

It is no surprise that we have a hard time with this, though. The stove is hot, the pain of loss and rejection powerful and intimate. There is only one question to ask ourselves about this life, and all questions about engagement collapse into our answer, whatever it may be.

Something Versus Nothing: the Existential Dilemma

Do we want something? Anything? Do we want to connect with people, our family and friends? Do we want to soak up experiences? Do we want to feel the wealth that incarnation offers us? DO WE WANT ANYTHING?

We can only have our desires met if we are Present to receive them. So if we want something, we have to show up, and risk pain and rejection. That is just how it is. As conscious adults, and even conscious children, we have a sense of returns for our effort. So the idea of not trying and receiving something anyway is incongruent. If we do not believe we have earned something, we cannot be Present to receive it. That is more about the nature of belief than the nature of trying.

So, given all of that, there is only one question. Are we going to try as much as we are possibly able to, or are we going to give up?

This is life and death. There are two options: choosing to engage in life on life's terms, or choosing death. Presence... and withdrawal. *The bountiful glory of life's experiences, including large amounts of uncontrollable and surprising pain and frustration,* **or the controllable future pain of having missed the opportunity to live**. Those are the choices.

That is it. Those are the two choices here. It is not possible always to choose life on life's terms. Sometimes we're too exhausted, sore, or burned out from life to be able to choose engaging at a given moment. But if we are going to live on this planet in these bodies for a full term, we need to hold that as the **Conscious Ideal** for our existence.

A Conscious Ideal is rarely necessary. It is necessary only when we want to have a base for constructing our lives around an idea in such a way that we can always refer back to it and find a Perspective we can use. In this case it is not only a good idea, and helpful tool, but a logical imperative if we are going to continue to draw breath.

I know I am not leaving much wiggle room when I leave "saying yes" to a Conscious Ideal. Conscious Ideals are rules that we have decided to adhere to "If We Are Able." Basic Conscious Ideals we usually see on a societal level are those that exist around killing people. We don't kill people, unless they are going to kill us. But if they are going to kill us, *we do what we have to.*

We are not bound to Conscious Ideals. A Conscious Ideal merely gives us our stance on something that is important to us. This is so that when we are distressed, we can get to it easily and often. In the case of "saying yes to engaging with life," it is something that we cannot do often enough, so having it close by as a Conscious Ideal gives us a powerful tool at the tip of our fingers.

Prioritizing a Perspective such as this can save us time and energy when we do not have an abundance of either, or are too stressed to think creatively. These are not optimal conditions, but life rarely offers us optimal conditions. When chaos is going on around us, and we are uncomfortable, it is a very important time to be engaged with our reality. It is also the time when we are the LEAST likely to do so. We want to engage with uncomfortable situations to see if there is a way we can Influence the situation. Without our presence, such information is very hard to come by, *and without engaging, Influencing a situation is impossible.*

What I am describing is an evolution of consciousness. It is an evolution because when you get into the "fight or flight" of a mental or emotional situation, I want you to quickly reach next to you and grab your Conscious Ideal of "saying yes to engaging" ...and remain Present in the discomfort for long enough to experience it fully.

This does not mean that we stay in an uncomfortable life. This does not mean that we stay places where we do not belong. That is not engagement. That is self-punishment. When in discomfort, we engage fully to understand and experience, and to see if the situation can be altered internally or externally. When that is fulfilled, then we can remove our presence.

You may ask "How long? How long do we have to be Present?" Long enough to know in our heart that we took in the experience, and did everything we could to transmute the negativity of the situation. This does not mean it has to be a long time, or that we will have succeeded. It means we gave it what we had. We will learn over time what that is, and we will learn to improve the length and quality of that time during our lives. I have had moments where I could last in discomfort no longer than ninety seconds before I picked up a bottle of alcohol (that was the way I left a situation). I have had moments of discomfort where I could sit in it and meditate in a sober fashion for days. I have had days when I would road rage out after three minutes stuck in traffic and actually punched and cracked the windshield of my own car. I have also had moments in traffic where I did a guided meditation with the beading sweat collecting between my skin and the seatbelt for an hour. I have no idea what made these situations different. It was not my job to know how my efforts would pay off, just to give it my best shot.

We all have that ability. We can all push ourselves. We can all learn to engage more. But, but…why do we have to? What's the big deal? (Is the childish whine in my voice loud enough?)

The Ideal of it may be clear, but there is more to the nuts and bolts of every situation than we can understand just by looking at an Ideal.

The Baseball Game Analogy

I have used baseball analogies a few times in this book, and this seems like a fine spot to use one again. I use the analogy because we are making a mistake about pain and the bounty of life. I think we truly view ourselves from the wrong Perspective pretty much all the time. So let's discuss striking out.

Whether or not you have ever played baseball, striking out is such a descriptive term that it is used anywhere someone has tried and failed. It is humiliating. So let's go to a baseball game. We are going to watch a few types of games as the audience of spectators.

Game 1: A player comes out, strikes out, and returns to the dugout. We watch everyone just stand there for three hours.

Game 2: A player comes out, gets a hit, and then decides to quit while he's ahead. We watch everyone just stand around for three hours.

Game 3: Players come in and out of the dugout, and all of them strike out, but they play the entire game during the three hours.

Game 4: Players come in and out of the dugout, get hits and strike outs, and play out the entire game during the three hours.

In all scenarios, you are the Audience. You are the crowd full of people. Game 4 is likely the most preferable game to watch. But which game is second? How do we want to spend our three hours?

For me it's Game 3, because we get to take part in player's strike outs. We get to cheer and watch and engage. I'm not just bored and killing time until the three hours is up. I'd rather watch fifty-four batters (that's a full game) strike out than one guy get a hit and then stop the game before anyone gets their feelings hurt.

Do you feel the same way? It's possible that you don't, but I'm going to move on with this as if you would rather watch the batters engage and try to have a full game.

Where we make a mistake with our lives, as we watch the analogy fulfill, is that we think of ourselves as JUST BATTERS. We are not. We are a mix of two things. The first is the people that we are over the course of our life, all different, with different skill sets encountering different situations. This aspect of these batters, and their memories, changes over time. Those are the batters. The second thing that we are, the permanent part of us that is Present throughout the whole of our lives, IS THE AUDIENCE OF SPECTATORS.

The Audience part of us is the part that is connected to the Universe ... the observant soul trying to get as close to experience as possible through our actions. We are the batters, we feel the pain, *but we owe ourselves a show here also*. We know this. We know this deeply and innately, so the extent to which we get bummed out by striking out has got to be tempered by the fact that we are still a part of the grand show we have come to exhibit.

We are not just the players experiencing pain and humiliation. We are not just the players succeeding, either. **We are the Audience that came to take part in something glorious.** We are the **Prime Watchers** of our experience. Whether you believe, as I do, that the Universe is also watching with us and soaking in the game does not matter. WE ARE WATCHING US. We know when we are giving the Audience a good show because we ARE the Audience. We know when we are phoning it in, not trying, and letting ourselves and everyone else down. We know because we are always watching.

Being the Prime Watchers of our experience is another reason we have to try. Not only can we not be Present for the fruition of our desires if we are not engaging, but we are also not giving ourselves the show we paid for, and we know it.

We do know it, right? We know when we are living half-assed and lying to ourselves. We may not know all the time, but we totally boo ourselves like the Audience boos the batter that doesn't take good swings in the batter's box. We boo ourselves.

But which one of those two aspects is the most "us"? Let's go back and think about the person on their deathbed. Do those complaints sound like they were upset about being struck out? *Or do they sound like they are sourcing from an underwhelmed Audience?* I'm going to go with the latter.

We minimize our presence as the Prime Audience, though, because that voice is SO DEMANDING. It always wants a show no matter how tired we are. And while it may console us when we strike out by telling us how hard the pitch was to hit, it wants us back up swinging immediately! Wow. It is unrelenting...as creation energy should be.

This is the reason that inspiration is such a vital asset to our toolbox. The Audience in our mind is demanding, the world daunting, and our abilities limited. That is a combination that necessitates we attend to our motivation often, and with tools that embolden our focus.

However, considering we are childlike in how we respond to information, many of the tools we use to get ourselves inspired are loud, authoritarian, and based on the idea of control and results. The problem with those is that they are inaccurate. Because of this, they may function as a tool only for a limited period. When we assume we have control, or we focus on certain results, we get ourselves into trouble. We get ourselves into trouble because our shattered expectations lead to frustration and shame.

Frustration and shame are feelings that stop engagement. They become a fear-and-punishment cycle that drives us from participation off into secluded areas where personal pain can gnaw our limbs down to the bone.

The Problem with our Expectations of Success and What We Really Want

What we want are promises. That is exactly what we cannot have. If we look for promises from the world of inspiration, we will find millions of them, because they are high sellers. However, they all lead to disengagement because they are false. They are short cuts. Short cuts sell, and are ALWAYS ATTRACTIVE.

The truth is that there is no short cut to wherever we want to get to, because where we want to get is happiness, and happiness is NOT A RESULT. Happiness is a way of doing things, *it is a manner of engaging that is fully invested in our action and appreciative of our results*, whatever they may be.

Focusing on results, and the promises of how we get to them, is not only is a falsehood because the promise of "being able to attain a result through effort" is false, but because it puts the weight of our happiness on a specific result, rather than the process of living and engaging.

Effort IS the reward. Engaging and striving IS happiness. Happiness does not come as a result of something specific achieved through our effort. It comes from the act of engaging the world around us fully. This is not "pleasure." Pleasure can have a cause and effect quite easily, but pleasure is trivial and momentary. I say it is trivial and momentary because it changes the second our Perspective changes, while happiness remains constant through the vast assemblage of our Perspectives.

This is why the inspirational slogans that point us toward results, and promise us control in direct relationship with objects of our desire, are so damning to our growth and happiness. The lie they sell us leads to misaligned focus (on results), and the expectation of specific results (which is uncontrollable). When these are not met our connection to giving effort suffers greatly, and we often disengage. It is hard enough to stay engaged without promises being broken and expectations not being met.

The Problems with Slogans of Control are that they lead to the following assumed connections.

Effort is directly related to achievement.

Achievement is directly related to happiness.

Safety is achieved by having that cycle solidified in our minds.

For the first relation:

We want slogans like "Take control of your life!" to be possible. They are not. We want to be able to "take charge," to "get results." We want guarantees that our effort will be rewarded with the achievement of a certain goal, and we will happily trade the truth and our long-term growth for some short-term belief and assurance.

We want to believe that quotes like "You'll find a way, or you'll find an excuse" are accurate. That if you really wanted something you could definitely have it if you worked hard enough. We deeply want to believe that the world is about effort leading to results. But it's not. It's just about effort. It's only about trying. The results are possible, but never completely under our control.

I remember coming out of high school, what I wanted more than anything was romantic connection. Now my understanding of the world was that if you had a specific list of characteristics going for you, *collecting* a mate was just part of what should happen.

So...I was gorgeous, healthy, fit, and strong. I had the physical thing going for me. I also had a job. In fact I had an exciting one with awesome perks at a sushi bar. That's two big check marks going my way. Also, I was an A student at a university. Finally, tack on that I was the lead singer of a band that had recorded an album.

I should have been beating them off with a stick. But I didn't even get nibbles. It made no sense. I would try for girls and women of all types and get rejected. My previous girlfriend had left me for a kid in high school and that had totally blown my mind.

I had all the things I was supposed to have--why was it not working? I didn't get it, and I was disheartened. I kinda gave up. Everything I had accomplished to get a woman didn't work for what I wanted.

And since my focus was on not getting the result I "was promised" I began to lose sight of the fact that results were not my focus. In my eyes, *the world had failed me*. It could do this **because I mistakenly thought it had promised me something**. It hadn't, and the grudge I held against life and giving effort was of my own making.

The truth is that the world doesn't fail any of us. Our expectations and these cheap promises create Perspectives that offer us consistent failure.

The second false correlation:

Our focus is normally on results; a desired end to effort, a goal. However, this goal is usually a means to an end, and we often forget this.

Unless the goal is "happiness," we are achieving it as a means to an end. The end is happiness. Every time. But the goal may be light years removed from happiness (oops). In fact, since happiness cannot be controlled, and we have little understanding of realities that we are not yet experiencing, this is likely to be the case.

My cousin wanted to be a pop star. But she didn't want to have to work out four hours a day. She didn't want to not have friends and be bossed around all day long. She didn't want to have no time to herself and be stalked by weirdos. Success at becoming a pop star would not have been success at all, because it would have been light years away from happiness. Many of our goals are like that.

"I wish everyone could be rich and famous, so they'd know that it isn't what it's about." --Jim Carrey

The third false correlation:

We want there to be a system for effort, so that we can make sense of what seem to be wastes of time and energy. We want it to make sense. We want to feel "safe" about the way we view how our engagement is going to work out. We want to understand why some things work out the way we envision them, and some don't. The fact that there is no solidity or sureness when it comes to how our effort translates into manifestations of reality drives us batty.

Thinking that there has to be a system is a crippling piece of mental jewelry. We need to take a good look at this want, and consciously dismiss it. We need to do this because it is the antithesis of faith. It is the opposite of trust. And while the promises that systems can give us are bound to fail, faith delivers a consistent reality. The reality may be complex and surprising (in fact that is very likely the case), and it may jostle our precious sensibilities, but it is never a lie. And, because it is honest, we will trust it more and more.

Once we can fully trust our faith, and understand our duty to engage during this lifetime, the happiness we have sought from results will be given us during the process. I love the process.

This is why we say life is a journey, not a destination. It is because effort is needed consistently, and results are delivered inconsistently. That which is within our realm of Influence is where our joy must be centered. All other appreciable items are glorious forms of gravy.

So how do we inspire ourselves without being misled? It's not difficult. It's not. The simplicity of the message we can use to inspire ourselves is almost embarrassing.

How We Do Everything Matters. That's it.

This is **Sophisticated Inspiration**. Just like Paid in Full is a sophisticated affirmation. It is the understanding that effort and engagement is creative and positive for the whole of existence. Let's go ahead and just jump into the visuals for this.

This is the Process: Sophisticated Inspiration

There is a process to living. Just like there is a Conscious Ideal to tell us why we must engage, there is Sophisticated Inspiration to tell us how to proceed. I used to say simply that "Everything Matters," but that makes it sound like the results matter, and that is TOTALLY FALSE.

How We Do Everything Matters. That is true. The energy that we put into our reality matters every time. We cannot control results and may not enjoy the results we get, but they get to be *our results* if we invest in them. This means that we get to take part in the authorship and Resonance of our experience. That matters, every time we do it.

So what do we have to do? What is this process that we have the opportunity to engage in? **We can connect to our effort, and self-substantiate internal results from the joy of giving effort.** We can be satisfied by giving effort. We can be invigorated by our engagement. We can know that whenever we engage with our souls, and invest our hearts, we move the grand design forward and make ourselves more alive.

When we engage, we feel more. We feel more joy, and we feel more pain. We are more alive. That is "Going with God." That is what the baby bird wanted when it broke out of its shell. Each time we engage…we break out of a shell.

It may seem like feeling our way fully into a traffic jam or waiting at the DMV is not mythic, but I can assure you, if you feel your way deeply into any moment, you are being born.

So this is the key to embodying Sophisticated Inspiration. YOU HAVE THE OPTION OF BEING BORN EVERY SECOND.

Please take your chances, show up, and be felt. Every birth creates more energy everywhere. Our engagement changes and expands the world every time we choose to be born into a moment.

After writing this, I got up and walked the rooms of my house to get the full effect, and I looked at all the items in my field of Influence and experience. I picked up a coffee cup my mate left when she went to work and I thought to myself, "Am I making this coffee cup more alive when I pick it up and focus my energy on it?"

The answer was YES. That coffee cup at the business end of my focus became more alive when I was born into that moment. The Resonance I experienced pulsated and rippled out in all directions.

HOW WE DO EVERYTHING MATTERS.

Once we take on Sophisticated Inspiration, there are few roadblocks to our ability to engage. The most common one is very persuasive, so I'm going to address it. It is persuasive because it is used by those who want to shift the importance of life back to results. It is natural for them to want to do this. It is also natural for us to want to listen because it seduces us through appealing to our need for control.

The basic statement that these voices (inside of us and external to us) make is this: "What you are capable of doing will not matter." It is a lie.

The Voter Dilemma (He Who Did Nothing Because He Could Only Do Very Little) and the Starfish Man

The Voter Dilemma is a literal thing in the society I live in right now. Many people I know are not huge fans of the government. The choices for laws and politicians that make it onto the ballots are shoddy at best. Many also believe that their vote is too small to matter. So they don't vote. They do not engage in the single most vital process to the forming of our society. That is insane.

Between every choice, whether we are fans of the choices offered or not, there is one that we prefer, and opting out of our ability to engage this choice is incongruent with living in a social world.

Every time we can have our voices heard, it matters. When we say "Our vote is too small to matter," we are saying "We are not guaranteed an outcome." True story. That's everywhere in life. It does not change in this area of engagement. "We do not like the choices." Yep. That happens in life too … often. Those facts are frustrating. They are disheartening. They make us all fussy and our heads get out of the game. They make us focus on results and not the process. They make us disengage.

What we don't realize is that "voter turnout" is what shows the health and vigor of a society, just like "engagement and investment" shows the health and vitality of an individual.

The frustrated souls focused on results do not want to be alone in that value. **When we engage and give effort without regard to results, we crash their systems of control.** When we engage for the sake of engaging, we begin to silence the internal and external voices that tell us that life is about destinations, rather than our individual journeys.

So please vote.

This dilemma reminds me of a story my mother told me as a boy. She was good with fables and stories that created Perspectives.

One day in a beach town there was a small tidal wave that rushed up onto the beach. The wave had displaced the starfish along the coast, and for tens of miles there were starfish stranded on the sand dying. A young man came upon the beach in fury at the scene of the dying starfish, and found an old man already there. The man was picking the starfish up, one by one, and tossing them back into the ocean. The young man said to the old man, "You aren't going to make a difference; there are too many," and he pointed at the expanse of dying starfish along the coast. The old man picked up a starfish, paused, and looked at the young man. He tossed the starfish back to his watery home and said, "Made a difference for that one."

We have the option to be born every second. There is no result that matters as much as our willingness to engage as often as possible in this holy orchestra.

I believe we often look at ideas like ascension and Rapture as a means of escape, of our "getting to the next level." This is natural, because from our learned Perspective we are "stuck in here," as if the human form was below our grand self-ideation. But the truth is that we are not even "in here." We lack presence. *The idea that we may want to get out of here is based on the false assumption that we ever arrived fully into this life and these bodies*.

We have little to no idea what our full presence in this life entails, because such a large percentage of it is spent in paralysis, distraction, and escapism. Our assumption that we are Present is not unlike our assumption that we are in control of our bodies (reminder, we do not digest our food; our stomachs do that for us, because our consciousness is not sophisticated enough to manage it). The belief is inaccurate, and has a crippling effect on our ability to Influence our reality. We cannot connect or Influence when we are not actively engaged.

Being "passively engaged" is an oxymoron. Our physical presence is not soul presence. Anything less than our soul presence is not enough. Soul presence takes place physically, mentally, emotionally, and spiritually. It is connected and aligned through the totality of our being. It takes effort and risk. And it is the only way we can connect and resonate with our experiences…to feel the Rapture of being alive.

Touch everything: that way we won't be dying alone. Alive with the process.

Thing is…I miss you. I miss everyone I meet. No one is Present for much of their time here. I am no different, honestly. I'm aware of it and still I'm trying to get close to 40-50% of my waking hours logged in being fully Present.

I was a drunk before. That was MUCH worse. I was Present about one to three percent of the time. I had people who loved me tell me they missed me while I was in the room with them. People could experience bits and pieces of me. I could experience bits and pieces of everyone else. I could enjoy them… from a safe distance.

I have thought about how "not Present" I was and tried to measure it against how Present I believe others are. I did this to make myself feel better about opting out of every situation. But the truth of the matter, especially with me, is that while many people do not have clear concepts of what presence means, I did. And while I was totally trying to not be Present, they were doing the best they could.

It's funny, my boy just came in the room as I was typing, and his brother was on the computer next to me totally immersed in gaming. He was trying to speak to me and could not make eye contact with me because of the video game running on the computer next to mine. I slowly reached my hand out, and moved his head toward me. Unconsciously, three seconds later, he was back facing the screen. I moved my chair in between him and the screen. Then he had to totally take me in (it didn't help that I was kinda giggling at him; he hates that). "I know it's hard not to look, but I'm alive and the screen is not, silly boy."

I want to say that to EVERYONE I MEET. We have the option to engage fully every second we are capable of thinking it. We get distracted and drift off after a few seconds, even if we are in meditation. Heck, one reason for meditation is to tap into how our mind drifts off so we can get to know it better and maybe have some Influence over it.

I like to try to imagine that we are in a football stadium. I imagine that each person has a mini light that illuminates when they are fully Present and engaged. I have never, in our society, seen a fully illuminated stadium. It is a dream of mine to have such a large number of people lit up in a moment that we can see masses of light and the waves of consciousness drifting through everything. It would be magnificent.

The truth is that there are minor flickers here and there rippling through sections, and that I cannot even keep my light on more than 40-50% of the time. What is awesome though, is that my family, and those I am close with...we can see each other's light. And when we all get our lights on together, we can do some amazing things. I see this with other groups too when they come together to illuminate an idea. The glorious thing about this is that it does not take more than a small percentage of people trying to light themselves up often to illuminate an entire section of our reality within the stadium. And if 10% of the stadium had their lights on at the same time, everyone would be able to see everything.

That is the nature of consciousness. It is illumination and inspiration. We may be afraid of what we'll see when we turn our lights on. We may feel like we do not have enough light to make a difference. We may not be paying attention. But we all have moments where we know we are alive and that our presence and engagement matters. In those moments, we can invest ourselves. We can take those moments and choose to be born.

We can all be more Present. We all grow from effort and contact. We all grow through experience…pain or joy. We all want to be known and felt, and we all want the Resonance of meaningful moments throughout our day. We ALL want it.

I have been giving Perspectives and ideas throughout this book. These ideas and Perspectives have helped me do what I can to be more Present, have more of an Influence, and express myself in a healthy manner. This section ends here because we have discussed enough to move on to the duties I believe we have the ability to consciously take on as engaged and conscious beings.

When we engage and invest ourselves, we have an opportunity to make the world a better place. The next section describes the exact ways in which we go about creating a healthier world. I want us to take part in that consciously.

Section 3

Chapter 21:

The Zombie Dream

This chapter is a living analogy. The most intense time of growth for me happened the moment I became willing to engage reality in an attempt to improve my life. I was intelligent, well-read, well-schooled, a healer, a therapist, a hard worker, and an experienced student of psychology and mysticism. But I had not been willing to "try" for the entirety of my twenties.

At twenty-nine, it had been long enough. My disengagement and escapism were coming to an end. I began therapy with the psychiatrist who listened to me well enough to realize that I had PTSD that needed to be medicated. She was a genius. Listening, and being intuitive, she got my mood swings managed quickly, and made NO attempt to take alcohol away from me. I still needed the ability to escape on my terms, and she knew it.

We began IET therapy, and went at it every week for about a year and a half. During that time I began to become alive, find my place in the world, and discover a home within my mind. She was an excellent therapist...and a good person to boot. She told me that with the type of treatment we were doing, the dreams I was going to have were pivotal for releasing trauma and anger.

These dreams played out as she described, but the overall picture that eighteen months of dreams created became an analogy that can describe how any consciousness comes to being engaged in healing itself and the world.

This is what we are here for. If you are reading this book, you are making the world better. Even if you are pouring effort into only the "idea" of making yourself better.

The purpose of everything I have described is going to be brought into effect during this, the third section of this book. Every Perspective will be used. The meaning of life, the Curriculum-based purpose of incarnation, Synergy of Commune, Psychological Determinism, Conscious Validation, Influence, Instinct, Conscious Ideals, etc. They will all be used to get at two Behavior Perspectives: the Rehabilitation of the Trauma of Incarnation, and the Transmutation of Fear Realities. That is what we are doing here.

The description of how we are becoming a full consciousness capable of habituating these behaviors has a theme. It was shown to me over eighteen months of analyzing dreams, and it has become clear to me that this is the best way to describe the movement of a human consciousness from one learning to engage with a hostile world, to a consciousness that has a healthy relationship with themselves and the world around them.

It is the Zombie Apocalypse. Yep.

The Zombie Mythos

Before I describe the sequence of my dreams over time, I am going to take a moment to make sure we are taking this mythos seriously. Zombies became a full-fledged horror object around the mid-'60s. This is not chance. Our world always creates our objects of myth. As our attention moved to more and more automated things, televisions and remote controls, automated factory parts, etc., our collective minds found their new source of horror: human beings that were numb, violent, unaware, emotionless, and whose only hunger was the brains of the living. This is not chance. It is a target-based fear.

I am not sure if we hatched this creation from a divine and shared source of something that was coming in the near future, or if its eventuality was a natural as the birth of Frankenstein's Monster, Dracula, and Wolfman. But I know how I see it, and since it is my dreams that we are going to be looking at, we can go ahead and use my interpretation (from early adulthood, long before the dreams).

Zombies are mind-numbed people. There are bits of this idea in every one of us. They are the lack of soul presence coupled with the embodiment of fear presence. Fear presence is the desperate drive to protect oneself and transfer all accountability, blame, anger, and pain onto others. Living in unconscious and aggressive "defense" against life, these human beings destroy all love in their path, and miss the opportunities that life offers. On top of all that, they turn those of us who are trying to live fully into fear-mongering half-wits. They do this by invoking our anger and fear, and by attacking us. They are not Present (living dead), acting on fear presence (hunters), who transfer inner violence to us (who eat us), and are fond of making us like them (destroying their brains). If they infect us with their fear (bite us), we may turn into one of them (zombie rebirth).

If you're afraid of zombies, it is likely because they are mindless killing machines who are destroying the world, and trying to eat your brain. *If you have an issue with people, it is also likely because they are capable of being mindless killing machines that are destroying the world, and messing with your mind.*

That's about as clear as I can make the mythos. It's the real thing. It translates into aspects of ourselves (bits and pieces) rather than a description about those infected and those not. But it certainly was my Perspective going into these dreams that such attributes could be isolated, and as a result I found a very rich set of descriptions to draw from.

Whether our personal correlative for "brains" is energy, love, joy, power, etc. ...there are people who can take that from us, and we all know it. That is what we fear: not only being killed by them, but being bitten by them and turning into one of them. We fear becoming the mindless murderer of innocence and the thief of peace.

So the dreams begin. I am working with my therapist, and allowing the presence of what I dislike. I am allowing myself to be uncomfortable. This is the beginning. I become Present in the world I cannot control.

Dream Sequence 1: This is the dream that I had first...my first Perspective. I had this dream previously in different times of my life, also. *This was my starting point.*

The first in the sequence of dreams was your basic horror story. It was the world I loved overrun by zombies, and almost everyone was dying or dead. The dream was disjointed, but mainly consisted of me running from place to place trying to find safe harbor, possibly helping some people along the way.

The dreams were exhausting and usually ended in a situation where I was powerless, trapped, or about to be eaten alive. I would wake up worn out and usually in a borderline state of panic.

My doc would ask me about the dreams, and I would say that I had a hard time just getting away from the zombies. She applauded me for not bailing on the dreams, or the work I was doing. She looked for any positives she could find. She would note my level of lucidity, or whom I had tried to save, or the places I went to seek safety. She would find meaning and validate my dream experiences.

That was the first round of dreams, and they were my initial Perspective about the world around me. I didn't feel safe, and was truly uncomfortable. I was often panicked. That was about the extent of my presence in the world.

Dream Sequence 2: This is the first jump in my level of involvement, and it happened after about two months of therapy.

In the second set of dreams I was much more active. I could find weapons, I could save people, and I could find safe harbor. I would spend the dream "gathering" allies and weapons, and settle in a large store with a ton of supplies. I would usually be in the act of fortifying the store when we, as a group, would get overrun. After that I'd lose track of everyone in the melee.

I would usually survive in this set of dreams. My doc let me know that my ability to engage the situation more effectively was a good sign, even though I didn't have any idea where it was going to end up. In this sequence I was learning to engage the dream on its own terms, and learning where my tools and safe harbor were. We all need to develop our tools, and have safe places to rest when dealing with this confusing and hostile world.

Dream Sequence 3: This is where my abilities started to become healthy habits, and I grew exponentially. This happened about a year in.

The third set of dreams was totally different in feel. It still had the area of safe harbor, and the people I was trying to save from the horror, but there was no real stress about it. I had plenty of tools, and was capable of mowing down hundreds of zombies, fending off wave after wave rather than being overrun.

These dreams were bloodbaths. I kept everyone safe. But, more than that, I was not at all worried about the oncoming hordes and went about dispatching them in a mellow, almost businesslike manner. Everyone was safe behind me. I never got out of control, or had more than I could handle.

My doc was joyous at this turn of events, and I began to understand the correlation. I was becoming accustomed to using my tools, and was no longer frightened by the presence of stressors. The items in my reality that had sapped my strength and frightened and upset me were waning. I was becoming more Present and effective. I was becoming skilled at managing my fear. I was becoming secure in handling what the world was throwing at me, and I was confident about my safety.

By this time my panic attacks were at a minimum, and I was developing healing treatments that I would later use in my practice. I was becoming creative and effective …potent. I assumed that this was the final stage of the process. I was wrong.

Dream Sequence 4: My limited expectations were outgrown. I was fully surprised about what the nature of my reality was becoming. This was fourteen months in.

In this sequence my abilities were unlimited. Also, by this time I was not having the dreams as often. Instead of having to fight off the zombies and find shelter, I could build shelter with a thought and keep the zombies at bay with a wave of my hand.

Another aspect to this was that not only were those I found and gathered safe, but I could build them a comfortable world behind me at the same time I was fending off the zombies. It was effortless, and almost joyous to watch a society grow behind me while I worked with ease in the situation that had before taken a ton of motion and mess.

The last part of this sequence that should be mentioned is that I could be bitten, even eaten for a time, and not be killed or turned into a zombie. I was invincible to damage and impervious to the risk of infection from being bitten.

This was at the time in my treatment where I had come to realize the development of healthy behaviors, and had begun creating ways of healing and helping the world. I had a safe space for myself and those close to me. I could improve the quality of life of those near me, and I no longer needed to fear the elements that were historically dangerous for me. I also no longer needed to use violence in my dreams. This is because my frustration and anger on a daily basis were a mere fraction of what they had been.

I was stable and powerful. I had Influence within my world, and I trusted it. As a result I had less fear and anger to contend with. I was moving not only into being able to survive and sustain my reality, but being able to improve my reality. I had made peace with being here. This was a great joy to me, and again, I thought I was done growing. I was not.

Dream Sequence 5: Transmutation. I had this dream only once, and then I NEVER DREAMED OF ZOMBIES EVER AGAIN. Ever. It also signaled the end of my need for therapy. My psychiatrist and I discussed this in one of our last sessions.

In this dream I could see the whole world. I was more than just powerful and safe. I was something else. I was engaged. I watched the world flail and come apart. I watched the infectious disease as it worked through everyone, and I was the embodiment of stillness in my heart...fearless. So I went to an open area, and called the zombies toward me.

I sat peacefully as they began to chew me to pieces. But it was different. I was feeding them, and I was regenerating my body faster than they could eat it. As each zombie hunching over me got its fill, its red and diseased and ragged bodies tearing into me, it would back off and wander away. As soon as it wandered away, it would begin to change color (filled with blue light). The zombies had fed on me, and gotten such a beautiful filling of healthy life that they began turning from zombies back into people. Then those people would spread the blue healing light to any zombie who came near them.

I watched as the world slowly spread the "non-zombie" virus across the globe that had originated in me. I watched it while being constantly devoured throughout the dream.

I knew that given who I had become, no matter what came at me, it would be changed forever for the better as a result of who I was, my engaged love for the world, and what I had to offer. I was now able to Transmute negative energy into healthy energy within myself. Then that ability spread to everyone else who took part in my experience, either directly or indirectly.

I know that we are all Present in this experience. I know that we all have tools, can find our way into reality through presence, and can Rehabilitate ourselves into a state of being that naturally Transmutes the pain and suffering of the world, turning it into an individuated and loving humanity.

I know this.

The changes that took place in the nature of the dreams during my eighteen months of treatment were correlatives for what I was experiencing in my relationship with life. The stages are, from what I've seen, consistent from person to person, for the most part.

1) We become Present and engage our fears, and begin to focus on learning tools and creating safety. This is the beginning

of self-examination and spiritual work. It is frightening and exhausting.

2) We become more adept and confident at using our tools to protect ourselves and those we love, and find safe places to rest and recover.

3) We become masters of our tools, and our confidence grows to the point where our worry gives way to creativity and energized production.

4) We can internally multitask. We can manage our fears and the incoming world around us while simultaneously managing our emotions and being creative to improve our lives. We begin to be able to do this with ease. It becomes a habit, and our focus strengthens.

5) We become a healing example for anyone who comes in contact with us. Our fearlessness and joy spreads, and the confidence of using tools and creating safety becomes illuminated for everyone.

This whole chapter is a lead in for the rest of this section. We are going to focus on Rehabilitating the Trauma of Incarnation first, then the Transmutation of Fear Realities. In the five sections above, we are working on the former for the first three, once we get to the fourth step, we are essentially rehabbed. Once we are rehabbed, the fifth step becomes easy to undertake.

I have talked about our purpose, the connected ideas of Experience, Resonance, and Rapture. But there is something that we can all do while we are going after our Rapture. In fact, it allows us to more fully engage. We transmute realities we do not like. We can take anything we are presented with, engage it, and improve it for the future. Simply, we can change the world and make it noticeably better while going about living a rich and resonant life.

Rehab and Transmute the world. That is what we are doing here.

Chapter 22:

Rehabilitation

Rehabilitation is a word we use to describe how we recover form a situation. We can rehab from addiction, illness, or injury. But we do not usually think of **our lives** as a situation where rehab is a primary Perspective. Maybe it is the assumed ownership of our bodies, or our assumed control over our lives, bodies, and behavior. Maybe it is that we do not want to deal with the fact that there is a built-in injury.

Whatever the reason, we do not consider life to be a rehab situation. Unfortunately, as a result, we do not take seriously the job of rehabilitating ourselves and managing our consciousness. So I am going to make the case for this Perspective in hopes that it may inspire movement in all of the areas we have discussed so far.

The Borrowing: The Case for Rehabilitation Focus

So…let's imagine a situation. Let's imagine being a drop of water. Let's imagine being a drop of water in the ocean, specifically. We do not feel separate from the rest of the water, and we are naturally moving with and through other drops of water that we share this vast ocean with. We are surrounded by similarity and comfort.

Then we are collected. We are taken, without our permission, and given to a situation elsewhere. This situation may be something we wanted, or it may be something that we were simply available for, being water. Neither of those reasons requires that we are ready for what happens to us.

We are poured from a faucet after being collected, and then we go into a coffeemaker. Then we are boiled. That hurts. Then we are jammed through coffee grounds at crazy high temperatures and all changed by the process into something we cannot recognize. We are different. We are uncomfortable. We are NOT what we used to be. This is not a natural situation, so we try to make the best of it. We even take on the idea that we are "coffee" and not "water." Then we are given a purpose. We are fuel for a human being. This human being drinks us (possibly mixes us with cream…well, hopefully), and we travel into his stomach and begin to be absorbed.

As we are absorbed, the coffee part of us and the water part of us begin to be separated and dissolved. The parts of us that we had begun to identify with get altered, and we are now part of another stream of fluid set to go out of the body after delivering the caffeine we had been carrying. Great, we're urine now. We're acidic, and as we carried caffeine into the body (and yummy coffee) we are now taking toxins out of the body (we did not overly thank the kidneys for saddling us with this job).

Then we are back mixed in with other water, but we are different. We are different because of our experience. We make the transition back into regular water through one of many processes and then…we're back in the ocean.

Seems kinda violent to me. We get collected and violently altered for a purpose, then used to deliver caffeine and

454   COFFEE FOR CONSCIOUSNESS

remove toxins from a separate conscious living thing. Then have to be purified to get back to what we were to begin with. Long, violent, unnatural process. But it is a process that created great joy, and had a purpose beyond what "being only water" could ever afford us.

Now let's imagine a different situation. We are consciousness. We are an aware bit of consciousness in an expanding universe. We move through all things and share space with other conscious energy. We are at one with all things...not separate.

Then we get collected. We get mashed together with other energy and slammed into living tissue. Organs and operating systems form in this tissue and we begin to form around a body. After nine months of growing in and breathing water we are jettisoned from our safe home and out into a cold, frigid, loud, bright, confusing world. Whoa. That's more violent than being boiled and poured over coffee grounds.

Then we have to try to get used to this body we're in. Every day, for years, we learn the most basic aspects of movement and nourishment. Then we learn the basics of family and communication. During these changes, we have to come to terms with a couple of things. We *have to realize that we are separate from other things*, and we have to come to terms with the fact that we do not own everything. This is totally unnatural for consciousness.

At about five, we begin a socialization pattern and are forced to attempt to assimilate into an outside standard for how we should behave. This is messy. Now we have to try to figure out what our family wants from us while simultaneously figuring out our place in society. We just figured out how to use these bodies and now we have to try to figure out how to get them to work with other people our age? I don't think we've gotten over the fact that everything does not belong to us, and now we have to learn to share with other people who are still bent out of shape about the same thing? Ouch.

Then we get pretty good at being a kid after about 5-6 years, and we hit puberty. Are you kidding me? Now all the things we just got used to are changing sizes? Now our mind doesn't work right and our moods are uncontrollable? Seriously? And wait, now that we're older our reactions have to be more under control because we're big and scary now?

Let me get this straight. I just got all this stuff down...moving and talking and trying to figure out how to share, and now everything is going to get WAY MORE UNCOMFORTABLE and I am not going to be allowed the same freedom to freak out about it because I am "older?" Temper tantrums were okay when I was two and had to deal with huge changes ...why on Earth are they not okay now? Just because I can break things? Oh...yeah, I guess that's the reason.

So now we have to deal with being betrayed by our bodies and having lost the solidity we felt with our mind. We have to try to move forward socially even though we are more confused than ever. We have to realize that we have doubts about our safety where we never had them before, and we have to deal with our own and others expectations on who we should be, when we don't even know who we are or what we want. We get to toy with that for a year or two, then...**WE ARE LEGALLY ADULTS**.

Now that we have no idea what's going on we are free to do almost anything, and may have the burden of taking care of ourselves--may have the burden of "trying" to take care of ourselves, that is. We move on to working and possibly a family while we are still working out the mechanics of everything and our Consciousness is helplessly playing a losing game of catch-up.

If we are exhausted, or stressed, or not well-schooled, or do not have the right environment or Influences, then Consciousness gets ignored completely. And while we may or may not be part of a more grand scheme of purpose (possibly experience feed for the Universe like the coffee was for the person), we are certainly capable of experiencing enjoyment and purpose inherently within our experience if we are lucky enough to get the **Perspective**. Which Perspective? The one that sees and understands all of the changes, remembers the oneness that exists (at least from time to time), and can use these Perspectives to fully engage in the present moments in as much joy as possible.

That is the rebirth that feeds the soul, and protects the consciousness through all coming rebirths, until our essence resource is returned to where it came from. This is **Consciousness Birth**.

Like the water becoming boiled water, then coffee, then urine, then going back to the ocean, we have been "reborn" over and over during the process of being alive. None of these births were of our planning, and all of them were violent surprises. This may seem inaccurate, because we can plan to have children, or get a job. That is true, but we cannot plan how we are going to feel when it happens, and how it feels is almost always a violent surprise. This is **Birth Trauma**.

Birth Trauma is the byproduct of our life changing, combined with our need to manage the change on every level of our being. The focus of rebirth is to learn to manage new realities as quickly as possible so that our existence can encompass a larger world that we have very recently and violently become a part of. Whether this is puberty, adulthood, parenthood, or tragedy, this is a violent occurrence.

I am going to take a moment to speak of things I did not know how to deal with, that were traumatic, and that took time to come to terms with. I know we all have these, so as you look over them, there's at least a slim chance you have had some of these happen to you (I'm laying the sarcasm on thick tonight).

1) I did not know how to work my body.

2) I did not know how to communicate.

3) I did not know what was going to be expected of me.

4) I did not know how to deal with non-family members.

5) I did not know how to deal with differences between myself and others.

6) I did not know how to deal with tragedy.

7) I did not know how to act around girls I was attracted to or what they wanted of me.

8) I was upset and surprised by inequality and corruption in the world.

9) I was upset and surprised by cruelty.

10) I did not know what to do to feel safe in the world.

11) I did not know how to deal with insomnia, bipolar disorder, or PTSD.

12) I did not know how to control myself with chemicals and addictions.

13) I did not know how to safely use money without risking my livelihood.

14) I was upset and surprised by the amount of pain and suffering in my life, and others' lives.

15) I was resentful at not having a reason for the suffering given to me.

16) I was resentful and angry about all of the above.

Those made me ask time and again "What am I doing here?" To this day, even now that I have transmuted the **Trauma of Incarnation** for the most part, I am surprised that I am still here. My mate and I have smiled and said, many times, "Why did we come here, again?"

Life is not a necessarily tenable situation for a soul to be in. That is the truth.

The Trauma of Being Born is repeated throughout our lives, but is very directly "Finding ourselves in an environment we cannot control (including our body), and the resulting feelings of loss and frustration." Every environment is a new world we didn't choose. Every new situation is another set of unexplained rules to familiarize ourselves with. **The frustration this causes has to be recognized**, like the first step in any 12 step program.

Think of the temper tantrums we see children having when they are not allowed to have everything they want at the exact second they want it. We have looked at this as "lack of patience," or "the selfishness of youth." Child psychologists have described it as "natural selfishness" and an "inability to empathize with the rest of the world and recognize other people." But what about looking at it from a totally different Perspective, one that doesn't have human life as the end-all-be-all of the soul?

Given their age, they can't imagine other people's needs. That is true. But what is likely also true, is that given their recent departure from *being connected to everything*, they simply cannot understand that everything in existence is not theirs. It's not just selfishness. **They do not understand separation**. They do not understand it because they have not been separated from Source energy long enough for it to have sunk in. When a toddler loses his mind crying because he cannot have something, does it look like selfishness? Or does it look like the ultimate betrayal of reality? HOW CAN EVERYTHING NOT BE MINE! WHY DID THIS HAPPEN! THIS IS WRONG ON THE DEEPEST LEVEL! Doesn't that seem more like the reaction toddlers have to being told "no"? **We have been ripped out of womb, after womb, after womb**: the Universal Source, the mother's womb, and childhood safety. We are separate, exposed, vulnerable, suffering, and in confusion. To compound that injury, we are not told that we need to recover from that damage, and we are not given any tools to work with going forward.

That last part...**can be fixed**. I am telling you that you have experienced a trauma and that you need to recover. I am also giving you many tools that may guide you on your way. I needed to tell myself this. I needed to say it out loud, even. You need to tell yourself this also. We all need to take Rehabilitation seriously. We have been separated from our natural state. **Incarnation is unnatural for a soul**. We are driving foreign machines, not of our direct choosing, and experiencing unforeseen difficulty and pain.

Much of this leads us to another aspect of Trauma that needs to be Rehabilitated: Accountability. We are the only ones who are accountable for our reality, and we control next to none of it. That. Is. Awful.

It is so powerful and frightening to be a part of this incarnation that I think the best way to describe treating it is rehab, and the best way to start is to see just how powerless we are coming into it. That way we can respect the fight to dig ourselves out, and the expectation of immediate success can be let go. That is Perspective.

Step 1: We admit that we are powerless over our situation. Our lives are not manageable.

The first step in 12 step programs, usually designed for behavioral issues rather than issues of habitual expectation or ignorance, is the best way to start looking at how huge our deficit is coming into the consciousness we have as an adult.

Ask yourself some questions:

1) Did you choose to be here?

2) Did you choose your parents?

3) Did you choose when and where you were born?

4) Did you choose the financial structure of your family?

5) Did you choose your abilities, or physical description?

6) Did you choose the opportunities you had?

7) Did you choose whether you were a man or woman, gay or straight?

8) Did you choose all of the good and bad things that happened to you?

No? Guess what...you are still the only one accountable for your life. You are powerless and your life is unmanageable. That is the first step. Your life is out of your control. That is an epic piece of understanding. It begs a response.

The next couple steps in the twelve steps encompass willingness to engage, and trust in the process (they call it a higher power; I have interest in that distraction). Those are the response steps. They are the embodiment of all of the tools I have presented, and they are a demand for Participation.

The rest of the 12 steps line up in one way or another with items in this book because they are intended to address the most common human problem. That is The **Inability to Manage and Regulate our Consciousness.** Everyone should know, understand, and take a crack at the 12 steps, addict or not, because no one is in control of their lives.

In the end, we have to deal with the fact that though we are powerless in the face of a chaotic uncontrollable existence, we are accountable. *We are accountable because we have the opportunity to Influence ourselves and the world around us with our Conscious Engagement.*

We are Accountable for our Presence, and that Presence changes the world.

We do have plenty of tools, though. The Rehabilitation is totally do-able. The goal, of course, is to be able to be as comfortable as possible in this foreign body. The goal is to be comfortable enough to form a relationship with our surroundings, internally and externally. The goal is to encompass as many Perspectives within this life as possible, comfortably, so that we can use them should we choose to.

There are so many little tools to tap into that I could easily fill another book with them. These are intended to upgrade the quality of our interface with reality. Our Interface with Reality is about our Conscious Focus and the object of our focus. *The enhancement of this relationship improves all other relationships.* That is why it is pivotal that we undertake habitually using tools like these.

The Church of Consciousness

For centuries, religious ritual has been centered on external involvement. Church every Sunday, prayer five times a day at specific times, ritualized fasting and meals, etc. I think all those things are nice ways of attempting to tap into our spiritual center. I don't know that they always worked. They were not always naturally resonant behaviors. They did not always focus on or successfully create a better relationship with our bodies and lives. So...I have some suggestions.

These suggestions all have a specific type of aim. They are experiences that improve our interface with reality. These are for everyone, men and women, young and old.

1) **Meditation**. Everyone should meditate. Period. The lesson of meditation is that there are many voices in our head, that we do not have to identify with all or any of them, and that there is an Observer Consciousness which we can identify with. Through that consciousness, we can learn about ourselves.

   Result: When we need to calm ourselves, use Conscious Validation, find Pivot Points, or alter our Perspective, we can utilize Observer Consciousness to sift through and quiet the many voices that would otherwise distract us from being able to Influence ourselves.

2) **Focused Movement**. Men and women often differ here (though there is crossover). For men we have martial arts, wrestling, and to a lesser extent sports ...and for women there is dance and yoga. All of these teach us to engage our bodies and use multiple habits of focus to enhance our physical abilities. This creates a direct relationship

between our soul's will and our physical form. Breath focus specifically is a part of any Focused Movement activity.

Result: We are capable of sensual experience over the whole of our body, and can trust our body to perform in a specific manner. This serves us when engaging in any task that needs to be accomplished, as well as when connecting ourselves to another person through sexual activity.

3) **Past Life Regression.** This is the first one in this section that may be a surprise, but I think that over time this will be a pretty common practice. I am stunned it isn't more popular now. This is not for kids, but it is for *everyone else* (not because kids aren't strong enough, just that they are not fully evolved into adulthood, so they have no business having adult experiences from another life).

The focus for Past life Regression has to do with Perspective, and fear. The fear aspect is the most obviously helpful. We can not only tap into seemingly irrational fears we have in this life and expose them, but in doing so we can often work through them (if the fear isn't healed, then the confusion over its irrationality is). The second fear dealt with is the fear of death. In a regression the therapist takes you through the death of that body. In that moment the fear of death can pass through you, as you experience the gorgeous peace and oneness that is felt upon a soul's passing back into the Universal field of energy. We can feel what it is like to die, and thus are no longer are in the grips of fearing it.

The Perspective part of the healthy effect of PLRs is that once we can see our lives from the outside, our ability to shift our focus around gets much easier. We can see our lives not just from "trapped inside," but from "moving through." This can remove resentment about our current, uncontrollable position.

Result: Fears get figured out and possibly eliminated. Our focus gets big... and our ability to shift our Perspective gets *noticeably stronger.*

Big note here: It does not matter if you do or do not believe in past lives. It does not matter if they are provable or not. It does not matter, because we cannot prove it true or false and it has really powerful positive results that are mind-expanding. I believe in it. But truthfully, it doesn't matter if you do or don't. It has an effect. That effect matters.

4) **Reiki.** Reiki is the common name for gathering and utilizing spiritual energy flowing through the body. This is for everyone. In fact, *kids are the best learners here.* Reiki is meant to create a healthy flow of energy within the body or any specific area that needs attention. Everyone can do this. Everyone. The energy that holds our atoms together and makes our bodies solid flows through all of us. It is concentrated magnetism and electricity. It can be photographed with Kirlian photography. Being able to use and manipulate it should be a part of everyone's early tutelage. Being trained to recognize and use spiritual energy is a huge thing. Feeling the effects of our will and focus running through our body is a powerful Validation for the existence and understanding of our spirit and its intrinsic power.

Result: Besides being capable of healing ourselves, it teaches us to be aware of Vibrational Realities. Being aware of the invisible information passing through us all the time makes us more capable of translating our Intuition, and tapping into our natural Source connections.

All of these naturally tap us into Source energy through our body and mind. They create a healthy interface that we can utilize in every area of our lives. These activities enliven our bodies, our minds, our immortal spirits, and our soul energy. That's what I mean when I suggest these activities as **The Church of Consciousness**.

Involving oneself with these activities gets us comfortable and confident in our bodies, as well as connected to the Source energy we came in with. This is vital to Rehabilitating the Injury of birth into a foreign body.

The question for the final piece of the Rehabilitation puzzle involves other people. It involves the presence of soul mates. Whether you are partial to that term or not, there are people in our world that we feel connected to and whose presence refines us by making us more aware of ourselves. Those are the people I am talking about.

While much of the other aspects of injury that we come in with can be dealt with by understanding where we are, and what tools we have to try to move ourselves around, there is a question that nags us that cannot be solved without the presence of friction and other people. That is the "Umm...who am I?" question. Our soul mates teach us who we are by pushing us, inspiring us, and triggering us at various depths of our consciousness. They are the catalysts for self-realization.

They are the tool by which we Rehabilitate the presence of that question. They do this by showing us the answer. They are our most powerful means of reflection and purpose.

Soulmate-Aided Refinement: The End of Confusion.

The "Who am I?" question is more of a big deal than we are capable of dealing with. It is a larger concept than one mind can organize. It's like opening a box of monsters in a dark room with no way out. We are incapable of escaping from what we find, so our mind builds safeguards to prevent us from messing around with such things. But no matter what our mind does to prevent this, there will be people in our lives capable of cracking open every lock, one by one, and forcing us to engage ourselves.

For every lock inside us, there are keys that other people have. Those people will be attracted to the lock within us, because the Universe loves matches (or we could call it psychological compatibility). The contact between us and our soul mates creates opportunities for growth. We must allow and fully experience the contact consciously to make the most of those opportunities. If we are not consciously experiencing, we are going to keep getting the opportunities to grow…repetitively. Unfortunately, they are not always pleasant.

I will say this clearly: If we are afraid to experience pain from contact with other people, *we are going to have to repeat the same soul mate connections until we allow the discomfort.* Whole books have been written on this. But we don't need a whole book, just a commitment to trying to experience our soul on its own terms through whatever experiences we come across.

This is a Lesson-Based Reality. We can learn from everything, and everything that gets to us, contacts us, or forces us into any type of reaction, can be a great lesson. Soul mates can be any type of person, from a mean boss, to a grandfather, to a lifelong friend, to a one-night stand, to a single moment of eye contact.

The thing they all have in common is that they "move" us. That is the first manner in which soul mates refine our conscious identity.

1) Friction and "Sanding"

Friction is contact that leads to a reaction. In the physical world, the very least that friction causes is heat (excitation of particles). The most is, of course, nuclear reaction. That's a pretty wide spectrum. But so is the scope of the revelations we are capable of having.

Being around our parents shapes our environment a ton (especially having their genetic code and other animal mannerisms). But they show us who "their children" are, not who *we* are. Around the time our sexuality kicks in and our desire becomes a type of identity, the world around us contacts us through our desire...and heats us up. I learned I liked aggressive, passionate women in 11th grade. This is not an odd revelation; many men like aggressive and passionate women. But it was REALLY important for me. It IS part of who I am, and I needed to have contact with such women to really understand this. But that was not the full extent of this journey.

The journey, over many years, led me to the woman I am with now. I had to find out within my preferred type of women, what I did and didn't like. That took many people, and many different types of contact. I call this **Sanding**. All soul mates Sand each other down, and help each other refine their wants.

This type of refinement takes place with friends, ideas, parenting, jobs, etc. It is how we find out what we can live with...*and what we cannot live without*. We begin to form clear wants and boundaries. This helps us stay focused on creating a world we enjoy.

This can only be done with two ideals in play. We have to experiment...and we have to be Present when we do so. That allows us to learn about ourselves, and that eases the "Who am I?" tension.

The second form is like Sanding, but more violent, taking more self control.

2) **Triggers and "Digging":** Following the discomfort

This is a process by which we are emotionally activated, and then search for the root cause of the issue rather than being distracted by the emotion.

Being triggered should be a joy. It is the first step on an emotional path that can lead us straight to an answer if we simply follow the discomfort. We can be triggered by anything from another driver's behavior to pet peeves we have with our significant others. *The triggers remain uncomfortable when we do not investigate them fully*. If we do not investigate, the triggers become more powerful, and can create of cycles of negativity. This is because they WANT to be learned. These are parts of us that are being ignored, and they *are not amused by our negligence*.

Seeing bullying triggers me. It triggers me...and then I say "Hmm...why does that trigger me?" Then I can follow *the most painful* avenue. "Well, it bothers me because it is preventable cruelty, but I cannot prevent it by myself. I am upset because I cannot stop people from being hurt. I do not like not being able to protect everyone."

Seeing drivers going slow in the fast lane makes me flip out. I ask myself why, and I come to "If they are driving in that lane slowly, then people are going to pass on the right, and I can't stop accidents from happening as new cars come in and merge. I am angry because I cannot drive everyone's car for them and I'm afraid of them getting hurt."

I get triggered by my mate's mood swings. I thought at first it was because I was afraid of her behavior. But then I remember back to other people I've been with who have been cruel to me, and though it was painful, it wasn't *that* bad. It happens. So I had to figure out what it was. I realized that no one can fully control their moods when I was young, but I didn't realize that I would react so strongly to "not being able to protect someone I loved from their moods." I am angry because I cannot protect her.

By being triggered and tracing the steps through what thoughts make me the most uncomfortable, I have come to learn something about myself. *I really like to protect people, and I really dislike not being able to protect people.* It infuriates me. Now I know more about myself. For the record, I didn't figure that out until I just typed it. So you just watched the learning experience. That's funny.

There is one more aspect to this that our soul mates help us with. That is being triggered repetitively by our soul mates. They do not just do so to get us to learn about ourselves, they do so to make us more adept at learning from being triggered. No one has triggered me more than my closest friends and significant others. They taught me how to have a reaction and then try to work with it. They make us strong so that we can learn ourselves better at every step.

Quick note. Having a soul mate and being triggered does not mean we belong with that person. It just means we have an opportunity to learn from them. The thing we may need to learn might be that we need to leave people who constantly trigger us. In fact, I'm pretty sure most of us have to learn that once.

3) **Acceptance of Our Role**: We have to accept that we are going to be the bad guy sometimes.

One aspect to soul mates and friction and triggering that goes unmentioned is that we need to make peace with the fact that we are going to trigger each other and act out at the expense of other people...specifically those close to us. This is one of the hardest parts of fully engaging. We do NOT like being the bad guy. It is Cognitive Dissonance Central. We need to get over this. Our dumbest decision and most brutal offense may be the thing that saves someone else's life, may be the thing that catalyzes change for them.

I had an awful relationship full of drugs and violence in my early twenties. The woman and I have not spoken since. What we naturally do in our society is assume that there is a good side and a bad side, or that the whole enterprise of the moment was garbage. But that is not the case. This is a Lesson-Based Reality. Because of this I know there is a good chance that our combustible and nauseating experience together definitely served as a positive for wherever our lives went afterwards. We were soul mates, *soul mates of the worst possible expression*. But I certainly did not repeat that relationship and my guess is that she probably didn't either.

This is how we learn our dark side, by being willing to play a role in someone else's refinement, even violently. Does this mean that we intentionally injure? Does this mean that we pass off accountability for our actions? NO. No-no-no. No. It means that we first understand that all of our behaviors are teaching tools for others...that the friction that occurs between connected people is always *an opportunity* first and *an effect* second.

I have had my worst drunken moments not with strangers, but with my mother and mate. That is awful. They have seen the absolute worst of me. The truth is, if we are vulnerable and open to our emotions around someone, they are going to see some really ugly stuff. This is just how it is. My ability to grow from my mistakes has to include that I accept whatever role I play in my mother's and mate's world through those brutalities. *If I don't get over my guilt I am pretty likely to bury what happened...and pretty likely to repeat it.*

The role of acceptance in soul mate refinement includes our mistakes. It includes our worst moments. It includes our betraying ourselves and those closest to us. What we make of those moments truly matters, so we must first embrace their reality, then accept their power with humility, and then Influence our behavior. To be able to accomplish that feat, we must understand that they are part of the process.

4) **Development**: Asking questions, and adding Perspectives.

We must find people we connect with and trust, and create a consistent dialogue. These people who can tap into and inspire our mind will be bountiful Sources for the creation of Perspective-based information.

In order to communicate with someone on a deep level, there have to be connections beyond mental. As a result of this fact there is always a Perspective that these friends have of us that can be of great insight.

The act of dealing with a subject matter as equals is like two sculptors going at a statue when each of them is blind to certain parts of the work. We chisel away using our tools...

language, tone, poetic and ornate expression, and our experience to get at something hidden. *That which is hidden is
our fully developed self* in relation to whatever idea is under
examination. This may seem simple, but when the topic is
suicide or whether to have children or not, it is vitally important. And while many conversations have the characteristic
of being mutable over time (like what makes a good football
coach, why our favorite band is our favorite band, etc.), not all
conversations have that quality.

I have been privy to many conversations that ended in
a final answer. This may take years, and a glut of vulnerable
communication, but it happens. These moments also refine
us. We have to be willing to form bonds with soul mates that
communicate with us and stretch our Perspectives. This helps
us rehabilitate the fury of *not knowing ourselves*, and *not being known* simultaneously.

To say that in another way...it helps answer the *"Who am
I?"* question, and the *"Who knows me?"* question at the same
time. That is so valuable, and another reason that Synergy of
Commune is vital to our development.

5)   **Becoming accustomed to Being Known**

The "Who am I?" question is focused on rehabilitating the
frustration over not knowing the identity of the individuated
parts of our soul energy as they express themselves through
our body and mind. Soul mates help us by recognizing us.
The aspect here that needs rehabilitation is our "Loss of Being
Known."

The Loss of Being Known is tricky, because it hides out
during our childhood. We automatically assume our parents and friends know us deeply during our formative years
(this is likely a survival-based feature). As we become more

aware of the world and more self-aware, the feeling of Being Known fades. We realize that there are huge facets of ourselves we have yet to uncover, and we gather the awareness that being known is difficult. This is not an accurate idea (other people may know us without our being aware of it), *but we still have to manage the sense of loss* that comes from its inception.

Once we feel the Loss of Being Known, at whatever time that happens, we have two things to rehabilitate. We have to find people who give us moments of Being Known (soul mates do this) to get closer to our soul energy state, and we must become comfortable with Being Known on a regular basis with the people we are closest to. Our **Prime Relationships** should be characterized by many moments, or even a consistent reality of Being Known.

Soul mates give us this feeling, that of Being Known. *That is why some people stay related to "bad" soul mates even though they are suffering as a result.* The horrific reality of not Being Known has not been rehabilitated, and *is so uncomfortable that rather than go without tiny bits of that feeling, we will remain in situations that can no longer yield us anything but pain.*

The fear of Being Known fully is equally horrifying. Allowing someone close to us, who has the ability to open up our box of monsters, is not an easy thing. **This is why in general we, as a collective, keep some soul mates close enough that we do not have to bear not Being Known, but retreat from anyone who may get all the way in and open us up to the fullness of our reality.** This fear has to be rehabilitated, and there is no sure way to get it done. It is scary, and messy, and not everyone is ready for it.

The payoff, however, is worth every brutal moment. For if you find a person that can open up your box of monsters, and help you feel safe in its presence, not only will you get to meet the deepest parts of yourself through them, you will be able to have a continuous feeling of Being Known. Because the person who opened the box knows such a large portion of you, as long as they are alive, you will be able to find your soul's reflection in them. That's pretty awesome.

The goal is to Rehabilitate to the extent that we feel *at home* in this life. We end up having to work with a huge number of issues throughout our lives, most of which have nothing to do with the Trauma of being born into a foreign body and the expectations that come with it. Most of our problems are mechanical and can be fixed. I say "fixed" because the issue of being born an individual, sourced from a collective, does not ever get fixed. We are born alone…and we die alone. That is and always will be true.

But there is much we can do to keep the sense of "wrongness" at bay. We can understand and relate to this individuated reality and we can use our Perspectives to limit the trauma of mortality and separateness.

We take an enormous amount of energy from a Source without boundaries and limits …and we squeeze it into a clumsy and vulnerable body. We take collective soul energy and make it separate and specific. This is not natural, and it is not supposed to be easy. Our frustration is expected. Our confusion is expected. Our "pretending to have this whole thing down" is unnecessary and damaging. It is damaging to ourselves and others, because in order to pretend like we've nailed it, we cannot be using all the tools afforded us.

When I am holding it together and pretending not to have a panic attack, rather than going over to a corner and breathing myself into a calm state, I am damaging myself, and not sharing the tool with others that may need it (or at least need to see that it is okay to use it).

The reason it is so important to ease the tension and make this body a home is that we are accountable for it and every consequence our actions create. We do not have control, but we are accountable, so we better be relaxed enough to use all of our tools at any given moment for the purpose of creating a better reality. This, of course, takes us to our next chapter: Transmutation.

Chapter 23:

Transmutation

Transmutation is the most important thing we can do during this lifetime. Transmutation is "taking something that we don't like, and changing it." I do not want to assign health or joy or positivity to this. Descriptions such as those are personal.

From the moment we are born, we are being given things. We are being given our genetics and our environment, our mind and abilities, our family and our neighbors. We are given food and culture and language. We are given the whole of existence, from our town, to the country we live in, to the entire global reality we are partaking in.

We are not going to like all of it. We're not. Whether something is "good or bad" really does not apply here. It is not a bad question to ask, but not something to get distracted by. The overall character of our life's movements carries enough focus with it to make those determinations over a long period of time, where the answers to such questions become obvious. That is the sophistication we want to use.

As we grow, we become more able to rise to the ideas we find to be filled with glory. Hopefully, as we grow, we also find healthy ways to deal with ideas and realities that we find repugnant. Much of what we find repugnant in our youth changes as we age. For instance, I REALLY like zucchini now. I like it a lot.

Fortunately, in our youth we do not have much power or understanding, so our repugnance over trivialities will not go far to create a worldwide ban on zucchini. On the other hand, our reactions toward violence and suffering as children may stick with us. The trick in every occasion is to learn situations deeply as we grow capable of reckoning with their existence. If we are capable of that, then we can move on to simpler, more direct steps.

Like It? Make More of It. Don't Like It? Think of a Better Way, and Become It.

As we move through our world we have many reactions to what we experience. Over time these reactions become more reliable for determining what we want more or less of in our world. But situations we like, as well as those we do not, have something very important in common. We must open our heart to their existence. We must engage them directly and fearlessly.

Both require this. Opening.

Like it? Open to it. Show gratitude, vibrate your joy, and make the tone quality of your appreciation clear to everything around you.

Then learn how to be a part of making more of it.

Don't like it? Open to it. Accept it, allow it, and understand it. Learn it. Learn how to relate to it.

Then learn how to Influence it without damaging yourself or those near you.

This is like Conscious Validation, in that we can go ahead and validate things in the world that we like, and then we have to manage and deal with everything else. The managing and dealing with ends up in Transmutation, or in Ignoring (if it cannot be handled)… just like with our "thought reality" in Conscious Validation. The reality has changed size and scope, but in both cases it consists of things we cannot change, and what we can do to Influence our future reality.

Transmutation is glorious because it changes our shared reality, rather than just our internal reality. Of course, since it's larger in scope and has more moving parts that are out of our control, it takes longer and is an even larger source of frustration.

When we like something it is easier to learn how to make more of it, but it still demands that we engage it. If we have great cooks for parents and love great food, it means we have a great set of resources to draw on. But if we do not engage, if we do not open to cooking and get curious and active in the kitchen, we are not going to "make more" of it. It is not passed down automatically, no matter how much we like it.

My parents were physically strong and I liked strong people. That didn't mean that I didn't have to work out. It meant that since I liked strength, I would engage the reality that creates the object of my gratitude…and get my butt to the gym. My parents were also quiet and kind people, that didn't mean I could just step into that. I had to learn my anger and impulses, and then learn how to manage them.

Transmutation is when we are presented with something internal or external that we are not fond of, and we engage in efforts to change it into something we do like. Our ability to achieve results here varies from "not too difficult" to "absolutely impossible." That is kind of a drag.

I have heard this called "alchemy." I am not against that term, but it tends to focus on the result, rather than the process of changing, so I am not going to use it. The result is not always obviously visible or attainable, and confusion in this area is detrimental to our ability to consistently engage.

Another aspect that is confusing and should be avoided is the presence of Universal Ethics. It is not because there is no right and wrong, or good and bad. We have already discussed that in the Vaya con Dios chapter. Some expressions and realities are better than others. But our habit when trying to mentally access these and make judgments is detrimental, because we devalue the presence of our likes and dislikes. *Devaluation of the self leads to confusion and disengagement.* So again, we don't want to try to make abstract descriptions like "right and wrong" a large part of our matrix when our focus is engaging in learning and influencing things.

I have limited this chapter to five types of Transmutation (of course there is a ton of play in types, and subsets). I think we will get a decent idea of what we are going after, internally and externally, to arrive at the starting point. Why is it a starting point? Because when we gain faith in our ability to Influence change in the world around us, we have begun living in a state of engagement. That creates a **Signature Impact**. A Signature Impact is what happens when ***WE make a dent in reality with who WE are***. It is a glorious thing. It is really nice to take part in some "Hey, I did that" moments while we are here.

1) **Emotion-Reactions**

This is an internal moment. We take a reaction like anger...and we accept it, allow it, and let it flow through us without transferring it to the rest of the world. It stops with us, so no one else has to feel it.

2) **Pain/Suffering**...change it into a lesson

This is internal. It is the ability to take a misfortune or tragedy and shift our Perspective on it from one of victimhood to one of being more experienced, more alive, and stronger as a result.

3) **Genetics**...Disease-Dysfunction Removal.

This is internal. We can take the character traits we were born with and change the level of Influence they have over our lives. This means that as a Pisces, or someone prone to fits of anger, I am capable of making dents in those traits and lessening their Influence if I want to.

Though the last three were internal, nothing is purely internal, because the practice of transmutation sets an example...a precedent for others to follow.

4) **Ancestry**...Reverse Cascade Healing

This is external. In general we have to have taken on some of the situations above and had some success before trying this, but that is not always the case. There is always guilt from parents, and grandparents. The guilt is centered on fears that they have let down the future generations. This can be healed by our health and joy in our lifetime. *If we are happy and healthy...it heals THEM.*

5) **Social Disharmony**...Vestigial Psychology

Vestigial Psychology is a social practice or identity we have that has outlasted its usefulness. Arranged marriages are a good example of one such practice that has disappeared from most industrialized societies.

There are examples for us *and for the world* in this section.

Micro-effect: I don't need to do this anymore.

"I don't need to be as afraid as I am, it doesn't protect me, and there is not really anything to truly fear...even death. I also don't need to continue having relationships with people that do not make me happy."

Macro-effect: We don't need to do this anymore.

"We don't need to wall off our borders and use religion to justify aggression and defense against others. It causes suffering."

So we line up the ideas and the changes, and we see how the abilities weave themselves into our lives through emotion. Our emotions make a great **Red Flag System**. Using this system we can examine what triggers us into anger or fear and begin to learn it so that we may Influence it in the future. In order to do this we have to form a healthy relationship with our emotions, but once that is relatively solid we can act on any topic of frustration we are presented with. And that action is what makes this lifetime so powerful. Not the results, simply our action.

This is beautiful focus...addressing the issues that come to us through our senses and emotions. It is glorious to be able to relate to them, engage them, and learn them *and ourselves through them*. It reminds me of the whole Course Curriculum focus I talked about in the second chapter. Input and reaction and Influence...so alive.

I remember when I first started focusing on this idea, and how we, *from the individual outward*, could have a massive effect on the world. I was pretty fired up, but I'm going to leave you the original document I wrote a few years ago. The excitement is palpable and still very deeply present for me. I used to write daily meditations for those who wanted to read my thoughts, so that is the format you are about to see.

"Because you are either stopping the chain of anger on this planet from moving on through time...or you're not."

HI! GOOD MORNING! Probably one of my more important mornings...so much so that the computers (two) have done everything they can to stop me from sharing this. I love that. Daily meditations yield things that are just lovely sometimes...the Age of Information is awesome.

So...we need to get some macro and micro ideas set up here about why this generation is here right now and what type of energy we are here to make available to transmute tension with. Each generation of people passes down trauma and pain, and frustration and hatred, along with whatever joys they can find. They do this in the same way life hits us individually with trials and suffering and stress. To the best of our abilities, we transmute those feelings into a healthy and loving life.

Our sensibilities are violated here in this world. This is part of what we signed up for (whether we believe in soul contracts or not...this is still the case. Things happen and we have to deal with them). In the last week or so, FOUR sets of friends have been burgled. This number is insane to me. What is not insane is the level of peace and the miniscule amount of animosity being dealt at the perpetrators by the families involved. If you ask me, this is one of the most important things we can do here now. We are being shown the injustices of the world through our existence here. What we can do...we can stop the chain of downward moving suffering that has been travelling through generations for hundreds of years.

Why us?

Because we have 1) the information; 2) the access to history; 3) the tools of consciousness with the love of joy and gratitude; and 4) an aversion to living in anger.

This is the time.

When we think about the changes in mass consciousness that are supposed to come with a shift...with our New Age stuff...THIS IS IT. This is our big task. Take the pain that is moving along the chronologic DNA on this planet and change the code. We are changing the DNA of life here, bond by bond, by choosing to live in joy over anger and in love over fear every time we are presented with discord. This is not limited to our pain from external circumstances, but includes our choices when we view the pain of others that are suffering in their battles whatever their contract was. OUR joy instead of anger. OUR love instead of fear. Whatever cause we fight for...that is the line we must defend. If we can fight for our causes and live in love without anger overwhelming us (I haven't met any that can pull this off), that's the way it needs to be. But we must keep a good eye on ourselves because we are either stopping the chain of anger on this planet from moving on through time...or we're not.

This is not martyrdom. This is not sacrifice. Why? Because we are able to do it without losing what those before us would have lost. This isn't taking a bullet. This is using the bulletproof vests we came in with. We are capable of taking the pain and allowing it without the need to pass it on and continue the cycle.

So enough with the long-winded "This is important!" activity in this chapter; let's get to the one-on-ones

The first is transmuting our internal reactions and realities.

Anger: Transmutation of Anger with the Knowledge of Its Basis in Fear

Anger is transferred from person to person in this society like a weird STD that we can give only to someone who didn't infect us with it, and always at inappropriate amounts. "Hmmm … I got this two-pound of herpes today at work from my boss; guess I'll just have to deal with it, you know, until my wife or children piss me off then I will unload that and the other five-pound bag of chlamydia I was carrying around also from general life dissatisfaction that came on this morning during the morning commute."

Anger is transferred from person to person. I get upset at my older son, and give him a talking-to, and it's not even a matter of ten minutes before he unloads it on his younger brother.

The issue is that anger is a secondary emotion. It arises from a basis of fear. It is "defense." All aggression is defensive. We are either carrying something that is not ours (aggression dropped on us by others) or we are having a secondary feeling (resulting from fear which does not want to be addressed due to Cognitive Dissonance).

But what happens is that in order to play the game of "anger hot potato" we are willing to create a cycle of transferring anger across our houses and lives continually. Ewww.

So we are either going to transfer it off of us because some-one transferred it onto us inappropriately, or we are going to transfer it off us because we do not want to have to deal with the fear we have associated with it. Dumping it is the only way to pull that off. One of the unfortunate things about transferring anger is guilt. We feel guilt because we know the person we transferred the violence onto did not deserve what they got…so it actually creates more discord and pain when anger cycles through people rather than being dealt with directly.

To stop the cycles that are created here there is only one answer. **We have to lean into the strike zone, and take one for the team**. That's it. We have to take the anger and trans-mute it for the good of the world around us.

This does NOT mean we bury it. This means we work with it. This means we use our tools to lessen its power. And if we can, we can heal its Source. *We do NOT give it valida-tion by allowing it to control our behavior*. We do NOT be-come slaves to it, mindlessly and unconsciously transferring it around like an STD.

So, how do we do that? How do we take anger, and turn it into something else? That's not the easiest thing to do, and it's even harder if we have to do it alone (having a healthy Prime Relationship can change our lives for the better here). But, the first step to everything is the same…we must open to it. We must fully feel the anger and whatever else comes with it.

I remember as a waiter I had limited time to manage my anger. If I held on to it, I would not be able to think clearly. So I picked up tools--some healthy, some unhealthy (I was young). They all had one thing in common that I realized lat-er: a head change.

So when I was a waiter and my manager would yell at me (likely for something that had nothing to do with me, transference-style) I did not have long to get through the injury. First I had to reality-check the situation. I just got yelled at, and I needed to do something with the energy that was just dropped on me. I had to feel it deeply. I felt shamed because customers and coworkers heard him yell at me. I felt confused because I was not the cause of his anger, yet received the aggression anyway. Finally I was upset because now I'd been thrown off track in my job and could not remember what I was doing. I did not have long to deal with this and then figure out where I was in my routine.

I could breathe. This is the best generic technique. But honestly, it does not always work. It just doesn't. Often it does, and we can definitely get better at engaging the whole of our body with our breaths, but it's not a guarantee.

I could also go stand in the freezer or go outside in the heat. Temperature and scenery change along with breathing can help. Or, I could go outside where no one was and punch a dumpster (this happened a lot). It was transference, and it still did damage to me and anyone who felt the Vibrations of the violence, *but it was better than directing it onto a person.*

I could also hold the anger and babysit it until I could vent. This is VERY HARD. **We never want to hold anger a second longer than we have to** (it is energetically draining, and toxic). But sometimes no one is around that we can share it with. And that is what venting is: addressing anger *with* someone, rather than at them or to them.

Venting involves the consent of another person to remove the anger and weaken its Influence over our reality. As long as we are holding it, a large amount of creative energy is being drained to guard it.

We need to be able *to have our anger,* assuming it has not dissipated over time, *and not transfer it* onto someone else. We need to stop the cycle by maneuvering ourselves into a situation where we can relieve our Held Anger. This is tricky.

When venting *with someone* they have to know their role and purpose. They have to know that you are both on the same team and dealing with the emotion of a third party (this includes our own triggers) *that has nothing to do with them.* They cannot help us vent if they are feeling defensive. We need to emote, in relation to a person intending to hear us, through Synergy of Commune. That is the best way for un-yielding anger to be released healthily.

I remember learning when I was young that women need-ed to vent to relieve stress. So for years I aided them in their stress relief by listening. At first I would try to help and make suggestions to fix "problems." After a while I realized that this was not helping, so I stopped and sat biting my tongue in frus-tration. This did not allow the transference of anger because I was biting my tongue and getting frustrated, so she felt guilty and I felt frustrated. **THAT DOES NOT WORK.**

As I got older I watched as women in general became less likely to vent, *because after trying with people for years who just bit their tongue, they were done feeling guilty for expressing themselves.* Then I realized that they were going to have to carry it around and be weakened by it…unless I could get it off them. I had the idea "Hey, why don't you just come and release all that at me. I know *it's not my fault,* and that *I don't have to do anything,* and that *you don't want me to get frustrated* by it. Why don't we just fix it together instead of allowing it to mess with our day?"

This changed everything. I didn't get frustrated, and I would take the full brunt of the release (not the anger, *just the release*). In fact, as long as we knew what was going on coming into the situation, she could direct some of the anger at me, and it was not a problem. I just needed to know exactly what I was supposed to do. I thought it was to listen and try to help...but that wasn't it. It was helping by allowing the fullness of the emotional release without having a single concrete thought about anything but the release of the emotion. I had to HONOR the emotion as it was released, *and not be distracted* by anything else. That is how we vent healthily. And that is how we keep anger from suffocating our reality.

Everyone's anger is different and moves through them differently. Everyone should go to anger management courses for basic training and learn meditation and breath control to help manage the presence of anger so that we do not continue to sap the creativity of our surroundings by drowning them in stress from cycles of anger being Present. But the main thing we need to get better at it is NOT transferring it to others.

The transmutation of anger, no matter where it came from, is simply saying *"I've got this now, and it's not going anywhere without my permission, or creating any more violent or negative realities. Its lifespan is done."*

The next group of ideas available for Transmutation is Pain and Suffering. We need to focus our Perspective on the fact that this is a Lesson-Based Reality. This takes some adjustment, as Pain and Suffering are powerful.

Also, this applies only to PERSONAL PAIN. We don't get to justify pain we don't feel. It is disrespectful to the experience of individuated existence and causes more pain. We do not say someone deserved pain so that they could learn, or that they should do X, Y, or Z with it. That is a form of violence. So, yeah, **don't do that**.

We are capable of growing and learning through pain and suffering. Focusing on that can transmute any pain or trauma we experience. It is not always possible to do this, but it does give us something positive to do with an awful situation should we find ourselves in one.

Transmutation of Pain and Suffering

Pain and suffering are the most deeply personal things we have to deal with. They are the results that we fear…and they cause any aggression we have. We feel pain at rejection and unfairness, and at guilt and shame, and failure and loss. All of these are going to happen to us.

Like the section on existentialism in the Rehabilitation chapter, *dealing with pain and suffering is a two-choice issue*. We have the option to shut ourselves down and give up, or we can change our Perspective of the situation and see it as the growth opportunity it is. This seems like an easy choice, but not all of these choices are equal, and some of them are not makeable. If someone loses a child, I would suggest NEVER EVER saying it can be a "good learning experience" for them, or that it's going to "make them stronger." And while I would never say it to anyone in that situation, it is nonetheless the truth.

Whether it is disease, paralysis, a toothache, a failure, a rejection, a divorce, or the tragic loss of someone close to us, our options are still the same. *Be a victim, or change the world*.

When we have gone through something horrific (I have mentioned my brother's cancer), we are granted access to an experience afforded to only a limited number of people. What do we do with all that pain and fury? We honor the experience...and we do the best we can with everything that has been dropped in our laps. Having rehabilitated ourselves from the anger over the unfairness of not having control over the presence of pain is necessary for this to work. Otherwise, we are going to get distracted by mental confusion, our sense that life has somehow betrayed us. That makes us disengage. WE don't want to do that.

So how do we make peace with pain? I have said that pain shared is pain halved, and that is true if we are committed to transmuting the pain. It still takes the first step. *We have to open our hearts to the pain, and allow its presence.* That is called the grieving process. It is vitally important. It is necessary for any transmutation to take place.

As we are engaged in our grieving process, we get to re-member...**this is OUR story**. How do we want to write how this event, or pain, will affect us? **What is our open-hearted creation in the face of tragedy and suffering?** We want to remain open to love. We want to learn any inherent lessons. We want to use this to know that even something this strong will not take us out of our Conscious Ideal. That Ideal where we say YES to life in spite of pain.

This gives us strength for two reasons. It gives us strength because we have emotionally handled bearing the presence of pain. Because we have grieved, and remained open to love and the world...rather than withdrawing. That is like exercising a divine muscle. It gives us strength also because we have a history to draw on, *a history that we survived.*

But this also gives us global strength... because everyone experiences deep pain and tragic events. *The more of us that have grieved and remained open to life, the more of us there are to share the burden of lessening pain through our shared experiences.* The fewer people that are engaging their lives through their victimhood (and we are all victims of some thing or another, even if it is just "birth"), the more we can aid each other in communal sharing of emotional burdens and fear, and the more strength we will be able to use to create new and glorious lives. That's pretty epic.

Pain and Suffering can be lessons. It is not always true that "What doesn't kill you makes you stronger." But it can be true. And if any one of us gets stronger by transmuting our suffering into strength, we all get stronger.

The next aspects of "items given" to us that we can address have to do directly with our family and that family history. It should be the hope of any parent to have a habit of giving their child a healthier, safer, richer world with more opportunities...one free from expecta- tion or the rigidity of roles. This, however, is not often the case, and we come from a long line of human history that usually puts "family" as the leading cause of life trauma. It is true that this is "suffering that we can turn into a lesson." But the importance of managing our lives through our bodies and souls (that are tied to a family of origin) has much a more far-reaching focus.

There are two parts to this. One is our Genetics. The other is our Ancestral Lineage of Behavior.

Genetics

You have a body. Stop and take it in for a moment; use your feelings to connect your body to your ancestors. Your father and mother exist within you. Your grandfather. You have a body that is like theirs. Your organs. Your mind. Your muscles and bones.

You also have knowledge passed down to you about your body from those that have been in theirs for some time. Your father and mother know the tendencies that exist. I'm sure you can list the strengths and weaknesses that run in your family without having to think about it too long. My body came in with longevity, great musculature and physical coordination, a weak stomach, and an active but unstable mind. I also got my grandfather's rage.

That's what I came in with. **It is not the identity I have to leave with**. The identity that you came up with for yourself... you do not have to leave with that either. Maybe there are parts that cannot be changed completely, but we have our Influence, and that is a powerful thing.

So what tools do we have to transmute something as solid as genetic programming? Heightened nutrition, healthy thinking, and focused engagement on our Genetic Expression.

Whether or not we believe our thoughts create our reality (theoretically possible at the very least), or that we can heal ourselves (placebo effect?), or that the blank DNA we have can be coded through habitual practice (again, there is research to support this), we can all alter our views of ourselves by dedicating time and effort to changing the status quo of our genetic imprinting. We do this by looking at characteristics of our family and self *that we do not want to pass on*, and we limit their Influence over our behavior.

So beyond the easy aspect of accentuating our inherited genetic strengths, we must find our weaknesses, and learn them well enough to minimize their power over us.

I grew up with a weak stomach. I could not deal with milk or fruit juice. It took me a long time to realize this. Afterwards, I simply eliminated certain foods from my diet that caused me extra problems. I have not thought of myself as having a weak stomach since...and none of my current family would ever think that of me. That is because I removed the Genetic Expression from the world. I stopped it from becoming a reality by forming healthy habits, and not dwelling on the supposed weakness.

This means that I did not have to Identify with my inherited weakness.

It took me some time to manage my mental instability, but I learned. And in learning, I gathered experience and tools for anyone (family or not) who could be suffering from the same issues. I learned where I needed to focus, and what I needed to not worry about. Through engaging this I became someone whom I don't consider to have any serious mental issues. Through my behavior and habits, I have created an Identity that does not include mental instability as a weakness. My genetics are off the hook for that. I've got it handled. I have tools now--tools that cannot be taken away from me.

So...think about all that you or anyone can be burdened with inheriting. Think of cancer, heart disease, Type 1 diabetes. There are means for influencing the effects of all of those on your life. Every problem has a proactive cure. Every possible Genetic Expression can be Influenced by our focus and engagement.

Is there a guarantee it will work? Of course not. Can I guarantee you that trying matters? Yes. It matters to not identify with or validate aspects of reality given to you that you do not connect with, or that you do not want to express through your incarnation here.

Our son has a food allergy that is serious enough for us to have an EpiPen in the house at all times. We have been telling him he'd grow out of it (suggesting that he does not need to Identify with it), which we totally believe. His teacher accidentally gave him what he was allergic to, and while he had a reaction, it was mild and he didn't need to go to the hospital. Last time he had contacted the item in question his throat closed, and different action needed to be taken.

The point is that we have more power than we are told. Just because our father or mother or entire family have something, that does not mean we have to Identify with it. *We have to engage the reality, but we can do so on our own terms.* We can learn, and Transmute anything in our field. The level of success we have may differ from person to person, but the idea of accepting our genetic flaws by rule is simply an outdated practice.

How many of us have already decided what was going to kill us? I would bet it's well over half of us. We know what runs in our family and has a habit of killing people off whom we share a last name with. But that is just the thing. It is a habit. It is not a promise that needs to be fulfilled. It is a reality that we can address.

Genetics are physical traits. But we also have a **Genetics of Behavior** to contend with in our families. This needs to be addressed for Transmutation.

Ancestral Lineage of Behavior

This section is not about genetics. This section is about behavior. My grandfather and father passed rage down to me. They could not help that. But in between my grandfather and my father, something happened to my family.

My father decided that the actual *expression of violence* was going to stop with him. As a result, the expression of anger and violence was so far removed from my reality that I was totally stunned when I found rage within myself at all. When my father took it upon himself to change the nature of what a "Mucci" would be doing, he changed the behavioral imprint of the ancestral line.

We can all stop and think about what our family does from a habitual standpoint. What patterns are we repeating as a family? This is an interesting question we all need to ask, because whether or not we are following in our family's footsteps, we are basing our movements off of their habits and modeling. This means that whether we are moving toward or away from them, our movement is still based on where they are and what they have been habitually validating. This may not exactly make sense, but if you imagine a devout Catholic family, they are likely to have Catholic children, or children that have rebelled against Catholicism. They are much less likely to have Hindu children (something very different), or children that rebel against Hinduism.

So…if our family of origin is putting forward certain habits, those are going to be focal points that *we need to be aware of objectively, without identifying ourselves with them.*

We need to see them, not take them on. They are already powerful enough.

We grow up thinking our parents and family are magic for the most part. We need that; it is a survival mechanism. It creates safety. But we have opportunities to break from that untouchable reverence for our family. We all need to break from this reverence because we need to assess what habits are present objectively, and which we want to continue. This takes healthy discernment. It is respectful to our parents' children to see what is influencing their reality, so that they can be healthier individuals with a larger Influence over the direction their lives take (*it always helped me to speak of myself in third person here, because while I may not always think I need to do this for myself, I would do anything to protect my parents' children. Makes almost no sense. Almost.*).

We must ask some questions. Our goal is to figure out what our final Perspective will be on our family of origin's issues (strengths, weaknesses, and habits) as fast as possible… without anger or judgment. I'm pretty sure my grandfather didn't tell my dad, "Yeah I am a wife-beating binge drinker, but I am dedicated to my work." My father had to figure that out over his childhood, and then struggle to find a way to forgive that while not following in his footsteps. This is a tall order if you don't know you're supposed to take it on (which, of course, he didn't). **We all should KNOW THIS,** but it is rare that parents teach their children to analyze them. My mother did a pretty good job there, as did my brother. I was lucky.

The questions we must ask:

1) *Who in my family is happy or unhappy?* First and most important question.

2) *Why are these people together?* This applies to any couples.

3) *What are they afraid of?* This is a tough one to trace. Most of the time fear is covered by anger and resentment, and a LOT of analysis has to go into finding the source. But it is important, because that source affects us too.

4) *How do they cope with stress?* To what extent do they face and manage their stress? How do they do it? To what extent do they bury their stress or escape reality rather than face it, and what means do they use for that?

5) *How healthy are their habits?* Eating, exercise, stress management.

6) *What are their beliefs, and how have they affected their lives?* Religion, power, ethics, money, behavior, etc.

7) *What are their strengths, and what are their weaknesses?*

This list is something every single person on the planet needs to be able to fill out fully. Until we can fill it out, we cannot ask the most important question.

HOW MUCH OF THIS DO I WANT TO CONTINUE IN MY FAMILY? What part of their worlds do I want to have a direct Influence on my behavior and decisions? What parts of their lives do I want to validate and continue? Which parts do I want to Transmute out of the family line so that my children will not have to contend with its Influence?

I didn't have to contend with violent behavior. My father went ahead and made that decision for me. It would be totally unnatural for me to act on my rage. I would have no idea how to do it *because no one modeled it for me.* My father made a decision, and the problem ceased to exist from there on down the family line.

I see many fathers making choices like this now. I see many mothers having more active nutritional views for their children (there are things many of us have simply stopped eating). I see many parents doing things differently than those that came before them, and this goes so much further than anyone could imagine. It creates a system by which children, by not acting out the unhealthy practices of their parents, can actually heal the wounds and lives of those that came before them. I call this **Reverse Cascade Healing. Reverse Cascade healing is when the success and growth of a generation in a family heals the guilt and shame of the previous generation by releasing them from the effects of their weaknesses and mistakes**.

So when we ask the necessary questions, and make decisions on what we want to validate and what we do not want to carry on with, we Transmute the Behavioral Ancestral Lineage of our family. When we become aware of this, and take it on as a reality we are accountable for, we heal in both directions in our field. We release the previous generations from guilt of what they could not give us, and our health heals them of their worry. We heal the next generation in more than one way. First, the decision to not continue an unhealthy manner of living likely leaves them with happier parents, and better behaviors to model after. But it also gives us the opportunity to give them as much of OUR story as we can. We can tell them what our fears are, and what are weaknesses are when they are ready to listen. We can tell them they need to analyze us and ask the same questions we did. We can save our children YEARS of analysis. Years.

We ask questions...we make adjustments. Everyone in our family is affected. That is the truth, and that is the power of this life opportunity we are gifted with.

Transmutation is about a story being written. Every event and negative thing in our lives is connected to a storyline. **We can Influence all of these storylines**. We can interject with an **Impact**, and make changes in the story by Influencing ourselves and the world around us.

Every item we wish to change contains its own story and its own plot. Understanding the thing we wish to change means understanding the plot of that particular story. Then once we understand it, we can make alterations in it. We cannot control the book *because we are not the only author*, but we can certainly take what we are being given, engage it, and invest our hearts in improving it in any way we can.

It is more difficult to look at the whole of society and think about what can be changed, so we are going to take a half chapter and look at what I call **Vestigial Psychology**. It is tougher to think about this aspect. It is tougher because we are capable only of forming Perspectives and feeding ideas on these items, as opportunities to directly affect change are rare and often take a collective of conscious and motivated individuals. They are possible, but the Perspective of their possibility must exist before the culmination of conscious action can come into being. We have to think of them before they can happen.

PART 2: EVOLUTIONARY INSURGENCE

I had to split this section of Transmutation off from the rest. This one is messy, and deserves extra attention. It is not easy to make statements about society without seeming judgmental and combative. As a result, it is likely to create some defensive and impassioned responses. In this area it is very difficult to manage a Perspective without enabling the "Universal Ethics" we need to stay away from. So I'm going to go slowly, as we all should when engaging with others about our shared culture. I need your charitable focus when reading this… that's what I'm asking.

This is about the Transmutation of Social Disharmony, not the Transmutation of evil. Social Disharmony can be seen through **violence, unrest, unhappiness, poverty, suffering, and disease** (there are more, but let's work with these six). We don't want those. It is unlikely that we can have a planet without having these in some form or fashion, but the quality of their presence can definitely be addressed and minimized through our engaged efforts.

We are going to try to identify beliefs about society and beliefs about what we think we should do individually. Then we are going to find out what beliefs lead to the six attributes of disharmony listed above. When we find beliefs, habits, Perspectives, or practices that fall under the category of "things that create disharmony," we're going to *figure out if the item in question is necessary* for our growing global society and consciousness. If they are deemed no longer necessary, they can be termed **Vestigial Psychology**. Vestigial Psychology is a part of our cultural psychology that is no longer necessary…like a tailbone for a tail that we no longer have.

If you remember the study with the apes and the banana, with the ladder and the accompanying cold spray of water when an ape went after the banana…that is a perfect example of Vestigial Psychology creating disharmony. This is not Universal Ethics, though. This is *our* decision to make. We can identify lots of things that cause disharmony, but then we have to make *an educated guess* about what would happen without it. Then we can hold a Perspective about it based on our findings. Seems kinda crass and silly, but when we get to religion, politics, healthcare, capitalism, war, and other more intimate beliefs that are social in nature, everything gets more difficult. Even John Lennon suggested lightly with the title "Imagine." He was just suggesting we try imagining doing without some of those things.

Are We Vestigial?

There are a lot of things we don't have to do anymore. Transmutation is taking something we can change through our focus, *and engaging in that change* in whatever way we can.

We can take something and make it the way we want it to be (or at least more like the way we want it to be). But when we get a close-up look at societal expectations, and group beliefs, the task gets more daunting. This is because the held-and-accepted knowledge of the times is reflected through everyone in the community, however large or small that may be. Our ability to work within the confines of our reality and simultaneously change our reality *does exist*. It seems like it cannot exist, like there must be a rebellion for change to take place, but that is not the case.

In order to engage in Transmutation of Social Disharmony, we need to find things that create it, and ask ourselves *if they are necessary*. Below I've listed ideas and practices and habits that create disharmony. Whether the ideas create disharmony or not is not the question. They DO create disharmony. The question is "Are they necessary?" I want to show how we ask that question. In the same way we looked at our family of origin, we need to look at our society of origin and the belief systems it has at its core.

I will outline how to present ourselves with the "Are they necessary?" argument by using Organized Religion as the key example, as it is present in every society.

Organized Religion

This one is a big issue. There are many religions that say their way is the only way, which is tough to logically fathom. There are religions fighting it out between each other viciously (you can watch the Middle East; they are great at this) that all hail from the same God (God of Abraham). Nazi Germany was Christian, killing off the Jews, and they SHARE THE SAME BOOK. Goodness.

Now not all religions are as vicious as the Western ones (although the caste system rules in Hinduism are pretty damning), but they all validate some system of behavior and ethics, and can thus easily result in judgment, condemnation, dehumanization, and therefore cruelty. So they all *can* lead to disharmony.

Does this mean that someone fully engaging in religion is going to be violent? No. Does it ensure that someone is going to let their accountability lie on the shoulders of a system of behavior external to them? No.

But are we going to be surprised when kids bully a young gay child until he kills himself, when Leviticus said homosexuality was a sin?

Are we going to be surprised when a young Christian soldier massacres a Muslim family in the Middle East and feels no remorse?

Are we going to be surprised when the upper caste in India forces the lower caste to live in their garbage?

Are we going to be surprised when racial genocide occurs? **No. We're not**. Why?

Here's why…

We know about the Salem witch trials, the Spanish Inquisition, WWII, the Crusades, and suicide bombers...and we know that religion's presence was at the root of *allowing* ALL of those. Was religion the cause? *No. People are the cause.* Really crappy people. But the allowance in times of turmoil is supplied by the presence of religion.

It allows us to break our own moral compass without the pangs of Cognitive Dissonance, because it supplies us with unquestionable authority in our actions. We're not surprised at the disharmony. It is common. What should surprise us is that religion has not evolved out of our system yet. This means there must be some pretty strong attachments to it... we need to individually decide if it is worth continuing those attachments.

So what does Organized Religion create that we should not do without?

It seems that we could take any holy book, make it a philosophical and psychological analysis of life, and keep it. The stories would still have great value. Seems to me that we can study and worship Jesus, or Buddha, without the need for organized religion. We can embody humility before a higher power without religion. We can engage in meaningful ritual. Ethics may be social, but we have internal compasses that react emotionally when we have ethical dissent from what we see, so that is something inherent in our being. Community and spirituality can be had without it. Faith can be had. We can also have a promise of an afterlife just by looking at the nature of consciousness. We can celebrate any holiday for its symbolic meaning within any religion. **We do not have to sign up for a package deal on ANY of this stuff. We do not have to accept anything we do not find totally in tune**

with our reality to have these attributes if we want them. Honestly, we do not have to go anywhere outside of ourselves and our surroundings to have access to all of these riches. We also do not need any other people to do this for us. We can do it all ourselves.

So what do we lose?

Certainty. Unquestionable doubtlessness. Rules and order from Authority. Righteousness. The idea of a chosen or superior people. The promise of justice. The promise of reward for behavior. The promise of Acceptance from an external Authority. The promise of afterlife punishment for those we dislike (it's tough to find a hell, purgatory, reincarnation in suffering, karmic damnation, or anything like that without religion). Dominion over land and animals (might be kind of important to lose this given the current global climate issues).

We want those things. I want them. I want to have them and feel safe that they are mine. I want them in the way that my ego wants to be fed. I want them to satisfy my desire for control.

It is okay to want them. It is okay. But that is what we are balancing the damage against. So they better be THAT important. The system that gives us those promises and certainties also facilitates violence and suffering...the worst kind of disharmony.

I don't know that all of the listed losses are healthy, but that is not for me to decide. That is for YOU to decide. That is honestly something everyone should decide. We can work together to help bring this out into the light.

Organized Religion is naturally divisive, and creates disharmony. We can assign our Value to the characteristics we want to keep, and withdraw from validating the system as a whole. The point is...*maybe we don't have to do that anymore*.

Maybe we can also do without certain ideas. Ideas like:

Capitalism as healthy (rather than an economy based on social progress)

The nobility of sacrifice

The connection between worth and production

The idea of divorce as failure (rather than rebirth or healthy change)

The usefulness of medicating problems

The Western medicine standard for treating and preventing illness

The idea that we need to work hard to deserve joy

The accepted cultural idea of beauty (rather than a personal one)

The idea of social punishment (jail) rather than rehabilitation under supervision (therapy)

Maybe we don't have to do any of this anymore.

This is a quick list and it is *my* list. It is one that I find worth questioning. We all have our lists, items we find puzzling and dangerous about our society. In those ideas we can investigate, and find for ourselves whether we need to value the system as a whole, or separate characteristics, and value just those characteristics as the basis for the creation of new social ideations.

The thing that makes something vestigial is evolution. Over time we grow into a form that no longer needs something. For instance, the appendix is often sighted as being vestigial (whether it is or not may be up for debate), but we let it be for the most part. When we do not let it be is when it is about to explode within us and kill us. Then we REMOVE it.

But since the items we are dealing with are shared culturally, we do not have a singular consciousness that can remove them. So how do we proceed? How can we be proactive about change in areas where people are defensive? How do we author change in a society that fears change? **Evolutionary Insurgence**.

Evolutionary Insurgence is the consistent expression of ideas that validate the movement away from Vestigial Psychology and toward the creation of something new.

Evolutionary Insurgence

Evolutionary Insurgence is not rebellion. It is aimed at re-moving the fear of change, while simultaneously removing aspects of our shared culture that are no longer healthy. For instance, slavery didn't end all at once. Slavery was outlawed because "all people were created equal"...but the equal-ity didn't show up for another ninety years, even on paper. That is because within the community that held such beliefs, there were very few successful insurgents speaking their mind about different Perspectives. In truth, that might not have been safe at the time. I am not faulting them for it. But it is safer now to be an insurgent than it has ever been given the na-ture of global communication and information-sharing. We are much freer to share our ideas than ever before and the

Perspectives we want to embody for the society we are creating can be taken on fearlessly.

There are Perspectives all across this country on religion, nationalism, guns, politics, and the oligarchy…as well as ideas on personal ideas like marriage, addiction, financial status, and ethnicity that can all be slowly adjusted over time if we give ourselves to them ideologically, and let that express through us.

All of the information we share, the conversations we have and the lives we live contain who we are and what we believe. This is an aspect of the world always expressing itself. What we want to change and what we want to create flows through our veins like blood and is soaked in every breath we draw. It is pervasive even if we do not voice it, teach it, or parent it.

But we can parent it. We can teach it. We can voice it. We are social creatures and our ability to share our thoughts and hearts is Present for all of us.

This is society embodying **Observer Consciousness**, and then hopefully being able to use **Conscious Validation** to remove the pieces that are the combination of *"no longer necessary"* and *"harmful."*

We are all part of the collective consciousness of our family, our community, our country, and the world. There is no rebellion, just a slow Validation of the changes we want and their eventual prominence as we become more and more conscious. This is how an individual can change the world every day, should we choose to engage in asking questions and living in accordance with our answers. We express and embody change.

So we finally wrap up with what it is our job to do as individuals, as parents of society and our children, and as expressive human beings in a growing collective consciousness. We are given our culture. The response to it is something we can carry with us. We can take elements with associated negativity and transmute them.

I have mentioned over and again that everything matters, that every expression is vital, and in this chapter, that we are a part of an evolving global consciousness. Our lives impact the world. Our families impact other families. We are pushing for the "Go with God" energy. We want expansion, and we want to remove the blockages to it. This is how we partake in the great drama of life, and make our individual voice heard.

Individual Accountability: The Single Mutation Theme

Transmutation is all about questions and answers (yes, it still is). It is about knowing what is present (by questioning), and our feelings about that presence (answers). In the last chapter we talked about emotion, genetics, and ancestral habit. While there is plenty of cross-over between last chapter and this one, now we are focusing on what exists around us.

Let's look around our life. Do we live in a house? Have a job or something like it? Have responsibilities when it comes to hygiene and taking care of ourselves? Yep.

What else do we have? We have expectations about our behavior, as well as laws enforcing them, from our culture.

We also have highly developed systems in our mind and body that create our reactions and behaviors within all of the other frameworks. We have habits. But we are a single entity, among many other single entities.

We are one person, one family, one set of behaviors, one worker, one parent, one driver, one set of habits, among billll-lions of others. We can ask ourselves questions.

1) What, among everything in my world, do I not like?

2) Can I change it, or stop doing it?

Two pretty simple questions. These questions can work through our thoughts, habits, ideas, behaviors, etc. It is not always possible to change things. It isn't. But we should still be asking these questions about the world around us.

And for everything that does not fall into the category of "things I do not like" ...that's where we have Gratitude. So let's take a moment and validate that reality.

If there are things we do not like, and that we do not have to keep doing, then we can be the single consciousness not validating that item within the consciousness of the culture. That is Personal Accountability. The first step to stopping a problem on a large scale is not being a direct part of the behavior. This means that if we do not like violence, that we do not partake in it, teach it, or allow it in our reality (to the extent possible). If we don't like unhealthy marriages or relationships, we had best not be in one.

I remember one time I had a friend that thought it would be all right to speak to me rather rudely. I said, "Okay, I don't stay friends with people who talk to me like that," and then I hung up the phone. That was it. Friendships where people talked to each in that manner lost one subscriber that day, and that person got rejected for behavior that did not find accord with the reality I wanted to create.

It's small, but it counts. Everything matters. Nothing is too small to matter. Every thought we validate and every action we allow or support matters. Every time we go out of our way to be kind, every time we take a moment and make the world better, we are creating a different society. *These are the single mutations within culture that lead to the evolution of a species*.

If one person does something different than expected, and it works, then more have the courage to try new things. And that is what we are. Besides being the **Single Mutation** within the species' consciousness, *we are the source of future courage for all healthy change*.

To transmute **Social Disharmony**, we engage our reality. We ask questions about our environment and answer honestly. In doing so we find what beliefs and practices are a part of our culture's **Vestigial Psychology**.

We take that knowledge, add it to all of the other things we want to create in our world (which we find using **Conscious Validation** of our habits), and we express it through our engaged **Participation**. In doing so, we begin an **Evolutionary Insurgence** within our culture. This starts with a **Single Mutation** and can grow to *whatever size the collective consciousness validates*.

This is how our choices and the ideas that we embody change the world. This is the sense of purpose that we feel is missing, until we understand our power. When we become related to our reality in a healthy manner, through knowledge and engagement, this power presents itself to us. It is ours.

It is impossible to feel powerless when we engage our world at this level. It is impossible to feel helpless or hopeless. Without those blockages to joy and inspiration, we grow unbounded and deliver our essence unto the world in the most holy way. Let us take part together, grow together, and move the world in the places where it is presently stuck. Let's keep our heart open, our mind calm, our focus clear, and our soul engaged. As close to grand-scheme purpose as we can get, **this is what we are doing here**.

Section 4

Chapter 24:

Use of Perspective

This last chapter is a dénouement. All of the heavy lifting is done. Perspective is the final description for our ability to expertly operate our consciousness within reality. Remember the tagline, "The Application of Perspective to Reality."

Everything we have talked about, the information and the analogies, those are all Perspectives. Each Perspective contains a focus... and that focus has a specific type of quality. One of the issues with the zombie-ish world we see is that we are not embodying *any* Perspective most of the time. We are often on autopilot, or in a state of confusion and fear. States of confusion keep us absent in our Perspectives, completely incapable of managing their usage.

What we want, after the past section, is to realize that we come into every moment having to rehabilitate the trauma of being Present (born into every moment), and with the opportunity to transmute anything we dislike into something better. That is the truth. **And for every moment, there is a Perspective**. These are the tools we *hope to have*, the glasses we see through to read the directions in the moments we are Present.

How Prepared Can We Be?

The amount of Perspectives we can habitually Option In to a moment is a measure of how prepared we can be to manage and Influence a moment. There is so much going on every second that we cannot control, internally and externally, that these *Perspectives are our salvation from complete powerlessness.*

It's interesting I use that word…powerlessness. But it's accurate. When we have nothing to bring to a moment to prepare for rehabilitating the difficulty of its presence, or changing it for the better, we are victims of our experience. Ouch. This is why being conscious of our limitations and aware of what little power we do have is so important. Perspectives prepare us.

The amount of Perspectives we can carry into a single moment is a measurement of our chances of successfully dealing with that situation in a way that creates harmony. It does not ensure anything; it just gives us a better shot. We carry umbrellas, coats, boots, sunscreen, and other items to prepare for weather, but our preparation is not going to help in every situation. Sometimes it will not help because it is the wrong tool-type (we have prepared for rain, rather than cold). Sometimes it will not be enough to cover the magnitude of what we are presented with (an umbrella is not going to cut it in a Category 5 Hurricane). Nonetheless, we want to gather as many tools as we can comfortably carry so that we can increase our chances of being prepared.

It is not always easy to hold all of these tools. It takes practice. Just like it would be difficult to fit every type of all-weather gear into a backpack, *it is difficult to fit every necessary Perspective into our Consciousness.* This is getting easier,

I believe, as we evolve into more fluent information-gatherers (thank you tech world, I guess?). But it is still difficult, even if we can manage carrying many Perspectives in our consciousness, to be able to grab the right one at the right moment. Even if we have the tool, it is difficult to pluck it from the vastness of consciousness and bring it to the focus of the moment so that it is a large Influence on our Now.

So what does this issue look like? I have rage issues. For this I have Perspectives. I have the following to keep me from acting out on my anger:

1) The memories of the bad consequences of acting out.

2) The peace and power felt from refraining from acting out.

3) Physical techniques, like breathing and moment-meditations to calm myself.

4) Muting devices, Perspectives that soften my voice and movements, so they do not reflect my inner fury. They are activated whenever my anger gets past a certain level.

5) Love. It washes over me and makes it difficult for me to act out against anything.

6) Self-allowance. I don't believe anything is wrong with me. My anger is welcome. I allow its authenticity.

This allows me *to not indulge my anger's hunger for expression* because I am not too busy fighting myself to see the full repertoire I have listed here. I can bring all of these tools to the moment. It does really well to keep me fastened down in my seat rather than up and rampaging.

I mentioned Pivot Points a long time ago. That is when these tools present themselves in correlation to a reaction type...like anger. But we can do more to prepare for reality than just waiting for reactions and then attempting to manage them. We can investigate the realities we are moving through during the day and find where we will need certain tools. If we do this, we can ensure the likelihood of their presence within our consciousness. If I know I am going to be in a situation where I am likely to get angry, I may be able to use other tools, like "Understanding," to stop myself before I even begin to react. That is **Perspective Sophistication**.

Perspective Sophistication happens when we can look forward into our upcoming moments and find the tools we will need. We do this so they are near our consciousness at the exact moments we will need them. It is art, not mastery.

I remember my old roommate had tension issues talking with his mom on the phone. The worst part about it was that he was NEVER prepared for her to call. He would get off working the night shift at 11 a.m., get home and pop open a beer. By his third he was tipsy and tired…and that's when she'd call. She hated it when he drank, so it always made him totally uncomfortable.

Then one day *he got it*. She was always going to call right when he was getting drunk. He was popping open his beer while I was sipping coffee, and he stopped before he put it to his lips and said, "I bet my mom is about to call. I'm going to be ready this time." And he was right. He set the beer down, prepared himself for everything she was going to say, and mellowed out. She called ten minutes later. He was sober and their talk went smoothly rather than stressing him out and exhausting him.

It is the art of being prepared.

So how prepared can we be? We generally know what our days are like. We know which tools we have to draw on from our previous successes. We know that we can stack all of the necessary tools up close to our consciousness and get used to carrying them around.

As a bipolar fella with PTSD and rage issues, *I was lucky.* I was lucky in that I was forced to carry as much as I could to ensure I had the highest odds of not incurring horrendous experiences and consequences. Not many people are forced, though, and that can be unfortunate for them.

It's unfortunate because carrying Perspectives requires we build an actual muscle in our consciousness. So, while I may get emotionally disturbed and have to use tools for the sun hitting me the wrong way, or the tone of voice a stranger uses with a cashier three aisles down at the grocery store, **I am also really prepared to handle it**. As a result I am more prepared to handle ANYTHING than the average person.

It does not have to be this way. I am afflicted, and simultaneously, more well-adjusted. Everyone can prepare. It is not admitting weakness to set yourself up for experiencing and expressing your strength, and exerting your Influence. Every moment is foreign to us unless we are prepared, so we need to prepare in one way or another to lessen the chance that we become a *victim* of that moment.

I often think "What eyes am I bringing to this moment?" I take stock of my mood and focus; then I see if anything needs to be moved around or invented. Much of Perspective and tool creation is Imagination. This means that being in a state of mind that allows our thoughts to flow creatively acts as a morphing tool that we can apply to any situation.

I think that the best therapists have this down. They can look into someone's life and create Perspectives for them to try-on and experience. This is the best way a therapist can give their client tools. Create a Perspective, then reinforce it and validate it often.

But we can do this for ourselves, of course. We do not need someone to give these treasures to us. The best part of that fact is that, as we imagine and prepare for our day, we can create tools for every situation and see how they work in concert with the tools we already have.

Imaginative Perspective Application

Our eyes go everywhere with us. But that's because our eyes can go anywhere. Eyes have been attached to every genius, every killer, and every general. They have been attached to every one of our family members. They are attached to people in every culture, and in every time. Our eyes are not as limited as we pretend they are. Our eyes are creative.

I focus on creating the best Perspective for every situation. If I cannot do it in advance, I focus on being able to do it at the time. *Also, I don't get hung up on reality*.

Where I place my eyes does not have to be true, or accurate, or possible. It is not about whether it's real. It is about whether it creates a tool that can help us with our world.

One of the repeat conversations we have with our friends has to do with their significant others, especially when we're young adults. The "should I stay or should I go" question is repetitive and frustrating because it lends itself to long drawn-out conversations made completely of waffling. But I found a way around it. Thank goodness, because those conversations were exhausting for me. I found a way to develop a tool out of an imaginary situation.

My friend would present a bunch of evidence (evidence that really does not matter, as it has not led to action) and ask me to look at the evidence with them, as if my looking at the same facts would create new facts. So, instead of engaging in that, I tried to find new facts. I asked my friend, "Hey, what if your boyfriend was forced through work to go to Canada for two years? He would be taken care of and make money. You'd also be taken care of and have time to get another roommate."

This ALWAYS led to a breakthrough because there was no pressure, and they could see whether or not they actually wanted to be around the person. It didn't lead to action on their part necessarily, but it certainly gave the situation new information. It gave my friend new facts, and new tools. Whether they used it... that, I couldn't control.

When I have panic attacks it often has to do with having to be somewhere later in the day. When I was a waiter I would get freaked out about working. I would start panicking over my 5pm -10pm shift at about nine in the morning. That is inappropriate, but it is my world, and that's what I had to deal with.

In my life now, I can get that same reaction over having to be somewhere. But, in general, I don't ever HAVE to go. Because of this...I realized a tool. *I could just lie to myself...* and use that Perspective.

Now when I get panicked about going somewhere, I just say "Okay, I don't have to go anywhere." Then, I imagine myself not going. That is a tool for dealing with my anxiety. I can believe it because I know that I don't HAVE to do it. Because of this I don't end up how I did before my waiter shifts, which is shivering, shaking, and crying. I actually mellow out, and go on about my day.

Because I get mellowed out by that Perspective, often I end up doing the thing that had been making me nervous. That is a POWERFUL result from a creative Perspective.

So the eyes I am using can be moved anywhere given the right circumstances. The circumstances are not always right, but *we can use our imagination to create the best circumstances possible.*

This book is a list of tools. Go through the glossary. I go through it all the time. Every Perspective, every story, every analogy, is a tool based on a Perspective. Literally every chapter is built to ease a burden by allowing greater focus on an idea, or presenting us with a usable tool.

The Beach of Quiet Emotion is the place where we want to be in order to find creative answers and healthy reactions. Conscious Validation is what we use to Influence our mind's habits. Healthy Expression is our goal. Synergy of Commune is how we want our relationships to express themselves. Observer Consciousness is how we watch and allow our thoughts to express themselves. Participation is the relationship we want with our world. Rehabilitation is the way we remove the trauma of surprise and loss in situations and our life overall. Psychological Determinism removes guilt and shame, as well as our confusion with our relationship to Free Will. Transmutation is how we can approach the entire world and attain a hopeful view of the future. Usable Mantras help us stay confident and available to all of these tools. Conscious Ideals give us a consistent answer when we get overrun by questions about the foundation of our Perspectives.

Knowing these Perspectives gives us a powerful tool going into any situation. It prepares us to create realities or react in the best way possible.

When we read a book like this, it is because we are trying to create something, not just understand. Conceptualizing is why we look into psychology or spirituality in the first place, but the reason we stay with it is because *we want to create something*. We want to create a healthy person who can express themselves, a person who has a very specific Influence on the world around them. The way we do this is finding a purpose that we can adopt and using our tools to align our world with that purpose.

Rehabilitation and Transmutation are the purpose. They translate into "This is supposed to be hard and I am trying to make it better." Perspectives are the tools we use in this endeavor.

The goal is to create a new person. We want to create a new presence. We embody the creation of a new reality through the Evolution of our Consciousness. The combination of a focused purpose, with the tools to achieve it, allow the individuated expression of a soul to Present itself to the world.

The Mosaic, the New Archetype: The Inclusive Being

I wrote a description of what I could see happening (in the close future) a few years ago. I started to delve into the necessary tools the average person would need to use in order to make it happen, and ended up writing this book. I like to think that the future is as close as it felt to me then, and still feels to me now after sixteen months of writing.

The idea I had created a new archetype. **The Inclusive**

Being. The Inclusive Being is "One World," "One Soul," "One Love," expressing itself through an individuated consciousness. The Inclusive Being contains the potential to access all Perspectives, and act in accord with that experience through his unique soul energy. The following is the essay I wrote that day....

Picture the face of humankind. Picture one face...one snapshot. One symbol for the human expression of universal energy that we all came from and are "in SOME way" trying to get back to. Take that snapshot and imagine every experience of every human being across all time being the components of an infinite and ever-growing mosaic that creates the original snapshot. An infinity of moments.

What we are is the mosaic of the first snapshot, the universal collective experience expressed by a million pictures of every reality we have ever incorporated put back together to form the original face. This is a "ONE," but upon closer look, it is a ONE with more richness and beauteous contrast. This is our method. **This is our expansion**. This is Entropy + REFINEMENT in the ONE.

We can bring up the pictures in the mosaic, our own and others, to use in every moment to have the most delicious new combination-experience that has ever happened. This new expression flowing through our consciousness is the application of our unique Perspective to reality. And each time we use it the mosaic gets bigger, as every new combination forms a new snapshot within the already existing mosaic. THAT IS EXPANSION.

It is true now that we are open to receiving and using multiple Perspectives simultaneously, where it may not have been in the past. The idea of the philosopher-king or poet-warrior was an attraction to me as a child. But it's not enough in this expanding world. *We want all Perspectives*. And I know we can have them.

Our job and joy is simply to learn the roles and Perspectives we are gifted. And we should try to learn all of them in as many different combinations as we can. If we are observant we will notice if it does or does not lead to a greater level of life experience and joy for us and those near us.

There has been a time in our lives when we were not bothered by whatever is bothering us. A time when we were not judging ourselves or another in the damaging way we are now. A time when we could flow with something without stressing. **That moment is now available to us, we can use it**.

THIS IS THE NEW ARCHETYPE. This is the Inclusive Being, who is able to use their life as an interchangeable reality matrix, where the Intuition and nature of our inborn desire to be happy and experience this delicious world can readily call up our greatest-fitting Perspective to handle any moment in the most meaningful way. This is, quite simply, using our consciousness, Intuition, history, and the influx of all those had by others in the universal grid of energy, **to become the Gods we know we are in order to make every moment of our lives divinely resonant**.

Every time the tool is used, it stimulates the "use this tool" part in everyone's brain. Perspective calls to us for use, and we call our collective consciousness forward when we use it.

One of my main goals for this book was the demystification of mind expansion. I have outlined it. It's not a huge deal. *Mind*

expansion is the ability to stretch our consciousness into more and more Perspectives. We have so many wants and so many questions. There is so much within us that is aching for experience, safety, love, and Resonance. This is the case of the soul cast into a body with no map to guide it.

This is because we are the map. We are the landscape. **We are the reality we seek, and the means to attain it all wrapped in one ball of energy.** How do we get at this profound experience? How do we continue to motivate ourselves to step more and more deeply into the incarnation at hand without distraction?

We engage and invest, in everything we are, all the time. We keep one hand on the wheel of our experience and one hand in our bag of Perspectives. We focus on pulling out the best tools for every situation, and using whatever keeps us creative and calm on the Beach of Quiet Emotion. We do this all simultaneously...and to the best of our ability. This achievement is possible in this new world we have created together.

So notice everything, keep your mind awake and engaged...and it will give you the life you've loved to want.

Glossary

A

Addict Checklist Ch.17-3
This is a set of questions to ask ourselves before trying to help an addict, whether with a physical relationship or chemical one.

The **Angst of No Promises** Ch.6
This is a state of being characterized by stress and disheartenment over the lack of certainty in life.

Ascend-In Ch.1
This is the act of fully embodying our incarnated reality.

Audience Ch.5
Anyone that is receiving or being Influenced by our expressions is our Audience.

B

Base Fears Ch.12-1
These are fears that occur simply because we live in an uncontrollable world where a necessary aspect of existence is that we are vulnerable to pain.

528 COFFEE FOR CONSCIOUSNESS

The **Beach of Quiet Emotion** Ch.10-3
This is the place in our consciousness where all emotional, physical, and spiritual sensations are heightened. It is a high-quality Vibration-space...a place of creativity. It is fragile, balanced, and calm.

Being of Conscious Assistance Ch.17-3
This is the type of assistance we want to give. It necessitates engaging in self-reflection and rigorous self-honesty. It is necessary to ensure we are actually "able" to help, rather than merely "wanting to."

Being Present (Presence) Ch.13
This is the ability to consciously engage and validate our reality, or exert Influence on the world around us.

Birth Trauma Ch.22
This is the trauma that comes with finding ourselves in ANY new situation. Adjusting to any new reality is akin to being born into an unfamiliar environment.

Body Sovereignty Ch.10-1
This is the role of the *vessel* our souls inhabit. It has a directive, separate from whatever temporary ones we may have, to seek health and life.

Break-In Moments Ch.9-2
These are moments where we can interrupt our consciousness and expand or reposition our Perspective.

C

The Church of Consciousness Ch.22
These are activities and experiences in our lives that serve as daily spiritual exercises. We can hold spiritual service for ourselves whenever we want.

Citizen Inferiority Complex Ch.12-1
This is the idea that huge corrupting agents stifle our ability to self-govern. It is the act of shifting accountability off ourselves onto an amalgam of evil controllers that we are powerless against.

Commune Imprinting Ch.1
This is a shared intimate reality (like a hug) that *captures a moment* and resonates.

Completing the Circuit of the Law of Attraction Ch.13
This is when our process of manifestation ends with the *enjoyment* of the received blessing or gift.

Conductor Consciousness Ch.8
This is how Observation Consciousness is capable of participating. Each motivating factor we have in our environment is analogous to musicians in an orchestra. When the Observer Consciousness engages the whole of the motivations present, he is capable "Conducting" the many pieces into harmony.

Conscious Ideal Ch.20
This is an ideal about our existence that we keep close by so that it can be a foundation for what type of Perspective we want to take on a situation. Saying "Yes" to life is a Conscious Ideal.

530 COFFEE FOR CONSCIOUSNESS

Conscious Validation Ch.9-1
This is the act of engaging with a subject or reality and investing in it on a specific level. We can engage our thoughts. If we do so, then we are capable of validating, altering, or dismissing them.

Contact Translation Ch.10-1
This is the true nature of sensation. It happens when our bodies are contacted by anything. When that specific information is translated to our mind for processing and either storage or usage, that is sensation.

Creation of External Validation Ch.11-2
This consists of forming a relationship with the Subconscious Mind through creating *and consciously validating* triggers of all types. Synchronicities are a common source of Commune between the conscious and subconscious mind.

D

Decision Validation Ch.9-3
This is a form of Conscious Validation that we perform when we become accountable for the entirety of an action *and its effects*. This means we accept our connection to unforeseen consequences.

Depersonalize the Mind Ch.11-2
This is the necessary act that needs to be taken often to move into Observer Consciousness from a reactive state.

Distance Goggles Ch.2
This is a larger Perspective of current situations, one that allows us to view them from outside our physical and mental impermanent realities.

E

Energy Bounty Ch.18
This is the energy that constantly spills out of someone who has plugged in to Source energy successfully. This is what is left over after someone has fueled themselves.

Evolutionary Insurgence Ch.23-2
This is the consistent expression of ideas that validate the movement away from Vestigial Psychology and toward the creation of new paradigm of behavior on a global scale.

Experience, Resonance, Rapture, repeat. Ch. 1
Experience: Contact with incarnate phenomena. **Resonance**: Integration of the phenomena. **Rapture**: Creation of new consciousness as a result...one that feeds itself into the grid of all consciousness and expands the self and the universe.

Expression Discipline Ch.15
This is a type of discipline that aims to use focus and attention to bring about a future made up of characteristics we want. It is positivity-centered, creative, and healthy.

External Mind Ch.8
This is brain activity, thinking, from reactions to any mechanisms of conscious or habitual thought, which form a part of the environment that our Identity/Observer Consciousness must contend with. The common mistake is that we identify with our thoughts. We must not do so. The mind is external to Identity.

F

Faith Ch.11-1
This is the *duty* we have to *act* upon our trust in something.

Fatal Flaw CH.10-2
In regard to the growth matrix, this is the mix of our emotional response to worldly fear and our assumption that others must be beyond it. It assumes that to emulate others will bring us comfort even though it does damage our soul. This is the moment we stop working with our body and *trust what we **think** is going on in other people's bodies*.

Free Will's Myth Ch.7
This is the idea that we are free to act beyond our environment's Influence on us. It is built on the idea that we are somehow separate from everything in our environment that motivates us.

Fulfillment of Gratitude Ch.13
This is "living in consistent enjoyment of what we have been matched with."

The **Fury of No Control** Ch.7
This is the name of the type of Cognitive Dissonance that attacks us when we are faced with the possibility that we do not completely author our behaviors and choices.

G

Garden Overrun with Weeds Ch.12-1
This is the state of being in a fear-dominated behavior matrix, where our creations and joys are hidden and protected from the world

behind a system of defenses. This defense separates us from external presence and love.

Genetics of Behavior Ch.23-1
These are traits passed down through family of origin that are as pronounced as physical traits.

Grid of Divine Vitality Ch.3
This is the river of energy flowing at all times that we may dip our souls into when we embody divine expression. There is always support there for conscious engagement.

H

The Hangover Option Ch.6
This is the option to choose the *certainty* of feeling bad over the *possibility* of feeling good.

Harmony of Intent Ch.19
This occurs when our emotionally active expressions (verbal or otherwise) match our beliefs.

Healthy Confidence Ch.19
Healthy Confidence is a positive relationship between our mind, our beliefs, and the evidence we can present to ourselves at a given time about our abilities.

Healthy Runoff Ch. 1
This is the excess positive energy that flows out to the rest of the world when we are living a good life. Akin to Energy Bounty, but on the macro scale.

Held Ideals Ch.17-3
These are easily referenced focus-purposes within our matrix of consciousness.

Host of Universal Creation Energy Incarnate Ch.2
This is the idea that our lives are the venue where a party for Universal soul energy takes place…a party where we are the Host that can provide what is desired.

I

Imaginative Perspective Application Ch.24
This is looking at our present situation, imagining the best Perspective to deal with the situation, and getting our consciousness as close to that Perspective as we can. This can be close to method acting.

Inability to Manage and Regulate our Consciousness Ch.22
This is the most common and powerful human problem. Period.

The **Inclusive Being** Ch.24
This is "One World," "One Soul," "One Love," expressing itself through an individuated consciousness.

Influence Ch.3
This is the effect that our *soul expression* can have on our moment to moment environment, as control over it does not exist. It is taking an active role in our many matrices of thought and behavior. *It is the part of our full environment of Influences that is authored by us*.

Insurgence of Consciousness Ch.12-3
This is the movement from within a society that changes the conscious integrity and focus of that society as a catalyst for evolution and global mind expansion. It is connected to Evolutionary Insurgence.

Interpersonal Alchemy Ch.12-3
This is the ability to take a parenting role in relationships that are surrounded by negativity, and transmute the negativity. It includes the ability to create while in pain... rather than reacting negatively and playing out an old script that may be causing disharmony.

Intuitive Hunger Ch.11-1
This is the Instinct delivered from the subconscious to the craving centers of our brain through its vast memory bank of flavors in reference to the body's needs.

J

Justified Righteousness Ch.12-1
This is a state of being, a Perspective taken on, wherein we can release our anger with a system of justification behind us such that we believe we are defending ourselves rather than attacking others needlessly.

K

The **Kitchen of How to Live** Ch.17-3
This is the analogy for the place where we, who have limited tools and knowledge from which to guide, must gather the tools we have and knowledge we have in order to guide others through complex processes.

L

Lesson-Based Reality Ch.9-3
This is the fact that growth comes through engagement, and that any experience teaches us and changes us.

List of Great Concerns Ch.14
This is the list I have of things I want to change about the world. You have one too.

Long-Term Life Goal Ch.17-3
This is an ethical imperative that we can harken back to in order to motivate ourselves to be careful. We do this so that we go through the necessary steps to protect those we are trying to help.

Loss of Being Known Ch.22
This is a trauma that we need to rehabilitate. We come into this life having not been separate, so being known was not a problem. Now that separation exists through our incarnation, we hunger for recognition.

Lucid Daydreaming Ch.9-2
This is the idea of habituating Break-in Moments or triggers into the practice of going about our day. We do this is in order to involve our consciousness in the working of our subconscious reality matrix.

M

The **Master's Conundrum** Ch.17-3
This is when our master-to-student relationship disintegrates (as our students become more capable), making us less powerful and necessary.

Mental Instinct Ch.10-2

This is a mechanism that justifies our feelings. It is the *natural and psychologically necessary* activity of the mind to seek evidence that supports the body's Present emotion.

The **Mold** Ch.16

The Mold is a set of ideas based on the same factors going into Psychological Determinism (genes and experience), but that create an ideal of how things or people *should* be. It is a set of expectations about reality that exists within us at all times.

N

The New Archetype Ch.24

This is the new type of person that is created when someone becomes capable of embodying the totality of the archetypes consciously, allowing that person the ability to flow between Perspectives to maximize experience and Influence.

O

Observer Consciousness Ch.3

This is the watcher in our brain, developed through meditation, that can objectively observe our reality…it is as close to an identity as we get.

Its loving attention is *soul presence*. Its ability to Influence our lives, and bleed through all environmental circumstances, is *soul expression.*

"On to the next Problem" Mentality Ch.13

This is when we complete a goal without validating it and resonating in its fulfillment before moving on to the next stressor.

Original Injury Ch.17-1
This occurs when our expectation of how groups of people should behave is not accurate and we feel betrayed by reality. This is the "person and group" version of Original Wound.

Overload Generation Ch.12-2
This is the generation whose prime function it is to bear out the fruits of the global test of intense social immersion. This is going on now.

P

PAID IN FULL Ch.19
This is an airtight and expansive affirmation. Its focus is to bring abundance.

Paralytic Mechanics Ch.20
These are systems we use to keep ourselves as safe as possible. They do this by convincing us to not engage.

Parenting the World Ch.5
This is an attitude. It describes how we relate to the world around us when we make ourselves accountable for expressing healthily, and for the nourishment for the growth of all.

Passive Validation Ch.9-1
This is the unhealthy practice of unconsciously validating what-ever happens to be passing through our minds. It is a form of non-engagement.

Perspective Map Ch.9-2
This is the map of our current focus and attention, including mood. It is a helpful survival and energy-saving mechanism. It can be altered.

Pivot Points Ch.9-2
These are moments, just *after* Break-In Moments, where we have the ability to maneuver from one Perspective to another. Their presence can be trained and triggered.

Pre-emptive Adjustment Awareness Ch.9-1
This is the trigger we can install in our consciousness on the fly when we need to make an adjustment to how we are behaving or perceiving.

Primary Caregiver Ch.8
This is the idea that we are the most influential consciousness when it comes to engaging our mind and behaviors, as we are constantly present for it. This means that we are the primary person responsible for our own care.

Prime Relationships Ch.22
These are relationships with lovers, followed by children, parents, siblings, and close soul family. **We want to *Be Known* in these relationships**.

Prime Watchers Ch.20
This is the idea that we are in the front row for watching the story of our lives unfold, rather than ONLY an active participant. If we have amazing lives, or boring lives, it affects us as an Audience.

The Process (Synergy Consciousness). Ch.1
The act of taking incorporated lessons and ideas in one area and using that energy in other areas to develop our reality. This is part of the creative foundation that we can tap into with every breath we take.

Psychologist's Checklist Ch.17-3
This is a set of questions we must ask ourselves before giving advice.

Psychological Determinism Ch.7
This is a theory postulating that every individual action is the result of two infinitely complex things...our environment and our specific momentary Perspective.

R

Red Flag System Ch.23-1
Our emotions are a red flag system. They tell us that something needs our conscious attention and engagement.

The **Reaction-Adjustment use of Cognition** Ch.9-1
Under the umbrella of Conscious Validation, this is the active conscious procedure wherein we allow the presence of a reaction, then adjust its makeup so that it is in line with *what we want our reaction to be*.

Reflexing Out Ch.10-3
This is the recoiling we do when we are emotionally activated in a negative way. This moves us from an area of high sensation to an area of low sensation to escape discomfort.

Relationship House Ch.17-1
Symbolic structure that is the objective correlative of a relationship, existing outside of the identities of the people involved.

Relationship Mold Ch.17-3
Like the Mold, this is the picture we have of every relationship in our lives. Our goal is to make it as dynamic as possible.

Relationship of Accountability Ch.5
This is the description of the degree to which we "take into account" our ability to impact the world around us as we move throughout our daily lives.

Remorse Perspective Ch.15
This is the Perspective we can use to go back and look at our mistakes without guilt interrupting our ability to learn from our mistakes.

Restriction Discipline Ch.15
This is a form of discipline that uses critique and punishment to shame the self into action, undermining the overall purpose of any goal. It is the opposite of Expression Discipline.

Romeo and Juliet Moment Ch.12-2
This is the moment when passion leads to change through unity and an example is set through which division is ended and growth ensues.

S

Sanding Ch.22
This is the natural refinement that takes place when souls contact each other. It is characterized by moments of friction followed by moments of refinement.

Semi-Malleable Host CH.10-1
That is what our human body is. It is something that is very difficult to alter…not something we control.

The Shoulder Surfer Ch.7
This is a small invisible being that lives on your shoulder. It has access to your entire subconscious mind, genetics, and complete recall of all your experiences.

Single Mutation Theory Ch.23-2
We become the first to change ourselves for the better, and that mutation has the possibility of changing the entire species.

Situation of Discernment Ch.15
This is a moment where we are capable of using ideals to create a reality that is more of what we want in our world, and less of what we don't, *while knowing that BOTH are going to be present.* This is a daily focus as it pertains to relationships and situations.

The **Smokehouse** Ch.10-3
The Smokehouse is a less sensitive plane of existence...with lower standards of living. In the Smokehouse, negative emotions are in less contrast with the surroundings, and *create less Cognitive Dissonance.* For people who have trouble processing emotions, the Smokehouse is more comfortable than the Beach of Quiet Emotion.

Sophistication in Communication Ch.5
This occurs when the Source (feeling), voice (expression), and reception of an idea (understanding) are all tied together with care.

Sophisticated Inspiration Ch.20
This is the Inspiration that grows out of Conscious Mind that understands that everything matters and that we are capable of influencing the world for the better at every step. It does not depend on tricks or coaxing.

The **Source Plug-In** Ch.18
This is our connection to Source energy that flows through us and engages our best qualities through presence and hope.

State of Inquiry Ch.8
This is the state of mind created by a healthy curiosity about our motivations at any given moment. It intends to track Motivation throughout our many matrices of consciousness. This is characterized by sentences like "What is affecting me right now?" and "I wonder why I did that?"

Stepping Into Your Power Ch.12-3
This is simply becoming creatively engaged in our reality as an "attitude" we move forward with. It turns moments of *weakness or failure* into moments of *opportunity*.

Subconscious Motion Tracker Ch.11-1
This is the theoretic ability of the subconscious Mind to take in the entirety of our surroundings at any given moment, explaining specialized reflex as well as pre and rapid cognition.

Synergy in Commune Ch.5
This is a mutual goal of understanding between people that are communicating.

T

Tone of Expression Ch.19
This is the character of our connection to a statement. The more we honor a statement of opinion or desire with the fullness of our being through action and intent, the more pure the tone.

Trauma of Incarnation Ch.22
This is the large overall Trauma of being born into a vulnerable and confusing body.

Triggers and "Digging" Ch.22
This is a process by which we are emotionally activated and then search for the root cause of the issue rather than being distracted by the emotion.

U

Upward/Outward Spiral Ch.9-3
This is the refinement of chaos into art and the accepting of Influence in all its forms, including an investment in the love of "glorious failure" within a Lesson-Based Reality.

Urgently Mortal Seriousness Ch.2
The stressed-and-struggling-for-survival focus that keeps us locked inside our present moment with no larger Perspectives available.

V

Vestigial Psychology Ch.23-2
This is a part of our cultural psychology that is no longer necessary... like a tailbone for a tail that we no longer have.

Vibration Ch.5
It is the *waveform identity* of a reality, that is, in itself, *a material reality*. It can have many characteristics and qualities.

Vibration of Intent Ch.5
A signature for the Source of an expression that is distinct. A material reality with physical presence that is connected to what we say and do.

Vitality Gasp Ch.13
Baby's unbridled laugh. It is our full immersion in a moment of joy.
Soulgasm.

The Voter Dilemma Ch.20
This is the dilemma created when a situation does not present any
options we like. Choosing between the "lesser of two evils" is a good
example of this situation. Yet, even though the options are not to our
liking, we still have the opportunity to engage and make the choice
that is "most" to our liking.

W

White Noise Ch.14
This is the cap of stress or fear that dampens our expression. It covers
and limits our unique expression as an instrument in the orchestra.

Wound of Passage Ch.10-3
This is the assault of stress caused by frustration and unmet expectation upon reaching adulthood. This happens when a child has fully
left the "nest."

Z

ZOOM OUT! Ch.9-2
The Zoom Out button is an operation we can perform after a Break-In
Moment has allowed us some Influence within our Perspective Map.
It grants us a larger Perspective, and in doing so relieves the stress of
the situation.